SHARE SOME *JOIE DE FRANCE*.

"Bal du Moulin de la Gallette" by Renoir, from the Museé d'Orsay, Paris.

France is a joyful celebration of life. From Art to Dance, Cuisine to Romance, you'll find that everything takes on a special magic when it has a French accent.

THE FINE ART OF FLYING
AIR FRANCE

The Best of

FLORIDA

Editors
Jim Burns, Catherine Jordan

Restaurant Editors
Steven Raichlen
with
Colleen Dunn Bates, Edward Guiliano

Contributing Editors
Lyn Farmer, Gordon and Janet Groene,
Scott Joseph, Jonathan Rogers, Patty Ryan,
Julie Ann Sipos, Karen Feldman Smith

Additional editorial assistance
Florence Lemkowitz

Page Makeup
Kevin MacDowell

Director
Alain Gayot

Publisher
André Gayot

PRENTICE HALL TRAVEL
New York ■ London ■ Toronto ■ Sydney ■ Tokyo ■ Singapore

Other Gault Millau Guides Available
from Prentice Hall Travel

The Best of Chicago
The Best of France
The Best of Germany
The Best of Hawaii
The Best of Hong Kong
The Best of Italy
The Best of London
The Best of Los Angeles
The Best of New England
The Best of New Orleans
The Best of New York
The Best of Paris
The Best of San Francisco
The Best of Thailand
The Best of Toronto
The Best of Washington, D.C.

Published by Prentice Hall General Reference
A division of Simon & Schuster Inc.
15 Columbus Circle
New York, NY 10023

Copyright © 1991
by Gault Millau, Inc.

All rights reserved
including the right of reproduction
in whole or in part in any form

PRENTICE HALL and colophon
are registered trademarks of Simon & Schuster Inc.

Please address all comments or advertising queries
regarding *The Best of Florida* to:

Alain Gayot, Vice President
Gault Millau, Inc., P.O. Box 361144
Los Angeles, CA 90036

Library of Congress Cataloging-in-Publication Data

The Best of Florida / editors, Jim Burns, Catherine Jordan :
 restaurant editor, Colleen Dunn Bates : contributing editors, Lyn
 Farmer ... [et al.] ;
  p. cm.
 Includes index.
 ISBN 0-13-085358-5 : $17.00
  1. Florida—Description and travel—1981- —Guide-books. 2. Miami
 (Fla.)—Description—Guide-books. 3. Orlando (Fla.)—Description—Guide-
 books. I. Burns, Jim, 1952-   . II. Jordan, Catherine.
 F309.3.B47 1991
 917.5904'63—dc20   91-10293

Printed in the United States of America

CONTENTS

INTRODUCTION 1
Before you go . . . includes an easy-to-use map of Florida's regions and a brief section on the history and heritage of the Sunshine State, plus a Toque Tally (an index by ranking) of all the best restaurants in Florida, complete restaurant indexes listed by cuisine and by area, a hotel index by area and price, and helpful explanations of Gault Millau's restaurant- and hotel-rating systems.

MIAMI 21
A tour of Florida's de facto capital. From posh Miami Beach to bustling downtown, we'll show you the finest dining, the loveliest resorts, the hottest nightclubs, the best recreation, and the most noteworthy attractions in this fast-growing international city. Plus, Key Biscayne and Hollywood.

THE KEYS 101
From Key Largo to southernmost Key West, discover the tropical delights of Florida's "out" islands.

GOLD COAST 127
A beach-lover's paradise on Florida's Atlantic side, this golden playground stretches from Fort Lauderdale to Palm Beach.

TREASURE COAST 177
Take in a bit of old Florida on this 100-mile stretch of Atlantic coastline, in the quiet towns of Jupiter, Stuart, Fort Pierce and Vero Beach.

SPACE COAST 185
The birthplace of speed, from Cocoa Beach to Daytona Beach on Florida's Atlantic side, with Cape Canaveral in between.

ORLANDO & CENTRAL FLORIDA 197
A guide to the brash, booming town that Disney built, with wise and witty advice on where to eat, sleep and play, both in the Vacation Kingdom and around Central Florida.

FIRST COAST 249
Explore the nation's oldest city, quaint Saint Augustine, and Florida's largest city, Jacksonville, on the state's northernmost strip of Atlantic coastline.

PANHANDLE 265
A stretch of the Old South in northern Florida, from the seaside city of Pensacola to the lazy-paced capital town of Tallahassee to the college town of Gainesville.

TAMPA BAY AREA 277
On Florida's Gulf side, we show you thriving Tampa, the lovely waterfront city of Saint Petersburg and culturally rich Sarasota, plus the surrounding islets and keys.

SHELL COAST 311
The sun-drenched southern strip on the Gulf, including Fort Myers, Naples and the enchanting islets of Sanibel and Captiva.

MAPS 335
Finding your way around. Detailed maps of Florida state, Miami & vicinity, The Keys and Orlando & vicinity.

INDEX 341

A DISCLAIMER

Readers are advised to remember that prices and conditions change over the course of time. The restaurants, hotels, shops and other establishments reviewed in this book have been visited over a period of time, and the reviews reflect the personal experiences of the reviewers. The critics and publishers cannot be held responsible for the experiences of the reader related to the establishments reviewed. Readers are invited to write the publisher with ideas, comments and suggestions for future editions.

INTRODUCTION

A MAP: FLORIDA'S REGIONS	2
FLORIDA REBORN	3
ABOUT THE RESTAURANTS	5
ABOUT THE HOTELS	16

FLORIDA'S REGIONS

The map below is an easy-to-use guide to Florida's many and varied regions. Each numbered area corresponds to a chapter in this book, in the order that they appear. We cover the state in a counterclockwise direction: first to **Miami** and **The Keys;** then up the **Gold Coast, Treasure Coast** and **Space Coast;** then to **Orlando & Central Florida;** then to the **First Coast,** west along the **Panhandle;** and down to the **Tampa Bay Area** and **Shell Coast.** From Tallahassee to Miami, Florida measures about 475 miles long. The distance from Miami to Orlando is 237 miles (a 5-hour drive); from Tallahassee to Orlando is 260 miles (4.5 hours); from Fort Myers to Palm Beach is 120 miles (2.5 hours); and from Miami to southernmost Key West is 150 miles (4 hours). (*See* pages 335 to 340 for more detailed maps.)

① MIAMI

② THE KEYS

③ GOLD COAST

④ TREASURE COAST

⑤ SPACE COAST

⑥ ORLANDO & CENTRAL FLORIDA

⑦ FIRST COAST

⑧ PANHANDLE

⑨ TAMPA BAY AREA

⑩ SHELL COAST

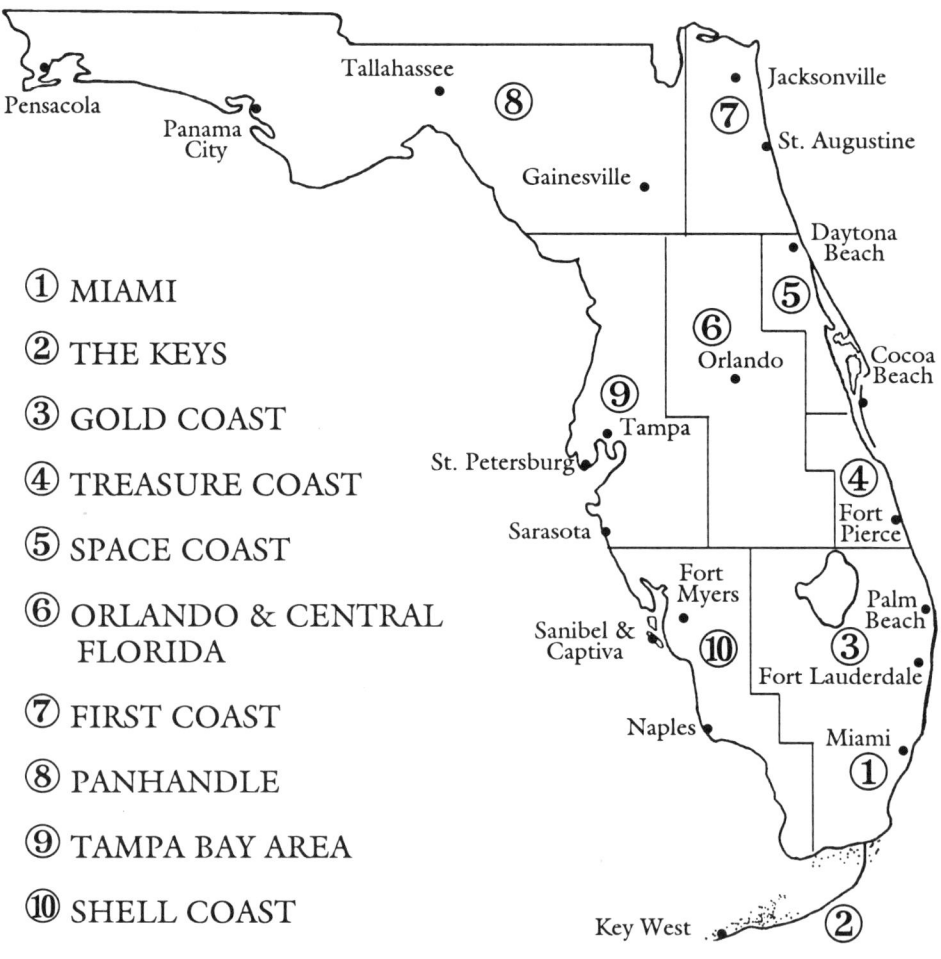

FLORIDA REBORN

THEY'VE FOUND THE FOUNTAIN OF YOUTH!

Remember that sleepy place your grandmother would escape to in the wintertime, and how she would ship a bushel of navel oranges and a "Wish you were here" note home for the holidays? That was the Florida of old. Then, at some point during the mid-1980s, everyone's image of the state as one vast retirement home exploded like a Fourth of July fireworks show at Walt Disney World. The nearly 40 million tourists who pack up from colder climes and head for the sunny Florida peninsula each year—with a collective $28 billion to blow on a good time—have given the state's personality an enormous booster shot of youth and vitality. And though suntans are still a major commodity in the state that brought the world Gatorade (the high-energy drink for athletes developed by researchers at the University of Florida), today's Florida has far more to offer than proximity to the Tropic of Cancer.

The state has a rich history that began centuries before the incognito arrival of one Walter E. Disney in the 1960s. (The clever cartoonist kept his identity a secret while negotiating for an enormous tract of land near Orlando—a maneuver to keep the price tag down to $6 million. Today, that piece of land is valued at roughly $6 billion.) After Spanish explorer Juan Ponce de León's discovery of "La Florida" (the little flower) in 1513, while in search of that elusive "fountain of youth," the Spanish came, saw and conquered the land. It was fought over for the next couple of centuries, by armies supplied variously by British, Seminole Indian, Confederate and Union interests. Not surprisingly, a very real regionalism still exists in Florida today, and the conflicting personalities of all of those warring factions—the Greeks, European Jews and Bahamian "Conchs" and Cubans who arrived later—still thrives like a lively chess game in Florida's diverse corners.

Following the Civil War, the farmers, fisherman and merchants of northern Florida grew fat off trading and agriculture, while the rest of the South suffered through Reconstruction. Tourism to Florida was restricted to wealthy fishing enthusiasts who came in from northeastern states by mailboat, for the annual tarpon migration. While the mid-century Disney conquest may well have been more important socially and culturally to Florida than that of any earlier conquistador, there were others responsible for building a tourism mecca that stretched all the way to Key West by 1912. The first was one Henry Flagler, who invested some $50 million in the Florida East Coast Railroad beginning in 1885. Along the way, he built several elaborate, world-class hotels that competed with those in Europe. Rival Henry Plant did the same along Florida's west coast, and voilà! A resort began to rise like a phoenix from the sogginess of Florida's jungleland.

The state received its next major boost decades later, when the TV series, *Miami Vice*, was beamed into America's collective living room in the mid-1980s. Suddenly Miami was an awfully sexy city, and Florida was once again in vogue. This more modern heyday, still in full swing long after *Miami Vice* has been taken off the air, hasn't been matched since the Art Deco days. To celebrate, the Miami Design Preservation League identified and certified an eight-block area of South Miami Beach buildings that had been built during the 1920s and 1930s. The reclaimed Art Deco District of the 1990s is the heart of a suddenly and decidedly hip Miami.

Treasures Unfathomable

As the state's charms spread beyond Miami and the Gold Coast (Fort Lauderdale and Palm Beach), the Florida Keys, whose more famous residents once included Ernest Hemingway, Tennessee Williams, Winslow Homer and Truman Capote, caught the world's imagination with more than its literary and art treasures. It was in 1985 that treasure hunter Mel Fisher uncovered more than $100 million in gold, silver and artifacts from the *Atocha* and *La Margarita* ships. Hundreds of millions of dollars worth of gold bars, chains, plates, coins and jewelry have been buried beneath Florida's coastal waters for more than 400 years. Experts estimate that up to 1,800 Spanish galleons, returning home from visits to Havana in the sixteenth and seventeenth centuries, were lost in Florida storms during that time.

Treasure hunting is at once big business and big dreaming—evidenced by the scores of ersatz hunters who comb Florida's beaches, metal detector in hand, gleefully digging up bottle caps. Still, their optimism is not entirely unreasonable: on land, pirates left an estimated $165 million in buried treasure, while fleeing Florida following various battles. Ship manifests indicate that the highest concentration of deep-sea booty is buried off the Treasure Coast, between Stuart and Vero Beach.

Throughout that region's Indian River groves and moving inland to Central Florida, a different kind of treasure can be found growing on trees. Though the citrus tree is a native of Asia and is believed to have been introduced to the Americas by Christopher Columbus, Florida is now the world's largest citrus-producing region. Some 50 percent of the world's grapefruits, 25 percent of the world's oranges, and 95 percent of the world's limes are produced in Florida.

Industry in the heart of the state shows increasing diversity: Florida's film industry is the fastest growing in the nation. Although Hollywood's film producers have been visiting Florida for decades, it is only lately that they have begun to set up shop here, turning Florida into an East Coast Hollywood. Disney-MGM opened a multimillion-dollar working production facility in Central Florida in 1989; Universal Studios opened a 440-acre complex in 1990 under the artistic direction of Hollywood producer Steven Spielberg.

INTRODUCTION About the Restaurants

Pleasures Unlimited

Recreation and leisure pursuits, however, will always reign over the Sunshine State. Florida boasts more spa resorts, tennis courts, holes of golf (Florida is the only state with more than a 1,000 golf courses), and full-service marinas than any other destination in the world. World headquarters of both the Association of Tennis Professionals (ATP) and the Professional Golfers Association (PGA) are located in northeast Florida's Ponte Vedra Beach. Ten years ago, that area was populated mostly by sea oats, swaying in relative solitude along deserted beaches. Today, a plethora of chrome-and-glass hotels, condo complexes and tinsel-rich playgrounds dot the landscape statewide. This can conspire to give parts of Florida the appearance of a carelessly designed strip mall, but much of Florida's rich heritage and unique environment has been preserved in the face of relentless development.

Tourism brochures, so eager to hawk Florida's well-developed tourism infrastructure, don't always manage adequately to sell the idea of the state's diversity. In spite of this 58,560-square-mile state's enormity, Florida's seductive peninsular shape that literally dangles off the continent guarantees that you'll never be more than an hour's drive from those lovely beaches. And with more than seventeen million acres of forests, and thirteen million acres of marshes, freshwater lakes and grasslands, the perpetually alluring coastline is only the beginning of the Florida experience.

Like an ingenue whose smarts are overshadowed by the knee-weakening impact of her loveliness, Florida's reputation has suffered from its own good looks. But we know better. Maybe we all should have listened to our grandmothers: they always did know Florida was a lot more than beautiful.

ABOUT THE RESTAURANTS

BOOM TIME IN THE OASIS

Kaboom! That's the sound of a break with the past, a sudden and powerful metamorphosis that is changing the face of Florida's culinary landscape—indeed, putting its food on the national map for the very first time. Until the 1990s, Florida's food scene was stagnant at best: here was a state with some of the freshest and finest produce, fish, fruit and fowl anywhere—and somehow none of this marvelous bounty ever made its way onto the diner's plate. Chefs clung steadfastly to the status quo—dishing out tired, uninspired food in old-fashioned, pretentious restaurant settings—and hoped no one would demand better. For a discriminating restaurant-goer, the standards for acceptability were appalling. The state of affairs is

INTRODUCTION About the Restaurants

illustrated perfectly by an experience we had in Tampa a decade ago: as we were served a mixed salad (straight out of the refrigerator) at a semigrand restaurant, the captain, in black bow-tie and dinner jacket, arrived to offer us "chilled forks for the salad."

While Florida wallowed in mediocrity like a sluggish alligator in the mud, a restaurant revolution was sweeping the rest of the country. New York and San Francisco remade themselves in the mid-1980s; Los Angeles, Boston and Chicago followed at the end of the decade. Today, Miami has finally begun to catch up with America's restaurant capitals, and is taking advantage of and building beyond the best contemporary innovations and trends we've seen in recent years.

Of course, Florida hasn't recultivated every inch of its culinary wasteland. The Sunshine State is still home to many classic French restaurants *à la* 1960 and numerous third-rate Continental affairs and greasy spoons. But the pots are bubbling madly in Florida's kitchens, and we can foresee the day when this grand 450-mile peninsula will be home to restaurants that rival those in New York and California. The contemporary breeze that has hit Miami and is blowing through Florida's other major cities is stirring up great change and excitement. Most notably, Florida is at last developing a distinctive, local cuisine.

Ten years ago, you could walk down Collins Avenue on the famed Miami Beach, and the only people you would see were grey-haired grandparents strolling in the sun. Five years ago in this area you'd find run-down or closed art-deco hotels and maybe a single restaurant. Today, this South Beach historic district is restored, spotless and packed with 35 restaurants—from sidewalk cafés to supper clubs, from Italian trattorias to Spanish *restaurantes*, from casual American eateries to sumptuous seafood houses. The crowds these days swing to young and free-spending.

Success breeds success, and Florida's restaurant scene is being fed by the prosperity all around the state. Already one of the nation's largest states and still the fastest growing, the combination of warm-weather resettlers and educated and well-paid corporate relocators—along with an ever larger number of the traditional tourists and retirees—has given Florida restaurateurs an increasingly sophisticated and demanding audience. Not only Miami, but Orlando, the Keys, Naples, Fort Myers, Tampa Bay and the Atlantic Gold Coast, from Palm Beach to Fort Lauderdale, are all booming.

The 1980s were also a period of homogenization across America. Every place began to look and taste alike. In New York, contemporary Italian restaurants such as Bice would open with success, and within a couple of years you could eat the same food at Bice in Chicago or Bice in Los Angeles, matching the original Bice in Milan. At new restaurants in New York, half the kitchen would hail from Los Angeles, and vice versa. The same food story was written daily; you could substitute the name of almost any major city for any other city. What was gained—in lighter fare, better produce, simpler preparations and strong influences from the Southwestern United States, California, Italy and Asia—was gained at the expense of regional cuisines. And that has been a great loss. Where can you go today in America and enjoy food like it is nowhere else?

Answer: Try Florida. Talented young chefs are utilizing local tropical ingredients to enhance the New American cuisine that has been widely embraced elsewhere: food

INTRODUCTION About the Restaurants

that is served raw; or grilled, smoked, blackened or cooked in a wood-burning oven; served on pizzas and in pastas. In Florida, thanks to a Latin American/Caribbean influence as well as a rediscovery of the traditional local foodstuffs of Florida's Native Americans, chefs are experimenting with mangoes, guavas, plantains, bonitos, chayotes, Key limes, papayas, coconuts, yucas, conchs, pompanos and Indian River soft-shell crabs.

If not every creation is successful, it's all in the name of progress. If not every chef has the skill and imagination to pull off or top what everyone is admiring at a neighbor's hotspot, this is certainly superior to the way things were. You cannot eat exactly the same meal in Miami as you can in New York, Los Angeles, Santa Fe, New Orleans, Paris or wherever, and thank goodness! With this, our first guide to the best of Florida, we are pleased to applaud the state as it wakes up, shakes off and moves into the exciting world of contemporary cuisine.

André Gayot

RANKINGS & TOQUES

Restaurants are ranked in the same manner that French students are graded, on a scale of one to twenty. The rankings reflect *only* the quality of the food; the decor, service, wine list and atmosphere are explicitly commented on within each review. Restaurants that are ranked 13/20 and above are distinguished with toques (chef's hats), according to the table below:

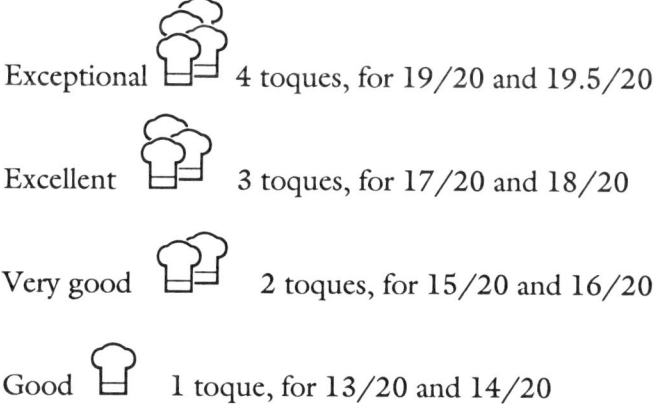

Exceptional   4 toques, for 19/20 and 19.5/20

Excellent   3 toques, for 17/20 and 18/20

Very good   2 toques, for 15/20 and 16/20

Good   1 toque, for 13/20 and 14/20

Keep in mind that we are comparing Florida's restaurants to the best in the world, and that these ranks are *relative*. A 13/20 (one toque) is not a very good ranking for a highly reputed (and very expensive) restaurant, but it is quite complimentary for a small place without much culinary pretension.

INTRODUCTION About the Restaurants

THE LAW OF THE MARKET

What decides the rating of a restaurant? What is on the plate is by far the most important factor. The **quality of produce** is among the most telling signs of a restaurant's culinary status. It requires a great deal of commitment and money to stock the finest grades and cuts of meat and the finest quality of fish. There is tuna, for example, and there's *tuna*. Ask any sushi chef. One extra-virgin olive oil is not the same, by far, as the next. Ditto for chocolates, pastas, spices and one thousand other ingredients. Quality restaurants also attune themselves to seasonal produce, whether it be local berries or truffles from Italy.

Freshness is all-important, and a telling indication of quality. This means not only using fresh rather than frozen fish, for example, but also preparing everything from scratch at the last possible moment, from appetizers through desserts.

What else do we look for? **Details** are telling: if sauces are homogenous, you know that the kitchen is taking shortcuts. The bread on the table is also a tip-off to the level and commitment to quality in a restaurant. Similarly, the house wine can speak volumes about the culinary attitude and level of an establishment. Wine is food, and wine lists and offerings can be revelatory. A list doesn't have to be long or expensive to show a commitment to quality.

Finally, among the very finest restaurants, **creativity** and **influence** can be determining factors. These qualities, however, are relatively unimportant for simply good restaurants, where the quality and consistency of what appears on the plates is of paramount importance. A restaurant that serves grilled chicken well is to be admired more than a restaurant that attempts some failed marriage of chicken and exotic produce, or some complicated chicken preparation that requires a larger and more talented kitchen brigade than is on hand. Don't be taken in by attempted fireworks that are really feeble sideshows.

PRICES & CREDIT CARDS

The price given at the end of each review is for a complete dinner for two, with an appetizer, main course and dessert per person, plus tax, tip and a bottle of wine. As it's hard to estimate the cost of wine; we assume a modest bottle at a modest restaurant and a good wine ($20 to $30 a bottle) at a more serious place. Lovers of the great Burgundies, Bordeaux or Champagnes will find their tabs higher than our estimates; conversely, those who eat lightly, sharing appetizers and desserts, will spend less.

Credit cards are abbreviated as follows:

AE: American Express and/or Optima
DC: Diners Club and/or Carte Blanche
MC: MasterCard
V: VISA

INTRODUCTION About the Restaurants

TOQUE TALLY

16/20

Mark's Place (*MIAMI*)

15/20

Chef Allen's (*MIAMI*)
Jordan's Grove (*ORLANDO*)
Ritz-Carlton Hotel Dining Room (*Naples, SHELL COAST*)
St. Honoré (*Palm Beach, GOLD COAST*)
Yuca (*MIAMI*)

14/20

A Mano (*MIAMI*)
Aragon Café (*MIAMI*)
Bern's Steakhouse (*Tampa, TAMPA BAY*)
Café Arugula (*Fort Lauderdale, GOLD COAST*)
Casa Rolandi (*MIAMI*)
Chatham's Place (*ORLANDO*)
Chef's Garden (*Naples, SHELL COAST*)
The Grand Café (*MIAMI*)
The Greenhouse (*Captiva Island, SHELL COAST*)
Il Porcino (*Fort Lauderdale, GOLD COAST*)
Jean-Paul's French Corner (*Sanibel Island, SHELL COAST*)
Louie's Backyard (*THE KEYS*)
The Mad Hatter *(Sanibel Island, SHELL COAST)*
Peter's La Cuisine (*Fort Myers, SHELL COAST*)
Regine's (*MIAMI*)
Sign of the Vine (*Naples, SHELL COAST*)
La Vieille Maison (*Palm Beach, GOLD COAST*)

13/20

Armadillo Café (*Fort Lauderdale, GOLD COAST*)
Armani's (*Tampa, TAMPA BAY*)
Café des Artistes (*THE KEYS*)
Café L'Europe (*Palm Beach, GOLD COAST*)
Café L'Europe (*Sarasota, TAMPA BAY*)
The Colony Restaurant (*Sarasota, TAMPA BAY*)
Le Coq au Vin (*ORLANDO*)
Donatello (*Tampa, TAMPA BAY*)
Il Tartuffo (*Fort Lauderdale, GOLD COAST*)
Jasmine Thai (*Tampa, TAMPA BAY*)
Joe's Stone Crab (*MIAMI*)
Park Plaza Gardens (*ORLANDO*)
Ramiro's (*MIAMI*)
Roberto's (*Palm Beach, GOLD COAST*)
Santa Lucia (*Fort Lauderdale, GOLD COAST*)
Siam Hut (*Fort Myers, SHELL COAST*)
Sterling's Flamingo Café (*Jacksonville, FIRST COAST*)
Toscanelli (*ORLANDO*)
24 Miramar (*Jacksonville, FIRST COAST*)
Victoria & Albert's (*ORLANDO*)
Victoria Park (*Fort Lauderdale, GOLD COAST*)
Windows on the Water (*Sanibel Island, SHELL COAST*)

12/20

Andrew's 2nd Act (*Tallahassee, PANHANDLE*)
L'Auberge du Bon Vivant (*Sarasota, TAMPA BAY*)
Brooks Restaurant (*Fort Lauderdale, GOLD COAST*)
Caffe Abbracci (*MIAMI*)

INTRODUCTION About the Restaurants

Café Marquesa (*THE KEYS*)
Café Seville (*Fort Lauderdale, GOLD COAST*)
Café Tu Tu Tango (*MIAMI*)
Chuck and Harold's (*Palm Beach, GOLD COAST*)
Dining Galleries (*MIAMI*)
La Ferme (*Fort Lauderdale, GOLD COAST*)
La Finestra (*Palm Beach, GOLD COAST*)
The Fish Market (*MIAMI*)
Flutes (*Fort Myers, SHELL COAST*)
The Forge (*MIAMI*)
The Gazebo (*Palm Beach, GOLD COAST*)
Il Tulipano (*MIAMI*)
Jamie's (*Pensacola, PANHANDLE*)
J. Fitzgerald's (*Tampa, TAMPA BAY*)
Joe Muer Seafood (*Palm Beach, GOLD COAST*)
Lá Trúc (*Palm Beach, GOLD COAST*)
The Lobster Pot (*St. Petersburg, TAMPA BAY*)
Margaux's (*Naples, SHELL COAST*)
Maxaluna (*Palm Beach, GOLD COAST*)
Max's Grille (*Palm Beach, GOLD COAST*)
Michael's on East (*Sarasota, TAMPA BAY*)
Mise en Place (*Tampa, TAMPA BAY*)
Morada Bar & Grill (*Palm Beach, GOLD COAST*)
Old City House (*St. Augustine, FIRST COAST*)
Osteria del Teatro (*MIAMI*)
The Pier House Restaurant (*THE KEYS*)
Runyon's (*Fort Lauderdale, GOLD COAST*)
Sangeet (*Fort Myers, SHELL COAST*)
The Sovereign (*Gainesville, PANHANDLE*)
Uncle Tai's (*Palm Beach, GOLD COAST*)
Villa Pescatore (*Naples, SHELL COAST*)
The Wine Cellar (*Jacksonville, FIRST COAST*)

11/20

Arthur's 27 (*ORLANDO*)
Atlantic's Edge (*THE KEYS*)
Baci (*Palm Beach, GOLD COAST*)
Beach Bistro (*Sarasota, TAMPA BAY*)
Bice (*Palm Beach, GOLD COAST*)
Bijou Café (*Sarasota, TAMPA BAY*)

The Bubble Room (*Captiva Island, SHELL COAST*)
Charley's Crab (*Palm Beach & Fort Lauderdale, GOLD COAST*)
Chris's House of Beef (*ORLANDO*)
Christini's (*ORLANDO*)
Dim Sum (*THE KEYS*)
Dominique's (*MIAMI*)
Dux (*ORLANDO*)
Gypsy Cab Company (*St. Augustine, FIRST COAST*)
The Heritage Grille Restaurant (*St. Petersburg, TAMPA BAY*)
The Heron (*Tampa, TAMPA BAY*)
Maison et Jardin (*ORLANDO*)
Mezzanote (*MIAMI*)
Ming Court (*ORLANDO*)
Mister Chu's (*Fort Lauderdale, GOLD COAST*)
Mucky Duck (*Captiva Island, SHELL COAST*)
The Pepper Mill (*St. Petersburg, TAMPA BAY*)
Portobello Yacht Club (*ORLANDO*)
Prawn Broker (*Fort Myers, SHELL COAST*)
Ragtime Tavern and Grill/Salud! (*Jacksonville, FIRST COAST*)
Sabal's (*St. Petersburg, TAMPA BAY*)
Salmon & Salmon (*MIAMI*)
Spring Creek (*Tallahassee, PANHANDLE*)
Stars and Stripes Café (*MIAMI*)
Studio One Café (*Fort Lauderdale, GOLD COAST*)
Victor's Café (*MIAMI*)

10/20

Akash (*MIAMI*)
Al Amir (*MIAMI*)
Anthony's (*Tallahassee, PANHANDLE*)
Arturo's (*Palm Beach, GOLD COAST*)
Basta's Cantina d'Italia (*St. Petersburg, TAMPA BAY*)
B.C. Chong (*MIAMI*)
Bugatti (*MIAMI*)
Café Baci (*MIAMI*)
Christie's (*MIAMI*)

INTRODUCTION About the Restaurants

Columbia Restaurant (*Tampa*, TAMPA BAY)
The Down Under (*Fort Lauderdale*, GOLD COAST)
Emiliano's (*Gainesville*, PANHANDLE)
Farmer Jones Red Barn (*Tampa*, TAMPA BAY)
Jimmy Ponce's Conch House (*St. Augustine*, FIRST COAST)
Harry's Continental Kitchens (*Sarasota*, TAMPA BAY)
Leonardo's (*Gainesville*, PANHANDLE)
Madrid (*MIAMI*)
Monty's Stone Crab (*MIAMI*)
Los Ranchos (*MIAMI*)
Ristorante Bellini (*Sarasota*, TAMPA BAY)
Sakura Gables (*MIAMI*)
The Sea Grill (*St. Petersburg*, TAMPA BAY)

The Strand (*MIAMI*)
Taste of Sze-chuan (*MIAMI*)
Thai Tony (*MIAMI*)
Unicorn Village (*MIAMI*)
The Wharf (*Tallahassee*, PANHANDLE)
Ziggy's Conch (*THE KEYS*)

9/20

Black Tulip (*ORLANDO*)
Raintree (*St. Augustine*, FIRST COAST)

8/20

Casa Juancho (*MIAMI*)
The Kapok Tree Restaurant (*St. Petersburg*, TAMPA BAY)

RESTAURANTS BY CUISINE

AMERICAN

A Mano (*MIAMI*)
Atlantic's Edge (*THE KEYS*)
Bijou Café (*Sarasota*, TAMPA BAY)
Black Tulip (*ORLANDO*)
Brooks Restaurant (*Fort Lauderdale*, GOLD COAST)
The Bubble Room (*Captiva Island*, SHELL COAST)
Café Arugula (*Fort Lauderdale*, GOLD COAST)
Café Marquesa (*THE KEYS*)
Chatham's Place (*ORLANDO*)
Chef Allen's (*MIAMI*)
Chuck and Harold's (*Palm Beach*, GOLD COAST)
The Colony Restaurant (*Sarasota*, TAMPA BAY)
Dux (*ORLANDO*)
Emiliano's (*Gainesville*, PANHANDLE)
The Fish Market (*MIAMI*)
Flutes (*Fort Myers*, SHELL COAST)

The Forge (*MIAMI*)
The Grand Café (*MIAMI*)
The Greenhouse (*Captiva Island*, SHELL COAST)
The Heritage Grille Restaurant (*St. Petersburg*, TAMPA BAY)
Jordan's Grove (*ORLANDO*)
The Kapok Tree Restaurant (*St. Petersburg*, TAMPA BAY)
Harry's Continental Kitchens (*Sarasota*, TAMPA BAY)
Louie's Backyard (*THE KEYS*)
Max's Grille (*Palm Beach*, GOLD COAST)
Michael's on East (*Sarasota*, TAMPA BAY)
Mise en Place (*Tampa*, TAMPA BAY)
Morada Bar & Grill (*Palm Beach*, GOLD COAST)
The Pier House Restaurant (*THE KEYS*)
The Pepper Mill (*St. Petersburg*, TAMPA BAY)
Runyon's (*Fort Lauderdale*, GOLD COAST)
Stars and Stripes Café (*MIAMI*)

Sterling's Flamingo Café (*Jacksonville, FIRST COAST*)
The Strand (*MIAMI*)
24 Miramar (*Jacksonville, FIRST COAST*)
Victoria & Albert's (*ORLANDO*)
Windows on the Water (*Sanibel Island, SHELL COAST*)
Ziggy's Conch (*THE KEYS*)

ASIAN

Dim Sum (*THE KEYS*)

CALIFORNIAN

Flutes (*Fort Myers, SHELL COAST*)
Sabal's (*St. Petersburg, TAMPA BAY*)
24 Miramar (*Jacksonville, FIRST COAST*)

CARIBBEAN

Café des Artistes (*THE KEYS*)
Louie's Backyard (*THE KEYS*)
Victoria Park (*Fort Lauderdale, GOLD COAST*)

CHINESE

B.C. Chong (*MIAMI*)
Ming Court (*ORLANDO*)
Mister Chu's (*Fort Lauderdale, GOLD COAST*)
Taste of Sze-chuan (*MIAMI*)
Uncle Tai's (*Palm Beach, GOLD COAST*)

CONTINENTAL

Arthur's 27 (*ORLANDO*)
Andrew's 2nd Act (*Tallahassee, PANHANDLE*)
L'Auberge du Bon Vivant (*Sarasota, TAMPA BAY*)
Beach Bistro (*Sarasota, TAMPA BAY*)
Café L'Europe (*Palm Beach, GOLD COAST*)
Café L'Europe (*Sarasota, TAMPA BAY*)
Chef's Garden (*Naples, SHELL COAST*)
Dining Galleries (*MIAMI*)
The Down Under (*Fort Lauderdale, GOLD COAST*)
The Gazebo (*Palm Beach, GOLD COAST*)
The Heron (*Tampa, TAMPA BAY*)
Jamie's (*Pensacola, PANHANDLE*)
J. Fitzgerald's (*Tampa, TAMPA BAY*)
Maison et Jardin (*ORLANDO*)
Park Plaza Gardens (*ORLANDO*)
Peter's La Cuisine (*Fort Myers, SHELL COAST*)
Raintree (*St. Augustine, FIRST COAST*)
Ritz-Carlton Hotel Dining Room (*Naples, SHELL COAST*)
Sabal's (*St. Petersburg, TAMPA BAY*)
Sterling's Flamingo Café (*Jacksonville, FIRST COAST*)
The Sovereign (*Gainesville, PANHANDLE*)
The Wine Cellar (*Jacksonville, FIRST COAST*)

CUBAN

Madrid (*MIAMI*)
Victor's Café (*MIAMI*)
Yuca (*MIAMI*)

FRENCH

Aragon Café (*MIAMI*)
L'Auberge du Bon Vivant (*Sarasota, TAMPA BAY*)
Café des Artistes (*THE KEYS*)
Le Coq au Vin (*ORLANDO*)
Dominique's (*MIAMI*)
La Ferme (*Fort Lauderdale, GOLD COAST*)
Jean-Paul's French Corner (*Sanibel Island, SHELL COAST*)
Margaux's (*Naples, SHELL COAST*)
Regine's (*MIAMI*)
St. Honoré (*Palm Beach, GOLD COAST*)
Studio One Café (*Fort Lauderdale, GOLD COAST*)
Victoria Park (*Fort Lauderdale, GOLD COAST*)
La Vieille Maison (*Palm Beach, GOLD COAST*)

INTRODUCTION About the Restaurants

HEALTH FOOD

Unicorn Village (*MIAMI*)

INDIAN

Akash (*MIAMI*)
Sangeet (*Fort Myers, SHELL COAST*)

INTERNATIONAL

Brooks Restaurant (*Fort Lauderdale, GOLD COAST*)
Café Arugula (*Fort Lauderdale, GOLD COAST*)
Sign of the Vine (*Naples, SHELL COAST*)

ITALIAN

Anthony's (*Tallahassee, PANHANDLE*)
Armani's (*Tampa, TAMPA BAY*)
Arturo's (*Palm Beach, GOLD COAST*)
Basta's Cantina d'Italia (*St. Petersburg, TAMPA BAY*)
Baci (*Palm Beach, GOLD COAST*)
Bice (*Palm Beach, GOLD COAST*)
Bugatti (*MIAMI*)
Café Abbracci (*MIAMI*)
Café Baci (*MIAMI*)
Casa Rolandi (*MIAMI*)
Christini's (*ORLANDO*)
Donatello (*Tampa, TAMPA BAY*)
La Finestra (*Palm Beach, GOLD COAST*)
Il Porcino (*Fort Lauderdale, GOLD COAST*)
Il Tartuffo (*Fort Lauderdale, GOLD COAST*)
Il Tulipano (*MIAMI*)
Leonardo's (*Gainesville, PANHANDLE*)
Maxaluna (*Palm Beach, GOLD COAST*)
Mezzanote (*MIAMI*)
Osteria del Teatro (*MIAMI*)
Portobello Yacht Club (*ORLANDO*)
Ristorante Bellini (*Sarasota, TAMPA BAY*)
Roberto's (*Palm Beach, GOLD COAST*)
Santa Lucia (*Fort Lauderdale, GOLD COAST*)
Toscanelli (*ORLANDO*)
Villa Pescatore (*Naples, SHELL COAST*)

JAPANESE

Sakura Gables (*MIAMI*)

MIDDLE EASTERN

Al Amir (*MIAMI*)

NEW AMERICAN

The Mad Hatter (*Sanibel Island, SHELL COAST*)
Mark's Place (*MIAMI*)
Old City House (*St. Augustine, FIRST COAST*)

NICARAGUAN

Los Ranchos (*MIAMI*)

PERUVIAN

Salmon & Salmon (*MIAMI*)

SEAFOOD

Charley's Crab (*Fort Lauderdale & Palm Beach, GOLD COAST*)
The Fish Market (*MIAMI*)
Gypsy Cab Company (*St. Augustine, FIRST COAST*)
The Heron (*TAMPA*)
Jimmy Ponce's Conch House (*St. Augustine, FIRST COAST*)
Joe Muer Seafood (*Palm Beach, GOLD COAST*)
Joe's Stone Crab (*MIAMI*)
The Lobster Pot (*St. Petersburg, TAMPA BAY*)
Monty's Stone Crab (*MIAMI*)
Mucky Duck (*Captiva Island, SHELL COAST*)
Prawn Broker (*Fort Myers, SHELL COAST*)
Ragtime Tavern and Grill/Salud! (*Jacksonville, FIRST COAST*)
The Sea Grill (*St. Petersburg, TAMPA BAY*)
Spring Creek (*Tallahassee, PANHANDLE*)
Villa Pescatore (*Naples, SHELL COAST*)
The Wharf (*Talahassee, PANHANDLE*)

INTRODUCTION About the Restaurants

Windows on the Water (*Sanibel Island*, SHELL COAST)
Ziggy's Conch (*THE KEYS*)

SOUTHWESTERN

Armadillo Café (*Fort Lauderdale*, GOLD COAST)

SPANISH

Café Seville (*Fort Lauderdale*, GOLD COAST)
Café Tu Tu Tango (*MIAMI*)
Casa Juancho (*MIAMI*)
Columbia Restaurant (*Tampa*, TAMPA BAY)
Emiliano's (*Gainesville*, PANHANDLE)
Madrid (*MIAMI*)
Ramiro's (*MIAMI*)

STEAKHOUSE

Bern's Steakhouse (*Tampa*, TAMPA BAY)
Chris's House of Beef (*ORLANDO*)
Christie's (*MIAMI*)
Farmer Jones Red Barn (*Tampa*, TAMPA BAY)
Runyon's (*Fort Lauderdale*, GOLD COAST)

THAI

Jasmine Thai (*Tampa*, TAMPA BAY)
Siam Hut (*Fort Myers*, SHELL COAST)
Thai Tony (*MIAMI*)

VIETNAMESE

Lá Trúc (*Palm Beach*, GOLD COAST)

RESTAURANTS BY AREA

MIAMI (P. 21)

Akash
Al Amir
A Mano
Aragon Café
B. C. Chong
Bugatti
Café Abbracci
Café Baci
Café Tu Tu Tango
Casa Juancho
Casa Rolandi
Chef Allen's
Christie's
Dining Galleries
Dominique's
The Fish Market
The Forge
The Grand Café
Il Tulipano
Joe's Stone Crab
Madrid
Mark's Place
Mezzanotte
Monty's Stone Crab
Osteria del Teatro
Ramiro's
Los Ranchos
Regine's
Sakura Gables
Salmon & Salmon
Stars and Stripes Café
The Strand
Taste of Sze-chuan
Thai Toni
Unicorn Village
Victor's Café
Yuca

INTRODUCTION About the Restaurants

THE KEYS (P. 101)

Upper Keys
Atlantic's Edge
Ziggy's Conch

Key West
Café Marquesa
Dim Sum
Louie's Backyard
The Pier House Restaurant

GOLD COAST (P. 127)

Fort Lauderdale
Armadillo Café
Brooks Restaurant
Café Arugula
Café Seville
Charley's Crab
The Down Under
La Ferme
Il Porcino
Il Tartuffo
Mister Chu's
Runyon's
Santa Lucia
Studio One Café
Victoria Park

Palm Beach
Arturo's
Baci
Bice
Café L'Europe
Charley's Crab
Chuck and Harold's
La Finestra
The Gazebo
Joe Muer Seafood
Lá Trúc
Maxaluna
Max's Grille
Morada Bar & Grill
Roberto's
St. Honoré
Uncle Tai's
La Vieille Maison

ORLANDO (P. 197)
Arthur's 27
Black Tulip
Chatham's Place
Chris's House of Beef
Christini's
Le Coq au Vin
Dux
Jordan's Grove
Maison et Jardin
Ming Court
Park Plaza Gardens
Portobello Yacht Club
Toscanelli
Victoria & Albert's

FIRST COAST (P. 249)

St. Augustine
Gypsy Cab Company
Jimmy Ponce's Conch House
Old City House
Raintree

Jacksonville
Ragtime Tavern and Grill/Salud!
Sterling's Flamingo Café
24 Miramar
The Wine Cellar

PANHANDLE (P. 265)

Pensacola
Jamie's

Tallahassee
Andrew's 2nd Act
Anthony's
Spring Creek
The Wharf

Gainesville
Emiliano's
Leonardo's
The Sovereign

15

INTRODUCTION   About the Restaurants

TAMPA BAY (*P. 277*)

Tampa
Armani's
Bern's Steakhouse
Columbia Restaurant
Donatello
Farmer Jones Red Barn
The Heron
J. Fitzgerald's
Jasmine Thai
Mise en Place

St. Petersburg
Basta's Cantina d'Italia
The Heritage Grille Restaurant
The Kapok Tree Restaurant
The Lobster Pot
The Pepper Mill
Sabal's
The Sea Grill

Sarasota
L'Auberge du Bon Vivant
Beach Bistro
Bijou Café
Café L'Europe
The Colony Restaurant
Harry's Continental Kitchens

Michael's on East
Ristorante Bellini

SHELL COAST (*P. 311*)

Fort Myers
Flutes
Peter's La Cuisine
The Prawn Broker
Sangeet
Siam Hut

Naples
Chef's Garden
Margaux's
Ritz-Carlton Hotel Dining Room
Sign of the Vine
Villa Pescatore

Sanibel & Captiva Islands
The Bubble Room
The Greenhouse
Jean-Paul's French Corner
The Mad Hatter
Mucky Duck
Windows on the Water

ABOUT THE HOTELS

A WORD OF ADVICE

Every sort of accommodation you can imagine can be found in Florida: there are fantasy beach condos, sprawling golf and tennis resorts, sumptuous spas, charming old inns, bed-and-breakfasts. Just read on—it's all here. A few words of advice:

- Be sure to make and confirm a hotel reservation well in advance—especially during peak seasons: mid-November to May in Central and South Florida; May to September in the Panhandle.

INTRODUCTION   About the Hotels

- During off season, rates can be as much as 30 percent to 50 percent lower than their peak-season highs. If you're on a tight budget, it might be wise to schedule your trip directly before or directly following high season.
- Many hotels offer sizable discounts and special weekend (Friday-to-Sunday) packages throughout the year; don't hesitate to inquire about these.
- In the hotel world, there is almost no such thing as an absolute rate. Room charges fluctuate by season, availability, quality of view, proximity to the ocean (at beachfront resorts) and so on. Don't be afraid to negotiate a lower rate, and don't take "no" for an answer until you're sure you can't negotiate any further.
- Don't assume that hotels falling under the "Top of the Line" or "Luxury" headings are truly luxurious: the place may position and price itself that way, but that doesn't mean it delivers the goods.
- Keep in mind that the rates we list do not include Florida's 6 percent sales tax. Also, most cities levy an additional hotel tax, ranging from 2 percent to 11 percent more.

CHOOSING A HOTEL

To help you easily find the hotel that best matches your budget, establishments in this book are listed in sections by price, from most expensive to least expensive: **Top of the Line, Luxury, Moderate** and **Practical**. **Inns** and **Bed & Breakfasts** are listed in separate categories. The symbol that accompanies each hotel review indicates in which price category the hotel belongs, and for the purposes of this book, we have defined the categories based on the average starting price of a single or double room:

   TOP OF THE LINE (From $200)

   LUXURY (From $150)

   MODERATE (From $100)

   PRACTICAL (Under $100)

Our opinion of each lodging is expressed in the text, where we describe and comment upon the decor, service, atmosphere, rooms, amenities, location and so on. Read the reviews carefully to select the hotel (within the appropriate price category) that best suits your needs and your tastes.

INTRODUCTION About the Hotels

HOTELS BY AREA & PRICE

MIAMI (P. 21)

Top of the Line (From $200)
The Alexander
Doral Saturnia International Spa Resort
Sheraton Bal Harbour
Sonesta Beach Hotel Key Biscayne

Luxury (From $150)
The Colonnade
Fontainebleau Hilton Resort and Spa
Grand Bay Hotel
Grove Isle Yacht & Tennis Club Hotel
Hyatt Regency Coral Gables
Sheraton Brickell Point on Biscayne Bay

Moderate (From $100)
Dadeland Marriott
David William Hotel
Doral Ocean Beach Resort
Doral Resort & Country Club
Hyatt Regency City Center
Inter-Continental Hotel Miami
Mayfair House
Miami Airport Hilton & Marina
Omni International Hotel
Sheraton River House Hotel
Turnberry Isle Yacht & Country Club

Practical (Under $100)
Doubletree Hotel
Dupont Plaza Hotel
The Edison Hotel
The Everglades Hotel
Harbor Island Spa
Hotel Place St. Michel
Hotel Riverparc
Hotel Sofitel Miami
Pan American Ocean Resort Radisson
Park Central Hotel
Ritz Plaza Hotel Miami Beach
Sheraton Royal Biscayne Beach Resort
Surfcomber

Inns
Miami Lakes Inn

THE KEYS (P. 101)

Top of the Line (From $200)
Little Palm Island (*Lower Keys*)

Luxury (From $150)
Hyatt Key West (*Key West*)

Moderate (From $100)
The Banyan Resort (*Key West*)
Cheeca Lodge (*Upper Keys*)
Hawk's Cay Resort and Marina (*Lower Keys*)
Holiday Isle (*Upper Keys*)
Marriott Casa Marina Resort (*Key West*)
La Mer Hotel (*Key West*)
Ocean Key House (*Key West*)
Pier House (*Key West*)
The Reach (*Key West*)
Sheraton Key Largo Resort (*Upper Keys*)

Practical (Under $100)
La Concha Holiday Inn (*Key West*)
The Curry Mansion Inn (*Key West*)
Duval House (*Key West*)
Eaton Lodge (*Key West*)
Faro Blanco Marine Resort (*Lower Keys*)
Island City House (*Key West*)
Marina del Mar (*Upper Keys*)
Merlinn Guest House (*Key West*)
Pelican Cove (*Upper Keys*)
La Terraza de Marti (*Key West*)

GOLD COAST (P. 127)

Luxury (From $150)
The Breakers (*Palm Beach*)
Chesterfield Hotel Deluxe (*Palm Beach*)
Diplomat Resort and Country Club (*Fort Lauderdale*)

INTRODUCTION About the Hotels

Marriott Harbor Beach Resort (*Fort Lauderdale*)
Pier 66 Resort & Marina (*Fort Lauderdale*)

Moderate (From $100)
Boca Raton Resort and Club (*Palm Beach*)
Colony Hotel (*Palm Beach*)
Hollywood Beach Hilton (*Fort Lauderdale*)
Marriott Hotel & Marina (*Fort Lauderdale*)
Ocean Grand (*Palm Beach*)
Palm Aire Spa Resort (*Fort Lauderdale*)
PGA National Resort (*Palm Beach*)
Sheraton Design Center (*Fort Lauderdale*)

Practical (Under $100)
Bahia Cabana Beach Resort (*Fort Lauderdale*)
Bahia Mar Resort & Yachting Center (*Fort Lauderdale*)
Boca Raton Marriott Crocker Center (*Palm Beach*)
Brazilian Court (*Palm Beach*)
Embassy Suites-17th St. Causeway (*Fort Lauderdale*)
Guest Quarters Suite Hotel (*Fort Lauderdale*)
Hollywood Beach Resort Hotel (*Fort Lauderdale*)
Inverrary Hotel and Conference Resort (*Fort Lauderdale*)
Jupiter Beach Hilton (*Palm Beach*)
Palm Beach Polo and Country Club (*Palm Beach*)
Riverside Hotel (*Fort Lauderdale*)
Sheraton Bonaventure Resort and Spa (*Fort Lauderdale*)
Sheraton-Yankee Clipper Beach Resort (*Fort Lauderdale*)
Sheraton-Yankee Trader Resort (*Fort Lauderdale*)
Traders Ocean Resort (*Fort Lauderdale*)

TREASURE COAST (P. 177)

Moderate (From $100)
Vistana's Beach Club

Practical (Under $100)
Club Med–The Sandpiper
Indian River Plantation
Sheraton Beach on Hutchinson Island

SPACE COAST (P. 185)

Moderate (From $100)
Marriott Daytona Beach (*Daytona Beach*)
Palm Coast Sheraton (*Daytona Beach*)
Radisson Suite Hotel Oceanfront (*Cocoa Beach*)

Practical (Under $100)
Cocoa Beach Hilton & Towers (*Cocoa Beach*)
Daytona Beach Hilton (*Daytona Beach*)
Holiday Inn Cocoa Beach (*Cocoa Beach*)
Indigo Lakes Hilton (*Daytona Beach*)
Perry's Ocean Edge Resort (*Daytona Beach*)
The Reef (*Daytona Beach*)
Royal Mansions Resort (*Cocoa Beach*)

ORLANDO (P. 197)

Top of the Line (From $200)
Disney's Grand Floridian Beach Resort
Marriott Orlando World Center
Sonesta Villa Resort
Walt Disney World Dolphin
Walt Disney World Swan
Walt Disney World Yacht and Beach Club Resort

Luxury (From $150)
Buena Vista Palace
Grenelefe
Grosvenor Resort
Hyatt Regency Grand Cypress
Omni International Hotel
Peabody Orlando
Stouffer Orlando
Villas of Grand Cypress

Moderate (From $100)
Compri Hotel Lake Buena Vista
Hawthorn Suites Villa Resort
Hilton at Walt Disney World Village
Vistana Resort

Practical (Under $100)
Harley Hotel
Park Plaza Hotel

Inns
Chalet Suzanne
Lakeside Inn

Bed & Breakfast
The Courtyard at Lake Lucerne
DeLand Country Inn

FIRST COAST (P. 249)

Luxury (From $150)
Marriott at Sawgrass (*St. Augustine*)

Moderate (From $100)
Amelia Island Plantation (*Jacksonville*)
The Lodge at Ponte Vedra Beach (*St. Augustine*)
Omni Jacksonville Hotel (*Jacksonville*)

Practical (Under $100)
The Bailey House (*Jacksonville*)

Bed & Breakfast
1735 House (*Jacksonville*)
Westcott House (*St. Augustine*)

PANHANDLE (P. 265)

Moderate (From $100)
Tops'l Beach & Racquet Club (*Pensacola*)

Practical (Under $100)
Marriott Bay Point Resort (*Panama City*)
Pensacola Hilton (*Pensacola*)
Sandestin Beach Resort (*Pensacola*)

TAMPA BAY (P. 277)

Top of the Line (From $200)
The Colony Beach & Tennis Resort (*Sarasota*)

Luxury (From $150)
Safety Harbor Spa & Fitness Center (*Tampa*)

Moderate (From $100)
The Don CeSar Registry Resort (*St. Petersburg*)
Harrington House (*Sarasota*)
Hyatt Regency Westshore at Tampa International Airport (*Tampa*)
Innisbrook Resort (*Tampa*)
Longboat Key Club (*Sarasota*)
Saddlebrook Resort (*Tampa*)
Sheraton Grand Westshore (*Tampa*)

Practical (Under $100)
Belleview MIDO Resort Hotel (*St. Petersburg*)
Longboat Key Hilton (*Sarasota*)
Tradewinds on St. Petersburg Beach (*St. Petersburg*)

SHELL COAST (P. 311)

Top of the Line (From $200)
South Seas Plantation (*Captiva Island*)

Luxury (From $150)
Marriott's Marco Island Resort (*Naples*)

Moderate (From $100)
Radisson Suite Beach Resort (*Naples*)
Registry Resort Naples (*Naples*)
Ritz-Carlton Hotel Naples (*Naples*)
Sonesta Sanibel Harbour Resort and Spa (*Fort Myers*)
Sundial Beach & Tennis Resort (*Sanibel Island*)

Practical (Under $100)
Naples Beach Hotel & Golf Club (*Naples*)
'Tween Waters Inn (*Captiva Island*)
Vanderbilt Inn on the Gulf (*Naples*)

MIAMI

RESTAURANTS	22
QUICK BITES	42
HOTELS	47
NIGHTLIFE	59
SHOPS	68
SIGHTS & SPORTS	86
BASICS	95

RESTAURANTS

Akash
11733 Biscayne Blvd.,
North Miami
• (305) 891-9919
INDIAN

10/20

It's a long way from North Miami to New Delhi. But the distance was recently slashed by the arrival of Akash, a posh Indian restaurant with a well-known sister in London. This isn't your usual ethnic hole-in-the-wall, not with its candlelit tables, heavy silverware and hovering service. The kitchen serves superior versions of time-honored Indian classics, including pakoras (Indian kreplach chock-full of cumin-scented potatoes), samosas (a sort of vegetable tempura fried in chickpea batter) and sag paneer (homemade cheese in a mildly spiced spinach-cream sauce). The house specialty is tandoori, meats marinated in yogurt and spices, grilled in an urn-shaped clay oven and served on sizzling platters. Don't leave without trying the pappadum (spicy lentil crisp), or one of the Indian breads, like kulcha (soft, chewy bread loaded with spiced onions). Rasmalai, rosewater-scented cheesecake, brings the meal to a dulcet close. Akash, which means "sky" in Hindi, is a pretty place with pink tablecloths, pink carnations, pink-and-gold banquettes and rose-colored carpets. Best of all are the eminently reasonable prices: two can dine regally, with wine or Indian Kingfisher beer, for about $50.
Open nightly 5 p.m.-10:30 p.m. All major cards.

Al Amir
1131 Washington Ave.,
Miami Beach
• (305) 534-0022
MIDDLE EASTERN

10/20

With its vertiginously high ceilings, mirrored pillars, marble floors, Moorish arches and trompe l'oeil murals of the desert, Al Amir doesn't look like the typical stateside Middle Eastern restaurant. The owners of New York's Al Amir obviously spent a sheikh's fortune opening this branch in the heart of Miami's Art Deco District. Why, then, do they undermine their efforts by employing such an overbearing, ill-informed staff? Nonetheless, there's good food to be had, such as lemony yabrak (rice-stuffed grape leaves), fatayer (spinach and pine nut pastries) and kafta istamboul (ground lamb blasted with garlic and grilled on a skewer). The fattouch (pita bread salad) owes its piquancy to a little-known spice called sumac. The cholesterol conscious will appreciate the variety of grilled items, including farouj michwi (baby chicken with lemon and herbs). The couscous, however, may be the worst we've ever tasted; even our waiter admitted its awfulness. But the homemade Middle Eastern pastries—all syrup and phyllo—helped make amends. Dinner for two, with wine, will run $70 to $80.
Open Sun.-Thurs. 6 p.m.-midnight, Fri.-Sat. 9 p.m.-1 a.m. Cards: AE, MC, V.

MIAMI Restaurants

A Mano

The Betsy Ross Hotel,
1440 Ocean Dr.,
Miami Beach
• (305) 531-6266
AMERICAN

By February 1991, Miami foodies were growing impatient: they had waited a year already for the opening of the new restaurant at the Betsy Ross Hotel. That month, not a moment too soon, the last pieces of gold leaf were applied to the peach and forest-green walls and the last mini-palm trees were planted in handsome hammered brass pots, and Norman Van Aken's new restaurant, "a Mano," opened to applause.

Finally, the Art Deco District has a dining room worthy of the area's name (except for the decor, which flaunts pure post-modernism; the designers of the high-ceilinged dining room put in enough unusual half-moon-shaped booths and enough *faux* marble trim to let everyone know that we're indisputably in the postmodern era). *A mano*, as you might have guessed, means "by hand" in Spanish, and this kitchen is serious about that. Van Aken takes a hands-on, cross-cultural approach to the cuisines of Cuba, the Caribbean, Latin America, Europe and even Asia. We find that he performs best in a tropical mode. Annatto oil (perfumed with an aromatic orange Caribbean seed) spices up a snapper escabeche. Rum sauce, fried plantains and Peruvian purple potatoes grace a meltingly tender pan-seared black grouper. Not that Van Aken is infallible. Some of his dishes work better in the realm of ideas than they do on the plate. "Very French toast," for example, features foie gras and Armagnac-caramel sauce, but the brioche french toast itself is too soft and far too rich to be eaten in the same breath as pan-fried goose liver. There's no faulting the bread basket, which might feature yard-long breadsticks or homemade Cuban bread. Desserts range from a simple but perfect flan to a peach poached in late harvest Riesling, served in puff pastry, with a dollop of honey. The $16-to-$26 entrée price will give pause to some, but its nice to see the trendy Art Deco District serve good food for its high prices. Dinner for two, with wine, will run $100 to $120. *Open Tues.-Thurs. & Sun. 6 p.m.-10:30 p.m., Fri.-Sat. 6 p.m.-11 p.m. All major cards.*

Aragon Café

Colonnade Hotel
180 Aragon Ave.,
Coral Gables
• (305) 448-9966
FRENCH

Once upon a time, diners looked to hotel restaurants for *grande* cuisine. Then came the boutique restaurant revolution and the rise of the owner/chef. Still, it's nice to return to a grandiose hotel dining room every now and then, for the well-spaced tables and ponderous silver that, in this age of belt-tightening, only the major hotels can afford. Consider the Aragon Café at the Colonnade Hotel. You could get dizzy gazing up at the barrel-vaulted ceilings. Portraits of Coral Gables's first ladies grace the walls. Fortunately, you get more than just an opulent decor. Pascal Oudin is a very clever chef, enveloping rabbit saddles in lobster mousse, fashioning lifelike demitasses out of white chocolate and filling them with mocha mousse, and

layering smoked salmon with leeks and anchovy butter to make an unusual terrine. Even the lowly potato pancake gets into the act, perfumed with lofty truffles. As in France, a plate of petit fours attends the formidable moment of reckoning. To experience the Aragon Café at its best, sign up for one of the monthly chef's dinners, a prix-fixe menu that pulls out all the stops. The service could be a tad more attentive. A grand dinner for two, with wine, will cost $120 to $150.
Open Mon.-Sat. 6 p.m.-10:30 p.m. All major cards.

B. C. Chong
3176 Commodore Plaza,
Coconut Grove
• (305) 567-0088
CHINESE

10/20

For reasons unclear to us, Miami has never possessed a great Chinese restaurant. So it was with great excitement that Asian food buffs awaited the opening of B.C. Chong in a Coconut Grove storefront. Here was a Chinese restaurant with a difference: a wall of glass with ringside views of the frenzied activity in the kitchen, and a menu that steers clear of clichés, favoring dishes seldom seen in these parts, like honey ham (steamed Smithfield ham), squid with black-bean sauce, and oysters with gluten casserole. The good news is that judicious ordering will fetch you Chinese food that's almost up to Bostonian or Philadelphian standards. The bad news is that Miami is a still a long, long way from Chinatown in New York. Good bets include the eight-treasure winter melon soup, the clams with onion-and-chili casserole and the river "chicken" (deep-fried frog with seasoned salt). We've never understood the popularity of the oily spring rolls. The setting is fancier than most Chinese restaurants—white-clothed tables, track lighting, a fresh gray-and-pink color scheme—and service is much friendlier than the Chinese norm. Dinner for two, with beer or wine, runs $50.
Open Mon.-Thurs. 11:30 a.m.-11 p.m., Fri. 11:30 a.m.-midnight, Sat. 5 p.m.-midnight, Sun. 5 p.m.-11 p.m. Cards: AE, MC, V.

Bugatti
2504 Ponce de Leon Blvd.,
Coral Gables
• (305) 441-2545
ITALIAN

10/20

If you must name a restaurant after a car, it might as well be a Bugatti. We like this yupscale pizza and pasta emporium, with its pink granite tables and chocolate- and cream-colored walls—it's just the place when you have a hankering for a colorful salad, a designer pizza or a stylishly served bowl of pasta. The first might be a superlative Caesar; the second a pizza Bugatti (topped with pesto and fresh vegetables); the third al dente penne (pasta quills) with a brandied leek sauce. In a cute twist on an Italian classic, melon balls come wrapped in thin strips of prosciutto. This is one of the few local Italian restaurants that serve bresaola (air-dried beef). It's no temple of haute gastronomy, but this neighborhood eatery is quick, fashionable and user-friendly. Dinner for two, with a glass of wine, will cost $40.
Open Mon.-Sat. 11:30 a.m.-10:30 p.m., Sun. 5:30 p.m.-10:30 p.m. Cards: AE, MC, V.

Caffe Abbracci

318 Aragon Ave.,
Coral Gables
• (305) 441-0700
ITALIAN

12/20

When a restaurant sports a name that translates as "Café Hugs," you can't help wondering initially if it isn't all fun and games in the kitchen. To the contrary, though this casually elegant, modern eatery hums with animated conversation and laughter most nights, from a crowd that gathers partly to see and be seen at a hot spot, the kitchen dishes up some very good Italian food.

Companion to Miami's Caffe Baci (which translates as "Café Kisses"), Caffe Abbracci is embraced by a progression of crowds throughout the evenings—starting with the quieter early dining set, followed by younger groups out for business or pleasure, and continuing into the wee hours with late-night revelers. This sleek place shares its relative's striking barrel-vaulted metal ceiling, and boasts its own marigold-colored walls, forest-green marble trim and a handsome burlwood bar. Proprietor Nino Pernetti and chef Mauro Bazzanini present dishes with justified confidence: bocconcino (melted buffalo mozzarella with porcini mushrooms and basil) and lumache nel nido (snails and mushrooms cooked in Barolo wine and served in a nest of polenta); or grilled swordfish marinated in lemon, ginger and olive oil. Alternatively, consider a straightforward veal scaloppine, or a less straightforward offering of sautéed shrimps with Tuscan white beans and sweet onion rings. If the menu can be used as evidence, chef Bazzanini apparently has a love of toasted pine nuts . . . and why not? Dinner for two, with a bottle of wine, runs about $80.

Open Mon.-Thurs. 11:30 a.m.-3 p.m. & 6 p.m.-11 p.m., Fri. 11:30 a.m.-3 p.m. & 6 p.m.-11:30 p.m., Sat. 6 p.m.-11:30 p.m., Sun. 6 p.m.-11 p.m. All major cards.

Caffe Baci

2522 Ponce de Leon Blvd.,
Coral Gables
• (305) 442-0600
ITALIAN

10/20

Baci means "kisses," and that's what patrons (at least the female ones) receive from Nino Pernetti, the dapper proprietor of Café Baci and its companion restaurant, Caffe Abbracci (*see* above). The consummate host, Pernetti helped pioneer the Coral Gables restaurant boom. While his food is really no better than that of any other Italian eatery in the Gables, the place never wants for takers, who love the decor, the conviviality and the hearty portions of mozzarella baci (buffalo mozzarella and tomato salad), risotto with Champagne and scaloppine amorose (sautéed veal with basil, pine nuts and cream). Delicate it's not, but the generous portions make up for any lack of finesse. Caffe Baci is a pretty place, with massive flower displays, peach-colored walls and a striking barrel-vaulted metal ceiling. Warning: do not come to the cafés Baci or Abbracci unless you have a high tolerance for noise.

Open Mon.-Thurs. 11:30 a.m.-3 p.m. & 6 p.m.-11 p.m., Fri. 11:30 a.m.-3 p.m. & 6 p.m.-11:30 p.m., Sat. 6 p.m.-11:30 p.m., Sun. 6 p.m.-11 p.m. All major cards.

Café Tu Tu Tango
3015 Grand Ave., Coconut Grove
• (305) 529-2222
SPANISH

12/20

Pablo Picasso never ate at the new Café Tu Tu Tango. We're not sure if he ever even made it to Florida, in fact, but if he had, he would have felt right at home here. At the fashionable new Cocowalk Mall, in the heart of Coconut Grove, is a Spanish artists' loft—complete with easels, paint cans, drawing paper, and even real, live, local artists dabbing oils on canvases. Brush jars on the tables hold the silverware; the pizzas are served on wooden painter's palates. In disarmingly spontaneous fashion, one moment, a pair of professional dancers might tango across the dining room; the next, a baritone might belt out an aria or a magician pull rubber balls out of thin air.

But no good loft party would become complete without food and ample wine. Tu Tu Tango's kitchen is ready to oblige with an extensive menu that uses the tapas of Spain as a starting point and circumnavigates the world. You want chips and salsa? You get chips and salsa, only the chips are fried plantains and Cuban sweet potatoes and the salsa is made with black beans. In keeping with its Floridian location, the tamales come flavored with conch. It would be impossible to cite all 42 items on the menu, but it would be a mistake to come here and miss gazpacho salad, the crab-filled croquetas, the pancetta and Gorgonzola pizza, or the alligator bites with Pick-a-Peppa cream sauce. Given the reasonable prices, the unusual entertainment, the whimsical surroundings, it's not surprising that Café Tu Tu Tango has been packed since the day it opened. What is surprising is that the food is as good as it is. Wash your meal down with white or red sangría (we prefer the former). Dinner for two with wine or beer will run $40.

Open Tues.-Sun. 11:30 a.m.-2 a.m. All major cards.

Casa Juancho
2436 S.W. 8th St., Miami
• (305) 642-2452
SPANISH

8/20

This is the house that Juancho built, although it looks like it might have been built by Disney. Imagine a Castilian castle on Calle Ocho in the heart of Miami. At your feet are rustic quarry tiles. Overhead are rough-hewn beams hung with country hams and garlic wreathes. Between them are enough hand-painted plates and hammered copper to stock a flea market for months. Bustling about are Spanish-speaking waiters, sporting green vests and scarlet cummerbunds, and strolling musicians in long black capes, their tambourines raised for tips. Alas, an army of performers and a warehouse of props doesn't guarantee good food. And however picturesque the atmosphere, Casa Juancho's food tastes like it came off a factory assembly line. Cordero Sepulveda turned out to be an overcooked slab of lamb topped with gluey gravy. We found the sangría so harsh that it could have doubled effectively as paint thinner. If you must eat here, order one of the rice dishes, like paella Valenciana or paella marinara (the latter made exclusively with fish). The tapas—pre-

pared in an open kitchen in the dining room—are marginally better than the entrées; jamón serrano (country ham) and tortilla a la española (potato-and-onion frittata) are good bets. We suppose there are worse desserts than the leche frita (fried-milk custard), but we haven't found it yet. These culinary infelicities don't seem to bother the public—late at night and on weekends, the place is packed. Dinner for two, with sangría, runs $60 to $80.
Open daily noon-1 a.m. All major cards.

Casa Rolandi
1030 Ponce de Leon Blvd.,
Coral Gables
• (305) 444-2187
ITALIAN

A warm, intimate ambience and lovely cooking smells draw you into this Italian restaurant in Coral Gables, and once you're inside, you discover that it produces good food to match. "Cent anni!" we say, "May it live to be 100 years!" A brick oven in an exposed kitchen provides an authentic backdrop for chef/owner Fabio Rolandi (a native of Lugano, Switzerland), and chef Alredo Alvarez to produce their fresh, simple and occasionally creative cooking. In the dining room, white walls lavished with blue and turquoise murals, and an arched ceiling crossed with wood beams and dotted with skylights, provide a cozy setting in which to eat it. The seafood carpaccio is a cool, luscious appetizer. The pastas are very good, including the black ravioli stuffed with shrimp. And we have a fond longing for the beet-and-potato gnocchi served with a sage and butter sauce. Kudos are in order for the tasteful introduction of a tropical influence here and there, something becoming the contemporary Miami culinary landscape, such a jumbo shrimp brushed with butter and achiote and baked in banana leaves. Dinner for two, with a modest selection from the good wine offerings, averages $90 plus tax and tip.
Open Mon.-Thurs. & Sun. noon-3 p.m. & 6 p.m.-11 p.m., Fri.-Sat. noon-3 p.m. & 6 p.m.-midnight. All major cards.

Chef Allen's
19088 N.E. 29th Ave.,
North Miami
• (305) 935-2900
AMERICAN

You're in South Florida now, and lest you doubt it, note that chef Allen has installed a video monitor in the bar so patrons can watch the kitchen activity. And that's not all. A hot pink streak of neon snakes across the dining room; guests dine under the soulless gaze of a life-size glass hammerhead shark; and there are more cellular telephones among the clients than in an AT&T showroom. Such is the setting for the contemporary American cooking of former New Yorker Allen Susser. He's at his best working with native Floridian seafood: rock shrimp are transformed into a peppery hash served on a crisp potato pancake, and pan-blackened snapper arrives on a bed of lentils and a chilled citrus-cream sauce. But while tasty, a few of the other dishes, notably the roast duck with chayote and plantains, are no more than the sum of their parts, not a culinary synergism.

MIAMI Restaurants

So while some dishes soar, others, though ambitious, remain more earthbound. Perhaps we're too critical. At least, we're certainly more so than the enthusiastic dining crowd that fills the place on weeknights. Whatever you have, save room for the nightly changing dessert soufflé, which must be ordered at the commencement of dinner and which never fails to rise. Another nice touch is the yard-long breadsticks. The service could be a touch more polished and a touch less familiar. Dinner for two, with wine, costs about $110.
Open Sun.-Thurs. 6 p.m.-11 p.m., Fri.-Sat. 6 p.m.-11:30 p.m. Cards: AE, MC, V.

Christie's
3101 Ponce de Leon Blvd.,
Coral Gables
• (305) 446-1400
STEAKHOUSE

10/20

Christie's is the quintessential uptown Republican chop house, a masculine haven of dark woods, ocher wall fabrics, brass rails, swiveled light sconces, simply framed prints and comfortable club chairs. Steak doesn't get much better than Christie's New York strip, fourteen sanguine ounces of lengthily aged, generously marbled, smokily charred beef. Said steak comes with a Caesar salad that's as laudable for its garlicky bite as for its generous size. Would that equal care went into some of the other accompaniments. The prime rib obscured the plate, as prime ribs are supposed to, but we couldn't help wondering if the jus had been prepared with a commercial mix. If the accompanying broiled mushrooms were fresh, as the menu insisted, the kitchen had perfected a method for making fresh mushrooms taste as if they were canned. But this is one of the few restaurants that still serves baked Alaska, that snowy meringue dessert from the Ice Age—those who appreciate a floor show with their meal will enjoy its ceremonious tableside flambéing. Our more cynical side suspected the speedy, solicitous service of having an ulterior motive: turning the tables. Dinner for two, with wine, runs $80.
Open Mon.-Fri. 11:30 a.m.-10:45 p.m., Sat. 5 p.m.-midnight, Sun. 5 p.m.-10:45 p.m. All major cards.

Dining Galleries
Fontainebleau Hilton,
4441 Collins Ave.,
Miami Beach
• (305) 538-2000
CONTINENTAL

12/20

In an age when food trends change as frequently as hemline lengths, it's reassuring to know that Miami has at least one restaurant where the dining experience has remained virtually the same for 40 years. Welcome to the Dining Galleries at the Fontainebleau Hilton, a monument to garishness and grandeur, to elegance edged with schmaltz. While the young turks of Florida cuisine are racing to discover exotic new fruits, underutilized seafoods and novel cooking techniques from Latin American countries, the chef here continues to turn out fettuccine Alfredo, Dover sole and filet mignon. As at most Continental restaurants (an ever-dwindling category), the simplest

One Word Captures the Moment.
Mumm's the Word.

Mumm Cordon Rouge. The only champagne to wear the red ribbon, symbol of France's highest honor. To send a gift of Mumm Champagne, call 1-800-238-4373. Void where prohibited.

Midnight magic.

You've never seen anything quite like the Rado® Black Anatom. The band is formed with scratchproof, jet-black titanium carbide links, interspersed with 18 kt. gold.

The anatomically-designed case top and crystal are scratchproof, too. The result: a watch that won't show the passing of time. But will, of course, measure each second with the precision of water-sealed Swiss quartz technology. Available for men and women.

RADO
Switzerland

Share Our Passion.
Throughout Central and South Florida.
For the Mayor's nearest you or for information,
please call 1-800-4-MAYOR'S.

MIAMI Restaurants

dishes—caviar, smoked salmon, stone crabs—are the best, and the complicated ones are to be avoided. But nobody comes here for the food anyway. No, the drawing cards of this Miami Beach landmark are the spacious tables draped with pink-and-green striped tablecloths; the live harp and orchestra music; the opulence of the museum-quality antiques, which include eighteenth-century pianos and Carrara marble busts; and the solicitousness of the tuxedoed staff. But for a restaurant this pretentious, the wine list is a disgrace. Never mind the shocking prices (Roederer Cristal Champagne goes for $180)—Merlots, Pinot Noirs and Gamay Beaujolais are lumped together under generic headings. Worse still, wines are listed without their vintages. Nonetheless, this is the perfect place to take your grandmother for her birthday or Mother's Day. Dinner for two, with wine, will run $150.
Open Tues.-Sat. 6 p.m.-11 p.m., Sun. 10 a.m.-3 p.m. All major cards.

Dominique's
Alexander Hotel,
5225 Collins Ave.,
Miami Beach
• (305) 865-6500
FRENCH

11/20

You may have heard of Dominique—he's the guy from Washington who serves alligator, rattlesnake and hippopotamus. Perhaps this flamboyant French restaurateur ought to drop by Miami Beach more often, to oversee his restaurant on the mezzanine of the Alexander Hotel. If he had visited on the night we were most recently here, he might have found (as we did) stale dinner rolls, soiled menus, chandeliers with burned-out bulbs and waiters who make TV wrestlers seem polished. The crowning indignity of our most recent meal was the $28 poitrine de canard (duck breast on foie gras, served with sweet onions and sautern sauces), which was remarkable solely for the absence of its foie gras garnish ("We ran out," the waiter explained lamely). It's too bad, really, because the setting is lovely. You enter the restaurant via a glass tunnel surrounded by tropical foliage. The dining room has the dark paneling, mirrored ceilings, mounted animals and fringed lampshades of an eighteenth-century French hunting lodge. We have eaten passably well at this upscale and generally old-school French restaurant. The kitchen is capable of preparing a decent rack of lamb, surrounded with the obligatory baby vegetables, and the chocolate and pistachio soufflés rise to the occasion (if you remember to order them at the beginning of dinner). The wine list, however, is an affront to wine lovers—selections are listed without their vintages, and when we inquired about the house wine, we were told, "It's dry and it's French." Dinner for two, with wine, runs $100 to $120.
Open daily 7 a.m.-3 p.m. & 5 p.m.-11:30 p.m. Cards: AE, MC, V.

MIAMI Restaurants

The Fish Market
Omni Hotel,
1601 Biscayne Blvd.,
Miami
• (305) 374-4399
SEAFOOD/AMERICAN

12/20

The Fish Market is one of Miami's best-kept restaurant secrets, a hotel dining room remarkable for its soaring gold ceilings, mirrors, mahogany trim, pink marble floors and soft candlelight. As the name suggests, this place specializes in local seafood, much of which is delicious: charred tuna served carpaccio-style, baked snapper with cilantro sauce, smoky grilled Florida lobster basted with truffle butter. Weight watchers will appreciate the five simply grilled seafood items served with a choice of four sauces, including a Mediterranean salsa. Ichthyophobes, despair not: The Fish Market serves one of the crispiest, juiciest racks of lamb in town. If you can, avoid the leathery smoked shrimp ravioli and tough dry-cured dolphin fish. But the complimentary olive pâté and roasted red peppers help make up for these infelicities. Seafood restaurants aren't usually known for their desserts, but the apple strudel here will make Austrians want to emigrate to Miami. The secret? The filling is cooked separately, and the rectangle of dough is crisply caramelized under the broiler. Service is courteous and reasonably attentive—and best of all, The Fish Market accepts reservations. Dinner for two, with wine, will run $80 to $100.
Open Mon.-Fri. 11:30 a.m.-2:30 p.m. & 6:30 p.m.-11 p.m., Sat. 6:30 p.m.-11 p.m. All major cards.

The Forge
432 Arthur Godfrey Rd.,
Miami Beach
• (305) 538-8533
AMERICAN

12/20

They sure don't build restaurants like they used to. Consider The Forge. This Miami Beach landmark has more brass rails than an ocean liner, more stained glass than a Tiffany lamp warehouse, more chandeliers than Versailles and more rare bottles in the wine cellar than there are gold bars in Fort Knox. In the old days, you could go to The Forge for such Continental standbys as roast rack of lamb and salmon with hollandaise sauce. But times change; these days, the lamb is apt to come in phyllo dough with a wild-mushroom duxelles, and the salmon might sport a spinach vinaigrette. Fortunately, the modernisms work; the food is appealing and tasty, neither too stodgy nor too weird. Keeping pace with health trends, the chef has introduced a series of spa dishes that are low in fat, salt and cholesterol. And it's a good idea to economize on the calories, because you'll need to compensate for the restaurant's signature dessert, a towering blacksmith pie (layers of chocolate and vanilla pudding topped with clouds of whipped cream). The wine list is as thick as the Miami phone book; big spenders will find Lafite-Rothschilds going back to 1822. The rest of us can settle for a collection of California boutique wines that is unsurpassed in South Florida. Dinner for two, with wine, will range from $120 to $150.
Open Mon.-Thurs. 5:30 p.m.-midnight, Fri.-Sun. 5:30 p.m.-1 a.m. All major cards.

MIAMI Restaurants

The Grand Café

Grand Bay Hotel,
2669 S. Bayshore Dr.,
Coconut Grove
• (305) 858-9600
AMERICAN

14

The news was whispered down quarry-tiled hallways and shouted on Regine's mirrored dance floor: "Suki's back!" After a two-year stint at the Trump Taj Mahal, chef Katsui "Suki" Sugiura has come back to the swank Grand Bay Hotel. And not a moment too soon! Once the crown jewel of Coconut Grove's hotel restaurants, The Grand Café had become just another hotel dining room. If anyone can restore it to its former preeminence, it's the former chef. Born in Japan and schooled in France, Suki takes his inspiration from six continents. He pairs grilled honey-cured salmon with marjoram sauce and a fennel salad. Prosciutto and figs become unexpected companions for herb-scented crabcakes. He's equally at home smoking five-spice duck and grilling black grouper with white asparagus and fried risotto. That's not to say he's above the occasional lapse, like the leaden basil tempura we tried recently, but all in all, his is a talent to reckon with. One dish the innovative Suki won't tinker with is the hotel's perfect crème brûlée. The split-level dining room offers loads of quiet elegance, with monumental flower displays, Oriental vases and Louis XV chairs, all patrolled by epauletted busboys and tuxedoed captains, who raise silver bell jars in perfect unison. Devoted sons and daughters take note: this is *the* place to bring mom for Sunday brunch. Two will spend $100 to $150 for dinner with wine.

Open Sun.-Thurs. 7 a.m.-3 p.m. & 6 p.m.-11 p.m., Fri.-Sat. 7 a.m.-3 p.m. & 6 p.m.-11:30 p.m. All major cards.

Joe's Stone Crab

227 Biscayne St.,
Miami Beach
• (305) 673-0365
SEAFOOD

13

Eat at Joe's. This local and tourist institution has reigned over Miami Beach since the early 1900s, and continues to deliver. Mostly, it delivers delicious stone-crab claws, which have been caught in the Gulf, cooked on the spot, immediately put on ice and rushed to Joe's, where they go straight to the table. So popular is this fish house that the Miami Beach tourist season is said to begin when Joe's opens and end when Joe's closes. Stone crabs have been around a long time, of course, but it took a retired waiter from New York, Joe Weiss, to turn them into a Sunshine State specialty. Noting that the flesh was watery when freshly cooked, Weiss had the idea to serve the coral-colored, black-tipped claws chilled, with a mayonnaise-based mustard sauce. The formula was a winner: Joe's grew from a six-table joint to a sprawling restaurant that serves 1,500 people a day. Stone crabs may be the focal point, but it would be a mistake to not try the oniony lyonnaise potatoes, the garlicky creamed spinach and the tomato-topped mountain of coleslaw. And, there is a full menu of seafood, meat, poultry and salads. To this, add a superlative bread basket and one of the best Key lime pies in Florida, and you've got yourself a great meal. Despite the 400 seats in a dining room remarkable for its hubbub, historic

photographs and good-natured waiters, there's always a line. The wine list is short but servicable. Two will spend about $80 for dinner, with wine.
Open Sun.-Mon. 5 p.m.-10 p.m., Tues.-Wed. 11:30 a.m.-2 p.m. & 5 p.m.-10 p.m., Fri.-Sat. 11:30 a.m.-2 p.m. & 5 p.m.-11 p.m. All major cards.

Madrid
2475 S.W. 37th Ave., Coral Gables
• (305) 446-2250
CUBAN/SPANISH

10/20

First, let's list what the Madrid doesn't have: floor shows, waiters dressed in Castilian garb and the decor of a castle in Spain. The owners of this unassuming place leave the fireworks to the tourist traps on Calle Ocho. What the Madrid does have is some of the best Cuban food in Miami: chewy Cuban rolls steaming hot from the oven, white-bean soup so hardy it can hold a spoon upright, and maduros (fried plantains) so meltingly sweet that you don't know whether to eat them as a vegetable or dessert. And that's not all. The arroz con pollo is the apotheosis of chicken and rice. The fragrant fried spiced pork could tempt a rabbi to forsake the kashruth. The rice pudding is exceptionally creamy, and, unlike at most Cuban/Spanish restaurants, the flan isn't too sweet. Regulars (the dining room is full of them) have their preferred day of the week to dine here for the rotating daily specials. When the food is this good, you don't need showy surroundings. Dressed in rec-room-style paneling, the Madrid's small, rambling dining rooms make you feel as if you're in a modest private home. Anglos tend to dine here from 6 to 8 p.m.; the Latin crowd arrives later. Dinner for two, with a pitcher of the fabulous sangría, will run about $40.
Open Mon.-Sat. 11 a.m.-11 p.m. All major cards.

Mark's Place
2286 N.E. 123rd St., North Miami
• (305) 893-6888
NEW AMERICAN

The critics' consensus as Miami's and, indeed, Florida's top restaurant, Mark's comes as something of a surprise. Entering this typically casual yet very stylish eatery in the new American brasserie style, with its white walls, brass railings, blond wood, booths and tables, ultramodern art and *de rigueur* art-deco lamps, you are caught up in a bustling crowd that promises a good time but not necessarily fine food. Or, perhaps you'll wonder at the suburban shopping-center scene outside contrasted by the valet parking. If Mark's were transplanted to California's Santa Monica or New York's Chelsea, it wouldn't be singled out for such gushing adoration, but rather quietly applauded for what it is: simply a place with fine food, prepared by a contemporary and inventive kitchen, served by a good staff. Springing up in a place like North Miami, however, Mark's deserves its rating and an extra point, for awakening a sleepy Florida to what's been going on gastronomically in most major cities across America for some time. Mark's kitchen has exploited the potential of Florida produce as no one has since the Indians. Talented Mark Militello, the 35-year-old chef/owner of Mark's Place, believes in ever-so-fresh ingredients and changes his menu daily, partly to include available Sunshine State canistels (egg fruits), conch, cassava root and fresh hearts of palm gathered by the Okechobee Indians. He combines these ingredients with feverish creativity on a menu that changes daily. A tangerine-fennel vinaigrette graces black grouper from the Florida Keys. Smoked pepper butter counterpoints the briny succulence of Banana River soft-shell crabs. Militello favors quick, low-fat cooking methods, but he's not above braising oxtails for hours to make an offbeat terrine of oxtail and foie gras. Not everything that comes out of this kitchen is inspired or faultless, however. Other dishes, such as the grilled swordfish basted with a mango-scotch barbecue sauce, are fine examples of the dangers of unbridled innovation, when a chef zealously combines various elements, flavors, techniques and products. If we dared to give any advice to this talented chef, it would be to moderate his ingenuity, because perfection lies somewhere between an inexorable torrent and a too-still river. Once, when we were served the most bland spaghetti with clams in memory, we wondered if the young kitchen staff hadn't missed the lesson on how to prepare flavorful pasta, say by utilizing clam broth. Desserts run from middling to oustanding, and often sport such whimsical names as "icky sticky coconut pudding." The wine list is heavy on American wines but provides something for everyone—more than twenty wines by the glass, as well as strong grand crus, California boutique wines, and even Sauternes and old ports by the glass. A superb dinner for two, with wine, will run about $150.

Open Mon.-Thurs. noon-2:30 p.m. & 6 p.m.-10:30 p.m., Fri. noon-2:30 p.m. & 6 p.m.-11 p.m., Sat. 6 p.m.-11 p.m., Sun. 6 p.m.-10 p.m. Cards: AE, DC, MC.

Mezzanotte
1200 Washington Ave., Miami Beach
• (305) 673-4343
ITALIAN

11/20

We've never understood why otherwise reasonable people would wait in long lines for a cramped seat in a dining room that's about as relaxed as a disco dance floor. So perhaps we're missing the point of the oh-so-trendy Mezzanotte, which has played to standing-room-only crowds since it opened in 1988 in the heart of SoBe (South Beach, the Art Deco District on Miami Beach). People aren't here for the service, which adheres to the "we're-doing-you-a-favor-by-waiting-on-you" school of stewardship. They certainly aren't here for conversation, which is made all but impossible by a roar reminiscent of a 747 at takeoff. They might be here for the workhorse northern Italian cooking served on stylishly oversize plates: cozze caprese (basil-

steamed mussels), mozzarella mezzanotte (fresh cheese with roasted peppers and basil), lombata mezzanotte (a flattened, breaded veal chop garnished with radicchio and Belgian endive) and the like, all of which is neither remarkable nor awful. But they're probably here just because everyone else is. As befits an art-deco hangout, pink neon light washes the black banquettes, glass-block walls and milk-glass light fixtures. Dinner for two, with wine, will run $60 to $80.
Open Sun.-Thurs. 6 p.m.-11:30 p.m., Fri.-Sat. 6 p.m.-1 a.m. All major cards.

Monty's Stone Crab
2550 S. Bayshore Dr., Coconut Grove
• (305) 858-1431
SEAFOOD

10/20

There are people—we among them—who believe that seafood should be eaten within sight of water. Monty's is happy to oblige, serving fist-size conch fritters and thick swordfish steaks along with a view of the bay and the bobbing masts of Club Nautica Marina. Okay, so it's a fern bar. You know the scene: natural woods, wicker furniture, blue-and-white curtains and a wall of glass overlooking the harbor. There are salad bars and there are salad bars, and this is one to be reckoned with, offering 42 different items. Cajun food may seem passé, but we'd gladly reorder the Cajun-spiced shrimp—six of the biggest shellfish we've ever seen, simmered in beer and piqued with cayenne. When they're in season, don't miss the sweet, juicy, ocean-fresh stone crabs. The open-air bar at the water's edge is a popular meeting place for hippies, yuppies and other Coconut Grove fauna. And, Monty's will even sell you all the stone crabs you can eat for $25.
Open Mon.-Thurs. 11:30 a.m.-11 p.m., Fri. 11:30 a.m.-midnight, Sat.-Sun. 11:30 a.m.-1 a.m. All major cards.

Osteria del Teatro
1443 Washington Ave., Miami Beach
• (305) 538-7850
ITALIAN

12/20

If imitation is the sincerest form of flattery, Dino Pirola must be one of the most sincerely flattered retaurateurs on Miami Beach. His restaurant, Osteria del Teatro, has inspired the opening of seven trendy Italian eateries within a six-block radius in SoBe (South Beach). But none can compare with Osteria for its congenial atmosphere and soulful food. Chef Daniel Theme puts modern twists on time-honored Italian classics. Saffron-tinged seafood partners homemade squid-ink tagliarini (unlike most SoBe restaurants, Osteria makes all its pasta). Huge grilled portabella mushrooms counterpoint melted fontina cheese. But Theme knows when to leave well enough alone—his crespelle (spinach-and-ricotta crêpes) and artery-clogging tiramisu are as timeless as a grandmother's minestrone. Located in the old Cameo Theater building, Osteria boasts an ultramodern decor: canvases stretched across the ceilings, striking neocubist paintings, burgundy-and-gray tablecloths. The clientele is older and classier than at Mezzanotte, and the service works like a charm.

MIAMI Restaurants

Dinner for two, with wine, ranges from $90 to $110.
Open Sun.-Thurs. 6 p.m.-11 p.m., Fri.-Sat. 6 p.m.-1 a.m. Cards: AE, MC, V.

Ramiro's
2700 Ponce de Leon Blvd.,
Coral Gables
• (305) 443-7605
SPANISH

13

Most Spanish restaurants in Miami are theme-park cafeterias. It's about time someone opened a serious Spanish dining establishment, one where the food does the showing off, not flamenco dancers and costumed waiters—especially when the someone is Luis Ramiro, the Spanish-born chef who runs this place (and another in Puerto Rico) with his two brothers. Seated on a brocade chair, gazing at the ornate moldings, at the paintings of Paris's Montmartre, at the tuxedoed maître d', you even begin to wonder where the connection with Spain comes in. It's probably in the matadorish flourish with which the waiters lift the silver bell jars, and the balletic dance they perform to and from the table.

Ramiro's menu is sufficiently classical to include anguillas—garlicky baby eels served with a wooden fork, as they would be in Spain—but in such minute portions that we considered ringing up our optometrist immediately to order a stronger prescription. The baby eels taste like clam-flavored spaghetti, but there are two black dots—the eyes—at one end. But before you set your mind on traditional Spanish food, know that Ramiro has a whimsical streak. An olive purée with squiggles of cream rests beneath an ingot-shape spinach flan. Salmon mousse sports a red-pepper tulip complete with an asparagus stem. Sounds precious? It *is* precious, but the predominantly Latin clientele loves it, and we can see why—though not every dish is a winner. The venison can be dry, and the plantain fritters can be downright leaden. Desserts have fallen far short of the restaurant's pretensions. The Spanish wine selection is comprehensive. Two will spend $80 to $100 for dinner with wine. *Open Mon.-Fri. 11:30 a.m.-2:30 p.m. & 6 p.m.-11 p.m., Sat. 6 p.m.-11 p.m., Sun. 6 p.m.-10 p.m. All major cards.*

Los Ranchos
Sweetwater Holiday Plaza,
125 S.W. 107th Ave.,
Miami
• (305) 552-6767
NICARAGUAN

10/20

On June 6, 1981, a young man in Texas named Julio Somoza turned on the TV news and saw the street fighting in Managua that would topple Nicaragua's ruler, his uncle Anastasio. Overnight, he became a man without a country. So he did what so many enterprising Latin American refugees have done: moved to Miami and opened a restaurant in Miami. Los Ranchos serves macho food in a macho setting: white stucco walls decked with cowhides and steer heads, sturdy wooden tables and Nicaraguan handcrafts. Carnivores will have a field day sampling from the menu, which offers every imaginable cut of grilled beef (Somoza favors Honduran grass-fed beef over the tenderer but less flavorful American grain-fed beef), homemade chorizo sausage,

cerdo (pork dyed Mercurochrome orange by a lime-and-annatto marinade) and such. If you're in the mood for a seriously meaty meal, try the lombito de costilla tatalolo, a smoky grilled beef tenderloin with the ribs attached, served with a trio of sauces, including chimichuri (Nicaraguan pesto). But even if you don't eat meat, you won't go hungry. You could make a feast of just the accompaniments: gallos pintos (red beans and rice), tostones (paper-thin fried plantain chips), maduros (fried sweet plantains) and salads. Start your meal with fried yuca with garlic salt, and end it with the airy tres leches ("three-milk") cake. Buoyed by the success of this place, Somoza has opened a second Los Ranchos in Bayside. Dinner for two, with Chilean wine, will run $60.
Open Sun.-Thurs. 11:30 a.m.-11 p.m., Fri.-Sat. 11:30 a.m.-11:30 p.m. All major cards.

Regine's
Grand Bay Hotel,
2669 S. Bayshore Dr.,
Coconut Grove
• (305) 858-9600
FRENCH

Regine's, on the thirteenth floor of the Grand Bay Hotel, may be the prettiest restaurant in Miami. But to come here just for the pink granite and black lacquer, the etched-glass partitions and mirrored chandeliers, the chinoiserie screens and sweeping views of Biscayne Bay would be to overlook artistry of a different sort: the cooking of Lisa Pethybridge. This soft-spoken chef syncopates French and Mediterranean melodies with regional American rhythms. Ancho chiles jazz up plank-roasted salmon with ravioli and cilantro butter. A pistachio crust counterpoints a superlative rack of lamb, served rosy, the way we like it. A hazelnut-pepper pesto harmonizes with medallions of beef tenderloin. Maître d' Giovanni Melis conducts the black-tie service with the precision of conductor Seiji Ozawa. The only dissonant note is the disco music, which starts thumping at 10 p.m.—this place is the Miami link of an international nightclub chain run by the famous French chanteuse Regine, so after dinner, you can work off the calories on one of Miami's dressiest dance floors. Dinner for two, with wine, will set you back from $100 to $120.
Open Tues.-Sat. 7 p.m.-midnight, Fri.-Sat. 7 p.m.-12:30 a.m.

Sakura Gables
440 S. Dixie Hwy.,
Coral Gables
• (305) 665-7020
JAPANESE

10/20

Miami lacks a world-class Japanese restaurant, so by default we'll name this neighborhood spot as our favorite. Every night, a well-heeled clientele packs the cozy pink dining room for the three Ts: tempura, teka-maki and teriyaki. The first is lighter than the run-of-the-mill batter-fried vegetables and shrimp. The second features circles of dark nori seaweed and vinegared sweetened rice around a bulls-eye of raw red tuna. The third is salty and sweet, the way we like it, served with one of Miami's

best miso salads. Some places have a mirrored ceiling over the bed—Sakura has one over the sushi bar. The chef breaks no new ground, but the fish is fresh and there's always a good selection. On the down side, the sushi bar backs up at peak hours, so you may have to wait a long time for a fix of hamachi or toro. There's another Sakura in Kendall. Dinner for two, with saké, will run $60.
Open Mon.-Thurs. noon-2 p.m. & 5:30 p.m.-10:30 p.m., Fri. noon-2 p.m. & 5:30 p.m.-11 p.m., Sat. 5:30 p.m.-11 p.m., Sun. 5:30 p.m.-10:30 p.m. All major cards.

Salmon & Salmon
2907 N.W. 7th St., Miami
• (305) 649-5924
PERUVIAN

11/20

No, you're not in the wrong place. Housed in a nondescript strip mall, this homey Peruvian restaurant looks like it's waiting to be foreclosed on. Suspended fishnets and a few kitschy landscapes decorate an equally nondescript dining room. The sole attempt at elegance is the burgundy cloths on the six tiny tables. But suppress your impulse to leave, because the cook serves some of the tastiest Peruvian food this side of Machu Picchu. You like soup? Try the aguadito, a steaming cauldron of clams, mussels, scallops and octopus in a pungent cilantro bouillon. You like curry? Don't miss the seafood cau-cau, its gravy fragrant with turmeric. The restaurant's namesake fish comes in thick steaks, smokily broiled, as buttery and moist as you could wish for. Potatoes a la huancayna wear a cold, creamy sauce of cheese, hard-boiled egg and garlic. To wash this uncommon fare down, try the lija (a sort of sangría made with Chilean wine and Inca Cola). With a bottle of Chilean wine, two will spend $40 to $50 for dinner.
Open daily noon-11 p.m. Cards: AE, MC, V.

Stars and Stripes Café
Betsy Ross Hotel, 1440 Ocean Dr., Miami Beach
• (305) 531-3310
AMERICAN

11/20

Norman Van Aken burst on the Florida food scene six years ago, at a Key West restaurant called Louie's Backyard. He subsequently wrote Florida's first truly modern cookbook, *Feast of Sunlight*. This venture, the Stars and Stripes Café at the Betsy Ross Hotel, takes guests on a gastronomic romp around the Caribbean and Latin America. Van Aken has a way with words, as evidenced by the smoked salmon "novel" with salsa cruda and a grilled tortilla, the "Ricky Ricardo" pizzatina (topped with black beans and chorizo) and the shell steak that's "born in New York and buried in bell peppers." A Bahamian chowder contains "hacked-cracked" conch, while the "burned" bananas with chiles, chocolate and ice cream turns out to be Van Aken's version of a banana split. Sometimes his imagination outstrips the abilities of his kitchen. But seated on the terrace of the newly renovated Betsy Ross, overlooking the Atlantic Ocean, one is

disposed to overlook any culinary peccadillos. Van Aken's latest venture is a more formal restaurant at the Besty Ross called A Mano, Spanish for "by hand" (*see* page 23). Dinner for two, with wine, will range from $60 to $80.
Open daily 11:30 a.m.-3 p.m. & 6 p.m.-midnight. Cards: AE, MC, V.

The Strand
671 Washington Ave., Miami Beach
• (305) 532-2340
AMERICAN

10/20

You never know who you're going to run into at The Strand. Actress and model Lauren Hutton is a regular, as are Mickey Rourke and Julio Iglesias. But whether you're a celebrity, a fan, a tourist or a local, you'll find a menu that is sufficiently highbrow to include mussels with grappa sauce and potato-leek pancakes with salmon caviar—and down-to-earth enough to list burgers and meatloaf. The roast chicken with mashed yams and beets is one of Miami's best. Desserts feature apple crisp and a nightly changing cheesecake. All in all, this is good, honest cooking that throws a few bones to the tenents of new American cooking. When Irene Griersing, Gary Farmer and Mark Benck opened this cavernous eatery in the heart of the Art Deco District on Miami Beach, friends and associates said, "You're crazy." It turns out they were crazy enough to attract weekend crowds of 300 and to rack up yearly sales rumored to be more than $1.5 million. Located on the site of the legendary Famous restaurant, The Strand boasts the expected art-deco trappings: mirrored walls, glass-block trim and Thonet chairs. Dinner for two, with wine, costs about $75.
Open Sun.-Thurs. 6 p.m.-1 a.m., Fri.-Sat. 6 p.m.-2 a.m. in-season (earlier closing off-season). All major cards.

Taste of Sze-chuan
1111 Kane Concourse, Bay Harbor
• (305) 868-8886
CHINESE

10/20

Take an Israeli owner, a Thai chef and a Chinese staff, put them all in one of the prettiest dining rooms in North Miami, and you get this idiosyncracy of a place in Dade County. The Israeli is one Moshe Zur, owner of seven Chinese restaurants in Tel Aviv. Legend has it that the Miami Beach mayor, Alex Doud, was so impressed with Zur's restaurants that he made him an irresistible offer to move to Miami. This place doesn't look like the average (read: frumpy) Chinese restaurant, with its stately black lacquered chairs and tables, the latter trimmed with mother-of-pearl bas-reliefs. Boughs of cherry blossoms strung with tiny lights decorate a split-level dining room remarkable for its curved forest-green walls. And the food? There are some remarkable dishes, among them Szechuan-style spareribs (bite-size nuggets blasted with garlic and ginger), calamari with fiery dried chilies and a mild chicken stir-fry that's eaten wrapped in lettuce leaves, burrito-style. And if the appetizer platter features the same batter-fried shrimp, chicken wings and spring rolls found at every Chinese hole-in-the-wall, here at least they are

garnished with a blazing sparkler. The sweet-and-sour dishes are as goopy and orange-red as the Cantonese fare most of us grew up on. Dinner for two, with wine, will cost about $50.
Open daily noon-2:30 p.m. & 5 p.m.-11 p.m. All major cards.

Thai Toni
890 Washington Ave., Miami Beach
• (305) 538-8424
THAI

10/20

East meets West at this chic Thai restaurant in the heart of Miami Beach's Art Deco District. Traditional Thai statuary stands among boldly contemporary tapestries and halogen track lighting. Brass forks and spoons stand out against striking black tabletops. Run by Japanese-born Toni Takarada, Thai Toni holds no culinary surprises, but the Thai classics are competently prepared and served with style. Fresh lemon grass perfumes a hot, sour and salty dish whimsically named Jumping Squid, while fresh basil leaves lend a licorice-tinted boldness to the green curry. Thai Toni chicken turns out to be an oversize saté, marinated with turmeric and coconut milk and served on a glowing brazier. The rice is dished out from an ornate silver tureen, just as it is in Thailand, but the beef in the Thai salad could be more tender. Crowds have not caused the servers to lose their graciousness. Dinner for two, with wine, runs $45.
Open Sun.-Thurs. 5:30 p.m.-11 p.m., Fri.-Sat. 5:30 p.m.-midnight. Cards: AE, MC, V.

Il Tulipano
11052 Biscayne Blvd., North Miami
• (305) 893-4811
ITALIAN

12/20

The setting is garish Biscayne Boulevard, but it might as well be a fashionable neighborhood in Turin or Milan, so authentic is Il Tulipano's northern Italian cuisine. The waiters (most of whom were born in Italy) describe house specialties in conspiratorial whispers, showing off platters of flawless vegetables, homemade pastas and mammoth porcini mushrooms. Asparagus teams up with arborio rice to make a verdant risotto. Agnolotti comes with three sauces—red marinara, green pesto and white cream—to mimic the Italian flag. Prosciutto, fresh rosemary and pounded chicken breasts are rolled into lovely, fork-tender spirals. Dessert might bring chilled zabaglione with mountains of enormous strawberries. And older red wines are decanted with ceremony. Innovative? No. Satisfying? Absolutely! The dining room offers the contemporary charm of white brick, oak cabinetry and tables adorned with crisply starched linens and Il Tulipano's namesake tulips. The Ferraris and Rolls-Royces parked out front attest to the restaurant's popularity with Dade County's glitterati. Dinner for two, with wine, runs $80 to $100.
Open Sun.-Mon. & Wed.-Thurs. 6 p.m.-11 p.m., Fri.-Sat. 6 p.m.-midnight. All major cards.

Unicorn Village

3565 N.E. 207th St.,
North Miami
• (305) 933-8829
HEALTH FOOD

10/20

At the risk of sounding older than we really are, we remember the original Unicorn restaurant, a funky hole-in-the wall with laid-back service and a strictly vegetarian menu. My, how times have changed! The new Unicorn Village is a health-food wonderland, complete with a state-of-the-art supermarket, craft shop and ultramodern restaurant that serves hundreds (if not thousands) of patrons each day. If you're expecting tasteless tofu dishes and gluey brown rice, think again. The menu jumps from pumpkin-seed polenta (topped with a roasted tomato-olive sauce) to a tofu tostada (spiced with pasilla chiles) to crisp pancakes made with udon noodles and shiitake mushrooms. Salad buffs will enjoy the powdery-pink creamy beet dressing. Nonvegetarians will be pleased by the naturally raised Coleman beef (served teriyaki-style or char-grilled with garlic mashed potatoes) and some of the tastiest roast chicken in North Miami. True, when you serve this many people, there's bound to be an industrial quality to much of the food. (The lightning speed with which the food arrives makes us wonder how much is prepared in advance.) But how many establishments cook for the masses *and* use organic produce, grain-fed meats and herbs and spices from five continents? As befits a health-food emporium, Unicorn Village boasts natural woods, purple floor tiles, luxuriant greenery and soaring cathedral ceilings; floor-to-ceiling windows offer spectacular views of the Intracoastal Waterway. The healthful fare and eminently affordable prices draw hippies, yuppies, seniors and everyone in between. Dinner for two, with a fruit smoothie or vegetable juice, will run about $40.
Open Sun.-Thurs. 11:30 a.m.-3 p.m. & 5 p.m.-9:30 p.m., Fri.-Sat. 11:30 a.m.-3 p.m. & 5 p.m.-10 p.m. Cards: MC, V.

Victor's Café

2340 S.W. 32nd Ave.,
Coral Gables
• (305) 445-1313
CUBAN

11/20

Since the day this Cuban extravaganza—and offshoot of New York's Victor's Café 52—opened, it has never wanted for business. That's because it's not just another Cuban restaurant, not with its multimillion-dollar decor. Past what may be the largest doors in Miami is the dining room, a soaring atrium under a huge barrel-vaulted skylight. Globe lights and tabletop candles cast a discreet glow, echoed by floor spots that peep from behind potted palms. Live mambo music, strolling guitarists, a pianist in the bar and a tile floor create an atmosphere that many find wonderfully lively but we find rather chaotic. The kitchen makes transcendent moros (black beans served with snow-white rice). The shrimp in the shrimp cocktail are almost as big as the lobsters in the north. The ropa vieja, meltingly tender shreds of braised skirt steak, are as good as this soulful dish gets. Other specialties include lechon asado (roast suckling pig), masitas de puerco fritas (fried spiced pork) and palomilla

(marinated grilled shell steak). Victor's is a good place for neophytes to try yuca con mojo, the standard Cuban accompaniment of starchy boiled cassava root basted with garlic and lime juice. But skip the fried plantains, which aren't nearly as sweet as those served at Madrid restaurant. The ornately decorated flan draws a lot of gasps, but we prefer the crema catalana (Cuban crème brûlée). A night at Victor's won't come cheaply—for one entrée, you could buy a full meal at most Cuban restaurants. Dinner for two, with wine, runs about $100.
Open Sun.-Thurs. noon-midnight, Fri.-Sat. noon-1 a.m. All major cards.

Yuca
177 Giralda Ave.,
Coral Gables
• (305) 444-4448
CUBAN

Miami may be rife with Cuban restaurants, but we've never had Cuban food like this before. No, one doesn't often encounter conch tamales with a jalapeño-cheese pesto, baby-back ribs with a guava barbecue sauce and yellowtail with crab empanadas and a pickled garlic rémoulade. Clearly Yuca has as much in common with the average Cuban restaurant in Miami as a yacht has with a dinghy. For its creative use of local produce and for the restaurant's positive impact on other restaurants, it earns an extra point. A yuca is a starchy tuber, of course, which chef Douglas Rodriguez converts into croquettes (served with Brie), soups (one is called "yucassoise") and pancakes (yuca blinis with osetra caviar!), not to mention traditional chips and french fries. Like a culinary Columbus, Rodriguez charts a bold course between the Old World and New, between traditional Latino cooking and contemporary American cuisine. Malangas and boniatas (Latin American root vegetables) are metamorphosed into gnocchi and served with picadilla (shredded-beef stew). A homey rice pudding nests in an audibly crisp almond tuile. But the restaurant's name is also an acronym for Young Urban Cuban American, an apt description of the hip, affluent, well-dressed, bilingual clientele that nightly besieges this Coral Gables storefront. This is the perfect dining spot for sophisticated travelers who, if they take the time to analyze what's on their plates, will find that Doug Rodriguez has created a brilliant synthesis of "Floridian" culture and horticulture. Even experienced eaters will regale their palates with—yes—truly new sensations. Success has already prompted Yuca to move to a new, chicly minimalist bi-level dining room, and the restaurant also now has a full liquor license. As at the theater, you can watch the action in the kitchen from the balcony. A tasty, remarkably inventive dinner for two, with wine, will cost about $110.
Open Mon.-Thurs. noon-2:30 p.m. & 6 p.m.-10 p.m., Fri. noon-2:30 p.m. & 6 p.m.-10:30 p.m., Sat. 6 p.m.-10:30 p.m., Sun. 6 p.m.-10 p.m. All major cards.

QUICK BITES

BARBECUE	42
CAFES & COFFEE SHOPS	43
CAFETERIA	44
HIGH TEA	45
HOT DOGS	45
LATIN AMERICAN	45

BARBECUE

Shorty's Bar-B-Q
9200 S. Dixie Hwy., Miami
• (305) 665-5732

Shorty's may have been the last restaurant in Miami to install air-conditioning. But for decades, its patrons have cheerfully endured the hot, humid air (pushed around by a battalion of paddle fans) and long waiting lines that invariably form at the restaurant's log-cabin portal. The reason is simple: Shorty's serves some of the best barbecue this side of Texas. We're talking real barbecue—the kind that is slowly smoked over smoldering hardwood. The skin on the chicken is dark, crisp, and blistered. The meat on the ribs is smoky, moist, and fall-of-the-bone tender. In an age when so few restaurants can muster even one decent barbecue sauce, Shorty's serves three: a barrel-aged hot sauce, a more conventional molasses/ketchup-based sauce, and a dark, thick, grainy, vinegar-based sauce reminiscent of Arthur Bryant's of Kansas City. To this add smoky baked beans, celery-seed-studded coleslaw, butter drenched corn on the cob, and a slab of white bread, and you've got the fixins for a serious feast. Shorty's doesn't discriminate and neither do its patrons: lawyers and truck drivers, doctors and dockers sit side by side at long communal tables under the watchful gaze of mounted animal heads and grandmotherly waitresses. Dinner for two with beer will run $25.
Open daily 11 a.m.-10 p.m. No cards.

MIAMI Quick Bites

CAFES & COFFEE SHOPS

Lulu's
1053 Washington Ave.,
Miami Beach
• (305) 532-6147

Elvis never dined at Lulu's. He would have felt at home if he had. The upstairs dining room is festooned with pictures of The King, while the downstairs room boasts antique license plates, hub caps, road signs and other Americana. Vintage rock and roll blares from a perfectly restored Seeburg jukebox for a dime a play. The King no doubt would have approved of the huge portions of home-style Southern cooking: catfish fingers, corn and okra fritters, and chicken fried steak, with plenty of mashed potatoes and boiled greens to go with them. The fried chicken is just greasy enough to let you know it's the real thing. And to wash it all down, the owners of Lulu's have gone to great lengths to obtain IBC root beer, the Rolls-Royce of soft drinks. Refined? No. Health conscious? Certainly not. But in an area plagued with chichi restaurants, Lulu's is mercifully unpretentious and fun. Dinner for two with beer runs $30 - 40.
Open Mon.-Thurs. 11:30 a.m.-12.30 a.m., Fri. 11:30 a.m.-1:30 a.m., Sat. 5 p.m.-1:30 a.m., Sun. 5 p.m.-12:30 a.m. Cards: AE.

News Café
800 Ocean Dr.,
Miami Beach
• (305) 538-6397

It's Sunday morning and they're already lined up on the sidewalk: bean pole–thin models, ponytailed youths in leather pants, silver-haired businessmen with their second wives and suntans. Welcome to the News Café, a gathering spot for Miami Beach boulevardiers. The food, although far from inspired, is better than it needs to be at this one-of-a-kind property, a deli-café-newsstand with a fabulous view of the ocean. Come here for quiches, frittatas, fruit and vegetable salads, thick sandwiches, fruit shakes, herb teas and espresso. Chocoholics take note: the News Café may be the only restaurant on Miami Beach to serve chocolate fondue. Expect a wait during peak hours (especially on the weekend); during the week, guests are welcomed to while away the afternoon over a newspaper and capuccino. Lunch for two, with beer, will run $15.
Open Sun.-Thurs. 8 a.m.-2 a.m., Fri.-Sat. 24 hours. All major cards.

Rascal House
172nd St. & Collins Ave.,
Miami Beach
• (305) 947-4581

It is said that the Rascal House serves 5,000 people a day, and we won't dispute that. Most of them are white-haired retirees with a penchant for such Eastern European specialties as kreplach soup, turkey paprikash and boiled beef flanken (short ribs) served in a pot of steaming broth. Belt-loosening deli platters, two-fisted sandwiches and Brobdingnagian desserts are the drawing cards, but you'll have to wait in line awhile before you can play your hand. Many a fancy restaurant could learn from the Bunyanesque bread basket. Yet all is not perfect in this

land of lox and latkes. The service is brusque, the noise level deafening, and on one visit, we spied a cockroach. The locals generally concede that the best meal is breakfast, but day or night you're apt to enter a packed house.
Open daily 7 a.m.-1:45 a.m. No cards.

Wagons West
11311 S. Dixie Hwy., South Miami
• (305) 238-9942

In a city as new as Miami, it's hard to find a vintage greasy spoon. Which is why we're always first in line for a booth or a stool at the perennially packed Wagons West at the Suniland Shopping Center. Isn't democracy grand? Silk-tie executives sit elbow to elbow with construction workers, wolfing down three-egg omelets, thick-cut french toast, and veritable mountains of corned-beef hash. We can't imagine what sort of person would eat chocolate-chip pancakes for breakfast, but our waitress assures us that these, too, are a lively seller. Don't expect much in the way of atmosphere: polyurethaned tables and barn-board walls plastered with corny sayings. The waitresses are just brusque enough to let you know that this is the real McCoy. Breakfast for two with coffee runs $10.
Open daily 6:30 a.m.-2:30 p.m. No cards.

CAFETERIAS

Biscayne Miracle Mile Cafeteria
147 Miracle Mile, Coral Gables
• (305) 444-9005

In this age of designer pizzerias and mesquite grills, cafeterias have fallen on hard times. Except, perhaps, in Miami, where these assembly-line eateries play to a loyal clientele of silver-haired senior citizens, necktied yuppies, and everyone in between. But why not jump in line at the Biscayne Miracle Mile Cafeteria in the heart of blue-blooded Coral Gables and see for yourself? For ten bucks you can eat yourself silly on towering biscuits, freshly baked corn sticks, turkey and roast beef carved to order, and collard greens cooked for hours, as they should be—a rarity in this age of the al dente green bean. Admit it: you've always harbored a secret craving for jello. This is the place to indulge it. Who cares that the desserts have aerosol toppings? When you've loaded your tray to capacity or beyond, a busboy in a gold jacket will help you carry it to your table. In case you misread the rather blatant body language, yes, he expects a tip. Dinner for two with soft drinks will run $20 to $25.
Open Mon.-Sat. 11 a.m.-2:15 p.m. & 4 p.m.-8 p.m., Sun. 11 a.m.-8 p.m. No cards.

MIAMI Quick Bites

HIGH TEA

Inter-Continental Hotel Lobby Lounge
100 Chopin Plaza, Miami
• (305) 577-1000

May we suggest the British version of Happy Hour—High Tea—artfully presented in the glorious lobby lounge of the Inter-Continental each afternoon from 3 p.m. to 5 p.m. Providing the backdrop for the elegant affair is the marvelous Henry Moore sculpture, "The Spindle," gracing the lobby. Even after tea concludes, the lobby is a lovely, elegant and somehow tropical setting from which to enjoy cocktails.
Open Mon-Fri. 3 p.m.-11 p.m., Sat.-Sun noon-11 p.m.

HOT DOGS

Arbetter Hot Dogs
8747 S.W. 40th St. (Bird Rd.), Miami
• (305) 226-9724

Picasso worked in oils. Arbetter paints with mustard and ketchup. His canvas is the humble hot dog, and in his hands, it becomes a work of art. Since 1972, the Arbetter family has obliged Miami's hungry hordes with beef and pork tube steaks generously heaped with sauerkraut, slathered with melted cheese, or piqued with spicy relish. Arbetter's pride and joy is a chili dog that ignites your throat as it fills your belly. He makes his chili daily, following a recipe he won't divulge for love or money. Hot dog emporiums aren't generally known for their cleanliness, but Arbetter's is so immaculate, you could almost eat off the floor. (Fortunately, the tables turn frequently enough that you don't have to.) There also outposts in North Miami and Cocoa. Lunch or dinner for two with sodas will run $10.
Open daily 10:30 a.m.-11 p.m. No cards.

LATIN AMERICAN

La Esquina de Tejas
202 S.W. 12th Ave., Miami
• (305) 545-5341

This boisterous eatery may be the only Cuban restaurant in Florida where you can order arroz con pollo (chicken with yellow rice) or tostones (mashed, fried plantains) and wash them down with a bottle of Château Lafite. We can't attest to the quality of the wine (we wouldn't chance $150 on a bottle that's been stored upright at room temperature), but we can vouch for the rib-sticking wholesomeness of La Esquina's Cuban soul food. We're not alone. Among others, Ronald Reagan enjoyed lunch here in 1983. Vast legions of Cuban Americans, not to mention Anglos, flock here for equally vast portions of paella, flan, dulce de leche (curdled caramel) and Cuban sandwiches—cold cut submarines cooked in a machine like a waffle iron. Feeling adventurous? Try the tasajo, shredded dried beef in a

MIAMI Quick Bites

tomatoey Creole sauce. The charms of the fufu (a wooden mortar full of starchy mashed plantain and fried pork rind) elude us. A counter lined with stools and tables draped with oil cloths give the vast "Texas Corner" the homespun feel of a luncheonette. Dinner for two with beer will run $20 to $30.
Open daily 7 a.m.-11 p.m. All major cards.

Islas Canarias
285 N.W. 27th Ave.,
Miami
• (305) 649-0440

Most people drive right by Islas Canarias the first time they visit. Located in a nondescript storefront in an equally nondescript strip mall, the "Canary Islands" is easy to miss. It's not until you taste the papas espagnolas (freshly fried potato chips), sopa de platanos (meaty plantain soup), chicarones de pollo (crisp chicken cracklings) and soothing natilla (egg pudding) that you begin to understand why the line for tables forms early and lasts most of the night. This is the sort of food mama would have made in the glory days of Havana, from tender boiled yuca with garlicky mojo (lime sauce) to camarones enchiladas (shrimp enchiladas) in a sonorous seafood sauce. The pudin de pan (a flanlike bread pudding) and other desserts prove the supremacy of Cuban sweets. The lacqueured wood tables are patrolled by a squadron of good-natured waiters in white shirts and black vests. The best news of all is the tab: two can eat themselves silly for $15.
Open daily 7 a.m.-11 p.m. No cards.

Momotombo
804 Ponce de Leon Blvd.,
Coral Gables
• (305) 442-8092

They're singing again at Momotombo. Can you hear them? Voices joined in soulful harmony; guitars strummed with passion; Nicaraguan folksongs to accompany repochetas, nacatamal and gallo pinto. Named for a volcano in Nicaragua, this restaurant hole-in-the-wall serves some of the best Latin American food in Miami. Repochetas are Nicaraguan grilled cheese sandwiches (made with tortillas instead of bread). Nacatamal is the Nicaraguan version of a tamale, an artery-clogging assortment of pork, shrimp, and spicy chorizo sausage steamed in masa inside a banana leaf. Gallo pinto, red beans and rice, makes a filling accompaniment to cangrejo (Nicaraguan crab chowder) or punta de filete en salsa jalapeña (sirloin tips with chili-cream sauce). For you to decide whether you want your fried plantains *verdes* (starchy and green) or *maduros* (soft and sweet). To wash them down, try a glass of zanahoria con naranja (carrot and orange juice) or cebada (a sort of eggnog). Decorated with formica butcher block and orange Naugahyde banquets, Momotombo isn't much to look at. But the soulful food and live music on the weekends speak loudly enough for themselves. Dinner for two with Nicaraguan beverages will run $20 to $30.
Open Sun.-Thurs. noon-10 p.m., Fri.-Sat. noon-11 p.m. All major cards.

HOTELS

TOP OF THE LINE (From $200)   47
LUXURY (From $150)   48
MODERATE (From $100)   51
PRACTICAL (Under $100)   55
INNS   59

TOP OF THE LINE (From $200)

The Alexander
5225 Collins Ave.,
Miami Beach 33140
• (305) 865-6500
Fax (305) 864-8525

From 1984 to 1989, The Alexander was the place where one's chances of meeting up with vice-cops Crockett and Tubbs, ersatz cocaine dealers and other various and sundry visiting Miami Vice glitterati weren't bad. The production offices of the one-time NBC television sizzler occupied an entire floor of the well-located, oceanfront Miami Beach hotel, and this is where its guest stars—from Sheenah Easton to Barbra Streisand—were generally put up. Since the TV series closed shop, The Alexander has been offering not only suites, but also one-, two- and three-bedroom condominium space within the property. Certainly the most upscale hotel in this area of town, The Alexander features a lobby graced not only with doormen that give a royal welcome, but also with Leroy Neiman oil paintings, bronzes, tapestries and antiques acquired from the Cornelius Vanderbilt mansion. The hotel sports the boldest staircase in town, and its pink edifice is the brightest spot on this stretch of an equally impressive horizon. The beach and pool area are extrordinary—a resort unto themselves. The most brazen of its older neighbors, this hotel still exudes an air of unquestionable elegance. *1-, 2- & 3-bedroom suites: $225-$1,000.*

Doral Saturnia International Spa Resort
8755 N.W. 36th St.,
Miami 33178
• (305) 593-6030
Fax (305) 591-9268

Step aside, O Golden Door, the Doral Saturnia has arrived. This spa resort, decidedly European and somewhat eerily removed from the bustle of Miami (save for the busy skies overhead, due to its proximity to Miami International Airport), the five-year-old Doral Saturnia has been acclaimed as one of the world's finest. With special-interest programs ranging from "Crash Cellulitis" to "Stress Management and Relaxation" and "Chef's Kitchen Spa Plan," the spa resort offers four- or seven-night programs promising to pamper, please—and push you to your

limits. Special features include 50 different aerobic exercise options, 26 private massage rooms and Fango Mud Treatments with plenty of therapeutic goop imported from Termi di Saturnia in Italy. The resort's Fat Point nutrition program is designed to be brought home as a way of lifetime maintenance of the progress made during a stay here.
Single packages: $1,630-$2,645; double packages: $1,260-$2,180.

Sheraton Bal Harbour
9701 Collins Ave,
Bal Harbour 33154
• (305) 865-7511
Fax (305) 864-2601

The Sheraton Bal Harbour has done an excellent job of marrying corporate and resort business within its 650-room structure. And let's not discount the 60 suites, poolside cabanas and patio lanais. The rooms are satisfactory, with nice views of the property. The hotel's layout aims to keep vacationers on the other end of the property from the three separate conference facilities, where beauty contests and trade shows are the usual fare. Boasting its very own gourmet delicatessen (where some of the best chocolate chip cookies in town are offered), ten acres of tropical landscaping, two pools and tennis courts, the Sheraton is adjacent to the very ritzy Bal Harbour Shops (Gucci, Cartier, Neiman-Marcus and Saks, to drop just a few shop names).
Singles & doubles: $195-$295.

Sonesta Beach Hotel Key Biscayne
350 Ocean Dr.,
Key Biscayne 33149
• (305) 361-2021
Fax (305) 361-3096

With its imaginative, attentive, summer-camp-like kids' programs (offered daily from 10 a.m. to 10 p.m.), Sonesta reigns as the best place in Miami for family vacationers. Key Biscayne, a self-contained group of small islands $1 away from Coconut Grove across the Rickenbacker Causeway, presents an excellent vacation spot for grownups, too. (President Nixon used to like it here: his answer to Kennebunkport during his presidency was Key Biscayne). The expansive, airy, 300-room hotel has tennis courts and an adjacent eighteen-hole golf course, with rooms and villas facing the beach, complete with the modern amenties you'd expect. Lest you get bored with the outdoors, daily shopping shuttles are offered daily.
Singles & doubles: $235-$295; suites $500-$985; 2- to 5-bedroom villas: $375-$950.

LUXURY (From $150)

The Colonnade
180 Aragon Ave.,
Coral Gables 33134
• (305) 441-2600
Fax (305) 445-3929

Since the turn of the century, when Henry Flagler's railroad began to cut through the Florida jungles, a handful of grande dames began springing up on the statewide hotel spectrum. Although only a few of these palaces remain in operation today, the Colonnade is at least one Florida hotel that has successfully managed to combine the luxury of the new with the seduction of the old. Situated in posh Coral Gables, the two-year-old

Colonnade Hotel was built on the site of the historic Colonnade Building. One of the first planned communities in the country, Coral Gables was the brainchild of one grapefruit farmer, George Merrick. Constructed in 1926 by the city founder himself, the fabulous domed Rotunda of the original building has been magnificently restored by artists from Mexico, Argentina and Guatemala. The five-story, European-style hotel features mahogany furniture, elaborate millwork, brass lamps and spit-polished marble floors. The rooms will make you happy, since they mirror much of the luxury found in the hotel's public areas. Coral Gables itself offers a wide variety of boutiques, galleries, antiques shops and restaurants, though the quiet suburb virtually closes up shop during the evening and weekend hours. For night activity, you can take a cab to the nightspots of Coconut Grove or South Beach.

Standard, medium, superior & deluxe rooms: $150-$230; suites $270 & up. Weekend & honeymoon packages available.

Fontainebleau Hilton Resort and Spa
4441 Collins Ave.,
Miami Beach 33140
• (305) 538-2000
Fax (305) 534-7821

One was not enough, so on this site there are two Fontainebleaus. One of them is the real thing, and the other, an enormous trompe l'oeil mural, is an illusion, a piece of art and a telling slice of information. It's illusion because it's only a painting, probably the largest trompe l'oeil in the world with its 13,016 square feet; it's art because this impressive mural is an important contribution to Miami's Art Deco District; it's informative in that it displays in detail what you cannot see behind the wall: the 1266-room Fontainebleau Hilton viewed from its mile-wide pool. Behind these pearly gates, it promises, there's a slice of waterfront heaven.

After all, enormity has its advantages. At the Fontainebleau, these include two pools, three whirlpools, 30 cabanas, seven lighted tennis courts, a full-service spa, an art gallery and shopping mall, a 200-slip boat dock and a multilingual hospitality center. Most of the guest rooms face the Atlantic Ocean, including the two-bedroom Frank Sinatra Suite (named after the frequent guest and performer); there are 60 suites spread among three separate buildings on the 60-acre grounds.

Built atop the remains of the famed 1920s Harvey Firestone mansion, the hotel has always been a pinnacle of luxury, imagination and flair: the goddess of the grande dames that characterized Miami Beach in the 1950s and 1960s. It is fitting then, that some eleven Miss Universes were crowned here during worldwide telecasts when the hotel acted as headquarters for the pageant. In 1978, when developer Stephen Muss bought the hotel, he engaged Hilton Hotel Corporation to manage it, and has since spent a cool $70 million to bring the hotel's former 1950s flash up to 1990s snuff. With its famous cave bars

MIAMI Hotels

outside, no less than twelve eating and drinking establishments and 1,200 feet of new sandy beach (which is swiftly replaced the moment it becomes even the least bit discolored), the Fontainebleau is a newer version of the kind of place it always has been—a place you can check into and never leave until you check out.
Singles & doubles: $155-$245; suites: $370-$650.

Grand Bay Hotel
2669 S. Bayshore Dr.,
Coconut Grove 33133
• (305) 858-9600
Fax (305) 859-2026

"Windward," the Alexander Lieberman metal sculpture, is a red shaft that points 29 feet up into the sky. Its name may be somewhat misleading; the interpretation of this esoteric statue erected—and that is the right word—in front of the Grand Bay Hotel is left to your imagination, or your unabashed fantasies.

An ambience of subdued elegance—in normal human-size proportions—characterizes the interior of this trademark of European influence, interfacing gracefully with modern touches to create one of Miami's best hotels. The Grand Bay promises to touch each of the senses during a stay here. Classical piano concerts are performed each evening in the lobby; afternoon tea is served daily. In a word, the Grand Bay is class.

Each of the hotel's six bi-level suites features a carefully themed international decor—African, Moroccan, South American, Italian, English and French—to match the hotel's equally cosmopolitan clientele. There are also 2 penthouse suites, 2 "Unique Suites" with private terraces, 12 "Bayfront Suites" and 27 "Grove Suites." Telephones and TVs are in the bathrooms; each suite boasts a wet bar. The 181 regular guest rooms are creatively designed and impeccably appointed: mineral water accompanies the turndown service; sitting areas include a love seat and a writing desk; fresh flowers and well-stocked mini-bars greet your entrance. Amenities include a 24-hour concierge service, shoe-shine service and a beauty parlor. Pointed toward Miamarina (a marina) and Biscayne Bay like an exclamation point, the hotel's coconut palms and other fruits of the tropics contrast just so with the old-world flair inside the hotel. Topping the whole enclave is the nightclub created by a poor Belgian girl who became the darling of the international jetset: Regine's.
Single & double rooms: $180-$225; suites from $290.

Grove Isle Yacht & Tennis Club Hotel
4 Grove Isle Dr.,
Coconut Grove 33133
• (305) 858-8300
Fax (305) 250-4090

The 49-room Grove Isle, situated among the glitzy high-rise residences of developer Marty Marguilies's private island just offshore at Coconut Grove, is one of Miami's worst-kept secrets. If only to gain access to the well-guarded retreat, as well as to wander through the impressive waterfront sculpture garden (pieces by Calder, Dubuffet, Noguchi, Lieberman and Heizer, among others), Grove Isle is well worth a stay. Hint: Don't be fooled by that lady on the bench; she's just another George Segal creation. There's plenty of recreation on the

property, and the island is just a stone's throw from the attractions, restaurants, shops and nightlife of Coconut Grove. Rooms are a notch above standard fare, with balconies, French-tile floors and a mini-bar to keep your Evian cool after the jog around the island's track.
Singles & doubles: $145-$220.

Hyatt Regency Coral Gables
50 Alhambra Plaza,
Coral Gables 33134
• (305) 441-1234
Fax (305) 441-0520

Tell your taxi driver to take the Douglas Road airport exit, and just keep driving. Neither of you will miss the Hyatt Coral Gables. It's hard to believe that there are only 242 rooms and 50 suites: the pink edifice of the Hyatt looks bigger than a New York grande dame. Perhaps this was no accident. The hotel was built around the same time that the gracious old Biltmore Hotel, just across the Gables, was undergoing a $50 million renovation. (The Biltmore, at the time of this writing, has gone belly up, leaving the Hyatt with only the Colonnade to compete with). The service, public decor and room appointments are lovely. Although there are plenty of delightful restaurants both within and in the vicinity of the Hyatt, it's located on the edge of a city whose charming streets are left very quiet on weekends and in the evenings.
Singles & doubles: $155-$210.

Sheraton Brickell Point on Biscayne Bay
495 Brickell Ave.,
Miami 33131
• (305) 373-6000
Fax (305) 374-2279

Just across the Miami River from downtown, Sheraton Brickell Point lies at the tip of Brickell Avenue, on the business end of Miami's "Golden Mile." Although it is theoretically within walking distance from downtown attractions, including Bayside Marketplace, there's a shuttle service, which we advise you to use, especially at night. Primarily a business hotel with 600 rooms, thirteen newly decorated suites and lots of meeting facilities, the hotel offers a lovely view of both Biscayne Bay and the river, depending on how high up you are. Rooms won't knock you out, but are perfectly servicable.
Singles & doubles: $145-$165; suites: $295. Weekend packages available.

MODERATE (From $100)

Dadeland Marriott
9090 S. Dadeland Blvd.,
Miami 33156
• (305) 663-1035
Fax (305) 666-7124

What? A Marriott in the middle of a residential area and across the street a popular suburban shopping mall? That was mostly the local response to the new Dadeland Marriott, which sprang up as part of an office complex a few years back. Since a Metrorail stop lies literally at the hotel's back door, and the Palmetto Expressway (running north and south through western Dade County) at the front door, at least this rather odd location does provide accessibility to the better-traveled tourist

MIAMI Hotels

areas. Bright and tasteful describes the building, with 303 guest rooms decorated to a Florida "T," especially on the two concierge levels.
Singles & doubles: $136.

David William Hotel
700 Biltmore Way,
Coral Gables 33134
• (305) 445-7821
Fax (305) 445-5585

Staying at the David William feels a bit like living in Coral Gables (it is surrounded by homes and apartments) and a bit like working in the ritzy, Spanish-flaired suburb (there are office buildings and places to power lunch inside the hotel). Off the fast track, and yet within walking distance from the shops of Miracle Mile, the hotel is ideal for business travel: there are kitchens inside all of the nicely appointed suites and hotel efficiencies. A great view of Coral Gables from the hotel's rooftop pool; both men's and women's spas are well-equipped and attractive.
Singles & doubles: $110; suites $150.

Doral Ocean Beach Resort
4833 Collins Ave.,
Miami Beach 33140
• (305) 532-3600
Fax (305) 534-7409

Although it has an appropriately chichi ring to it, the Doral got its name in a rather unassuming way: Doris and Al, the founders, joined their first names together and a hotel mini-empire was born. The original resort, a half hour's drive inland, became famous for its golf tournaments. The 420-room (and -suite) beachfront property offers reciprocal privileges to guests at both the Doral Resort & Country Club and the Doral Saturnia International Spa Resort via a surprisingly spacious, comfortable and air-conditioned motor coach. Probably your best bet within this seventeen-story glass tower is to get a room facing the bay, since the night lights are stunning. All rooms have either a double or a king bed. All Doral guests can board the *Doral IV* an 80-foot motor yacht, which docks across the street for cruises up and down the Intracoastal Waterway, as well as the famous Starlight Roof nightclub, offering a delightfully expansive, glittering view of Miami Beach.
Singles & doubles: $105-$190; suites: $235-$750. Special packages available from $129-$489.

Doral Resort & Country Club
4400 N.W. 87th Ave.,
Miami 33178
• (305) 592-2000
Fax (305) 594-4682

Don't even consider this one unless you use words like "birdie" and "scratch golfer" in your everyday conversation. An overstatement, perhaps, but since this hotel's primary claim to fame is the irresistibility of its 99 holes of golf, those checking in at the self-proclaimed largest self-contained golf resort in the United States should most certainly accept the sport as a way of life during a stay here, all other pursuits playing second fiddle to assigned tee times. Actually, the Doral activity folks do an excellent job of coordinating plenty of on-property diversions, as well as transportation to shopping areas, attractions and the other two Doral hotels. With 650 rooms and suites housed in

MIAMI Hotels

eight private lodges, tennis instruction offered by Arthur Ashe and several excellent restaurants and lounges, we concede the Doral is a lovely place not only to golf the week away but also to pass the week waiting for your spouse to sink that eighteenth hole for the eighteenth time.

Singles & doubles: $95-$155; suites $195-$415. Special packages available from $119.

Hyatt Regency City Center
400 S.E. 2nd Ave., Miami 33131
• (305) 358-1234
Fax (305) 358-0529

Check in here, if you like being in the thick of things. Concertgoers tromp through the lobby on a regular basis to attend performances at the James L. Knight Center. It's a rare day when the Riverfront Exhibition Center goes without a show, a college graduation, or a celebration of some sort occurring. Valet parkers beware these events: harried-looking security people just wave you on elsewhere, which can be daunting for those returning to their rooms with golf clubs or fishing gear! The downtown Hyatt is Miami's closest answer to a New York hotel with its own subway station. Still, the rooms are nicely decorated and spacious, particularly on the Regency Club levels, where the gratifying perks and excellent service make it worth what one must go through to return to the room each evening.

Singles & doubles: $129-$159; Regency Club: $159-$179. Weekend packages available.

Inter-Continental Hotel Miami
100 Chopin Plaza, Miami 33131
• (305) 577-1000
Fax (305) 577-0384

The bayfront address of the Inter-Continental Hotel Miami at Miami Center (the Pavillon Hotel before it went bust) notwithstanding, you'd be hard-pressed to orient yourself anywhere near Biscayne Bay from within the heavily marbled lobby. Most of the hotel's 644 guest rooms (including 30 deluxe suites, two presidential suites and two magnificent bi-level penthouse suites) provide magnificent water views. There are also nice amenities in the rooms. The less publicity-conscious of the rich and famous love this place, and it has benefited greatly in recent years from the bustle of neighboring Bayside Marketplace and a generally spruced-up downtown.

Singles & doubles: $139-$259; suites: from $249. Weekend packages available.

Mayfair House
3000 Florida Ave., Coconut Grove 33133
• (305) 441-0000
Fax (305) 447-9173

Despite the promise made by the white-gloved, gray-tuxedoed doormen, the Mayfair House exudes a decidedly folksy attitude. It's from one of the suite terraces, each of which is graced with a private Japanese hot tub, that David Letterman once broadcasted his Late Night show, shouting into the busy Coconut Grove streets in an attempt to scare up a little comedy. We can only conjecture that he also enjoyed the two sinks in the bathroom, his own private dining area, and the lavish, distinctive decor of the suites. Surrounded by the élan of Mayfair in the

Grove, hands down Miami's ritziest shopping enclave, the open-air corridors, graced with airy ferns and decorated with colorful tiling, are certainly appealing to those who shun air-conditioning. This 181-suite hotel offers a lovely rooftop sundeck for an afternoon of poolside pursuits, and the seashore beckons only a few minutes' walk away. If you enjoy a bit of sun on your terrace, or a good view, be sure to request one of the few that's optimally placed for lounging.
1 & 2-bedroom suites: $140-$800. Packages available.

Miami Airport Hilton & Marina
5101 Blue Lagoon Dr., Miami 33126
• (305) 262-1000
Fax (305) 262-5726

If a Hilton is a Hilton, and an airport hotel is an airport hotel, then the Miami Airport Hilton & Marina does a better job than most. Situated on an artificially constructed peninsula surrounding a 100-acre freshwater lake, the Hilton offers sailing and watersports (albeit with an expressway in the background), a nice, quiet pool and tennis courts for day and night play. The top three floors of the hotel contain the Towers rooms, where concierge service, a private lounge and a host of personalized amenities await. There's a fitness center, a business center and complimentary shuttle service to and from the nearby airport.
Singles: $125-$165; doubles: $140-$195.

Omni International Hotel
1601 Biscayne Blvd., Miami 33132
• (305) 374-0000
Fax (305) 374-0020

The best thing about the Omni—on top of its spectacular glass elevators—is the location. Three minutes from the Port of Miami, and ten minutes (in opposite directions) from the airport and the nightlife of South Beach, the twenty-story, 531-room luxury hotel offers a spectacular view of both downtown Miami and Biscayne Bay. The hotel boasts the largest public room in Miami (ask any local who graduated from high school after the late 1970s where the senior prom was staged). Rooms are fine, with the standard fare of amenities.
Singles & doubles: $110-$145; junior suites: $165; suites: $205-$285.

Sheraton River House Hotel
3900 N.W. 21st St., Miami 33142
• (305) 871-3800
Fax (305) 871-0447

Since you aren't allowed to stop at the Miami International Airport until your party is actually standing in front of you, you may have to drive around again and again. If you accidentally exit while looping around, you'll find yourself at valet parking for the Sheraton River House. Stop by. Have a drink. Stay a while. Or, check in between flights. One of the oldest of the airport hotels, the River House has recently been refurbished, redecorating its 408 rooms and bi-level suites. The rooms are quite comfortable, and sound-proofed against those noisy jets.

MIAMI Hotels

Men's and women's health clubs, three lighted tennis courts and a jogging trail relieve the between-flight tedium.
Singles & doubles: $95-$140; suites: $150-$500.

Turnberry Isle Yacht & Country Club
1999 W. Country Club Dr.,
Aventura 33180
• (305) 932-6200
Fax (305) 932-9096

If you want to straddle Miami and Greater Fort Lauderdale, Turnberry Isle stands tall as a delightful place to do it. Also, as its magnificent ocean club is generally the venue of choice for local brides with a couple of bucks to spend on the extravaganza, it's the best place to crash a wedding. If that's not your style, bring your golf clubs instead, for there are two eighteen-hole golf courses (plenty of shopping nearby for golf widows). The snazzy 117-slip marina lends just the right nautical touch, while 24 multisurfaced tennis courts complete the resort feeling. We like the rooms, some of which have splendid views. Downtown Miami and downtown Fort Lauderdale are about equidistant for evening jaunts to the nightspots.
Singles, doubles & triples: $125-$155; suites: $200-$950.

PRACTICAL (Under $100)

Doubletree Hotel
2649 S. Bayshore Dr.,
Coconut Grove 33133
• (305) 858-2500
Fax (305) 858-5776

The Doubletree Hotel has plenty of competition in Coconut Grove because of its newer and much snobbier neighbors, so it doesn't even try to play the *Who's Who* game with its guest list. However, if you're neither rich nor famous, and just want to get a feel for what it must be like to actually live in the heart of the Grove, check out the Doubletree. The 172-room hotel has a pool and two tennis courts, with access to sailing, fishing cruises and harbor cruises just across the street at Sailboat Bay. The rooms and eighteen suites are well appointed and comfortable, many offering splendid bay views.
Singles & doubles: $59-$69; suites: $109.

Dupont Plaza Hotel
300 Biscayne Blvd. Way,
Miami 33131
• (305) 358-2541
Fax (305) 377-4049

Let's face it: in the shadow of the semicircular, multicolored Centrust Tower and the fascinating Southeast Bank building, two of Miami's most sophisticated landmarks, the Dupont Plaza doesn't exactly get your blood flowing. The building, which looks something like a dormitory in a poorly endowed university, features 292 guest rooms, each of which could use some redecorating. Still, film crews from Italy seem to favor the hotel and its central location, checking in and using a half floor or so for production offices. One bright spot: the Dupont Plaza does offer decent valet service.
Singles & doubles: $75; bi-level penthouse suites: $100; 1-, 2- & 3-bedroom suites: $150-$450.

MIAMI Hotels

The Edison Hotel
960 Ocean Dr.,
Miami Beach 33139
• (305) 531-0461
Fax (305) 532-2224

Don't even think about the Edison if you're looking for a little peace and quiet. The Edison, with its bustling Tropics nightclub, lies right in the thick of South Beach action, like a traffic cop without his white gloves on. A parade of neon-clad beautiful people begins on Ocean and Fifth at around 8 on Friday night, and doesn't stop until just before dawn on Monday. The building itself is magnificently redone, with blue trimmed arched windows and the requisite pastel peach exterior. The 65 rooms are one the small side, with small bathrooms and full tubs. Like most of the art-deco hotels, The Edison remains popular with the European set.
Singles, doubles & triples: $75-$95.

The Everglades Hotel
Biscayne Blvd. at 3rd St.,
Miami 33132
• (305) 379-5461
Fax (305) 577-8445

The 371-room Everglades Hotel, located at the entrance to the Port of Miami and facing festive Bayside Marketplace, has long been a favorite among cruise passengers enjoying pre- or postcruise visits to the city. Many of its rooms offer spectacular views of the skyline, so booking here during Grand Prix, Orange Bowl and other downtown festivities is probably your best bet for the price.
Singles & doubles: $79; suites: $100. Weekend, cruising & fly/drive packages available.

Harbor Island Spa
Larry Paskow Way,
North Bay Village 33141
• (305) 751-7561
Fax (305) 754-6244

A local television station recently named North Bay Village one of Miami's safest neighborhoods. Indeed, staying at the cloistered Harbor Island Spa is almost like visiting some well-hidden retreat, far away from the bustle of Miami. Situated along one of the more northern of the islands paralleling Miami, the spa is highly regarded for the quality of its fitness and nutritional programs, lifestyle awareness and improvement programs—not to mention the fact that it's not too far from the ritzy Bal Harbour Shops, where you can indulge a little after a hard day on the treadmill. Rooms echo the spa lifestyle.
Singles & triples: $75-$220.

Hotel Place St. Michel
162 Alcazar Ave.,
Coral Gables 33134
• (305) 444-1666
Fax (305) 447-1318

Despite the size of the rooms (they're small, but they have high ceilings) and how hard it can be, especially during the season, to snag one (there are only 30 of them from which to choose), the Hotel Place Saint Michel remains a delightful, romantic, European-style inn that makes for a wonderful visit to the heart of old Coral Gables. Featuring a popular piano bar and lovely, European style bistro downstairs, the Place Saint Michel has two wings. Rooms are decorated with armoires, ceiling fans and period furniture (except for the beds, which are firm and brand new). Rates include a basket of fresh fruits and cheese on arrival,

Italian chocolates, turndown service and your morning newspaper.
Singles & doubles: $90-$125; suites: $125.

Hotel Riverparc
100 S.E. 4th St.,
Miami 33131
• (305) 374-5100
Fax (305) 381-9826

Only those who read the sign figure this one out: Miami began right here. Fort Dallas, today a festive raw bar and nightspot overlooking the Miami River, is adjacent to the 130-room tower of the hotel. It is at the fort, established during the Seminole Indian wars, that just before the turn of the century Cleveland heiress Julia Tuttle gathered together a handful of hangers-on to put together a city. (Of course, the arrival of the railroad helped). Today, the deluxe rooms and suites all offer views of the river where it all began, as well as a nice spectrum of the downtown and Brickell Avenue business areas. Those who had to leave their car phones at home will be glad to know that there are three phones in every room. Similarly, the nonstop activity of the James L. Knight Center and Riverwalk next door at the Hyatt can be accessed at slightly lower prices for those staying at the Riverparc.
Singles & doubles: $85-$105; suites: $105-$290.

Hotel Sofitel Miami
5800 Blue Lagoon Dr.,
Miami 33126
• (305) 264-4888
Fax (305) 262-9049

This hotel promises to offer "a taste of France at the Miami airport," with 285 European-style guest rooms, a French bakery and take-out, and a small but well-stocked French gift shop, Le Petit Bijou. Sunday brunch here is a real joy, replete with improvisational actors attired as French characters who stroll from table to table to strike up conversation. The hotel offers a complimentary shuttle to and from the airport, as well as two tennis courts and a fully equipped fitness club. The rooms are fine, featuring amenities beyond the airport average.
Singles & doubles: $75-$130. Weekend packages available.

Pan American Ocean Resort Radisson
17875 Collins Ave.,
Miami Beach 33160
• (305) 932-1100
Fax (305) 935-2769

Situated along a somewhat less vibrant stretch of North Miami Beach, the Pan American Ocean Resort Radisson nonetheless remains delightful, a full-service resort, popular for generations among the visiting European crowd. Although the beachfront unfolds white and expansive (the hotel takes up 400 feet of private beach), and shopping at Aventura and The Waterways is close by, the location necessitates quite a trek to downtown, South Beach, Coral Gables and other good spots. Still, prices are good, and the self-contained resort presents an excellent family value. Accommodations include 146 spacious rooms, most with balconies or terraces facing the Atlantic.
Singles & doubles: $90-$160.

MIAMI Hotels

Park Central Hotel
640 Ocean Dr.,
Miami Beach 33139
• (305) 538-1611
Fax (305) 534-7520

If the Park Central looks familiar, it's probably because every New York film-location scout in existence has stumbled upon its 1920s sculpture garden, grand lobby and grander piano, and its colorful entryway. Right in the center of the Art Deco District's self-imposed weekend parade, the hotel has 80 rooms and suites, each of them artfully decorated with paddle fans, palm-printed carpets and black-and-white stills from the 1920s and 1930s. Although there are hotel patio bars along Collins Avenue where you can enjoy evening cocktails, the Park Central's dark and graceful lobby is a great compromise for those who insist on being air-conditioned under the August sun.
Singles & doubles: $60-$125.

Ritz Plaza Hotel Miami Beach
1701 Collins Ave.,
Miami Beach 33139
• (305) 534-3500
Fax (305) 531-6928

The newest of the renovated art-deco buildings lending their lovely edifices to the South Beach hotel scene, the Ritz opened just last year. Up the street a piece from pastel heaven, the Ritz boasts 133 cleverly decorated rooms, an Olympic pool, a festive poolside terrace bar and a cozy bar; for business travelers, complete services are available.
Singles & doubles: $65-$175.

Sheraton Royal Biscayne Beach Resort
555 Ocean Dr.,
Key Biscayne 33149
• (305) 361-5775
Fax (305) 361-0360

Though you might be put off initially by this plain-looking hotel; it nonetheless enjoys a great location for an outdoor retreat. Experience the Sheraton in one of the seventeen lanais, where cocktails and cooking at sunset are preferred evening endeavors. The 192-room hotel also has two-room oceanfront suites overlooking a quarter-mile of private beach, and ten championship tennis courts, four of them lit for night play. The oft number-one-rated public golf course in Florida is just a putt away from the Sheraton, with complimentary transportation and tee times arranged through the resort. A special feature for watersports enthusiasts: complimentary windsurfing instruction offered daily; attendance is advisable before striking out on your own along with the pros at Hobie Beach.
Singles & doubles: $85-$330. Packages available.

Surfcomber
1717 Collins Ave.,
Miami Beach 33139
• (305) 532-7715
Fax (305) 532-7280

Although the Surfcomber theoretically falls beyond the northern boundary of South Beach's Art Deco District, its 194 refurbished rooms are most definitely part of the Miami Design Preservation League's insistent push to keep the area updated and lively. Recent additions to the certifiably art-deco structure include air-conditioning, televisions and telephones in all guest rooms, a fitness center, a sidewalk café and an excellent location right across the street from a fine stretch of beachfront.
Singles & doubles: $40-$80.

INNS

Miami Lakes Inn
Main St.,
Miami Lakes 33014
• (305) 821-1150
Fax (305) 821-1150
ext. 1150

When these people say "get away from it all," they really mean it. Miami Lakes is basically in the middle of nowhere, just south of the Golden Glades Interchange in northwestern Dade County. And yet, it is a great little neighborhood and a lot of fun for those who have already "done" Miami and are truly looking for a getaway. The official resort of the Miami Dolphins, the Miami Lakes Inn is the pride of Main Street, a quaint little neighborhood of 70 shops and theaters. Take your clubs for a walk to the eighteen-hole championship golf course, where it's not unlikely that you'll run into Dolphins quarterback Dan Marino or coach Don Shula, who lives in the neighborhood. We like the rooms, too.
Singles & doubles: $119-$170; suites: $199-$450.

NIGHTLIFE

BARS	59
CABARETS	62
COMEDY & MAGIC	62
DANCE CLUBS	63
JAZZ	66
POOL HALLS	66
PRIVATE CLUBS	67

BARS

Clevelander Poolside Bar
1020 Ocean Dr.,
Miami Beach
• (305) 531-3485

Meeting for cocktails at the Clevelander is a very "South Beach" thing to do. The outdoor establishment looks like something out of *The Jetsons,* with lots of strangely tilted concrete umbrellas and wandering fountains, into which several people are likely to stumble during the course of any given weekend. Known for its frozen drinks and proximity to the ocean, the indoor bar is

perhaps best enjoyed on hot summer nights, when air-conditioned is the temperature of preference in these parts.
Open daily noon-5 a.m. Reggae Sun. 8:30 p.m.-midnight. Happy hour nightly 5 p.m.-7 p.m. No cover. All major cards.

Doc Dammer's Saloon
Colonnade Hotel,
180 Aragon Ave.,
Coral Gables
• (305) 441-2600

Doing its "dammdest" to beef up the sad little nightlife scene in Coral Gables, Doc Dammer's was named for one of Miami's original realtors. Edward "Doc" Dammer gave away free "gifts" (like china sets and phonographs) as part of his Coral Gables sales pitch. Doc Dammer's the bar offers great free hors d'oeuvres, good music and a knockout Happy Hour. The bar and grill re-creates the era of its namesake with original photographs and memorabilia from boom to bust in Coral Gables.
Open Sun.-Thurs. 7 a.m.-midnight, Fri.-Sat. 7 a.m.-2 a.m. All major cards.

Hungry Sailor
3064 1/2 Grand Ave.,
Coconut Grove
• (305) 444-9359

The Hungry Sailor puts the "1/2" after its address so that you'll know you have to walk through a semihidden arcade to reach its doors. (You can enter from Main Highway or Grand Avenue.) Just follow the smell of the burgers and the sound of the reggae, which is most always played live. A small, friendly establishment full of University of Miami students, Grove-ites (1960s holdover types notwithstanding) and jazz, blues and reggae lovers of all shapes and sizes. Added bonus: the Hungry Sailor allows you to escape the exuberant underage crowd that seems to have taken over the Grove streets on weekends and school holidays.
Open nightly 9 p.m.-2:30 a.m. Live reggae Tues.-Sat. Brazilian music Sun. No cover, but 2-drink mininum Tues.-Wed. All major cards.

Penrod's Beach Club
1 Ocean Dr.,
Miami Beach
• (305) 538-1111

Ladies, if you enjoy entering your legs and other bodily parts in competitions, this is the place for you. String bikinis are the daytime dress code, especially if you have a particularly hot bod and have just excused yourself from a mean game of volleyball on the beach just outside. If you arrive around sunset (when the outlying rays begin to disappoint), you'll find a much mellower crowd at Penrod's than you will during the late-night hours. Dance music is offered nightly on the second floor, live bands are featured poolside on the weekends, and the first floor is a lively sports bar with frequent games and competitions. Think Spring Break with a cover charge.
Open daily 11 a.m.-5 a.m. Shows Fri. 5 p.m.-11 p.m., Sat. 2 p.m.-7 p.m., Sun. 4 p.m.-9 p.m. Cover $3 Mon.-Thurs. & Sun., $5 Fri.-Sat. All major cards.

MIAMI Nightlife

Stuart's Bar & Lounge
Hotel Place St. Michel,
162 Alcazar,
Coral Gables
• (305) 444-1666

Hands down, Stuart's is the most romantic bar in Miami. Set up for a blind date? Have a second date? An anniversary? Telling your husband you're finally pregnant? Stuart's is the place for you. With European café tables for two, enormous picture windows and a mahogany bar, Stuart's delights. You may order appetizers from the menu of the adjacent restaurant, and select from an excellent wine list. On the weekends, a jazz trio plays unobtrusively in the background, and black-and-white-aproned waitresses absolutely whisper their hellos and adieus.
Open nightly 5:30 p.m.-midnight. All major cards.

Sundays on the Bay
5420 Crandon Blvd.,
Key Biscayne
• (305) 361-6777

10880 Collins Ave.,
Miami Beach
• (305) 945-6065

Both branches of Sundays on the Bay are named appropriately: spots where private sailboats and cruisers, following a long day plying the waters of Biscayne Bay, tie up for the afternoon, so their weary captains and crews can drink and dance until nightfall. We have never been to Sundays when someone or another hasn't ended up in the water, as it's hot and crowded and people just sort of ignore the "fourth wall" of the outdoor establishment. At night, the crowd runs to the young and annoying ("No bogus I.D. accepted," the ad screams), although there are all sorts of drink specials and college nights that continue to attract the precollegiate crowd.
Open Mon.-Thurs. & Sun. 5 p.m.-midnight, Fri.-Sat. 5-p.m.-3 a.m. All major cards.

Tavern in the Grove
3416 Main Hwy.,
Coconut Grove
• (305) 447-3884

Grab a beer at the Tavern, a nice place to be when things get out of hand on Main Highway, as they tend to do around about midnight on weekends in the Grove. All those kids cruising up and down the streets, blasting disco music from their car stereos? They're not allowed in unless they're over 21. A good, old-fashioned bar, still reasonably priced in a neighborhood that's gone to the chic dogs, the Tavern has lots of friendly events scheduled, like dart tournaments and Schnapps night (Tuesdays).
Open nightly 5 p.m.-3 a.m. Cards: AE, MC, V.

Tobacco Road
626 S. Miami Ave.,
Miami
• (305) 374-1198

The oldest bar in Miami, Tobacco Road is housed in a well-preserved architectural gem in the heart of what was once known as the "Roads" section of town. Tucked behind Brickell Avenue, whose chrome and glass skyscrapers loom in the background, Tobacco Road is a great place to enjoy Miami, old and new. At night, it tends to get a bit loud, with live jazz bands booked nightly both upstairs and downstairs.
Open nightly 5 p.m.-3 a.m. Showtimes vary. No cover weeknights, $3-$5 weekends. Cards: AE, MC, V.

MIAMI Nightlife

CABARETS

Club Tropigala at La Ronde
Fontainebleau Hilton,
4441 Collins Ave.,
Miami Beach
• (305) 672-7469

Here's your chance to sneak a peek at the Fontainebleau—even if you're not a guest. Elaborately costumed, Las Vegas–style reviews offer a cast of dozens, plenty of sequins, feathers and false eyelashes. If you miss the show, you can enjoy a very reasonably priced dinner, and salsa and dancing to Top 40 music. The Fontainebleau is in great shape for an old dowager, and the best of the hotel gets displayed at La Ronde.
Open nightly 7 p.m.-3 a.m. Shows Wed.-Sun. 8 p.m. & 10 p.m. Cover $13.50. All major cards.

Les Violins Supper Club
1751 Biscayne Blvd.,
Miami
• (305) 371-8668

Every wonder what Miami was like back in the fifties? Les Violins will remind you of Ricky Ricardo's fictional "Tropicana" nightclub on "I Love Lucy." There's no place else in town where $39 buys dinner, an elaborately costumed Mediterranean show and dancing the night away to Latin Big Band sounds.
Open Tues.-Sun. 7 p.m.-3 a.m. Shows nightly 10:30 p.m. All major cards.

COMEDY & MAGIC

Mental Floss
3138 Commodore Plaza,
Coconut Grove
• (305) 448-1011

This one's a tough call. It all depends. Mental Floss, relying on the quick wit of the cast members performing improvisationally during any given show—plus the cooperation of the audience—can be absolutely brilliant. It can also be a snore, downright embrassing not only for the comics, but also for each and every audience member. Skits are performed on the spot, and are based on input supplied by (and sometimes yanked out of) the audience. "Experimental Floss," an improvisational show performed by new members of the comedy troupes, is generally a total wash. "The difference between college and professional football," a taped message insists when you phone for tickets and reservations. Sometimes, though, both the rookies and the pros put on a show about as enjoyable to watch as professional bowling. Don't let us discourage you, though. When these people are hot, they're sizzling. Exiting an "on" show at Mental Floss, you won't remember when you've laughed so much. On top of that, Mental Floss is the only professional comedy club in town offering original comedy created exclusively by local performers.
Performances Fri.-Sat. 8 p.m., 10 p.m. & midnight, Sun. 8 p.m. Cards: AE, MC, V.

MIAMI Nightlife

Peacock in the Grove Café
2977 McFarlane Rd.,
Coconut Grove
• (305) 442-8877

Peacock appears to have somewhat of an identity problem: depending on when you visit, it's a comedy club, a dance hall, a jazz room, a lunch spot, a late-night eatery or an elevated daytime bar from which to enjoy the ongoing show passing by in the streets below. Depending on who's playing, performing, spinning and/or walking by, Peacock can be a lot of fun.
Open nightly 5 p.m.-3 a.m. Cover varies.

DANCE CLUBS

Club Nu
245 22nd St.,
Miami Beach
• (305) 672-0068

Club Nu's interior designers are a bit overzealous. The club completely changes it's decor on a regular basis, with themes ranging from Egyptian to an "environmental" celebration of women. (Please don't ask us what this means; you must see it for yourself). Housed in an old, art-deco casino (which despite heavily publicized protests from the Miami Design Preservation League has been more or less totaled), Club Nu hosts minor and on-the-edge rock stars (Grace Jones, Oingo Boingo), which generally draw large crowds, several times a week. Call for a schedule and current decor update.
Open nightly 10 p.m.-5 a.m. Cover $10 before midnight, $15 after midnight. Cards: AE, MC, V.

Dick Clark's American Bandstand Grill
Bayside Market
401 Biscayne Blvd.,
Miami
• (305) 381-8800

A cross between "Happy Days," "American Graffitti" and "Miami Vice," Dick Clark's lets you sing, dance, record a rock 'n' roll song of your own and make a general fool of yourself, while the lights of Miamarina (where TV's Sonny Crockett lived and boated) shine in the background. Dick Clark's is three bars laced together with an excellent selection of memorabilia on display. (If you must have an Elvis Poster or American Bandstand T-shirt of your own, there's also a gift shop on the premises).
Open Sun.-Thurs. 11 a.m.-midnight, Fri.-Sat.-2 a.m. All major cards.

Ensign Bitters
Corner Virginia St. &
Grand Ave.,
Coconut Grove
• (305) 445-2582

Art-deco styling, a marble dance floor, snake-shaped bar, lots of aquaria and plenty of tiling add up to a "casual, yet elegant" bar for the snobby but civilized among us looking for a wildly good time. Music runs to Top 40, with live entertainment on weekends and music videos beamed onto oversize TV screens. Jackets preferred.
Open Mon.-Thurs. 11:30 a.m.-3 a.m., Fri. 8 p.m.- 5 a.m., Sat. 8 p.m.- 5 a.m. Cover $20 Fri.-Sat. All major cards.

MIAMI Nightlife

Industry
1445 Washington Ave.,
Miami Beach
• (305) 532-0922

What an interesting fate for the art-deco Cameo Theater on Washington Avenue, in a section of South Beach that the queazy could still consider seedy. On weeknights, it hosts performance art and poetry readings. But come Saturday night, it becomes Industry, a progressive dance club catering to a naughty, rowdy tribe of youngsters from good families. Like promgoers in the high-school gymnasium, this gang doesn't seem to notice the impromptu decorations (a rather odd selection of slides and video images projected onto the walls of the architectural masterpiece), nor do they notice that the Cameo is an architectural masterpiece at all (the music's much too loud to inspire awe of any sort).
Open Fri.-Sat. 11 p.m.-5 a.m. Cover $7. No cards.

El Internacional Discoteca
3090 W. 16th Ave.,
Hialeah
• (305) 556-7788

Visitors to Miami, want to "dirty dance?" The problem with dancing salsa, merengue and the ubiquitous lambada is that they each take a certain level of skill. If you're leading overzealously, you quite literally have someone's life in your hands. El Internacional is the club of choice among those who have reached a certain skill level at Spanish dances. Once you walk through the front doors, get ready to spend an evening in Buenos Aires, Madrid . . . would you believe Havana during the fifties?
Open Tues.-Sun. 8 p.m.- 4 a.m. Cards: AE, MC, V.

Island Club
701 Washington Ave.,
South Beach
• (305) 538-1213

Although it's anyone's guess as to how these rituals evolve, the line at the Island Club winds around the block deep into the wee hours of the morning—but only on Mondays. During the rest of the week (although it offers live rock music nightly), Island Club looks like the off-season in the Caribbean, a lonely few playing ping-pong and pool to the strained tunes of a CD jukebox.
Open nightly 5 p.m.-5 a.m. Cards: AE, MC, V.

The Kitchen Club
100 21st St.,
Miami Beach
• (305) 538-6631

Is your nose pierced? Would you like it to be pierced? Check out the Kitchen Club, where there are plenty of safety pins artfully linking together various bodily protrusions; where there's a veritable stable of black leather milling about to the none-too-rhythmic rhythm; where the hair mousse of choice is shellac and the music runs to the progressive. On the edge. About to jump out a window.
Open Wed.-Sat. 10 a.m.-5 p.m. Cover $3-$6. No cards.

MIAMI Nightlife

Lime in the Coconut
Corner Virginia & Grand Aves., Coconut Grove
• (305) 448-1409

If you're not in the mood for pretense, but still want to check out Mayfair, try Lime in the Coconut. Visiting bands play everything from disco to classical and original rock, and if you go at happy hour, two-for-one drinks let you do Mayfair on the cheap.
Open nightly 4 p.m.-2 a.m. Happy hour Wed.-Fri. 4 p.m.-7 p.m. Showtimes vary. Cards: AE, MC, V.

Stefano's
24 Crandon Blvd., Key Biscayne
• (305) 361-7007

A hotspot among those in the know and those who live on "The Key" (sometimes referred to as Key Rats), Stefano's is somewhat removed from the rest of Miami's night scene. (It's no easy bar hop to either South Beach or Coconut Grove from the Key). Still, choose Stefano's for an evening, especially when there's a band scheduled. Wednesday night is lambada night; Thursday night, reserved for Latin dancing exclusively.
Open Tues.-Sun. 5 p.m.-5 a.m. Live band Tues. & Thurs.-Sun. Showtimes vary. All major cards.

Stringfellow's
Mayfair Shops, 3390 Mary St., Coconut Grove
• (305) 446-7555

If Regine could do it, so could equally jet-set clubber Peter Stringfellow, friend to Robin Leach, a couple of ex-Beatles, Eddie Murphy and oh so many other celebs. With establishments roaring in London, New York and Beverly Hills, Stringfellow opened his Miami restaurant and nightclub in 1988. Although it's posh in ambience, with all the latest in video and lighting disco paraphernalia, remember the Happy Hour (5 p.m. to 8 p.m.) bargain, and for ladies at least, the ladies-night bargain.
Open Tues.-Sat. 8 p.m.-5 a.m. Cover $20. No cover for dinner guests. All major cards.

Village Inn
3131 Commodore Plaza, Coconut Grove
• (305) 445-8721

A holdout from the "old" Bohemian grove—when the music and ambience were original, and the owner remained unindicted on income-tax violations—the Village Inn is dark, crowded and full of real, genuine people just about every night. Around the corner from the late-night eatery of the same name, there's generally a live band playing, and you can dance with two or three of your closest friends on a cozy dance floor.
Open nightly 10 p.m.-3 a.m. Cover varies. All major cards.

MIAMI Nightlife

JAZZ

Café des Arts
3138 Commodore Plaza,
Coconut Grove
• (305) 336-3634

918 Ocean Dr.,
Miami Beach
• (305) 534-6267

Both of these cozy restaurants offer an interesting twist to their jazz selections: generally, they host Brazilian artists. The Grove Café serves forth a wonderful rooftop ambience from its fourth-floor, downtown Grove locale; at the South Beach Café des Arts, the spicy, sultry music blends with the sounds of the Atlantic Ocean just across the street.
Open nightly 5 p.m.-midnight. All major cards.

Lucky's
Park Central Hotel,
640 Ocean Dr.,
Miami Beach
• (305) 538-1611

The jazz pianists who tickle the ivories at the stylish, 1930s-style Lucky's make you feel as if you had moved through time. Whether you're dining at Lucky's or just enjoying cocktails, the lounge is a class act not to be missed on a bar hop up and down Ocean Drive.
Open nightly 5 p.m.-midnight. All major cards.

Sports Rock Café Miami
Bakery Center,
5701 Sunset Dr.,
South Miami
• (305) 666-6607

Despite a change of hands (athletic club members and lunch guests arrived one day to find the doors locked), Sports Rock has bounded from hard times to offer an evening of fun and games in the suburbs. Located in South Miami, which becomes rather hopeless when most of the stores and restaurants close at sundown, Sports Rock offers live jazz, both indoors and outdoors, as well as pool, basketball and all sorts of quasi-athletic pursuits that bargoers enjoy.
Open Thurs.-Sat. 5 p.m.-2 a.m. No cover. Cards: AE, MC, V.

Tropics International
The Edison Hotel,
960 Ocean Dr.,
South Beach
• (305) 531-5335

Tropics rumbles with an eclectic menu of jazz, rock, blues and Latin music to be enjoyed poolside, the rhythm of the Atlantic Ocean's waves just across the street harmonizing nicely. Go early in the summer months, when, unless you snag a table indoors, you're in for a real sweat-in.
Open Mon.-Thurs. & Sun. 7 a.m.-1 a.m., Fri.-Sat. 7 a.m.-3 a.m. Hours & showtimes vary. Cover $3. All major cards.

POOL HALLS

Society Billiards
2895 McFarlane Rd.,
Coconut Grove
• (305) 441-8787

1253 Washington Ave.,
Miami Beach
• (305) 674-0005

In Coconut Grove, Society Billiards has the coldest air and beer in town. A cavernous structure (formerly a church), the pool hall offers an afternoon or an evening of great tunes and a chance to rack 'em up. The Art Deco District branch of New York–based Society Billiards is similarly sophisticated, offering not only the 34 pool tables, but also eleven satellite televisions tuned into sporting events the world over.
Open daily noon-2 a.m. No cards.

MIAMI Nightlife

The Irish Pub
1430 Alton Rd.,
Miami Beach
• (305) 534-5667

Dark, dirty and loads of fun, Irish Pub has been in the neighborhood since 1938. Pool tables, darts, pinball (yes that's pinball, not just those newfangled video games) and frosted mugs of beer, ale and stout are served in the shadows—even when it's bright, white-hot outside and most everybody else is at the beach. Located on the wrong side of the island (the west side) in the middle of a tired old section of town, the pub is a blast from the past that's managed to remain a neighborhood hangout, even among the University of Miami med-school students, and various other yuppie types who live on this side of The Beach. This is not a place to come alone or with a date, but instead with a large group of people you love in tow.
Open daily noon-1 a.m. No cards.

> **EXPLORING ON FOOT**
>
> Two of Miami's best neighborhoods at night are Coconut Grove and Little Havana. In the Grove, dozens of sidewalk cafés and nightspots hum with activity. The heart of Miami's Cuban community, Pequeña Havana sizzles with good, cheap eateries and Latin nightclubs.

PRIVATE CLUBS

Regine's
2669 S. Bayshore Dr.,
Coconut Grove
• (305) 858-9500

You've got three ways to get yourself into Regine's for a delightful evening of dancing and tasty $9 well drinks: check into the Grand Bay Hotel; make and keep dinner reservations at Regine's; or cough up $300 for the annual membership. Considering what a cool place the artfully decorated nightspot is, none of these seems extreme. Do what you can to get in and you'll enjoy a night in Miami you won't soon forget, towering over Coconut Grove with all the beautiful people.
Open Tues. & Thurs. 8 p.m.-3 a.m., Fri.-Sat. 8. p.m.-5 a.m. All major cards.

Semper's
Waldorf Hotel,
860 Ocean Dr.,
Miami Beach
• (305) 673-6730

Semper's is a gloriously decorated (read: Victorian, art-deco, Nouveau Funk) private club that has an interesting membership system—just have two member friends make a call on your behalf—meant to keep out the riff raff without being out-and-out snotty. Once you get inside, it's all worth it. On weeknights in particular, and early enough so it's not stiflingly crowded, it's a delightful place to kick back, observe the Michelle Pfeiffer lookalike on the piano, order a martini and pretend its the 1930s. Or the 1920s, or the 1940s. Or the early '90s. Whatever era strikes your harmonic.
Open Mon.-Thurs. & Sun. 8 p.m.-2 a.m., Fri.-Sat. 8 p.m.- 5 a.m. No cover. All major cards.

SHOPS

ANTIQUES	68
BEAUTY & HEALTH	70
BOOKS	72
CHILDREN	73
CLOTHES & JEWELRY	73
DEPARTMENT STORES & SHOPPING CENTERS	77
FLOWERS	79
FOOD	79
GIFTS	81
HOME	82
SPORTING GOODS	84

ANTIQUES

Antique Auctions

Miami Antique Auction Co.
2644 S.W. 28th Ln., Miami
• (305) 856-3097

Located in a rather unassuming neighborhood—on the wrong side of the Metrorail tracks south of Coconut Grove—Miami Antique Auction Co. is part of a larger smattering of interesting furniture and collectibles warehouses. Offering French and English furniture, decorative arts, bronzes and carved woods with no minimum, no reserve and no buyer's premium. *Hours vary; phone ahead for details.*

Antiques Markets

Alhambra Antiques Center
3640 Coral Way, Coral Gables
• (305) 446-1688

With a couple of dozen dealers under one air-conditioned roof, in Miami this means you don't have to sweat while searching out that one particular thing, or whatever you're in the market for. Specializing in French and English furniture, decorative accessories, original paintings and lots of fun vintage jewelry.
Open Mon.-Sat. 10 a.m.-6 p.m.

Antique, Jewelry & Collectibles Show
Coconut Grove Exhibition Center, Bayshore Dr. at 27th Ave., Coconut Grove
• (305) 444-8454

One weekend each month, Coconut Grove Cares organizes a wonderful antiques show, featuring dealers from the Southeast, at the bayfront Exhibition Center and Dinner Key. Literally hundreds of dealers fill the front hall with all kinds of items, ranging from fun junk to très cher fare; the back room hosts separate shows with their own themes, dolls of the world and historic toy trains among them.
Open Sat. noon-9 p.m., Sun. noon-6 p.m.

Art Deco & Art Nouveau

Frances Cary Antiques
11077 Biscayne Blvd., Miami
• (305) 891-6196

Not quite inside the Miami Design District, Frances Cary nonetheless carries a designer's treasure trove of art-deco and art moderne collectibles. A member of the International Society of Appraisers, Cary promises competitive prices on all items.
Open Mon.-Fri. 9 a.m.-5 p.m.

Last Tango in Paris
1214 Washington Ave., Miami Beach
• (305) 532-4228

Somehow, browsing through cluttered rows of art-deco and mid-century modern collectibles is just more fun to do in South Beach than anywhere else in town. You can also find an excellent selection of vintage clothing, jewelry and accessories on display here.
Open Mon.-Sat. 10 a.m.-5 p.m.

Morgenstern's Antiques
2665 Coral Way, Miami
• (305) 854-2744

If you've just bought one of those Spanish-style mansions overlooking the banks of the Coral Gables Waterway, you'd best get yourself to Morgenstern's. Featuring a huge selection of modern Latin American and Cuban art mixed up just so with old Oriental rugs, tapestries, paintings and porcelain, Morgenstern's gets much of its stock from local estates.
Open Mon.-Fri. 9 a.m.-5 p.m.

MIAMI Shops

Valerio Antiques
Mayfair Shops,
3390 Mary St.,
Coconut Grove
• (305) 448-6770

Art-nouveau and art-deco items are priced sky-high, but many of them are worth it. Excellent selection of lamps, glassware and collectibles—including Lalique, Tiffany and Galle glass; bronze and ivory are often in plentiful stock. If you don't want to pay the prices, Valerio's wonderful displays will at least provide some food for thought for your home decor. The helpful sales staff also provides a wonderful education in both eras.
Open Mon.-Sat. 10 a.m.-6 p.m.

Books, Maps & Prints

Americana Bookshop & Gallery
175 Navarre Ave.,
Coral Gables
• (305) 442-1776

"Call me, I actually know what I'm doing," says John Detrick, owner of Americana Bookshop. If you're in the market for used and rare books on Old Cuba, Florida history and military trivia, Detrick is indeed the man to see while in Miami.
Open Mon.-Fri. 10 a.m.-5:30 p.m.

Jewelry

Surfside Watch & Silver Vault
9458 Harding Ave.,
Surfside
• (305) 865-4474

If you're in the market for vintage watches, Surfside's the place for you, with a huge variety of Vacheron, Cartier and Rolexes for sale. Surfside is also in the market to buy; depending on your timing, you can also pick up some great buys on art glass and sterling silver pieces.
Hours by appointment.

BEAUTY & HEALTH

Beauty Salons

Georgette Klinger
Bal Harbour Shops,
9700 Collins Ave.,
Bal Harbour
• (305) 868-7516

Spend the day at Georgette Klinger, while her surgical team of stylists works on you from head to toe. As is the way here at Bal Harbour, the ambience is posh and the idea is to pamper you.
Open Mon.-Thurs. & Fri. 10 a.m.-9 p.m., Tues.-Wed. & Sat. 10 a.m.-6 p.m., Sun. noon-5 p.m.

Gessner & Camp Salon
1731 Ponce de Leon Blvd.,
Coral Gables
• (305) 442-1065

The salon business in Coral Gables is tough. So when Detlev Gessler and Paco Camp got enough local attention to open a place of their own, they went out of their way to make sure nobody would forget it. Hand-crafted metal sculptures surround the stations, and the walls have metric nodules screwed in every foot or so, making the salon seem as peaceful as a submarine. They also made a commitment to 100 percent

environmentally correct products; even the coffee cups they give you are recycled. And the haircuts? They're the talk of the town.
Open Tues.-Sat. 10 a.m.-7 p.m., Sun. 10 a.m.-5 p.m.

Nails at the Beach
1300 Collins Ave., Miami Beach
• (305) 532-1129

Get your nails done in the heart of the Art Deco District (something red and shiny would probably honor the era properly). Gel nails, tips, silk nails and unusual "Nailart" are offered at reasonable prices.
Hours by appointment.

Scents, Soaps & Toiletries

Subtilite
Mayfair Shops, 3399 Virginia St., Coconut Grove
• (305) 444-3950

Specializing in the La Prairieline of skin treatments made by the famous clinic in Montreux, Switzerland, Subtilite also offers Zarolia perfumes in hand-blown glass bottles and a variety of other fragrances and cosmetics.
Open Mon.-Sat. 10 a.m.-9 p.m., Sun. noon-5:30 p.m.

Terry's Wholesale Perfumes and Colognes
20286 Old Cutler Rd., Miami
• (305) 378-9682

It's definitely worth the drive way south of downtown (Old Cutler Road presents a beautiful one, anyway) because this wholesale perfume and cologne shop has prices that can't be beat at the duty-free shops. Be sure to check the dates of arrival on purchase; perfume does lose its scent with time.
Open Mon.-Sat. 10 a.m.-6 p.m.

Tanning Salons

Grove Fitness Tanning Salon
2901 Florida Ave., Coconut Grove
• (305) 442-2107

So it rained the whole time you were in Miami and you just can't go home without a tan? No problem. The folks at Grove Fitness will take care of you in no time, promising visible results in only one session without burning.
Open Mon.-Fri. 6 a.m.-10 p.m., Sat. 8 a.m.-6 p.m., Sun. 10 a.m.-6 p.m.

Vidal Tan Soon
9601 S. Dixie Hwy., Miami
• (305) 665-3394

Vidal offers 100 percent, pure UVA tanning (that's supposed to prevent burning rays), as well as European body wraps and toning tables that help make sure your Florida suntan sticks as long as possible.
Open Tues.-Sat. 10 a.m.- 6 p.m.

BOOKS

B. Dalton
Bayside Marketplace,
401 Biscayne Blvd.,
Miami
• (305) 579-8695

You've got to get a book to read on the beach, right? Well, this national chain has loads of titles, from Marcel Proust to Dave Barry. The other major branch of this popular bookstore is at Omni International Mall, 1601 Biscayne Boulevard, Miami, (305) 358-1895.
Open Mon.-Fri. 10 a.m.-9 p.m., Sat. 10 a.m.-6 p.m., Sun. 11 a.m.-5 p.m.

Books & Books
296 Aragon Ave.,
Coral Gables
• (305) 442-4408

Books & Books owner Mitchell Kaplan can almost singlehandedly be credited with bringing the Miami Book Fair to Miami more than seven years ago. A very special place to browse, socialize and chat, Books & Books offers rare books, impromptu recommendations and regularly scheduled poetry readings upstairs.
Open Mon.-Fri. 10 p.m.-8 a.m, Sat. 10 a.m.-7 p.m., Sun. noon-5 p.m.

Bookstop
7710 N. Kendall Dr.,
Miami
• (305) 592-7292

We mention Miami's Bookstop branch because of its sheer size. Here's the kind of place where you want to whisper while browsing because you feel as if you're in a library. On top of the usual selections, there's an interesting collection of rare books and dozens of hard-to-find magazines. A "Reader's Choice" card, valid for one year and priced at $10, offers a 10 percent discount.
Open daily 9 a.m.-10 p.m.

Joe's News
1549 Sunset Dr.,
Coral Gables
• (305) 661-2020

This is where South Miami's literary crowd meets to ignore the posted signs that warn against heavy browsing. At Joe's, you'll find plenty of cheapskates who'd rather stand and read than buy the great selection of international magazines and newspapers, maps and pipe and tobacco products.
Open Mon.-Sat. 8 a.m.-9:30 p.m., Sun 8 a.m.-9 p.m.

Waldenbooks
Mayfair Shops,
2911 Grand Ave.,
Coconut Grove
• (305) 448-0261

Omni International Mall,
1601 Biscayne Blvd.,
Miami
• (305) 358-5764

How many titles are printed in a year? Some 40,000? Seems impossible that so many new books come out annually, that is until you do some browsing at this national chain. Whatever recent title you're looking for, most likely, will be here on the shelf.
Open Mon.-Fri. 10 a.m.-9 p.m., Sat. 10 a.m.-6 p.m., Sun. 11 a.m.-5 p.m.

CHILDREN

Clothes

Baby Baby
Mayfair Shops,
3390 Mary St.,
Coconut Grove
• (305) 445-7890

In contrast to baby stores that try to make infants looks like teenagers and toddlers like young execs, Baby Baby specializes in the kind of classic baby and little-people fashions that a very rich grandmother would buy.
Open Mon.-Sat. 10 a.m.-9 p.m., Sun. noon-5:30 p.m.

Baby Ling
230 Miracle Mile,
Coral Gables
• (305) 446-8182

Specializing in children's formal wear—including flower-girl dresses and tuxedos in a variety of sizes. Row after row of traditional children's clothing in a really enormous store, Baby Ling reminds of a mid-sized department store, for kids only.
Open Mon.-Fri. 10 a.m.-6 p.m.

Miami Oxygene
Bal Harbour Shops,
Collins Ave. at 96th St.,
Bal Harbour
• (305) 868-4499

If labels like Catimini Trotinette, David Charles and Fino Fino are important on your kids' clothes, head to Mini Oxygene. To match the miniature designs from Paris, London, Italy and Spain, there's a multilingual sales staff.
Open Mon. & Thurs.-Fri. 10 a.m.-9 p.m., Tues.-Wed. & Sat. 10 a.m.-6 p.m., Sun. noon 5 p.m.

CLOTHES & JEWELRY

Beachwear

Alice's Day Off
5900 Sunset Dr.,
South Miami
• (305) 477-0393

This store has the greatest picture windows in South Miami, two skies-the-limit glass plates with mannequins sporting the teeniest bikinis. Good selection of towels, sandals, sunglasses, beach bags and other leisure paraphernalia as well.
Open Mon.-Sat. 10 a.m.-8 p.m.

Connie Banko
5898 S. Dixie Hwy.,
South Miami
• (305) 667-1535

All the women who have long wished they could buy a different size bikini top than bottom will adore Connie Banko, who custom-makes swimwear for the disproportionate and just plain picky among us.
Hours by appointment.

MIAMI Shops

Jewelry

Coral, Pearls & Gems
447 41st St.,
Miami Beach
• (305) 531-0087

242 Miracle Mile,
Coral Gables
• (305) 445-2644

Both locations offer excellent selections of custom-designed diamonds, also offering a full selecton of gold, precious stones, pearls and one-of-a-kind designs. Balogh's also carries an interesting selection of precious vintage jewelry picked up at estate sales through Florida.
Open Mon.-Sat. 9:30 a.m.-5:30 p.m.

Lisa Loren Jewelers
• (305) 854-1422

Sylvia and Berne Abrams, who now work out of their homes after closing the World of Mayfair, have, for more than ten years, been offering customers watches, gold and silver jewelry, designer creations and custom-designed jewelry at up to 40 percent off store prices. Servicing many rich and famous customers by appointment only, Lisa Loren can offer such low prices because of her low overhead.
Hours by appointment only.

Miami Jewelry Center
7271 Red Rd.,
South Miami
• (305) 661-7621

A small, family-owned and -operated jewelry store in the heart of the Red/Sunset shopping district, Miami Jewelry Center rates among the city's fastest and most reliable outlets for all types of sales, repairs and appraisals.
Open Mon-Fri. 9:30 a.m.-5:30 p.m., Sat. 9:30 a.m.-4 p.m.

Menswear

Abiti Boutique
Mayfair Shops,
3390 Mary St.,
Coconut Grove
• (305) 446-4805

If you are a man who can't seem to match two socks together, go see Melissa Gottlieb; the owner of Abiti will dress you from head to toe in Gianni Versace, topping you off with a host of understated touches.
Open Mon.-Sat. 10 a.m.-9 p.m., Sun. noon-5:30 p.m.

F.G. Bodner
Mayfair Shops,
3390 Mary St.,
Coconut Grove
• (305) 448-7581

Remember the Zoot Suit that all those *film noire* types wore so well? F.G. Bodner recreates the look, 1990s style, with lots of the good, old-fashioned service you expect when you're spending just a bit too much money on men's clothes.
Open Mon.-Sat. 10 a.m.-9 p.m., Sun. noon-5:30 p.m.

Franco B.
350 Miracle Mile,
Coral Gables
• (305) 444-7318

Franco B. specializes in outfitting the Coral Gables gadfly, with ceremonious service, alterations performed on the premises, an a fine selection of Italian suits and accessories.
Open Mon.-Sat. 10 a.m.-7 p.m.

MIAMI Shops

Luomo
Aventura Mall,
Biscayne Blvd. at N.E.
197th St.
Aventura
• (305) 937-2702

The advantage to Luomo: you can get lavished with attention for much less money than is required at Gianni Versace or Maus & Hofffman. Specializing in Canali, Valentino, Confar and Reporter with custom tailoring available on site.
Open Mon.-Fri. 10 a.m.-9:30 p.m., Sun. noon-5:30 p.m.

Maus & Hoffman
9700 Collins Ave.,
Bal Harbour
• (305) 865-7411

With outlets in Fort Lauderdale, Palm Beach and Naples, Maus & Hoffman remains a favorite among well-dressed Florida men, offering hand-tailored jackets, slacks and shirts from Hickey-Freeman and Oxxford. The Bal Harbour outlet features a wonderfully colorful and splashy selection of Hermès Paris silk cravats.
Open Mon. & Thurs.-Fri. 10 a.m.-9 p.m., Tues.-Wed. & Sat. 10 a.m.-6 p.m., Sun. noon -5 p.m.

Recycled Clothing

Deco Dermots
1436 N.E. 163rd St.,
North Miami Beach
• (305) 940-1587

Ever wonder about those people who get their jeans faded and ripped just right? At Deco Dermots, you can buy used Levi's that way—for under $10. Also an excellent selection of antique costume jewelry priced at $2 a piece.
Open daily 1 p.m.-6:30 p.m.

Dust & Glitter
3490 Main Hwy.,
Coconut Grove
• (305) 448-6020

5863 Sunset Dr.,
South Miami
• (305) 667-4025

The main philosophy at Dust & Glitter seems to be: we dust, spot, dry clean and display in funky, creative ways; you pay more for it. The South Miami branch is much more fun than the Grove store: it is larger, and put together to look like a collection of department stores would if you took a walk back in time over the last six or eight decades.
Open Mon.-Fri. 10 a.m.-6 p.m.

Miami Twice Vintage Department Store
6562 Bird Rd.,
Miami
• (305) 666-0127

Miami Twice boasts not only the largest inventory of vintage clothing in South Florida, but manages to do it at very reasonable prices. Having just expanded from a mere boutique into an out-and-out department store, Miami Twice also sells an always cleverly displayed selection of vintage jewelry, collectibles and furniture.
Open Mon.-Sat. 10 a.m.-6 p.m.

Tania Sante's Classic Collectibles
6556 Bird Rd.,
Miami
• (305) 662-4975

You have to hit Tania's on the right day. When you do, take a walk through your grandma's attic and find just the perfect outfit to wear to South Beach tonight—something they couldn't ever have re-created at F.G. Bodner for ten times the price.
Open Mon.-Sat. noon-6 p.m.

Shoes

Thee Leathery
3460 Main Hwy.,
Coconut Grove
• (305) 448-5711

Thee Leathery has a full selection of Timberland Classic Boat Shoes, a must-have for those planning oceangoing excursions during Florida visits. There's also an excellent selection of other shoes (including Bass Weejuns, Sebago Docksiders and Sperry Top-Siders), as well as belts and purses.
Open Mon.-Sat. 10 a.m.-6 p.m., Sun. noon-5 p.m.

Margapita
2290 Mary St.,
Coconut Grove
• (305) 448-6740

It's hard to nail Margapita down to a price range; a nice pair of Italian pumps goes for around $150, a pair of alligator boots is priced at an appalling $3,000. Elegant, expensive and worth it, Margapita also carries a stunning line of Rene Caovilla evening shoes.
Open Mon.-Sat. 10 a.m.-9 p.m., Sun. noon-5:30 p.m.

Robert's Western Wear
5854 S. Dixie Hwy.,
South Miami
• (305) 667-6647

Put on your Stetson and head over to Robert's Western Wear if you're in the market for boots. Robert's carries an excellent selection of Lucchese, Justin and Tony Lama boots, to name a few, in both men's and women's sizes.
Open Mon.-Sat. 10 a.m.-6 p.m.

Womenswear

Carolyn Lamb
Florentino Plaza,
3444 Main Hwy.,
Coconut Grove
• (305) 443-4631

You might be surprised to find this outpost of chic designs dwarfed behind an enormous Fuddrucker's (a hamburger joint). Sleek and unusual dancewear, bright casual clothes that make great souvenirs and elegant cocktail outfits, suits and sweaters by Japanese, New York and West Coast designers.
Open Mon.-Sat. 10 a.m.-6 p.m., Sun. noon-6 p.m.

Carlyon Collection
Mayfair Shops,
2nd Floor,
3390 Mary St.,
Coconut Grove
• (305) 446-7678

Carlyon is to clothing what Leo Castelli is to painting and sculpture. Owner Miguel Mier has retained local designers to create a variety of unique items: hand-slashed leather jackets, capes and dresses, custom-created jeweled handbags and a treasure trove of wearable ethnic art.
Open Mon.-Sat. 10 a.m.-6. p.m., Sun. noon-6 p.m.

Caron Cherry
Mayfair Shops,
3390 Mary St.,
Coconut Grove
• (305) 443-9966

It is the rare shop where those spending $30 on a scarf are treated just about the same as others dropping $10,000 on an evening gown. As opposed to the kind of posh boutique that specializes in one or two lines of clothing, the postmodern Caron Cherry carries all sorts of labels regularly brought back by Cherry from shows all over Europe.
Open Mon.-Sat. 10 a.m.-9 p.m., Sun. noon-5:30 p.m.

MIAMI Shops

Four Way Street
5814 Sunset Dr. (at Red Rd.),
South Miami
• (305) 665-5077

Situated within the Red/Sunset shopping district, Four Way Street offers a nice selection of jeans and casual sportswear that grown-ups can actually wear right along with the juniors. There's usually a 50-percent-off rack in the back featuring cast-off Edwins, Paris Blues and the like. Natural leather bags and belts are generally reasonably priced.
Open Mon.-Sat. 10 a.m.-6 p.m.

Gucci
Bal Harbour Shops,
Collins Ave. & 96th St.,
Bal Harbour
• (305) 868-6504

With typically quiet elegance, the small but well-stocked Gucci outlet at Bal Harbour displays the world-renowned designer's shoes, bags, luggage, scarves and other accessories.
Open Mon. & Thurs.-Fri. 10 a.m.-9 p.m., Tues.-Wed. & Sat. 10 a.m.-6 p.m., Sun. noon-6 p.m.

DEPARTMENT STORES & SHOPPING CENTERS

Aventura Mall
Biscayne Blvd. at 197th St.,
Aventura
• (305) 935-4222

We were tempted to dismiss Aventura Mall as just another sprawling suburban shopping mall, but being that Aventura is such a nice suburb, there is indeed something special about Aventura Mall. Its 200 shops are anchored by Macy's and Lord & Taylor (among others), and parking is generally plentiful.
Open Mon.-Sat. 10 a.m.-9 p.m., Sun. noon-5:30 p.m.

Bakery Center
5701 Sunset Dr.,
South Miami
• (305) 662-4155

Marked by a trompe l'oeil mural at its center, the shopping and entertainment center sits on the site of the old Holsum Bakery, listed on the National Register of Historic Places. Currently the structure even has a minimuseum, the Miami Youth Museum, where kids can have at it, while moms take a look around. Hands-on cultural art exhibits and guided tours in English and Spanish are offered daily, with a permanent exhibit depicting life in turn-of-the-century Cuba. There are plenty of shops and restaurants not only inside the huge, pink concrete elephant, but in the neighborhood surrounding Sunset Drive, where the street is often closed to traffic for art shows and festivals.
Open Mon.-Sat. 10 a.m.-9 p.m, Sun. 10 a.m.-6 p.m.

Bal Harbour Shops
9700 Collins Ave.,
Bal Harbour
• (305) 866-0311

Even Bal Harbour's security guards are overdressed in red, white and black, and helmets with bronze points. Neiman-Marcus, Saks Fifth Avenue and dozens of chic designer outlets make this mall the place where you'll most likely run into lots of well-heeled poodles accompanying their mistresses on shopping forays. The outdoor, bi-level mall is a shady structure splendidly

MIAMI Shops

laid out for cool shopping even in the dead of summer.
Open Mon. & Thurs.-Fri. 10 a.m.-9 p.m., Tues.-Wed. & Sat. 10 a.m.-6 p.m., Sun. noon-5 p.m.

Bayside Marketplace
401 Biscayne Blvd., Miami
• (305) 577-3344

Located on sixteen acres overlooking Miamarina and Biscayne Bay, Bayside Marketplace has been the heart of downtown Miami since its opening. With a total of 140 shops and restaurants, there is also an open-air crafts alley, where locally crafted items are for sale, all at tourist prices, so shop around a bit before buying.
Open Mon.-Sat. 10 a.m.-10 p.m., Sun. noon-8 p.m.

Caribbean Marketplace
5927-29 N.E. 2nd Ave., Little Haiti
• (305) 758-8708

A $1.2 million, private-public joint venture meant to stimulate Miami's Caribbean roots and culture, the Caribbean Marketplace originally opened as a place for Little Haiti residents to meet and shop. Following a repositioning, the market now offers a variety of ceramics, Haitian paintings, exotic African fashions and tropical fruits and ice cream that characterize the outdoor bazaars of the Caribbean.
Open Mon.-Sat. 10 a.m.- 5:30 p.m.

CocoWalk
3015 Grand Ave. at Virginia St., Coconut Grove
• (305) 444-0777

This brand-new shopping complex opened in early 1991, and houses 30 shops, ten restaurants and an eight-screen AMC cinema.
Shop hours vary; generally open Mon.-Thurs. & Sun. 10 a.m.-10 p.m., Fri.-Sat. 10 a.m.-midnight.

The Falls
8888 Howard Avenue Dr., Kendall
• (305) 255-4570

Although it's a totally manufactured visual experience, The Falls presents one of the most alluring shopscapes in South Florida. Surrounding a variety of ponds, streams, footbridges and waterfalls are a petite Bloomingdale's, and 60-odd specialty shops: your typical upmarket chocolatiers, clothiers and boutiques.
Shop hours vary. Outdoor mall open daily 10 a.m.-midnight.

Historic Cauley Square
22400 Old Dixie Hwy., Cutler Ridge
• (305) 258-3543

Housed in an old railroad building protected by the National Register of Historic Places, Cauley Square surprises as you exit Miami to the south (toward the Florida Keys) on U.S. Highway 1. A variety of shops vend Florida crafts and artworks, ladies' apparel, old-fashioned curtains, antiques and collectibles. Located two miles south of the Cutler Ridge Mall.
Open Mon.-Sat. 10 a.m.-4:30 p.m.

Mayfair Shops in the Grove
2911 Grand Ave., Coconut Grove
• (305) 448-1700

Mayfair features an award-winning design, featuring elaborate tilework, fountains, wrought-iron detailing and hundreds of airy ferns divided into two wings, Mayfair West and Mayfair East. While the large anchors are Burdines and Mayfair House, there are also dozens of fashion, jewelry and accessory shops, as

well as galleries, restaurants, a fitness center and hair salon. Because most of the mall is open air, you can stroll through it even after hours for a bit of window shopping on your way to and from the many chic nightspots and cafés it houses. Be forewarned though, the layout is Byzantine, so don't get lost.
Open Mon.-Sat. 10 a.m.-9 p.m., Sun. noon-5:30 p.m.

Miracle Center
3301 Coral Way,
Coral Gables
• (305) 444-8890

On top of the 50 shops, eleven-screen movie theater, restaurants, bars and health club, the newly constructed miracle center has the coolest elevators in town. Talk into the speaker, and a voice simulator repeats what you just said. We're not sure what the point of it is, but it's a great way to kill time and get to know your fellow passengers on the way up. Miracle Center is the only major mall in town in which the shops remain open on Sunday evenings.
Open daily 10 a.m-9 p.m.

FLOWERS

Floral Group, The Designers
2125 Biscayne Blvd., Miami
• (305) 599-3098

When the Floral Group truck arrives at your door, you know what's coming next is something you've never seen before. The outfit owns its own foliage farms and hothouses in Haiti, where it grows and imports orchids and rare tropical flowers.
Open Mon.-Sat. 9 a.m.-4 p.m.

FOOD

Bakeries

The Cookie Bar
Bayside Marketplace,
401 Biscayne Blvd., Miami
• (305) 381-6874

You can smell the ten different daily specials baking away at The Cookie Bar almost from the moment you enter Bayside. On top of delivering marvelous platters locally, these folks will ship anywhere within the United States.
Open Mon.-Sat. 10 a.m.-10 p.m., Sun. noon-8 p.m.

La Petite Pâtisserie
Fuller Street at Main Hwy.,
Coconut Grove
• (305) 442-9329

A delightful selection of fresh-baked goods to take out. Enjoy your purchases at tables set up, sidewalk café–style, just outside.
Open Mon-Sat. 8 a.m.-6:30 p.m., Sun. 8 a.m.-2 p.m.

MIAMI Shops

Fruit Stands & Shippers

Athens Tropical Fruits and Novelties
6976 Collins Ave.,
Miami Beach
• (305) 865-9119

Here's the ultimate Florida souvenir: a dozen mixed mangoes and papayas shipped back home. Athens takes care of everything, including recipe suggestions.
Open Tues.-Sat. 8 a.m.-8 p.m., Sun. 11 a.m.-5 p.m.

Ferris Groves
530 Arthur Godfrey Rd.,
Miami Beach
• (305) 538-0350

Attached to a natural-foods market and restaurant, Ferris Groves deals in all sorts of local produce: avocados, limes, pineapples, grapefruits and mangoes, all of which can be shipped locally, throughout the United States or to Canada and Europe.
Open daily 10 a.m.-10 p.m.

Norman Brothers Produce
7621 S.W. 87th Ave.,
Kendall
• (305) 274-9363

If you're a South Miami/Kendall housewife and you've just finished Jazzercise class on a Saturday morning, you're going to need to jump in your Volvo and head over to Norman Brothers right away. Have a peach-and-yogurt shake as you pick out your beefsteak tomatoes, vine-ripened on Homestead's farms. Also enjoy the bakery, deli and fish market.
Open Mon.-Sat. 8 a.m.- 7 p.m., Sun. 10 a.m.-6 p.m.

Gourmet

Epicure Market
1656 Alton Rd.,
Miami Beach
• (305) 672-1861

Epicure makes us happy by carrying a harmonious combination of things we instantly want to buy. Check out the specialty bakery on the premises, an excellent selection of international wines and cheeses and a take-out deli with all sorts of exotic items.
Open Mon.-Fri. 9 a.m.-7 p.m., Sat.-Sun. 9 a.m.-6 p.m.

Poppi's in the Grove
Mayfair Shops,
2911 Grand Ave.,
Coconut Grove
• (305) 444-7716

The most complete specialty food store in South Florida, Poppi's offers over 70 different kinds of beer from twenty countries, and the same amount of cheeses, wines and Champagnes. The only food store in the Grove with its own specialty bakery, Poppi's bakes breads and such that change daily—and can be enjoyed on wrought iron tables posted just outside.
Open Mon.-Fri. 8:30 a.m.-8 p.m., Sat. 9 a.m.-8 p.m., Sun. 9 a.m.-6 p.m.

MIAMI Shops

Roney's Health Emporium
2385 Collins Ave.,
Miami Beach
• (305) 532-0015

A Miami Beach favorite since the late 1960s, Roney's has an abundant selection of macrobiotic foods, organic produce, cookbooks and natural cosmetics. You can even pick up a pair of Birkenstock sandals in a variety of sizes.
Open Mon.-Fri. 10 a.m.-7:30 p.m., Sat.-Sun. 10 a.m.-6 p.m.

Scotty's Grocery
3117 Brid Ave.,
Coconut Grove
• (305) 443-5257

Scotty and Grace McDaniel think buying groceries should be a very exacting science. In the family since the 1930s, the charming, perfectly designed and sparkling gourmet delicatessen and grocery store is the pride of Coconut Grove. They cater *and* they deliver, a lost art in these parts.
Open Mon.-Sat. 8 a.m.-8 p.m., Sun. 9 a.m.-7 p.m.

Trattoria Pampered Chef
3145 Commodore Plaza,
Coconut Grove
• (305) 567-0104

This excellent café cooks up all sorts of baked goods to eat in or take out—and tops it all off by vending many of its secret ingredients. Also for sale is an enormous assortment of imported caviars, wines, Champagnes and cheeses, plus just the right cookware to go home and whip up a few goodies ourselves.
Open Sun.-Thurs. 11 a.m.-midnight, Fri.-Sat. 11 a.m.-1 a.m.

GIFTS

Afro-Caribbean Import Export
741 N.W. 62nd St.,
Miami
• (305) 757-1022

Situated north of the downtown area, this delightful and imaginative shop makes you feel that you're somewhere in the Caribbean. There's a wide variety of items available at generally low prices, each originating in Africa, the Caribbean, Central or Latin America. Best bets: jewelry, wood carvings, pottery and baskets.
Open Mon. & Wed.-Sun. 10:30 a.m.- 6:30 p.m.

Botanica La Caridad
651 Washington Ave.,
Miami Beach
• (305) 538-7961

Botanica La Caridad reigns as the best place in town from which to transport yourself into the eerie world of the Afro-Cuban Santeria religion. Purchases here can include religious statues, pictures, bells, altars, incense, candles and the occasional spiritual consultation that promises to identify enemies or bring back long-deceased loved ones.
Open Mon.-Fri. 10 a.m.-6 p.m.

H&H Gift Collection
126 Miracle Mile,
Coral Gables
• (305) 441-8911

This place is a lot of fun. There's costume jewelry by the basketful to be dug through and tried on. Some pieces are priced from $3 and up, including authentic-looking imitations. Any piece can be beautifully gift wrapped and shipped around the

MIAMI Shops

world. There are designer and vintage pieces, and some of the real McCoy as well.
Open Mon.-Sat. 8:30 a.m.-7 p.m.

Mato
3399 Virginia St.,
Coconut Grove
• (305) 443-2322

Mato carries a little bit of this, a little bit of that; prices range from about $40 to upward of $400 for gifts, housewares, rugs, toys, electronics and pieces of art.
Open Mon.-Sat. 10 a.m.-9 p.m., Sun. noon-5:30 p.m.

Spy Shops International
2900 Biscayne Blvd.,
Downtown
• (305) 573-4779

What better gift for the man who has everything than some high-tech surveillance equipment? Say what? Spy Shops International has become quite the tourist attraction in recent years among the "007" crowd, vending all sorts of espionage-oriented goodies, counter-surveillance systems—even anti-kidnapping and armored vehicles. Gadget-lovers and terrorists alike will go wild at this place.
Open Mon.-Sat. 10 a.m.-5:30 p.m.

Torrah Treasures
1309 Washington Ave.,
Miami Beach
• (305) 673-6095

For a glimpse at some Jewish folk-song books, Hebrew games and Hasidic religious articles, Torrah Treasures is a cloistered little old-world shop where the employees and shoppers alike converse in Yiddish.
Open Mon.-Fri. 10 a.m.-6 p.m.

Zanjabil
3442 Main Hwy.,
Coconut Grove
• (305) 448-3830

It's hard to put your finger on exactly where the bulk of the imports at Zanjabil originate. There are leather handbags, tropical fashions, incense, perfumes, primitive art and Dhurrie rugs, to take just a brief inventory. Framable greeting cards and colorful locally created posters make great souvenir items as well.
Open Mon.-Thurs. 10 a.m.-11 p.m., Fri.-Sat. 10 a.m.-midnight, Sun. noon- 10 p.m.

HOME

Fabrics

Calico Corners Decorative Fabrics
16810 S. Dixie Hwy.,
South Dade
• (305) 253-5400

It's off the beaten path, but if you venture down south to Calico Corners, you'll find a wonderful selection of fabrics in stock at savings of 30 percent to 60 percent off retail—savings which increase if you happen to hit a frequent sale. For re-upholstering furniture, Calico Corners happily provides custom labor.
Open Mon. & Wed. 9 a.m.-9 p.m., Tues. & Thurs.-Sat. 9 a.m.-6 p.m., Sun. noon-5 p.m.

Furniture

Antares
2640 S.W. 28th Ln.,
Miami
• (305) 854-1211

Although it's situated neither in a posh shopping mall nor anywhere near a ritzy antiques district, Antares manages to catch your attention as you drive by on U.S. Highway 1 by placing a rather odd-looking piece of furniture on its back porch, right beneath the Metrorail tracks. Specializing in interpretive contemporary furniture, Antares is the kind of place that the Arquitectonica firm (which designed most of Miami's signature funky buildings) and the set designers for Miami Vice probably frequented.
Open Mon-Sat. 10 a.m.-5 p.m.

J&J Rattan
4652 S.W. 72nd Ave.,
Miami
• (305) 666-7503

If it's made out of rattan or wicker, and meant to go in or around your home, J&J has it. To add a distinctly tropical touch to your home decor, start out at the furniture store, then head over to the pottery, plant and wicker shop across the way. Situated within a warehouse shopping development, J&J offers a good opportunity to stroll through the complex and see what other bargains you can pick up in the suburbs.
Open Mon.-Sat. 10:30 a.m.-5:30 p.m.

Luminaire
331 Ponce de Leon Blvd.,
Coral Gables
• (305) 448-7367

Luminaire specializes in Italian and French contemporary furniture—the kind of stuff that makes you look like you're very wealthy, but not a bit conservative. Home and office furniture and accessories from Luminaire add up to a distinctly Miami feeling.
Open Mon.-Sat. 10 a.m.-5:30 p.m.

South Beach Furniture Company
121 5th St.,
Miami Beach
• (305) 532-2997

The custom and expertly refinished art-deco and mid-century modern furniture pieces at South Beach Furniture Company are perfect for somebody who's just rented an apartment—preferably with black-and-white tiled floors and a porthole window—on Ocean Drive. Even if you haven't, stop in and see where it all began.
Open Mon. & Wed.-Sat. noon-7 p.m., Sun. 2 p.m.-5 p.m.

Garden

Botanical Garden Center
19110 Krome Ave.,
Homestead
• (305) 235-0118

Don't be surprised to find a major agricultural outpost just south of metropolitan Miami. Krome Avenue is not only a hub of activity for fresh local produce and rare tropical fruits and vegetables, but it is also well known as being the best place to find abundant local foliage. Local landscape architects favor the Center, probably because it offers row upon row of colorful

flora at rock-bottom prices. If you're a-shopping for plants, it's worth the drive out to Homestead.
Open Mon.-Sat. 8:30 a.m.-5:30 p.m., Sun. 8:30 a.m.-4 p.m.

Denmark's Art Stone
12351 N.W. 7th Ave., Miami
• (305) 681-6641

The name is deceptive. Denmark's Art Stone boasts an enormous selection not of Danish items, but of Mediterranean balusters, natural-cut coral stone, statuary, mosaic table sets, cast quarry, terra-cotta and other items so popular in the many Mediterranean-styled yards and gardens of South Florida homes.
Open Mon.-Sat. 10:30 a.m.-5:30 p.m.

Miccosukee Indian Chickee Huts
18799 S.W. 8th St., Miami
• (305) 223-5055/ 559-2849

The thatched huts of the South Florida Indians are used still as typically Florida-style garden ornamental garden structures throughout Miami. Miccosukee crafstman Pete Osceola will custom-design and build the huts, called chickees, to order.
Hours by appointment.

SPORTING GOODS

Bicycling

Bicycle Center
13799 S. Dixie Hwy., South Dade
• (305) 238-5080

With its many shaded bike paths, triathlon events and verdant parks, Miami is a biker's dream. One of the city's largest bicycle sales and service facilities, Bicycle Center carries name-brand bikes, a large selection of mountain bikes, a pro shop and an exercise and fitness department. There's a full line of clothing and accessories, plus a very helpful and particularly knowledgeable sales staff.
Open Mon.-Sat. 9 a.m.-7 p.m., Sun. noon-5 p.m.

Kendall Cycle Fair
13870 N. Kendall Dr., Kendall
• (305) 385-7755

Featuring an excellent, speedy service department, and a large selection of kids' bikes, adult trikes and mountain bikes, Kendall Cycle Fair is worth a drive out to the suburbs.
Open Mon.-Sat. 10 a.m.-7 p.m.

Fishing

Crook & Crook
2795 S.W. 27th Ave.,
Coconut Grove
• (305) 854-0005

Featuring one of the city's largest supplies of marine hardware, fishing tackle and electronics, Crook & Crook has been in business in the Grove for more than 30 years. Sort of a de facto Miami-area mariner's hub, Crook & Crook is a good place to stop by to pick up information and brochures about fishing, yachting and sailing charters.
Open daily 7 a.m.-9 p.m.

South Bay Marine Store
3375 Pan American Dr.,
Coconut Grove
• (305) 859-2124

Located adjacent to the Dinner Key Marina (which boasts a large fleet of charter vessels), South Bay is a complete tackle and marine supply outfit. Live bait, dive gear, beer and ice, fishing licenses and a large selection of fishing rods help boaters stock up for a day on Biscayne Bay and out in the ocean.
Open Mon.-Thurs. 8 a.m.-5:30 p.m., Fri. & Sun. 8 a.m.-6 p.m., Sat. 7 a.m.-7:30 p.m.

Golf

The Golf Shoppe of Miami
4542 S.W. 75th Ave.,
South Miami
• (305) 262-1601

Since Florida boasts more holes of golf per capita than any other state, it's a good place to pick up discounted equipment. The Golf Shoppe offers a huge selection of clubs, shoes, gloves, new and used balls and men and women's golf clothes.
Open Mon.-Fri. 9 a.m.-6 p.m., Sat. 9 a.m.-5 p.m., Sun. 11 a.m.-4 p.m.

Windsurfing

Windsport Catamarans & Windsurfers
610 N.W. 167th St.,
North Miami Beach
• (305) 651-6556

Windsport offers a decent selection of Hobie catamarans, windsurfers (most every brand) and small sailboats at warehouse prices (that's because the place actually is in a warehouse, and its hours aren't too reliable, but the prices are good). Located below the Golden Glades Interchange (the confluence of Highway I-95 and the Palmetto), Windsport isn't so easy to reach the first time around, so you may have to persevere and loop back again.
Hours vary.

SIGHTS & SPORTS

AMUSEMENTS	86
ARTS	87
EXCURSIONS	87
LANDMARKS	87
NEIGHBORHOODS	88
PARKS & GARDENS	91
SPORTS	92
TOURS	94

AMUSEMENTS

Miami Metrozoo
12400 S.W. 152nd St., Miami
• (305) 251-0400

One of the only "cageless" zoos in the country, Metrozoo lets you watch an abundance of wildlife in its own natural habitat. Rare white Bengal tigers born on site and koalas are among those species making up this 290-acre habitat. A one-half acre free-flight aviary containing 300 exotic birds is another highlight of the zoo.
Open daily 9:30 a.m.-5:30 p.m. Adults $8.25, children 3-12 $4.25.

Miami Seaquarium
4400 Rickenbacker Cswy., Key Biscayne
• (305) 361-5705

At the Seaquarium (located on Virginia Key), you can visit with a 10,000-pound killer whale, and a performance of the dolphin, "Flipper" (of TV fame), to wrap up a day at the beach. There are other daily shows in which sea lions and dolphins share the spotlight with the headliners.
Open daily 9:30 a.m.-6:30 p.m. Adults $14.95, children under 13 $10.95.

Parrot Jungle & Gardens
11000 S.W. 57th Ave., South Dade
• (305) 666-7834

It's a natural, subtropical garden of exotic trees and plants, which is home to delightful parrots who perform daily. Opened by naturalist Frank Scherr in 1936 (and operated by his family until 1988), the park now has more than 1,100 birds and 1,000 plant species. Eighty of Parrot Jungle's photogenic flamingos are featured in the lead-in footage of the television show *Miami Vice*. The gardens boast the oldest cypress hammock in Florida

(south of Lake Okeechobee), the biggest ficus tree on Florida's "Gold Coast" and bananas that grow upside down.
Open daily 9:30 a.m.-6 p.m. Adults $10.50, children 3-12 $5.25.

ARTS

Miami City Ballet
905 Lincoln Rd.,
South Beach
• (305) 532-4880

Once a thriving department store, a gutted structure now serves as the rehearsal hall for the new, already acclaimed Miami City Ballet. Since 1985, under the artistic direction of Edward Villella, the ballet company has performed at various venues throughout town and internationally; onlookers are welcome to sit in front of its picture windows to watch rehearsals.
Rehearsal times vary. Call for information.

Museum of Science and Space Planetarium
3280 S. Miami Ave.,
Coconut Grove
• (305) 854-4247

A rather disappointing facility (except perhaps for those under 12 years old), the museum features hands-on exhibits and hosts traveling shows. Here's a switch: the adjacent 65-foot dome of the Space Transit Planetarium offers rock-and-roll laser shows on weekend nights that are quite creative and interesting.
Open daily 10 a.m.-6 p.m. Laser Showtimes vary. Adults $5, children 3-12 $3.50.

EXCURSIONS

Shark Valley Tram Tours
Everglades National Park,
The Everglades
P.O. Box 1729,
Miami
• (305) 221-8455

The 1.4-acre Everglades National Park is just an hour's drive (about 35 miles) west of Miami. At Shark Valley, you can pick up a tram that traverses some fifteen miles of the park in two-hour excursions, resting midway at a 50-foot-high observation tower.
Open daily 8:30 a.m.-4 p.m. Reservations required.

LANDMARKS

The Barnacle
3485 Main Hwy.,
Coconut Grove
• (305) 448-9445

Tours of The Barnacle, built in 1891 by Commodore Ralph Munroe, are given daily. Munroe was one of the first photographers in Florida, and he left behind an extraordinary legacy of pictures of early Florida. His frame house, built from wreck timber, cut in Munroe's own sawmill, features a skylight of ceiling windows that provide an elaborate cooling system.
Open daily 9 a.m.-4 p.m. Tours Mon.-Fri. at 10:30 a.m., 1 p.m. & 2:30 p.m. Admission $1.

Brigade 2506 Monument
Calle Ocho at S.W. 11th Ave.,
Little Havana

The monument to Brigade 2506 marks perhaps the saddest chapter in Cuban-American history. In 1961 a group of exiles, trained by the U.S. government, launched the disastrous Bay of Pigs invasion from South Florida. Many of the Cuban-American soldiers were captured by their own family members who remained loyal to Fidel Castro. The United States was forced to pay Cuba millions of dollars in food and supplies to buy the freedom of those imprisoned during the unsuccessful coup attempt. A fire burns perpetually at the monument, which has come to represent all oppressed Latin American countries.

NEIGHBORHOODS

CORAL GABLES – One of the country's boldest architectural developments in the 1920s, Coral Gables was the brainchild of George Merrick, who envisioned a city-within-a-city built on his family's grapefruit plantation. Today, the Spanish Revival buildings of the community comprise some of Greater Miami's priciest real estate, housing not only private families, but also banks, restaurants, hotels and country clubs. Four elegant entrances to "The Gables," all planned by architect Denman Fink, have defined the city boundaries since 1927. These Spanish-style gates include Douglas Entrance (Douglas Rd. & 8th St.), **Granada Entrance** (Granada & 8th St.), **Commercial Entrance** (Alhambra Circle at Madeira Ave. & Douglas Rd.) and **Country Club Prado Entrance** (at Country Club Prado and Tamiami Trail). Also worth a look are the fourteen Denman Fink plazas, each with a cooling fountain bubbling at its center. The most prominent of these plazas are the enormous **Balboa Plaza** (Coral Way & S. Greenway Dr.), **Columbus Plaza** (Columbus & Indian Mound Trails) **DeSoto Plaza** (Sevilla & Granada Aves.), **Ponce de León** (the first of the structures erected; Coral Way & Granada Ave.) and **Granada Plaza** (Granada & Alhambra Aves.). In Merrick's "Commercial District," the distinctive **Coral Gables City Hall** (405 Biltmore Way, Coral Gables; 305-446-1657), another Denman Fink structure, is listed on the National Register of Historic places. Features of the Spanish Renaissance building (significantly damaged in the 1925

> **A RICH HERITAGE**
>
> In Florida, local architecture does not, as popular belief may once have had it, begin with Cinderella's castle and end with a beachfront condominium whose construction necessitated the destruction of a mangrove swamp. On the contrary, nearly 700 Florida members are listed on the National Register of Historic Places, 28 of which are historic districts with anywhere from five to 2,485 contributing structures or archaeological sites. These were selected from more than 44,000 sites of historical or archaeological significance that have been filed with the state.

hurricane and later restored) include a coral-rock edifice, which comprises a semicircular wing. Twelve columns support a stone balustrade, where an ornate panel features the coat of arms of Coral Gables. A 500-pound bell sits atop the building's clock tower. The Chamber of Commerce distributes free self-guided auto tours.

KEY BISCAYNE – The drive over the **Rickenbacker Causeway** from the mainland to **Key Biscayne** is the most beautiful in Miami. Pick up the hump-backed, elbow-shaped series of causeways (begininning with the Rickenbacker) to Key Biscayne at the southern foot of Brickell Avenue. Populated by posh homes and condos, golf and tennis clubs, hotels and public beaches, the island is largely residential. Former president Nixon, in fact, owned a waterfront winter home here in the 1970s. There's plenty to do when you enter the Keys via the Rickenbacker Causeway, where a $1 toll is charged, and which is guarded by a perpetually revolving shark statue.

On Foot

ART DECO DISTRICT – The nation's youngest historic district and the first of the twentieth century to be placed, on the **National Register of Historic Places**, the **Art Deco District** that sprang up in the 1920s and 1930s today encompasses the most important bevy of remainders from this era. Spanning from Sixth Street to Dade Boulevard between Lenox Court and the beach, the one-square-mile district boasts more than 800 noteworthy buildings in the art-deco tradition, as well as classical examples of Streamline Moderne and Spanish Mediterranean Revival styles. The art-deco look was greatly influenced by the buildings of Chicago's Century of Progress (1933) and the New York World's Fair (1939). The designs created by America's art-deco architects reflect the joy and hope that swept the nation at the beginning of the Machine Age. The motif was further adapted to the Miami climate, blending classical design with tropical features and colors. **The Miami Design Preservation League** (661 Washington Ave., South Beach; 305-672-2014) conducts the tour; Monday to Friday 10 a.m. to 6 p.m., Saturday 10 a.m. to 2 p.m. Contribution $5.

BRICKELL AVENUE – A walking tour of **Brickell Avenue** begins at its southern end, where scattered flower vendors, posted beneath the I-95 overpasses, hawk bunches of "rosas" and other fragrant flowers to passing businesspeople. It's here that Miami's answer to New York's Park Avenue begins. Brickell Avenue, splayed out before **Biscayne Bay**, is flanked by flashy condominiums and posh office buildings. Brickell Avenue is separated into a residential area and a business district, both characterized by towering bayfront buildings. The residential section is the more southerly of the two, highlighted by the arresting "Atlantis," which is pierced by a thirty-seven-foot-square "hole" cut between the tenth and fourteenth stories. Atlantis—with its metallic blue detail work, red triangle roof and yellow balconies—was one of the whimsical, tropical, Latin, Arquitectonica design firm's first projects. This first bayfront masterpiece that catches your eye as your stroll down Brickell Avenue did, however, gain the most attention for Arquitectonica, the firm whose work came to characterize the Miami of the mid- to late 1980s. That "hole" in Atlantis's center actually houses a residential Jacuzzi, as well as a winding red staircase and a bushy palm tree. The brilliant, rainbow-striped **Villa Regina** just to the north is the showpiece of Israeli architect, Yaacov Agam. Next, the elevated **Brickell Palace** is an elevated design masterpiece that descends like an enormous stairway into Biscayne Bay. The business portion of Brickell begins at about **Seventh Street**, and continues over the **Miami River Bridge** into the downtown area. For more information, contact the **Greater Miami Convention & Visitors Bureau** (701 Brickell Ave., Ste. 2700, Miami; 305-539-3000).

COCONUT GROVE – One of Miami's original settlements that has always drawn both social recluses and the creative set, **Coconut Grove** (beginning at El Jardin, 3747 Main Hwy.) is a delightful Miami suburb shaded by banyan trees and fronting Biscayne Bay. Zane Grey, the Western novelist, wrote many of his thrillers in this verdant, tropical setting, where Everglades champion and writer Marjorie Stoneman Douglas and poet Robert Frost were neighbors. To drop names of a few more luminaries who either settled or wintered in Grove cottages, beyond the sidewalks lined with orange gumbo limbo trees: Harriet Beecher Stowe, Thomas Alva Edison and William Jennings Bryan. Begin a walking tour on the Grove's Main Highway, where the private Carrollton Sacred Heart school blocks the view of El Jardin, the city's earliest-known Mediterranean Revival structure. Stop in at the school's public relations office for permission to look at El Jardin, built in 1917. The highway affords a full view of the estate's gate house, also part of the school. The Coconut Grove Playhouse farther down Main at 3500 opened as a motion picture house in 1927. It was restored in 1956, when it became the Player's State Theater, and is now a popular regional venue and theater school.

LITTLE HAVANA – Between 1960 and 1980, some 500,000 Cubans fled Fidel Castro's communist regime in Cuba. Another large exodus occurred in 1980, when Castro emptied his prisons, allowing them to join other departing Cubans in the Mariel boatlift. At that time, all who were met by family at the docks were granted immigration status in the United States; others were sent to refugee camps, pending further investigation on a case-by-case basis. Miami's Little Havana, or Pequeña Havana, a three-and-a-half-square-mile neighborhood defined by **N.W. 37th Avenue**, the **836 Expressway, Miami Avenue** and **South Dixie Highway**, has been the center for the exiles' philosophical, political and cultural affairs since the early 1950s. To reach Pequeña Havana from the downtown area, follow I-95 north to the 836 Expressway West. Exit 37th Avenue (Douglas Road) south to S.W. Eighth Street (Calle Ocho), where you can begin a walking tour of the area conducted by the **Kiwanis Club of Little Havana** (900 S.W. 1st St., Ste. 202, Miami; 305-324-7349/545-5643) also the organizers of **Carnaval Miami**, the largest annual Hispanic Festival in the United States.

PARKS & GARDENS

Bill Baggs Cape Florida State Recreation Area
Key Biscayne

Miami's highest hill (the William Powell Bridge!) challenges bikers who set out to explore Key Biscayne. You can cycle all the way out to Crandon Beach, and then on to Bill Baggs Cape Florida State Recreation Area, marked by the Cape Florida Lighthouse at its tip. The oldest structure in South Florida, the lighthouse was built in 1825 to warn passing ships of the dangerous reef off shore. It was attacked and destroyed by Indians in 1836, and later rebuilt. Today, visitors can climb to the top, where a fascinating museum and great view await.

Fairchild Tropical Gardens
10901 Old Cutler Rd., Coral Gables
• (305) 667-1651

The largest tropical botanical garden in the continental U.S. is right here. Dedicated in 1940, the facility includes more than 8,000 research volumes on tropical vegetation. During World War II, airforce pilots received tropical island survival training here, and instructions to be used in the event they were shot down on combat missions. Over the past half century, some 6,700 varieties of tropical plants have been brought in and planted. Through a mail-order botanical program, volunteers ship more than 30,000 seeds annually to those wishing to cultivate tropical foliage.
Open daily 9:30 a.m.-4:30 p.m. Hourly tram tours. Adults $5, children under 13 free. Tram tour $1.

Matheson Hammock Park and Marina
9610 Old Cutler Rd., Coral Gables
• (305) 669-6979

The star attraction of Matheson Hammock (aside from the alligator signs telling us to beware while passing a pond) is a pleasant bike path shaded by a descending mangrove tunnel that leads to the bay. Actually little more than a shallow lagoon overlooking the marina, families with children favor Matheson's beach for quiet swimming and sunbathing. Occasionally, instructors set up shop on the bayside to teach windsurfing. A walking path continues out of the park and north to Cartagena Plaza, also called Cocoplum Circle, where a pair of bronze shoes punctuates a flower-filled circle.
Open 6 a.m.-dusk. Parking $2.

Venetian Pool
2701 DeSoto Blvd., Coral Gables
• (305) 460-5356

Float on your back in the Venetian Pool and consider the poolside orchestras who played here for all sorts of Hollywood types—among them, Johnny Weissmuller and Esther Williams—in the pool's heyday. Now open to the public, vines cover the old rock quarry's stucco walls, and cold, clean water runs through dark caves punctuated by waterfalls. The pool is a "don't miss" while in Miami.
Open Sat.-Sun. 10 a.m.-4:30 p.m., Mon.-Fri. schedule varies. Adults $4, children under 12 $1.50.

MIAMI Sights & Sports

Villa Vizcaya Museum and Gardens
3251 S. Miami Ave., Coconut Grove
• (305) 579-2813

A fabulous Italian Renaissance palace built in 1916 by industrialist James Deering, Villa Vizcaya's construction took about 10 percent of the work force of the young city of Miami. The path cutting through the tropical hardwood hammock leads to the mansion itself. The Great Stone Barge, a private island just offshore that Deering built as a breakwater and boat dock, seems to float behind the palace. Guided tours are offered daily. From November through April, "Moonlight Walks" are offered in Spanish and English on the night of the full moon.
Open daily 9:30 a.m.-5 p.m. Adults $8, children 6-18 $4.

SPORTS

Basketball

Miami Heat
721 1st Ave., Miami
• (305) 577-4328

Miami's own National Basketball Association Team, the Heat plays 41 home games per season at the newly constructed Miami Arena.
Season runs Nov.-April. Call for ticket information & schedule.

Bicycling

Dade Cycle
3216 Grand Ave., Coconut Grove
• (305) 443-6075

Servicing Coconut Grove for more than three decades, Dade Cycle not only offers an excellent same-day service and repair department, but also boasts the largest fleet of rental bikes in South Florida. A free bike route map accompanies all rentals.
Open daily 9 a.m.-6 p.m.

Fishing

Blue Waters
16375 Collins Ave. (Castaways Dock), North Miami Beach
• (305) 944-4531

Private accommodation arrangements for parties of up to twenty, on oceangoing sailfish, marlin and shark charters. Fast, 50-foot, air-conditioned sport fisher.
Chartered daily by advance reservation. Call the 24-hour information line for details.

Captain Dan's Deep Sea Fishing Charters
1020 MacArthur Cswy., Miami Beach
• (305) 372-9570

Captains Dan Kipnis and Wayne Conn love beginners, welcoming one and all aboard their 67-foot *Reward II* for full-day, half-day and chartered fishing parties. Don't forget the Dramamine if you're prone to seasickness.
Chartered by advance reservation. Scheduled parties Mon.-Sat. 9:30 a.m.-1:15 p.m. & 1:45 p.m.-5:30 p.m., Sun. 9 a.m.-1 p.m. & 1:30 p.m.-5:30 p.m.

New Moon III
16375 Collins Ave.
(Castaways Dock),
North Miami Beach
• (305) 949-9762

Full- or half-day oceangoing fishing charters aboard a newly customized, 50-foot sportfisherman. Accommodating parties of one to six fishermen.
Chartered daily by advance reservation. 24-hour information line.

Top Gun
575 Crandon Park Blvd.
(Crandon Marina),
Key Biscayne
• (305) 361-8110

The *Top Gun* specializes in oceangoing billfish parties by charter. A fully-equipped, 46-foot Hatteras, she makes full- or half-day excursions for one to six people.
Chartered daily by advance reservation.

Football

Miami Dolphins
2269 N.W. 199th St.,
Miami
• (305) 623-6262

The Dolphins made their move to the brand-new Joe Robbie Stadium (leaving the Orange Bowl for the University of Miami), and home games are frequently sold out. Available tickets can be purchased in advance or at the stadium's Gate G prior to each game.
Season runs Sept.-Dec. Call for ticket information & schedule.

Greyhound Racing

Biscayne Kennel Club
320 N.W. 115th St.,
Miami Shores
• (305) 754-3484

Got a little racing in your blood? One of the most popular diversions along Florida's Gold Coast, the Kennel Club features seasonal greyhound racing.
Open Oct. 31-Dec. 25. Call for schedule information.

Flagler Greyhound Track
401 N.W. 38th Ct.,
Miami
• (305) 649-3000

Flagler picks up where Biscayne left off, offering seasonal greyhound racing.
Open June 10-Dec. 31. Call for schedule information.

Horse Racing

Calder Race Course
210th St. & N.W. 27th Ave.,
Miami
• (305) 625-1311

Although it's a trek north and west from downtown up to Calder, horse-racing is a fascinating seasonal event.
Open May-Jan., Tues.-Sun. 1 p.m. post time.

Sailing

Adventure Yacht and Sailing
2480 S. Bayshore Dr.,
Coconut Grove
• (305) 854-3330

Even for the unskilled sailor, spending a day on a small sailboat in Biscayne Bay is thinkable. Adventure offers instruction and rental of Hobie Cats (catamarans) and other small sailboats for an hour, half- or full-day period.
Open daily 9:30 a.m.-sundown.

Castle Harbor Sailboats
Dinner Key Marina at Bayshore Dr.,
Coconut Grove
• (305) 858-3212

Offering larger craft for the more experienced crew, Castle harbor rents 23- and 27-foot sailboats for groups of up to six.
Open daily 9 a.m.-sundown.

Florida Yacht Charters & Sales
1290 5th St.,
Miami Beach
• (305) 532-8600

Florida Yacht Charters & Sales has a crafty way of trying to sell you a boat: by teaching you to captain one. Offering sailing lessons and sailing vacation courses, the outfit also vends a variety of sailing vessels.
Open daily 9 a.m.-6 p.m.

TOURS

By Air

Dade Helicopter Jet Service
950 MacArthur Cswy.,
Watson Island
• (305) 371-3218

This one is definitely not for the fainthearted, nor those even vaguely afraid of heights. A chopper will whisk you across Biscayne Bay for seven- and fifteen-minute sightseeing and photo sessions, touring Miami Beach, the port area, downtown, Key Biscyane and Coconut Grove along the way.
Open daily 9 a.m.-6 p.m. Cost $49-$89 per person.

By Bicycle

Miami Beach Bicyle Center
923 West 39th St.,
Miami Beach
• (305) 531-4161

A bicycle path stretches for more than twenty blocks through the Art Deco District, and renting a bicycle built for one or more, and riding along The Boardwalk to the north is a popular diversion. From Fifteenth Street to the southern end of the island (South Pointe Park and Penrod's Beach Club at First Street), the beach attracts young and beautiful locals, as well as Europeans, who frequent the nearby art-deco hotels. For those traveling by car, there's metered street parking. The boardwalk stretches from 21st Street north to 46th Street (along the concrete "Condo Canyon"), attracting strollers, joggers and bicyclists who want to check out the famous hotels along the ocean.

MIAMI Basics

By Boat

Biscayne National Underwater Park
S.W. 328th St. &
Biscayne Bay,
Homestead
• (305) 247-2400

One of the only national parks in the country that is fully submerged, Biscayne National Underwater Park can be explored via two 52-foot glass bottom boats. The vessels whisk you across Biscayne Bay through mangrove creeks and out to 25-foot-high tropical coral reefs. Snorkeling, scuba and canoe rental can also be arranged from these docks.
Open daily 8 a.m.-6 p.m. Prices vary.

SeaEscape
Pier 6, 1080 Port Blvd.,
Downtown
• (305) 379-0000

SeaEscape sets sail daily from the Port of Miami for one-day itineraries to Freeport in the Bahamas. Included are three meals, casino gambling and Las Vegas–style entertainment. Depending on the day, this trip can be very crowded and uncomfortable, or else a lot of fun. If you've never been on a longer cruise, it might be worth the trip. However, you can also watch the mega-cruise ships that make Miami home port from Watson Island off the south side of I-395, the MacArthur Causeway the on-ramp to the north on Biscayne.
Departs daily 10 a.m. Evening cruises Tues. & Fri. Fare $29-$79.

BASICS

GETTING THERE	95
GETTING AROUND	96
AT YOUR SERVICE	97
GOINGS-ON	98

GETTING THERE

Cab fare from the airport to downtown is between $12 and $15. Regularly scheduled service aboard **The Airporter** goes to **Cutler Ridge, Homestead** and **The Keys**. Fares range from $12.50 to $25. Call (305) 247-8877, or the 24-hour reservation line, (305) 247-8874. **SuperShuttle** tours the airport terminal every fifteen minutes around the clock, charging $5 to $18 for door-to-door service to hotels and homes; count on a higher fare for the Keys, Orlando or West Palm Beach. SuperShuttle service is also available from **Miami International** to **Fort Lauderdale** or **West Palm Beach** airports. Call (305) 871-2000 for information and reservations.

GETTING AROUND

By Bus

Miami is linked by a transit system that includes buses, the **Metrorail** elevated rail system operating from downtown to **Hialeah** in the west and as far south as Kendall, and **Metromover**, a two-mile elevated system that loops around downtown and connects to **Metrorail at Government Center**. Regular bus fare is $1 each way (exact change required), and 50 cents for senior citizens, the physically disabled and students who have valid ID. Metromover fare is 25 cents, 10 cents for seniors, the physically disabled and students with rail permit. Most routes operate from 6 a.m. to midnight; every 90 seconds for Metromover and every eight seconds to fifteen seconds for bus and rail. For information, call (305) 638-6700. **Tri-Rail** operates Monday to Saturday along fifteen stations from West Palm Beach to Miami, with free transfers to Metrorail for service to downtown and south Miami. Fare is $2 each way, $1 for seniors, handicapped, children and students with valid ID. Weekly passes are available. **Old Town Trolley** (305-374-8687) shuttles between Bayside and downtown for $1; **Greyhound Bus Line** has seven stations in Greater Miami. Call (305) 374-7222; Spanish (800) 531-5332.

By Car

When driving around Miami, it's important that you have a complete address, for example, not simply Eighth Street, but N.W. Eighth Street, or Terrace, or Avenue. The city relies on a grid system with Flagler Street dividing north from south, and Miami Avenue dividing east from west. Avenues run north-south; streets east-west; there are also terraces, lanes and circles, and outsiders get quite befuddled when faced with an address on N.W. South River Drive. Highway I-95 is the chief in-town north-south artery; Highway I-395 serves Miami Beach via the **MacArthur Causeway**; the **Florida Turnpike** is the fastest north-south route, bypassing the city and ending in Homestead. The **Airport Expressway** is an extension of the **Julia Tuttle** causeway, linking the beaches with the airport, then U.S. Highway 27. The **Palmetto Expressway** rings the downtown area and is a good route from **Miami Lakes** to the **South Miami-Kendall** area. Rental car agencies include **Alamo** (305-633-6076), **Avis** (305-637-4900), **Budget** (305-871-2722), **Dollar** (305-887-6000), **General** (305-871-3575), **Hertz** (305-275-6430), **National** (800-328-4567) and **Thrifty** (305-871-2277).

By Taxi

Taxi rates throughout Dade County start at $1.10, $1.40 per mile after that. From the airport to downtown is a twenty-minute ride costing $12 to $15; to Miami Beach add another five to ten minutes and $10 to $15 for a total of up to $30. Call **Metro Taxi** (305-888-8888) or **Yellow Cab** (305-444-4444).

USEFUL TELEPHONE NUMBERS

The area code for all South Florida telephone numbers is (305).

Alcoholics Anonymous ....(305) 887-6762
Cirrus ATM locations throughout Florida .... (800) 4-CIRRUS
Coast Guard emergencies ....(305) 535-4314
Crisis/Suicide prevention ....(305) 358-4357
   (Spanish-language) ....(305) 358-2550
Dade County Bar Association ....(305) 371-2220
Florida Bar Assn. lawyer referral...................(800) 342-8011
Dade County Medical Association ....(305) 324-8717
Deaf Services (305) 444-2266 (voice), (305) 444-2211 (TDD)
East Coast Dental Society ....(305) 667-3647
Emergency 911
Fishing and hunting licenses ....(305) 375-5820
Greater Miami Visitor Information
   Center ....(305) 245-9180, (800) 852-8675
Greater Miami Convention & Visitors
   Bureau............................(305) 539-3000, (305) 641-1111
Jacksonville Memorial Medical Center ....(305) 325-7429
Library, main..(305) 375-2665
Lighthouse for the Blind ....(305) 856-2288
Metro-Dade Transit Agency ....(305) 638-6700
Miami Beach Resort Hotel Association
   (24-hour reservations for hotels,
    car rental, admissions) ...(305) 531-3553, (800) 531-3553
Parking information, garages ....(305) 373-6789
Parks and Recreation ....(305) 579-2676
Police, non-emergency ....(305) 595-6263
Port of Miami............. (305) 371-7678, Fax (305) 375-4605
Post office, main branch ....(305) 470-0222
Professional Translating Services...................(305) 371-7887
Ticketmaster...(305) 358-5885
Tri-Rail....................... (800) 874-7245, Fax (305) 763-1345
U.S. Passport Agency ....(305) 536-5395
Weather, surf condition ....(305) 661-5065
Western Union ....(305) 691-7912, (800) 325-6000

MIAMI Basics

FOREIGN EXCHANGE

Currency exchanges are found throughout the airport. **Barnett Bank of South Florida**, (305-825-5900), offers exchange at the airport and all branches. **Deak International** (155 S.E. 3rd Ave., Downtown; 305-381-9252) is a major exchange, and the **Fontainebleau Hilton Resort and Spa** (4441 Collins Ave., Miami Beach; 305-674-1907). Also offering currency exchange are **Jefferson National Bank** (301 Arthur Godfrey Rd., Miami Beach; 305-532-6451; or 18170 Collins Ave., Miami Beach; 305-935-6911); **Southeast Bank** (200 S. Biscayne Blvd.; 305-375-7500); and **Sun Bank** (777 Brickell Ave.; 305-591-6000).

WEATHER & WHAT TO WEAR

January and February are the coldest months in South Florida, with overnight temperatures usually no lower than the high 50s. Daytime temperatures are in the 70s in winter and the high 80s in summer. The rainy season is June to October, with June having the most rainfall. March and December are the driest months. Lightweight resort wear is a good bet all year; carry a sweater or jacket to indoor events even in the hottest weather because the air-conditioning might be chillier than you think.

GOINGS-ON

January

- **Orange Bowl Football Classic**, New Year's Day. Major sports event, televised nationwide; (305) 642-5211.
- **Three Kings Parade**, January 6, Little Havana. Celebrates Epiphany, Latin style; (305) 447-1140.
- **Beaux Arts Festival**, second weekend, University of Miami; (305) 284-3536.
- **Deco Weekend**, second weekend in January. Relive the 1920s with vintage cars, music and styles in the nation's largest "Deco" neighborhood; (305) 672-2014.
- **Redlands Art Festival**, second weekend, Fruit and Spice Park; (305) 247-5727.
- **Homestead Frontier Days and Rodeo**, late January to early February. Serious competition among some of nation's best riders and ropers; (305) 247-2332.

February

- **Homestead Championship Rodeo**, early February, Homestead. National rodeo stars vie here for money and fame; (305) 372-9966.
- **Miami Film Festival**, Miami; (305) 377-3456.
- **Miami Beach Festival of the Arts**, early February, Miami. Street festival celebrates music, theater and dance; (305) 673-7733.

MIAMI Basics

- **Cornucopia of the Arts**, Vizcaya. A spectacular Renaissance palace and garden setting forms the backdrop for this celebration of arts and culture; (305) 579-5238.
- **Coconut Grove Arts Festival**, mid-February, Coconut Grove. One of the state's best celebrations of arts, foods and culture; (305) 447-0401.
- **Miami International Boat Show**, mid-February, Miami. One of the nation's largest; thousands of displays in and on the water; (305) 531-8410.
- **Buskerfest**, late February, Bayside Marketplace. Zesty mayhem featuring street performers, foods and crafts; (305) 577-3344.

March

- **Scottish Festival and Games**, early March, Miami. Traditional Scottish contests in colorful costume on lovely Key Biscayne; (305) 757-6730.
- **Carnaval Miami,** early March, S.W. 8th Street, Miami. A ten-day fiesta, with Latin rhythms, food, dancing and a wildly colorful parade; (305) 324-7349.
- **Calle Ocho Festival**, mid-March, Little Havana. Latin street party is America's largest Hispanic blow-out, climaxing pre-Lenten Carnaval; (305) 324-7349.
- **Italian Renaissance Festival**, mid-March, Vizcaya. Medieval contests, feasting, costumes, entertainment in a stunning "doge's palace"; (305) 579-2500.

April

- **Miami Grand Prix**, April 6-7, Miami. Internationally renowned grand prix drivers race through downtown streets in this Monaco-style classic; (305) 665-7223.
- **Artist Days at Vizcaya**, Vizcaya; (305) 579-2500.
- **Dade Heritage Days**, Miami; (305) 358-9572.
- **Coconut Grove Music Festival**, early April, Coconut Grove. Sunny parks spill over with music of all kinds in this old and artsy section of the city; (305) 661-6571.
- **Greater Miami Billfish Tournament**, Miami; (305) 598-8127.
- **Taste of Miami**, mid-April, Bayfront Park. City's great restaurateurs sell samples of their best creations; (305) 375-8480.
- **Coconut Grove Seafood Festival**, mid-April, Coconut Grove. In a lush park, samples of the area's famous seafood harvest are sold; (305) 442-4084.

May

- **Hispanic Theatre Festival**, begins mid-May, Miami; (305) 446-1116.
- **Haitian Festival**, Miami; (305) 347-1320.
- **Great Sunrise Balloon Race and Festival**, Homestead. Meet at Harris Field to watch balloons life off at sunrise. Food, souvenirs, fun; (305) 245-6150.

June

- **Miami-Bahamas Goombay Festival**, first weekend in June, Coconut Grove. Bahamian and Caribbean rhythms, costumes, food, dance; (305) 372-9966.

July

- **Pops by the Bay**, entire month of July, Miami Marine Stadium. Outdoor concert on beautiful Biscayne Bay; (305) 945-5180.
- **Colombian-American Festival**, Bayfront Park. Features the culture, music and food of one of Miami's Latin American populations; (305) 576-9433.
- **Miccosukee Music and Crafts Festival**, late July, Miami. Indian food, music and crafts shown in the Miccosukee Indian village; (305) 223-8388.

September

- **Caribbean-American Festival**, late September to early October, various locations around Dade County. Enjoy Reggae, goombay, jerk chicken, goat souse and other culinary treats, plus music and dancing; (305) 387-4694.
- **Oktoberfest**, late September to early October, north of downtown. Beer, oompah and gemutlichkeit in Miami's version of the Munich original; (305) 374-7610.

October

- **Hispanic Heritage Festival**, entire month of October, Miami. Call for schedules of contests, historic re-enactments, arts, crafts, music and food events; (305) 541-5023.
- **West Indian Carnaval Extravaganza**, first weekend in October, Miami Beach. Bands, arts, rides and food from throughout the Caribbean; (305) 770-1833.
- **Banyan Festival**, Coconut Grove; (305) 444-7270.

November

- **Miami Air Show**, early November, Opa-locka Airport, Miami. One of the nation's largest; big-name aviation groups, racers, and stunt performers; (305) 685-7025.
- **Sunstreet Festival**, mid-November to December 7, Liberty City's African-Americans present gospel singing, talent shows, street parties and parades; (305) 696-5648.
- **Santa's Enchanted Forest**, mid-November to January 1. Tropical Park becomes a wonderland of lights, rides, food booths and entertainment; (305) 893-0090.

December

- **Art in the Heart of Miami Beach**, first weekend in December, 41st St., Miami Beach. Juried art show features works of 150 artists; (305) 538-8874.
- **Boat Parade**, second weekend in December, Intracoastal Waterway. Boats compete for Best Christmas Display prize. Event ends with gala at Bayside; (305) 935-9959.
- **Holiday Spirit of Vizcaya Gardens**, Vizcaya; (305) 579-2808.
- **Miccosukee Indian Arts Festival**, last week in December, Miami. Native American costumes, dance, crafts, foods, alligator wrestling; (305) 223-8380.
- **King Mango Strut**, December 30, Coconut Grove. This wacko parade parodies the more famous King Orange parade the following evening; (305) 441-0944.
- **King Orange Jamboree Parade**, December 31, downtown; (305) 642-1515.

THE KEYS

INTRODUCTION	102
UPPER KEYS	102
LOWER KEYS	108
KEY WEST	110

INTRODUCTION

There is nothing in the United States quite like this sunwashed chain of coral islets that stretch endlessly into the Gulf of Mexico, like a school of tropical fish streaking toward Cuba. Beginning with Key Largo and continuing south 115 miles to Key West, which dangles at the southernmost tip of the continental United States, the entire chain is connected by the Overseas Highway (U.S. Highway 1). For this book, we divide the islands into the **Upper Keys**, from Key Largo to Vaca Key; **Lower Keys**, stretching from Marathon Key south until the chain ends in the Gulf, and **Key West**, which, because of its magical allure over the decades for the famous, infamous and nonfamous alike, merits its own section. Spend a few days swimming, sailing and sunning on these paradisial bits of reef, share a rum drink or two with a local and you'll understand that peculiar blend of natural splendor and artificial honkytonk that makes the Keys so unique. (For a detailed map of the Keys, see page 340.)

UPPER KEYS

RESTAURANTS	102
QUICK BITES	103
HOTELS	104
NIGHTLIFE	105
SHOPS	106
SIGHTS & SPORTS	107

RESTAURANTS

Atlantic's Edge
Cheeca Lodge,
Mile Marker 82,
Islamorada
• (305) 664-4651
AMERICAN

11/20

The last time we dined at the Cheeca Lodge, its restaurant was a glorified fish house. My, how times have changed! A recent multi-million-dollar face-lift has left this Islamorada landmark looking as pretty as a Beverly Hills beauty parlor. A swank new dining room stands where the fish house once did, all candlelit tables, rattan chairs and potted palms. Soups now make a fancy two-pronged attack—the broth is poured over the rest of the

ingredients at the table—and entrées now travel in the company of fashionably al dente dwarf vegetables. And this may be the only place in the Keys that serves a midmeal sorbet (actually more of a sherbet). We couldn't fault the creamy richness of the roasted-corn-and-lump-crab chowder, the painterly presentation of the braised snapper and the fresh flavors of the Key lime dessert sampler. Nonetheless, there's something so stilted and belabored about this restaurant, it makes us long for the simpler fare of yore. In any event, the ocean views afforded by the enormous bay windows are incomparable, and the kitchen is happy to grill, braise, pan-fry or blacken any fish that guests of the hotel may land. Dinner for two, with wine, will run $80.
Open Mon.-Thurs. 7 a.m.-2:30 p.m. & 6 p.m.-10 p.m., Fri.-Sat. 7 a.m.-2:30 p.m. & 6 p.m.-11 p.m., Sun. 7 a.m.-3 p.m. & 6 p.m.-10 p.m. All major cards.

Ziggy's Conch
Mile Marker 83 1/2, Islamorada
• (305) 664-3391
SEAFOOD/AMERICAN

10/20

The Conch, a.k.a. Ziggy's (the name of the founder), isn't much to look at, with its mustard-colored walls, mounted game fish, terrazzo floors and blaring TV set. And its food isn't exactly innovative: save for the prices, the menu doesn't seem to have changed one whit in 30 years. But despite these shortcomings (or perhaps because of them), this Islamorada institution attracts a cultlike following. The food could be described as Italo-American seafood: fried fish platters, lobster de jonghe (spiny lobster broiled with artery-clogging doses of garlic butter) and mammoth oysters carpeted with creamed spinach or melted cheese. Conch, the restaurant's namesake, comes in fritter form, chowder, "cracked" (pounded, pan-fried steaks) and even in a rich sauce of shallots, brandy and sherry. The regulars wait to hear the daily specials before ordering. If it's offered, don't miss the lobster paisano (a tomatoey, garlicky stew). But we wouldn't eat the saccharin-flavored Key lime pie if it were free. Ziggy's is the sort of place where the waitresses wear white dresses and sensible white shoes and hard liquor flows more freely than wine. Dinner for two, with cocktails or beer, ranges from $60 to $80.
Open Fri.-Wed. 5 p.m.-9:45 p.m. Cards: DC, MC, V.

QUICK BITES

Alabama Jack's
58000 Card Sound Rd., Upper Key Largo
• (305) 248-8741

"We've been here 'bout as long as there's been a here to be at," says the crusty bartender at this equally crusty open-air seaside bar and eatery. The pelicans among the nearby mangroves seem to bob their heads in agreement. It'd be stretching things to say that Alabama Jack's patrons come for the food alone; the chief

attractions are the clog dancers and the live country music on weekends. But the kitchen serves a conch chowder that's loaded with sweet shellfish, and the crisp, sweet, pepper-studded conch fritters are about as good as this Florida delicacy gets. On the down side, we doubt that even those hungry pelicans would eat the leaden crabcakes. Perched at the edge of the blue, blue waters of Barnes Sound, Alabama Jack's does a lively business with boaters. It gives you a feel for what the Florida Keys must have been like before the proliferation of condos and trailer parks. Lunch for two, with beer, runs $10 to $15.
Open daily 11 a.m.-7 p.m. No cards.

HOTELS

Moderate (From $100)

Cheeca Lodge
U.S. 1 at Mile Marker 82,
Islamorada 33036
• (305) 664-4651/
664-2893

To cruise boaters and sailors plying the Gulf waters of the Keys, the blue-tiled roofs and 525-foot-long fishing pier jutting into shallow waters of the Cheeca Lodge are a familiar landmark. The 27-acre resort is a marvelous retreat, one of the most thorough getaways in the Keys, tucked among 27 tropically landscaped acres. There are a golf course, six tennis courts lit for night play and a beautiful, white-sand, 1,000-foot-long beach (the latter of which is a rare commodity in the Keys, which are set upon brittle coral rock). You can choose your accommodations—and your price range—at Cheeca Lodge, which offers not only 203 guest rooms, most of them waterfront, but also well-appointed suites and marvelous ocean-view villas.
Singles & doubles: $100-$200; suites: $175-$225; villas: $500-$700.

Holiday Isle
84001 Overseas Hwy.,
Islamorada 33036
• (305) 664-2321
Fax (305) 664-2321,
ext. 658

The most prominent landmark of the 77-room Holiday Isle resort is an enormous fish hanging upside down from the adjacent docks. The second most prominent landmark is the traffic that surrounds Holiday Isle most every weekend afternoon. The resort's Tiki Bar is the gathering spot of choice for those returning north to Miami on Sunday afternoons; the favored place to grab one more margarita before heading home. A favorite among not only last ditch revelers but also avid sportfishing enthusiasts (Holiday Isle's charter fleet is enormous), the playground for grownups is known more for its festive (and often loud) ambience than for the quality of its accommodations or service. The buzz of jet skis and wave runners and the beat of calypso music continue well past dusk. Still, a brief stay at Holiday Isle typifies the Keys experience.
Doubles: $120; suites: $325.

Sheraton Key Largo Resort
U.S. 1 at Mile Marker 97,
9700 S. Overseas Hwy.,
Key Largo 33037
• (305) 852-5553
Fax (305) 852-5553 ext. 548

On the Gulf side of Key Largo, the 200-room and -suite Sheraton, barely an hour's drive from Miami, offers a good, relatively inexpensive way to experience the Keys on the quick. It has a private fishing pier, two pools, tennis courts and a clean (if minuscule) private beach. Still, it's a quick drive over to Pennekamp—where you can enjoy that beach, or hop on a glass-bottomed boat or dive boat heading out to the reef.
Singles & doubles: $125-$230; suites: $270-$395.

Practical Hotels

Marina del Mar
U.S. 1 at Mile Marker 99,
Key Largo 33037
• (305) 451-4107
No fax

For scuba divers and snorkelers who want to explore the majestic John Pennekamp Coral Reef State Park, Marina del Mar has the best location of any resort in the Keys. Located on the Gulf side of Key Largo, the resort offers not only plenty of dockage for private boats, but also a nautical store, a dive shop and dive instruction on the premises. The main building, though rather plain-looking, houses nicely appointed and always clean rooms, most of which offer private balconies with nice views of the marina. Charter and rental boats are available, as are bicycles and motor-scooters for rental.
Singles & doubles: $64-$145; suites: $110-$295.

Pelican Cove
U.S.1 at Mile Marker 84.5,
Islamorada 33036
• (305) 664-4435
No fax

Pelican Cove is one of those hotels that sacrificed architectural innovation to ensure that all its rooms fronted on the ocean. The rooms, suites and efficiencies, therefore, fan out like drum majorettes in a straight line along the Atlantic. All the facilities are decent enough, and the Jacuzzi suites in particular are loads of fun. There are a saltwater swimming lagoon, tennis courts, a boat ramp with dockage and yet another Florida Keys–style, artificially constructed sandy beach.
Singles & doubles: $95; suites $125-$315.

NIGHTLIFE

The Tiki Bar
Holiday Isle Resort,
Mile Marker 84 1/2,
Islamorada
• (305) 664-2321

A tour of the Florida Keys would be incomplete without an evening at The Tiki Bar. This institution has always managed to line them up for miles on weekend nights when everybody's heading home. There is, after all, only one road out, and the Tiki Bar marks just about the halfway point. There's always a live calypso or reggae band rocking the thatched roof, while suntanned patrons line up at the open-air bar for its famed frozen drink, the rum runner, a potent combination of light and dark rum, grenadine, blackberry brandy and banana liqueur that

could well be described as liquid nirvana. (At last count, the Tiki Bar had served 27 million of those deadly drinks.) Take your rum runner to one of the picnic tables out back and watch the jet skis carve up the Atlantic. Lunch is served here, too.
Open Sun.-Thurs. 10 a.m.-12:30 a.m., Fri.-Sat. 10 a.m.-2:30 a.m. No cards.

SHOPS

Clothes & Jewelry

H.T. Chittum & Co.
U.S. 1 at Mile Marker 82.7,
82748 Overseas Hwy., Islamorada
• (305) 664-4421

This store is sort of a more tropical Banana Republic, carrying lots of island safari-type clothing, as well as bait and tackle, handmade gaffs, trolling lures and custom-made knives. A great place to buy gifts for the fisherman, hunter or general outdoor enthusiasts in your life.
Open daily 8:30 a.m.-6 p.m.

Maggie's Sand Dollar
U.S. 1 at Mile Marker 81.8,
81888 Overseas Hwy., Islamorada
• (305) 664-8807

These small shops on Islamorada and Marathon keys sell bathing suits and more bathing suits (sort of the uniform for the Florida Keys), plus a nice selection of dresses and casual wear for both men and women. The service at both Maggie's Sand Dollar stores is particularly attentive and friendly, as is the custom in these parts. Marathon Key branch is located at 2315 Overseas Highway, Marathon, (305) 743-6677.
Open Mon.-Sat. 10 a.m.-5 p.m.

Gifts

Island Silver & Spice
U.S. 1 at Mile Marker 82,
81981 Overseas Hwy., Islamorada
• (305) 664-2714

Picture a tropical department store. There would be all sorts of resort wear, plus lots of tropical home-decor items, generally painted with flowers and shells. And there would be lots of T-shirts to make souvenirs for the folks at home. That's Island Silver & Spice, worth a stop if you're in Islamorada.
Open daily 10 a.m.-5:30 p.m.

The Rainbarrel
U.S. 1 at Mile Marker 86.5,
Islamorada
• (305) 852-3084

You can't miss this sprawling, eclectic collection of crafts studios, shops, gardens and galleries from the highway. It's a great place to pick up souvenirs that aren't simply of the standard, anonymous variety. More than 300 artists and craftspeople exhibit in this community, and you can find all sorts of woodwork, sculptures, hand-carved marble, stained glass, leather goods, paintings and handmade jewelry, much of it signed by the artist, generally at reasonable prices.
Open daily 9 a.m.-5 p.m.

Shell World
U.S. 1 at Mile Marker 97.5,
Key Largo
• (305) 852-8245

If you're in the market for shark's teeth, Shell World promises the biggest selection in the Keys. Also plenty of shells, black and red coral, local artwork and resort wear.
Open Mon.-Fri. 10 a.m.- 5:30 p.m, Sun. noon-4 p.m.

SIGHTS & SPORTS

Parks

John Pennekamp Coral Reef State Park
U.S. 1 at Mile Marker 102.5,
Key Largo
• (305) 451-1621

John Pennekamp Coral Reef State Park, adjacent to the Key Largo National Marine Sanctuary, is situated around a massive coral reef that can be readily explored. From the safety of a glass-bottomed boat, or behind a snorkel mask, or through hundreds of scuba bubbles, a fascinating array of marine life awaits. Some 650 species of tropical fish and 40 species of coral inhabit the 21-mile-long, 8-mile-wide park. The park was named for a Miami newspaper man and conservationist.
Glass-bottomed boat tours daily 9 a.m., noon & 3 p.m. Adults $10; children $6. Snorkel boat tours daily 9 a.m., noon & 3 p.m. Adults $16. Scuba dives (for certified divers only) daily 9 a.m. & 1 p.m. daily. Cost $30.

Theater of the Sea
U.S. 1 at Mile Marker 84.5,
Islamorada
• (305) 664-2431
Fax (305) 664-8162

You can't miss Theater of the Sea from the highway: the masts of a re-created tall ship loom over the horizon. Among the attractions at one of the oldest marine parks in the country are the dolphin swim (you can swim along with dolphins, with a trainer and guide), sea shows and a marine petting aquarium. Be sure to call ahead to make a reservation for the dolphin swim.
Open daily 9:30 a.m.-4 p.m. Adults $10.25, seniors $9.23, children 4-12 $5.50. Dolphin swim $50.

Sports

Admiral Dive
U.S. 1 at Mile Marker 103.2,
Key Largo
• (305) 451-1114

The first thing most visitors to the Keys will want to do is get certified to scuba dive. Aboard the 65-foot *Admiral I*, many individuals manage to accomplish this feat in a day. For snorkelers and scuba divers alike, the full-service dive store and PADI (Professional Association of Diving Instructors) facility makes daily trips to the magnificent reefs surrounding Key Largo.
Hours by charter. Packages $69.95 per person.

Club Nautico
527 Caribbean Dr.,
Key Largo
• (305) 451-4120

Florida's largest boat-rental outfit, Club Nautico has a Key Largo outfit with a fleet of 16-, 18-, 20-, 23- and 25-foot power boats, for those who want to go on fishing, waterskiing, sightseeing or diving expeditions of their own.
Open daily 8 a.m.-4:30 p.m.

Keitz's American Diving Headquarters
U.S. 1 at
Mile Marker 106,
Key Largo
• (305) 451-0037

Harry Keitz arranges snorkeling charters to the reef at Pennekamp (where he promises visibility for between 60 and 100 feet), and offers free instruction.
Hours by charter. Tours daily 9 a.m., noon & 3 p.m. Prices vary.

Witt's End Sailing Charters
U.S. 1 at Mile Marker 100 (Marina del Mar), Key Largo
• (305) 451-3354

How about sailing aboard a 51-foot ketch without having to do any work? Up to six guests can learn to sail, dive or snorkel aboard the *Witt's End*, as well as take sunset cruises and half-day, full-day or weekend-long sails. If you want to charter the boat for a week or longer, a special itinerary can be designed.
Schedule by charter. Prices vary.

LOWER KEYS

HOTELS

Faro Blanco Marine Resort
1996 Overseas Hwy.,
Marathon 33050
• (305) 743-9018
No fax

Many of the place names in the Florida Keys have stuck since Spanish explorers first plied these waters in the late sixteenth century. Faro Blanco (meaning "white lighthouse"), however, is actually one of the newest resorts in the area, offering accommodations on both the Atlantic and Gulf sides of Marathon. Boating guests have the luxury of being able to pull their boats virtually right up to the front door, and the sprawling retreat has already proven popular among fishermen, sailors and water-sports enthusiasts of all shapes and sizes with its elaborate marina facilities. For something different (and surprisingly luxurious), check out the hotel's "Houseboat Suites," situated on the ocean side of the resort; bayside, there are small cottages and condominiums with up to three bedrooms. With two restaurants and a lounge, your boat in the backyard and glorious sunsets every night, Faro Blanco is one of those places you won't want to leave at all once you check in.
Cottages: $55-$99; houseboats: $65-$175; lighthouse rooms: $135-$175; condominiums: $175-$225. Cards: AE, MC, V.

Hawk's Cay Resort and Marina
U.S. 1 at Mile Marker 61,
Marathon 33050
• (305) 743-7000
Fax (305) 743-7000 ext. 3625

Located at the tip of Duck Key, a private island accessible by a small bridge just off Marathon, Hawk's Cay is one of the best for family vacationers in the Lower Keys. A subject of debate in the media in recent years, the resort is home to a dolphin training facility that allows guests to join the creatures in their tanks and swim right along with them. The 178-room and -suite resort offers many other diversions: glass-bottomed boats, wave runners, tiki boats and surf-sailing equipment on property, plus a 50-slip full-service marina and dive shop. The guest rooms, lounges and restaurant are clustered around an enclosed, artificially constructed lagoon, lending a distinctly tropical air to the whole resort. Included in the rate is a lavish breakfast buffet.
Singles & doubles: $125-$200; suites: $225-$440.

Little Palm Island
Rte. 2, Box 1036,
Little Torch Key 33040
• (305) 872-2524
No fax

From the moment you step into the private launch, the mood is set. It blissfully doesn't include such modern niceties as telephone, television or radio (that's why you escape here), but each of the suites has a whirlpool bath, bar and swell amenties beneath its thatched roof. The accent at this Little Torch Key resort is on restful solitude, which might include a bit of sailing, or a rum drink by sunset at the Tiki Bar. Do bring a saddlebag full of money, or you'll find the prices downright uncivilized.
Suites: $410-$500.

SHOPS

Marine Jewelry
U.S. 1 at Mile Marker 54,
Quayside Village,
Marathon
• (305) 289-0628

Although the name may sound like a contradiction in terms, Marine Jewelry has a splendid display of jewelry, including 14-karat gold enameled conch shells and authentic Spanish treasure coins on chains. There are also some lovely queen conch pearls and an abundance of coral jewelry.
Open Mon. 10 a.m.-5 p.m., Tues.-Sat. 10 a.m.-9 p.m.

SIGHTS

Strike Zone Charters
U.S. 1 at Mile Marker 28.5,
Big Pine Key
• (305) 872-9863

Strike Zone offers four-and-a-half-hour island tours of the Looe Key National Marine Sanctuary, with its unusually clear waters and wild coral formations, where bird hammocks, old shrimp plantations and the exotic marine life co-exist. Also explorable beneath the seas are several wrecked ships, among them the 1744 British frigate H.M.S. *Looe.*
Fish-fry picnics & dive excursions daily by reservation. Adults $29.

KEY WEST

RESTAURANTS	110
QUICK BITES	112
HOTELS	113
NIGHTLIFE	119
SHOPS	121
SIGHTS	123

RESTAURANTS

Café des Artistes
1007 Simonton St.,
Key West
• (305) 294-7100
FRENCH/CARIBBEAN

Hoping to topple Louie's Backyard from its perch as Key West's premier place to dine (and, in the opinion of many, succeeding at this), Café des Artistes has chosen to be as French in manner and taste as the semitropical setting and availability of ingredients will allow. You can still dine in your shorts and sport shirts, as you can everywhere on the island, and if you eschew the surroundings of the main dining room, you can savor the sea breeze on the restaurant's open terrace. Among house specialties we have raved about are the carpaccio de boeuf, served with delicate Parmesan shavings and sprinkled with basil and capers; and chard rôti aux framboises, the half duckling roasted crisply and served with a fresh raspberry sauce. Dinner for two, with wine, will eat up a worthwhile $90.
Open daily 6 p.m.-11 p.m. Cards: AE, MC, V.

Café Marquesa
Marquesa Hotel,
600 Fleming St.,
Key West
• (305) 292-1244
AMERICAN

12/20

Who says a Key West restaurant needs an ocean view to be successful? Not Dennis O'Hara, the chef and manager of this popular place. Even on Sunday night, his postmodern dining room, with its marigold walls, white columns, trompe l'oeil murals and open kitchen, plays to a full house, for O'Hara has been fortunate enough to find diners who care more about what they see on their plates than the view out the window—and he always gives them something surprising to look at. Three kinds of soup arrive in three tiny bowls. An open lasagne boasts a vegetarian walnut filling. The individual ribs of a sesame-and-honey-coated rack of lamb radiate from the center of the plate

like sun rays. Squiggles of caramel sauce and chocolate give a stylish twist to flan. We're not saying it all works—leathery duck topped a lackluster salad, and lobster ravioli were disappointingly bland (this is one of the rare restaurants where the entrées outshine the appetizers)—but for the most part, O'Hara's food is as enjoyable as it is inventive. Beer drinkers will be intrigued by the brews from Togo (West Africa) and Peru. Dinner for two, with wine, will run about $80.
Open nightly 6 p.m.-11 p.m. Cards: AE, MC, V.

Dim Sum

613 1/2 Duval St., Key West
• (305) 294-6230
ASIAN

11/20

You don't need a degree in culinary arts to know that any style of cooking on the Pacific Rim is the nation's latest restaurant food fad—and the Burma-born proprietors of Dim Sum are on hand to make sure that Key Westers stay on top of the trend by getting their fill of gado gado, dragon noodles and khauk swe chicken. Mind you, if Dim Sum were located anywhere but a small island that lacks sorely in good Asian fare, it might even escape our notice completely, but since dragon noodles are a rare treat in Key West, we are perfectly happy eating them at Dim Sum. Among the dishes, gado gado is an Indonesian steamed vegetable salad with a creamy peanut dressing. The dragon noodles boast a chili sauce that will light up your mouth like a Fourth of July sparkler; and the khauk swe chicken features soft egg noodles in a rich coconut-milk gravy. You can wash these tasty dishes down with one of five kinds of tea, Asian beers or China Cola, a natural cola made of casia bark, peony root and Malaysian vanilla. Bananas steamed in coconut milk bring the meal to a sweet conclusion. Tucked away in a cozy courtyard off Duval Street, Dim Sum has the peaked roof, straw ceiling, bamboo trim and silhouette paintings of a private home in Southeast Asia. The service is as personable as it is multinational and prompt. Dinner for two, with beer, will run $60 to $70.
Open Wed.-Mon. 6 p.m.-11 p.m. All major cards.

Louie's Backyard

700 Waddell Ave., Key West
• (305) 294-1061
AMERICAN/CARIBBEAN

Is there anything more delightful than brunch on the terrace at Louie's Backyard? Before you, the sun glints and sailboats bob on the glass-smooth Atlantic. Overhead, an enormous sea-grape tree shields you from the sun's rays. And delights of the edible sort highlight the contemporary American menu. No ho-hum eggs Benedict here; instead, you're offered poached eggs and home-smoked shrimp on buttermilk biscuits with an almond-tomato hollandaise. Herbed mascarpone and homemade pumpernickel accompany exceptionally silky smoked salmon. Pancakes are made with gingerbread batter and accompanied by boiled cider. Does life get better than this? But now that we think about it, there may be something as delightful as brunch on the terrace: dinner upstairs, in the rose-and-turquoise Café

at Louie's. Working out of a "theater" (open) kitchen, chef Susan Ferry weaves Asian, North African and Latin American ingredients into a modern Caribbean cuisine, featuring such dishes as a Caribbean fruit and vegetable salad graced with an orange and lemon-grass vinaigrette, and local shrimp in a marinade of annatto (a fragrant orange spice) and lime. The service is well meaning but a trifle affected. Both restaurants fill quickly, so be sure to request a terrace table when you make a reservation. Brunch for two, with mimosas, will cost about $50; dinner with wine, $100.
Open Mon.-Sat. 11:30 a.m.-2:30 p.m. & 6 p.m.-10:30 p.m., Sun. 11:30 a.m.-3 p.m. & 6 p.m.-10:30 p.m. All major cards.

The Pier House Restaurant
The Pier House,
1 Duval St.,
Key West
• (305) 296-4600
AMERICAN

12/20

When the setting's this spectacular, a restaurant doesn't need to serve remarkable food—but though you can't get much more spectacular than The Pier House's oceanfront views and Caribbean sunsets, the cooking actually lives up to the scenery. You're in the Caribbean now, and lest you doubt it, know that the egg rolls house conch, that the Caesar salad contains smoked shrimp and that a black-bean cake and pico de gallo (a chop of fresh tomato, jalapeño and cilantro) accompany the smokily grilled sea scallops. And while we're on the subject of smoke, the smoked rack of lamb with curried jus and homemade chutney transforms a commonplace entrée into an inspired creation. The secret? The Pier House does all its smoking over buttonwood, a tree native to Key West. A daily fish special features two fish (perhaps tuna and dolphin), two coatings (perhaps blackening spices and blue cornmeal) and two sauces (perhaps avocado cream and roasted peppers). Also worth noting are the crusty sourdough bread and the textbook Key lime pie. One small complaint: The salad chef needs to lighten up on the vinegar. The best seats in the house are those on the terrace, but if bad weather forces you inside, you'll find a comfortable, clubby dining room accoutred with brick and glass, peach-colored chairs and candlelit tables. Two will spend about $100 for dinner with wine.
Open Mon.-Sat. 11:30 a.m.-2:30 p.m. & 6 p.m.-10:30 p.m., Sun. 10:45 a.m.-2 p.m. & 6 p.m.-10:30 p.m. All major cards.

QUICK BITES

Camille's
703 1/2 Duval St.,
Key West
• (305) 296-4811

The setting is Key West in 1991, but it might just be Berkeley or Ann Arbor in the late '60s. The funky elegance of this Duval Street storefront, with its flowered purple tablecloths and faded gallery prints, has given this place a loyal local following. This is *the* place to bring a big appetite and a small purse for a formidable breakfast: three-egg omelets, homemade pastrami hash, chunky home fries and freshly baked Cuban bread, drenched with butter and flattened in a Cuban sandwich press. Come lunchtime, Camille's serves a mean grilled-cheese sandwich made with avocado, tomato and bacon. And all day long, laid-back waitresses will keep your coffee cup filled. In a town with this many tourists, you know you can trust an establishment patronized by the locals. Breakfast for two, with coffee, will cost $10 to $15.

Open Mon.-Wed. & Fri.-Sat. 8 a.m.-3 p.m., Sun. 9 a.m.-1 p.m. No cards.

Half Shell Raw Bar
Lands End Village at the foot of Margaret St., Key West
• (305) 294-7496

The Apalachicola Bay oysters and "top neck" (littleneck) clams served at Half Shell Raw Bar are probably no better than those served at innumerable other Florida raw (seafood) bars. They just taste that way, seasoned as they are by the view of the fishing boats, the scents of the ocean (and diesel exhaust!) and the magical light of Key West at sunset. This boisterous bar, with its varnished picnic tables, is equally popular among locals and tourists, who pile in for steaming cups of conch chowder, cracked conch steak, fried oysters and stone crabs with one of the better mustard sauces in Florida. The Half Shell also serves a dish we could eat for the rest of our lives: smoked conch (smoking seems to bring out the natural sweetness of this Caribbean mollusk). The sangría won't kill you, but we prefer to stick to the beer. Lunch for two, with beer, will run $15 to $20.

Open Mon.-Sat. 11 a.m.-11 p.m., Sun. noon-11 p.m. Cards: MC, V.

HOTELS

Luxury (From $150)

Hyatt Key West
601 Front St., Key West 33040
• (305) 296-9900
Fax (305) 292-1038

They call the Hyatt a "boutique resort," and when we checked in, we learned exactly what that meant. It has to do with being small, impeccably laid out and absolutely committed to overseeing the smallest detail of your Key West experience. It seems as though employees here are required to have lots of freckles, great attitudes, be on their way to hotel school and look great in white shorts. For a resort of this size (only 120 rooms), the Hyatt offers stacks of amenities, including three restaurants and lounges, a raw bar, a multilevel sundeck and a small but tidy beachfront offering abundant water sports. The Hyatt also rents the nicest-looking fleet of motor scooters in town. Rooms are

spacious and well appointed, with paddle fans, terra-cotta floors and one of the most creatively stocked mini-bars we have seen.
Singles & doubles: $159-$285. Packages available.

Moderate (From $100)

The Banyan Resort
323 Whitehead St.,
Key West 33040
• (305) 296-7786
No fax

Named for the two majestic, twisted banyan trees that between them manage to shade the grounds of eight Victorian homes, The Banyan Resort makes for a delightful stay in Key West. It is located just down the street from Hemingway House, where the young author lived for nearly 30 years, changing the face of American literature somewhere in between. Five of The Banyan's eight homes are listed on the National Register of Historic Places; they are joined together by botanical gardens, a fish pond and a variety of tropical birds that call the place home. The 38 rooms are each air-conditioned and comfortably furnished with period antiques. Just one block west of Duval Street, and slightly south of Mallory Square, the resort is ideally located for those who prefer tranquillity over tumult.
Singles & doubles: $115-$145.

Marriott Casa Marina Resort
1500 Reynolds St.,
Key West 33040
• (305) 296-3535
Fax (305) 296-4633

Tennessee Williams and Truman Capote were known to sunbathe here on this six-acre resort that opened on New Year's Eve of 1921. The southernmost of Florida railroad baron Henry Flagler's grande dames, the Casa Marina has hosted celebrities, statesmen, artists and socialites—not to mention the writers in this literary community—in 314 guest rooms. The hotel sits on the ocean side of the key, with vaulted, black cypress ceilings, intricate paneling, piazzas, loggias and arched windows looking over the water. A recent restoration program added 63 new suites, each remaining true to the Spanish Renaissance theme which Flagler insisted on. Rooms vary in size and quality, so take our advice: spring for a room with a view of the water, in the main building. Or, better yet, reserve one of those with a lanai in the new West Wing or a suite in the new East Wing.
Singles & doubles: $135-$345.

La Mer Hotel
506 South St.,
Key West 33040
• (305) 296-5611
No fax

Part of the Old Town Resorts group, La Mer is a funky little eleven-room Queen Anne–style home. Built in 1903, the house features the turret and latticework fencing typical of the day, all graced by swaying palms that hide it from the traffic of Front Street. La Mer is Key West the way it used to be, attracting the easygoing set who shun the busy resorts of Duval Street and the beaches. Rooms are comfortably furnished in cane and rattan furniture, and they're totally unassuming in their flair.
Doubles: $104-$144. Cards: AE, MC, V.

Ocean Key House

Zero Duval St.,
Key West 33040
• (305) 296-7701
No fax

Ocean Key House is more just plain fun than anything else. If you're hoping to be square in the middle of some lively action, it'll be hard for you to decide where to request your room or suite. If you choose the Mallory Square side, you're right outside Mallory Square (where the wild and wacky sunset celebration takes place each and every night) and the cruise ship docks. On the gulf side, you've got the spectacular Dockside Bar and Raw Bar, which is hopping whenever one of Key West's famous festivals is underway, and of course the improbably clear blue-green water filtering by from the outlying Straits of Florida. Upon entering the Ocean House, you may find the cramped, unassuming lobby off-putting; note that the rooms can be equally small and unwelcoming. If you stay here, treat yourself to a suite, each of which has a two-person (at least) Jacuzzi. The complimentary Continental breakfast offered daily isn't just your standard fare: fresh baked muffins and pastries, fresh squeezed orange juice and steaming mugs of coffee are prepared each morning in the hotel's own bakeshop.
Rooms: $125; suites: $285-$450.

Pier House

One Duval St.,
Key West 33040
• (305) 296-4600
Fax (305) 296-7569

The Pier House, which of all the major resorts on Key West held the longest-standing and best reputation on the island, recently has been restored to its past grandeur. Following a major refurbishment program, the resort not only has 129 newly decorated guest rooms and thirteen suites, but also five glorious "Honeymoon Suites" which rank among Florida's finest accommodations. (To show it all off, Pier House's new ads features great-looking, scantily clad people lounging around the grounds). On the Gulf side of the island, the private terraces of one wing of the Pier House offer the most idyllic place in town from which to enjoy the sunset. There's also a new spa offering massage, loofah rubs, herbal wraps, aerobics and exercise circuits. Even if you can't afford the Pier House, make sure you take a walk through the grounds and grab a Piña Colada during your visit.
Singles, doubles & suites: $135-$525.

The Reach

1435 Simonton St.,
Key West 33040
• (305) 296-5000
Fax (305) 296-2830

The Reach doesn't look like much from the outside. Its designers saved it all for the guests. Situated on the Atlantic side of the island, The Reach consists of 150 Caribbean-style, white terraced guest rooms (including 80 wonderful suites, complete with Mexican tiled floors), each cleverly positioned to face the ocean. Amenities include a complete health club and massage by appointment. Among the newest of the island's major resorts, The Reach is positioned away from the spirited bedlam

of Duval Street, but on a three-and-a-half-mile-long island, nothing is too far away from anything else. Inside the rooms, though the buildings are the requisite late-1980s, built-hotel, soft Bermuda pink, the decor is an understated white on white, plus paddle fans (for comfort) and coffee brewers (for convenience). Make yourself a cup, and watch the morning sunrise over the beach, where the sailors and windsurfers are setting up for the day. Situated on the southern tip of the island, the hotel marks just about the exact spot where the continental United States ends in the Atlantic Ocean. When it comes mealtime, make sure you have reservations elsewhere on the island, as the hotel's own, The Reach, doesn't have anything outstanding to offer for lunch or dinner.
Singles & doubles: $99-$575.

> *We're always happy to hear about your discoveries and receive your comments on ours. We want to give your letters the attention they deserve, so when you write to Gault Millau, please state clearly what you liked or disliked. Be concise but convincing, and take the time to argue your point.*

Practical (Under $100)

La Concha Holiday Inn
430 Duval St.,
Key West 33040
• (305) 296-2991
No fax

Don't let the "Holiday Inn" in the title fool you. This hotel has character, and loads of it. Originally built in 1925, La Concha has endured the test of time—sort of. It was at the heart of the social scene during the Hemingway era, when well-heeled heiresses grabbed the train to Key West for a cool tropical fling en route to fishing expeditions in Havana. Like the rest of the island, La Concha suffered terribly throughout the depression, and was dealt its final blow when the railroad was destroyed in a 1939 hurricane. Even when the hotel eventually closed down, its bar, The Top, continued to offer a dazzling view of Key West—despite a rather seedy ambience—to those who made the trek through the abandoned hotel. Enter Holiday Inn, who in 1987 entered into an agreement with the local Spottswood family who still owned the property, and commenced a $20 million renovation on the hotel. Today La Concha is a delight, its rooms decorated with paddle fans and period antiques. Located in the heart of the action of Old Town in the middle of Duval Street, La Concha is neither on or near a beach. But its higher floors still offer the best view in town on an otherwise pancake-flat island.
Singles & doubles: $70-$275.

THE KEYS Key West – Hotels

The Curry Mansion Inn
511 Caroline St.,
Key West 33040
• (305) 294-5349
Fax (305) 294-4093

Built in the late 1800s by a Conch (pronounced "konk," here meaning a native Bahamian, and also used for Key West natives), the Curry Mansion is one of the most inviting of the island's storybook gingerbread houses. A twenty-room guest house, the Victorian mansion's architecture and decor are so exquisite that the home is also open for tours. Each room is furnished with marvelous period antiques, but as with most of the small guest houses in Key West, the rooms vary greatly in size and comfort. Be sure to inquire about the various rooms' features while making your reservations. Outside, the Curry Mansion's most prominent feature is the white latticework of its widow's walk, which offers a lovely panorama of the surrounding neighborhood. Caroline Street is only a block east of Duval Street, but it offers a shaded retreat removed from the hoopla of central Old Town.
Singles & doubles: $90-$175.

Duval House
815 Duval St.,
Key West 33040
• (305) 294-1666
No fax

We mention Duval House because it is just as charming as most of the other Victorian mansions–cum–tiny inns in the area, but its prices are well below standard. That's because Bob Zurbrigen, the owner, is a handyman, tried and true. When there's a paint job to be done (and there frequently is when you've opened a 100-year-old-house to the public), Zurbrigen and partner Ben Connors do it themselves. The seventeen guest rooms feature paddle fans and wicker headboards, each room presented within a different color scheme, although they differ greatly in size and proportion (an issue the owners will happily discuss with your over the phone).
Singles & doubles: $43-$68; triples: $53-$78. Cards: AE, MC, V.

Eaton Lodge
511 Eaton St.,
Key West 33040
• (305) 294-3800
No fax

A traditional inn where intimate personal attention is a standard, the nineteenth century Eaton Lodge is listed on the National Register of Historic Places, a Conch house with lush gardens and English-style grounds. If you're expected at the Eaton Lodge, an old London taxi will meet you at the airport. On the outside, there are the louvered shutters typical of the island; the lobby is graced with a chandelier. There are only eleven guest rooms, each with its own bath and a nice private terrace.
Singles: $55-$105; doubles: $60-$120; triples: $70-$120. Cards: MC, V.

Island City House

411 William St.,
Key West 33040
• (305) 294-5702
No fax

The three buildings that make up this resort were once a natural cypress wood Alfonso Cigar factory, a Victorian Mansion and a historic carriage house. The property was then bought by its current owners and transformed into the Island City House, after three years and $750,000 of work. The resort is joined together by decks and gardens, a pool and a Jacuzzi, all capped off with a white picket fence. Located three blocks away from the bustle of Duval Street, the 24-parlor suite compound is one of the most popular retreats in Key West. All of the interior wallpapers, curtains, upholstery and bedcovers are of Victorian prints; floors are hardwood pine. Each room has its own small kitchen and its own paddle fan, the old-fashioned way to cool down during those tropical Key West nights.
Singles, doubles & triples: $65-$175.

Merlinn Guest House

811 Simonton St.,
Key West 33040
• (305) 296-3336
No fax

Located on Simonton Street, which runs parallel to Duval, the anassuming Merlinn Guest House is a great value. It combines the charm and hospitality of the Victorian bed-and-breakfasts in town with a good selection of rooms in four different clusters. The newest of these is the Tree House, which has a private sundeck, high ceilings, pine floors and a private bathroom. There is a parlor decorated in Orientalia, where guests congregate in the evenings to read and listen to music. Decorated by a former New York designer who moved to Key West and opened the inn, the property's public spaces are far more attractive than are the rooms. This is intentional at Merlinn, which feels this is where most of a guest's time will be spent while staying here. Speaking of the guests, Merlinn's attracts mostly gay male visitors, reflective, of course, of Key West itself.
Singles, doubles & triples: $45-$87. Cards: AE, MC, V.

La Terraza de Marti

1125 Duval St.,
Key West 33040
• (305) 294-8435
No fax

Called La-Te-Da by those in the know, this delightful little 20-room resort and restaurant was named for Cuban patriot José Marti, who once stayed here. Clustered around a pool and the most popular poolfront restaurant in Key West, La-Te-Da's rooms exude elegance: Oriental rugs, stereos, microwaves, bottled water, Godiva chocolates at bedtime and pink carnations strewn about. Right in the thick of the whimsical social scene and action typical of Key West (La-Te-Da hosts the most popular Sunday brunch in town and twice weekly Tea Dances), the hotel attracts a heavily gay male clientele, but will be enjoyed by anyone who loves a good party. With that in mind, if you need quiet, make sure to request a room in the back, away from the pool area; it often resounds with laughter and party chatter well into the wee hours.
Doubles: $48-$183.

NIGHTLIFE

Bars

The Afterdeck
700 Waddell,
Key West
• (305) 294-1061

With an intimate bar and only a handful of tables, The Afterdeck, located by the beach behind Louie's Backyard, is a great place to wind up (or down) an evening. Though it's on the wrong side of the island for the best sunset view, it dependably draws a crowd at happy hour. It's also a beautiful setting for after-dinner drinks; even after closing there's swimming at a small public beach just next door.
Open daily 11:30 a.m.-2 a.m. All major cards.

Captain Tony's Saloon
428 Greene St.,
Key West
• (305) 294-1838

Old Hem would be proud that his old haunt still stands. Ernest Hemingway, that is. A small, cozy, smoky institution of a place, Captain Tony's is staunchly supported by Key West natives as being *the* original Sloppy Joe's, Hemingway's favorite watering spot. Locals say he drank here, caroused here, created a ruckus here, wrote here. We'll stand by what the locals say, because we have a feeling this place would have been old Hem's choice over the "other" one any day. There's that authentic, slightly seedy atmosphere hanging in the air, and you can spend most of the night soaking it up. "Captain Tony" Tarracino, by the way, is also Key West's mayor. Ask him about the skeleton on display, and he'll tell you it belongs to "a former wife." Sounds like something Hemingway might have said.
Open Mon.-Sun. 10 a.m.-2 a.m. No cards.

Full Moon Saloon
1202 Simonton St.,
Key West
• (305) 294-9090

Yes, there is some action that continues into the wee hours even when you're not on Duval Street. The Full Moon Saloon is a great place to get away from the crowds on Duval, and they serve a great fish sandwich along with your cold beer even when it's getting close to breakfast time.
Open daily 11 a.m.-4 a.m. All major cards.

Gringo's Cantina
509 1/2 Duval St.,
Key West
• (305) 294-9215

Gringo's deserves a very special award for its margaritas, which appear to be about a gallon in size, and are always salted just right. A great place to kick off cocktails for the evening.
Open daily noon-midnight. All major cards.

Sloppy Joe's
201 Duval St.,
Key West
• (305) 294-5717

The famous Sloppy Joe's bar, featured in all sorts of stories about Ernest Hemingway's drinking, carousing and creating famous characters, still thrives—but down the street from this spot. *This* Sloppy Joe's likes to tell visitors that Hemingway did his ample drinking here and even worked here at one time; but locals in the know pooh-pooh that claim. They all stand by the first Sloppy Joe's of the 1920s and 1930s (now called Captain Tony's, just down the street), as being the *real* watering hole in which Hem slaved over his beers and books, and in which he left a cache of unfinished manuscripts. Everybody agrees, however, that Hemingway definitely hoisted a few here at some point, and why not?

This newer, bigger, more open bar, which appeals to a rowdy crowd day and night, isn't the spot for an inspired writer to concentrate; he'd do better to chug a few and forget the manuscript. Go in the late afternoon for something long and cool, and you'll generally be in the company of a higher common denominator than you would late at night.
Open daily noon-4 a.m. No cards.

Jazz

The Top
Holiday Inn La Concha,
430 Duval St.,
Key West
• (305) 296-2991

What was originally a ritzy nightclub and later a seedy dive with a great view of the island is now a wonderful little jazz bar. The Top, re-vamped when Holiday Inn took over the La Concha in the late eighties, is a great place from which to watch the sunset, or enjoy after dinner drinks. Sunday afternoons are also particularly lively.
Open daily noon-1 a.m. Shows Thurs.-Sat. 9 p.m.-1 a.m., Sun. noon-6:30 p.m. All major cards.

Music Clubs

Jimmy Buffett's Margaritaville
500 Duval St.,
Key West
• (305) 296-3070

Bands change weekly here at the nightclub owned by the folk singer whose "Margaritaville" is thought to be the "real" Key West. Music runs from bayou/Cajun to the island reggae and calypso. Once in a while, Mr. Buffett himself appears before a crowd of locals who generally seem to know all his words by heart.
Open daily noon-4 a.m. Showtimes nightly 10:30 p.m. All major cards.

Schooner Wharf
202 William St.,
Key West
• (305) 292-9520

Located on the waterfront, the Schooner offers a nice alternative to Duval. Reggae, progressive and dance bands play nightly, and this is probably the best place in town to dance.
Open daily 11 a.m.-4 a.m. Shows daily 9 p.m.-1 a.m. No cover. No cards.

SHOPS

Accessories

Shades of Key West
305 Front St.,
Key West
• (305) 294-0329

335 Duval St.,
Key West
• (305) 294-0519

Shades of Key West carries a wide selection of name-brand sunglasses, plus specialty items like over-the-head chains that work especially well on fishing and boating expeditions when unsecured sunglasses tend to end up in the water.
Front St.: open daily 10 a.m.-6 p.m. Duval St.: open daily 10 a.m.-8 p.m.

Sunlion Jewelry
208A Duval St.,
Key West
• (305) 296-8457

If you just must have one of those pieces of eight you saw at Mel Fisher's museum this morning, Sunlion is the place for you. Less pricey purchases include an abundance of golf charms and chains, plus some interesting hand-crafted jewelry from local artisans.
Open Tues.-Sat. noon-7 p.m.

Beauty

Russell House
611 Truman Ave.,
Key West
• (305) 294-8787

At Russell House, a mere $119 can indeed make you feel beautiful. It starts with a jazz-exercise class, and moves on to a dip in a Roman tub, full body massage, hydrating facial, makeup job, shampoo, cut and style, a light lunch and a free gift.
Open Tues.-Fri. 9 a.m.-4 p.m.

Books & Newsstands

Key West Island Bookstore
513 Fleming St.,
Key West
• (305) 294-2904

Because this is the bookstore of choice among so many members of Key West's literary community, don't be surprised to run into a world-famous author or two during a visit here. Used, rare, first-edition and autographed copies from local writers are on display at Key West's only literary-oriented bookstore.
Open daily 10 a.m.-6 p.m

L. Valladares & Son
1200 Duval St.,
Key West
• (305) 296-5032

The oldest newsstand in Key West, L. Valladares carries an abundance of out-of-town and foreign newspapers, plus more than 300 paperbacks and a marvelous selection of magazines. There's also a special section reserved for books on Key West and the works of local authors.
Open daily 8 a.m-8 p.m.

Fabrics

Key West Hand Print Fabrics
201 Simonton St., Key West
• (305) 294-9535

It's most interesting to browse through this store after a fascinating tour of the fabric factory on the premises. A huge display of decorator and fashion fabrics, plus sundresses, belts, hats, shoes and island wear are available in brilliant floral colors and designs. Because they are dyed and crafted by hand, items here tend to be quite pricey.
Open daily 10 a.m.-6 p.m.

Gifts

The Bottling Court
Front St. at Simonton, Key West
• No phone

In 1893 it was Jack's Saloon, hangout for the local wreckers, fishermen and sponge divers. In 1920 it became the local Coca Cola bottling plant. Today it is The Bottling Court, a "historic" little collection of shops and boutiques. As long as you don't mind overly cute, touristy bric-a-brac, you'll enjoy a stroll through its air-conditioned walkways. At least it makes for a cooler afternoon of shopping than do the streetfront shops on those sweltering summer days.
Open Mon.-Sat. 10 a.m.-9 p.m., Sun. 11 a.m.-7 p.m.

Fast Buck Freddie's
500 Duval St., Key West
• (305) 294-2007

If you shop nowhere else while in Key West—nor in all of Florida for that matter—be sure to make it to Fast Buck Freddie's. Sort of an out-of-whack department store, Fast Buck somehow manages to capture the spirit of Key West in all of the items it hawks, from watercolor greeting cards, to men's and women's resort wear, to a wonderful housewares department. Because of an overzealous design team and an equally fervent buying department, Fast Bucks is rather hard to describe; there's always something different to poke through and pick up.
Open daily 10 a.m.-6 p.m.

Island Needlework
527 Fleming St., Key West
• (305) 296-6091

Island Needlework's unique touch is that many of its designs and patterns are hand-painted. Belts, rugs and a variety of needlework are also for sale prefab.
Open Mon-Sat. 10 a.m.-4 p.m.

Whitehead Street Pottery
1011 Whitehead St., Key West
• (305) 294-5067

Situated inside a renovated, 100-year-old Cuban grocery store, Whitehead Street Pottery vends original stoneware, porcelain and Raku-fired vessels.
Open Mon. & Wed.-Sun. 10 a.m.-6 p.m.

SIGHTS

East Martello Museum
3501 S. Roosevelt Blvd., Key West
• (305) 296-3913

Key West's triangle of fortresses were built in anticipation of the island's role in the Civil War. The East Martello Museum is housed in the Martello tower, whose spiral staircase afforded the Union soldiers who held the island a sweeping view of the nearby waters. (You can climb to the top today to enjoy a similar view). The museum itself presents a fascinating walk back in time, with a display that includes deflated inner tubes and rickety rafts that Cuban refugees have "sailed" into Key West during the last few years. There is also a marvelous display of first edition books written by members of Key West's resident writers colony.
Open daily 9:30 a.m-5 p.m. Adults $3, children 7-12 $1.

Ernest Hemingway Home & Museum
907 Whitehead St., Key West
• (305) 294-1575

It is here that Ernest Hemingway wrote many of his major novels: *For Whom the Bell Tolls, Green Hills of Africa, A Farewell to Arms* and the *Snows of Kilimanjaro* among them. That great writer resided here from 1931 to 1961. Guided tours are offered; a gift shop vends Hemingway T-shirts, books and other memorabilia. Descendants of the author's six-toed cats, which roam the grounds and reproduce regularly in a fashion that would have made old Hem proud, can be had for $100.
Open daily 9 a.m.-5 p.m. Adults $5, children $1.

Great Southern Gallery
910 Duval St., Key West
• (305) 294-6660

Though the name might be a bit of an overstatement, Great Southern has a nice selection of local works. There is also a good selection of art supplies, and art classes and seminars are held regularly on the premises.
Open Thurs.-Mon. 11 a.m.-6 p.m.

John James Audubon House and Gardens
205 Whitehead St., Key West
• (305) 294-2116

John Audubon visited Captain John H. Geiger in 1832 at what is now the Audubon House, to work on many of his wildlife paintings. It is now a museum displaying an extensive collection of original works—including an extensive collection of porcelain birds—by the artist and naturalist.
Open daily 9:30 a.m.-5.p.m. Admission $5.

Island Arts
1128 Duval St., Key West
• (305) 292-9909

Although it's way down on the southern end of Duval where few shopping forays extend, don't miss Island Arts. All sorts of locally crafted pottery, sculpture, paintings and handcrafts are on display, from a painted, sequined and beaded suitcase to a nice selection of Raku-fired pottery.
Open daily 10 a.m.-5:30 p.m.

Arts

Key West Lighthouse Museum/ Southernmost Attractions
938 Whitehead St., Key West
• (305) 294-0012

The Key West Lighthouse Museum (one of Florida's oldest brick lighthouses) celebrates the island with a marvelous view of its environs (only to those who make it up the 88 steps)! The museum is at the center of a cluster of attractions within walking distance. Nearby is the site of the Southernmost Point in the continental United States (which is well marked for frequent photo opportunities). The public beach here, Southernmost Beach, provides an equally popular afternoon escape. An old Bahamian Gingerbread house here, called (you guessed it), Southernmost House, is also worth a visit.
Open daily 9:30 a.m.-5:30 p.m.

Mel Fisher Maritime Heritage Society Museum
200 Greene St., Key West
• (305) 294-2633

On display is a glittering, abundant collection of Spanish pieces of eight, gold bars, jewel-studded crosses and other gems—just a fraction of the $250 million booty Fisher's Treasure Salvors came upon when they discovered the shipwrecked *Atocha* and *Margarita* after fifteen years of trying. (Fisher lost a son and a daughter-in-law during the expedition).
Open daily 10 a.m.-6 p.m. (Last ticket sold at 5:15 p.m.).

The Red Barn Theatre
319 Duval St., Key West
• (305) 296-9911

The Red Barn stages seven productions a year, all featuring local performers. After the first week in July, when the theatre closes down for the summer, new works of local playwrights are often produced; traditionally to rave reviews in this literary community. If you're interested in other theater, check out the program at the Waterfront Playhouse (305-294-5015), or the Tennessee Williams Fine Arts Center (305-296-9081).
Performances Wed.-Sun 8 p.m. Tickets $12.50.

The Wrecker's Museum
322 Duval St., Key West
• (305) 294-9502

Housed in the oldest home in Key West, The Wrecker's Museum commemorates a colorful period in Key West's history: the salvaging days. Built around 1829, the museum is situated in a nine-room pine structure, and features a display of photos and artifacts depicting the island's history.
Open daily 10 a.m.-4 p.m.

Landmarks

Fort Zachary Taylor State Historic Site
End of Southard St., Key West
• (305) 292-6713

Located on one of the best white-sand swimming beaches in Key West, Fort Zachary Taylor is a "must-see" for Civil War buffs. It is from the National Historic Landmark that Union forces enforced their blockade, an era commemorated inside the red brick structure with a fascinating museum.
Open daily 9:30 a.m.-5 p.m.

Mallory Market
Whitehead St.,
Key West
• (305) 296-4557

Some might call it a tourist trap, but we think it's charming. Sure, you'll find the usual selection of T-shirts with bawdy slogans and shells that have seen more of a Taiwanese warehouse than a Florida beach. But Mallory Market's shops and attractions also include an enormous selection of locally produced sponges, fresh-juice and ice-cream stands and the oldest attraction on the island, the Key West Aquarium.
Open daily 10 a.m.-7 p.m.

Sports

Reef Raiders Dive Shop
109 Duval St.,
Key West
• (305) 294-3635

The Galleon Resort,
617 Front St.,
Key West
• (305) 294-0442

Captains Franco Piacibello and Craig Heiges hope that expert divers and aficionados alike will board the *Nautilus* dive boats. They offer an abundance of custom programs, including full scuba certification courses, night dives, wreck dives, private charters and treks to the outlying Dry Tortugas.
Two snorkel and scuba trips daily: 10 a.m.-1 p.m.; 1:30 p.m.-5:30 p.m. Prices vary.

Tours

Conch Classic Air Tours
Key West Airport,
Key West
• (305) 296-0727

The Conch Classic Air Tours open cockpit biplane looks like something out of *The Great Waldo Pepper*! (You will too, when you don your complimentary goggles and scarf). What a way to see Key West. On an island characterized by its flatness, it's impossible to get this kind of glorious view except if you're brave enough to go aerial. By special request, the pilots make reef tours, photo flights—and also upon request, will even perform some pretty daring (some would say frightening) acrobatic stunts with you in the front seat.
Hours by appointment. Prices vary.

Conch Tour Train
301 Key Lime Sq.,
Key West
• (305) 294-5161

We prefer the train, which has chugged around Key West for more than 30 years, to the trolley, especially in the summer months when a steady breeze is a necessity on any tour of Key West. Depending on the driver/guide you're assigned on the one-and-a-half hour journey, the look you get at Key West could vary greatly. (We're convinced they make up a good half of the local lore they impart along the way). But it's an awful lot of fun anyway, and a great way to get an overview of the island before you strike out on your own.
Open daily 9 a.m.-4 p.m. Adults $11, children $5.

Key West Seaplane Service

Key West Airport,
5603 W. Junior College Rd.,
Key West
• (305) 294-6978

Once you've seen the Keys from underwater, aboard a motor scooter, by foot and by trolley, you'll want to try a new angle. Key West Seaplane offers custom seaplane tours that head 68 miles out into the Gulf of Mexico, where Fort Jefferson (the Civil War prison) awaits. There are also snorkeling and bird-watching tours available; real adventurers can camp on the island while the seaplane awaits.
Hours by advance reservation. Prices vary.

Old Town Trolley Tours

1910 N. Roosevelt Blvd.,
Key West
• (305) 296-6688

The trolley not only gives an insightful, 90 minute tour of the island, but also lets you off at various stops. When you're finished having a look around, another trolley will pick you up.
Open daily 9 a.m.-4:30 p.m. Adults $11, Children 4-12 $5.

GOLD COAST

FORT LAUDERDALE 128
PALM BEACH 154

FORT LAUDERDALE

RESTAURANTS	128
QUICK BITES	137
HOTELS	139
NIGHTLIFE	145
SHOPS	148
SIGHTS & SPORTS	150

RESTAURANTS

Armadillo Café
4630 S.W. 64th Ave., Davie
• (305) 791-4866
SOUTHWESTERN

13

When chefs Kevin McCarthy and Eve Montella opened Armadillo Café in 1988, they were considered radical pioneers and more than a little crazy—know-it-all urbanites didn't see how a hip Southwestern restaurant could possibly make it in rural Davie, the capital of South Florida's horse country. Now all those urbanites are trekking out here regularly for a taste of this inventive, accomplished cooking. Southwestern food was all but unknown in these parts, so McCarthy and Montella weren't bound to follow any public perceptions. The result? A sinuous blend of Southwestern and Caribbean influences, unlike anything you've ever tasted. Florida blue crabcakes with a pineapple-chile salsa, lobster quesadillas, lobster and corn chowder with oyster mushrooms . . . local ingredients combine with various cooking styles to create vivid tastes. McCarthy deftly pops a sombrero on a classic French dish, duck à l'orange, by smoking the duck and dressing it with a citrus, honey and lime sauce. Montella is responsible for the desserts, which are uniformly fabulous: bitter-chocolate fritters, chocolate-pecan torte, mocha crème brûlée and more. The food is well matched with a striking collection of American wines (including brief tasting notes on each), along with a few worthy foreign vintages and a good selection of beers from the American Southwest. As lively and informal as the food, the setting is notable mostly for its savvy, casually dressed crowd and paper-covered tables topped with a supplies of crayons. Dinner for two, with wine, runs $50 to $75.
Open Sun. & Tues.-Thurs. 5 p.m.-10 p.m., Fri.-Sat. 5 p.m.-11 p.m. Cards: DC, MC, V.

GOLD COAST Fort Lauderdale – Restaurants

Brooks Restaurant
500 S. Federal Hwy., Deerfield Beach
• (305) 427-9302
AMERICAN/
INTERNATIONAL

12/20

Every day, customers ask about the name. Who is Brook, or Brooks, and where is she, or he? It turns out that owner Bernard Perron just saw the name somewhere and liked the sound of it. Fortunately, his restaurant isn't run as capriciously as it was named. Perron now spends most of his time at Boynton Beach restaurant, Benvenuto, but the family keeps the business going: daughter Lisa manages the large facility (cozily luxurious but fairly nondescript, with heavy furnishings and tones of dark green and aqua), her husband is the chef, and her brother is the sous-chef. Such nepotism can be a recipe for disaster, but here it works with amazing harmony. If the term "hodgepodge" didn't have such pejorative connotations, it would describe Brooks's culinary style ideally. The appetizers couldn't be any more eclectic: a light crabcake with lobster sauce, Asian fried dumplings with prawns, fettuccine with Gorgonzola and fresh tomatoes, Bahamian conch chowder. The entrées also jump around the globe, though you'll also find such reliable French classics as veal with apples and Calvados and duck with port and mustard. The grilled meat dishes are especially good. The small wine list boasts a superb collection of older French and Californian bottles at fair prices. Dinner for two, including wine, averages $100.
Open Sun.-Thurs. 6 p.m.-9:30 p.m., Fri.-Sat. 5:30 p.m.-10 p.m. Cards: AE, MC, V.

Café Arugula
3110 N. Federal Hwy., Lighthouse Point
• (305) 785-7732
AMERICAN/
INTERNATIONAL

(14)

Dick Cingolani is Fort Lauderdale's version of that Napa Valley, California cliché, the stockbroker-turned-winemaker. After retiring from the advertising business in the early 1980s, he traveled the world and finally succumbed to the siren call of the restaurant business. Today he owns three successful eateries, all within walking distance of one another in a small community a few miles north of Fort Lauderdale. At Café Arugula, his flagship, Cingolani serves what he calls a "cuisine of the sun," combining influences from California, the Mediterranean, Spain and the Caribbean. He pairs mussels, for instance, with Cajun smoked ham, and he combines escargots with chorizo, sherry, tomatoes and peppers. A red snapper filet is dusted with ground pecans and sauced with a cilantro-lime butter. Swordfish is seared over an oak fire and served on a bed of sautéed spinach and a tomato-saffron sauce. The kitchen works masterfully with assertive flavors, keeping the preparations simple and letting the ingredients speak for themselves. (For a time, the food veered sharply toward the Southwestern, but Cingolani channeled those creations into his excellent, inexpensive Border Café next door.) Desserts, made by Cingolani's daughter, are a standout, particularly the raspberry crème brûlée and the bitter Mexican chocolate torte. The wine list is remarkable for its fair prices,

service is first-rate, and the decor is restrained and classic: red plush chairs, roomy banquettes, well-spaced tables and unobtrusive light fixtures. Not only is this one of the best restaurants in South Florida, it's also one of the most comfortable. Two will spend about $110 for dinner with wine.
Open Sun.-Thurs. 5:30 p.m.-10 p.m., Fri.-Sat. 5:30 p.m.-10:30 p.m. Cards: AE, MC, V.

Café Seville
2768 E. Oakland Park Blvd.,
Fort Lauderdale
• (305) 565-1148
SPANISH

12/20

In many parts of South Florida, restaurants that claim to serve Spanish food actually serve Cuban food with Spanish overtones. Not so at Café Seville—this is the real thing, from the warm, informal atmosphere, to the dark-oak decor, to the extensive list of Spanish wines. The menu shuns invention in favor of tradition, and the place manages the neat trick of combining the sophistication of Seville with the casual feel of a café. As at so many good restaurants in Spain, you can settle in for a full meal or stop by for a quick nibble on the small dishes called tapas: escargots with garlic and tomatoes, grilled pork with mustard, shrimp sautéed with garlic, sherry and red pepper, and much more. Spanish food is too often identified with heavy meat dishes, so it's nice to see a menu that showcases Spain's considerable culinary diversity. Duck and rabbit show up alongside the expected pork, and there's a fine paella, but best of all are the admirable fish dishes, like the yellowtail with white wine, leeks and tomatoes. On the down side, the Spanish fondness for overcooking isn't helped by the kitchen's penchant for heating plates to a sizzle—the food keeps cooking even after the waiter has gone. The moderately priced wine list includes a number of the new, fruity Spanish wines. Dinner for two, with wine, runs $70 to $80.
Open Mon. 6 p.m.-10:30 p.m., Tues.-Fri. 11:30 a.m.-2 p.m. & 6 p.m.-10:30 p.m., Sat. 6 p.m.-10:30 p.m. Cards: AE, MC, V.

Charley's Crab
3000 N.E. 32nd Ave.,
Fort Lauderdale
• (305) 561-4800
SEAFOOD

11/20

Charley—or rather, Chuck Muer, who also owns Chuck and Harold's in Palm Beach (*see* page 157) and Joe Muer Seafood in Boca Raton (*see* page 159)—is no bold innovator, but he's a master of giving the public what it wants: good seafood cheerfully served at fairly reasonable prices. The Palm Beach branch sits practically on the ocean and has a good water view, but the Fort Lauderdale outpost has the more picturesque site, along the Intracoastal Waterway; diners arrive by car or water taxi, or tie down their own boats at the dock. The multilevel dining area, much of which is open to the fresh air, is big enough to serve as a dry dock, but we prefer to sit outside on the deck, an unmatched setting on a balmy tropical night. The menu can't compete with the view, but it does offer some appealing fish dishes. The most unusual of the several types of grilled fresh fish (which are always excellent) is tilapia, a two-pound specimen originally from Africa but now farm-raised in North Carolina; the kitchen braises it with squash and thyme. The crabcakes are among the best in town, the seafood paella is as good as at any local Spanish restaurant, and the seafood pasta is exceptional. But many other dishes, especially the nonfinned ones, are run of the mill. Although amiable, service can lag when the crowds descend. The wine list isn't as comprehensive as it could be, but it is reasonably priced. Still, the bill adds up quickly: two will spend about $120, with wine.

Open Sun.-Thurs. 11:30 a.m.-2:30 p.m. & 5 p.m.-10 p.m., Fri.-Sat. 11:30 a.m.-2:30 p.m. & 5 p.m.-11 p.m. All major cards.

The Down Under

3000 E. Oakland Park Blvd.,
Fort Lauderdale
• (305) 563-4123
CONTINENTAL

10/20

Given its name, you might logically assume that The Down Under serves trendy Australian cuisine—perhaps charred filet of wallaby with a kiwi-mango chutney. But the truth is much more mundane: it's simply located down and under an overpass that spans the Intracoastal Waterway. Now more than two decades old, this was one of Broward County's first great dining establishments. Leonce Picot and Al Kocab initially conceived it as a convivial tropical bistro, but with the city's rapid growth, what began as an upscale tavern turned into a full-fledged restaurant with a lengthy menu and one of the best wine lists in the country. The setting is still a big draw, with its spectacular view of pleasure-boat traffic, its open-air charm and its cozy (almost cramped) decor: dark-wood trim, hanging plants and a potpourri of antiques. Sadly, though, The Down Under hasn't aged as well as its wines. Though the service remains top-drawer, the original French-oriented menu has given way to generic Continental cuisine. Inconsistency seems to be the kitchen's watchword: on the one hand, it turned out a wan, lifeless beef Wellington; on the other, it proved its ability to be creative with a perfectly cooked shrimp stir-fry given considerable zest with cilantro, chilis and sweet Indonesian soy sauce. Avoid the thin, often overcooked crabcakes, and be warned that some of the fish dishes can be tasteless, but by all means order the tasty duck confit. Fortunately, the kitchen's shortcomings probably won't prevent you from having a most enjoyable evening, thanks to the view, the service and, most of all, the extraordinary wine list, rich with hundreds of mature, reasonably priced wines that were purchased young and aged in a temperature-controlled warehouse. Dinner for two, with wine, runs about $110.

Open Mon.-Fri. 11:30 a.m.-2 p.m. & 6 p.m.-10 p.m., Sat.-Sun. 6 p.m.-10 p.m. All major cards.

La Ferme

1601 E. Sunrise Blvd.,
Fort Lauderdale
• (305) 764-0987
FRENCH

12/20

In a fast-paced city that changes dramatically in a single year, a restaurant must be doing something right to maintain a clientele for more than a decade. Factor in the public's increasing preference for Italian food over French, and La Ferme's continuing success seems downright remarkable. Marie-Paule Terrier is an important part of that success—she is a constant, efficient and charming presence in the front room, watching over diners like a cultivated governess. The cooking is done by her husband, Henri, who neatly balances the old and the new, with a resultant cuisine that is comforting yet just inventive enough to avoid stodginess. It's a perfect match for the provincial bourgeois decor (the huge room looks like it was decorated by a French Ethan Allen, with dark woods and heavy, upholstered chairs); the setting and the food transport you to a well-provisioned French country inn. A salad of sweet, barely cooked Florida crab is nicely set off by slices of creamy avocado. Fettuccine serves as a blank canvas for salmon and wild mushrooms. Terrier delves into the bounty of Florida's waters to come up with such unusual dishes as poached ray fish. Duck gets any number of fruit-based sauces, all of them intensely flavorful but none overly sweet. At dessert time, Terrier chucks invention and pays honor to his schooling and sense of tradition: his fruit-flavored soufflés are justifiably recommended by the staff, his chocolate torte is a silken, flourless bit of heaven, and his apple tart is the best for miles around. The fairly priced wine list scores highly with collectors for its fine selection of older vintages. La Ferme is an unexpected treasure along one of Fort Lauderdale's most commercial stretches. Dinner for two, with wine, costs about $90. *Open Tues.-Sun. 6 p.m.-10 p.m. All major cards.*

Il Porcino

8037 W. Sample Rd.,
Coral Springs
• (305) 344-9446
ITALIAN

To the uninitiated, the porcino is just another mushroom, but to the enlightened, it is no more merely mushroom than the truffle is merely a fungus. Its admirers are legion, but few display more devotion to *Boletus edulis* than Luciano Balzano, who, with his cousin Filippo Ascione, runs this quiet restaurant in the western suburbs. Its location is the only aspect of Il Porcino that is suburban—in every other way, it is consummately cosmopolitan, from its modest, homey decor (white walls hung with a few Italian prints, neutral furnishings), to its first-rate service, to its small but choice collection of Italian wines. Best of all is the food, an adventurous combination of traditional concepts and new techniques. It would be a crime to come here and not try porcini, preferably in the restaurant's signature dish, superb risotto with porcini. But if that doesn't suit you, don't worry: lightly sautéed porcini accompany nearly every plate that leaves the kitchen. Don't leave without trying the terrific carpaccio

made from thinly sliced bresaola (air-dried beef) dressed with capers, radicchio and truffle-infused olive oil. Pastas have never disappointed us, particularly the nightly specials, such as pumpkin-filled ravioli or gnocchi tinted with squid ink and served with a creamy tomato sauce. The owners hail from the Ligurian coast, so fish is treated with the respect it deserves, as evidenced in such tasty, carefully prepared dishes as snapper with tomatoes, black olives and basil and salmon with a mustard-cream sauce. The veal dishes also reveal the chef's firm hand with herbs and light hand with sauces. So successful has this place been that Rino Balzano, Luciano's brother, left not long ago to open a new branch of the family business, Il Tartuffo (*see* below). Fortunately, this expansion has not caused Il Porcino to let its quality slip—it remains a faithful replication of an Italian country restaurant, tucked unexpectedly into a quiet Fort Lauderdale suburb. Two will spend about $90 for dinner with wine.
Open Mon.-Sat. 5 p.m.-11 p.m., Sun. 5 p.m.-10 p.m. Cards: AE, MC, V.

Il Tartuffo

2980 N. Federal Hwy.,
Fort Lauderdale
• (305) 564-0607
ITALIAN

Rino Balzano considers the truffle to be the eighth wonder of the world, and he pays homage to his beloved fungus by spiking many of his dishes with a splash of truffle oil or a smear of truffle paste. In autumn, when fresh truffles are in season, a bowl of Piedmont's prized white gold holds a place of honor by the door. Like its sibling, Il Porcino (which is run by family members—specifically Balzano's brother and cousin), this place boasts a contagious Italian ebullience: the minute you walk in the small, pristinely white room (reminiscent of a Greek Isles restaurant), you're adopted by the sort of Italian family that Walt Disney might have created. The short menu is augmented by daily specials, perhaps lobster ravioli or gnocchi with cream sauce. Balzano trolls the fishing fleet daily, bringing in an unusual haul that might include razor clams (which were routinely thrown back until he showed skippers how tasty they were). The core of his cooking philosophy is the restrained use of intensely flavored sauces on carefully cooked pastas, fish and meat. Yellowtail partners with a light sauce of tangy black olives and fresh, briefly sautéed tomatoes; salmon gets a lift from fresh sage; and chicken is combined with potatoes, peas and prosciutto. Make sure to save room for the best tiramisu in South Florida. The wine list boasts a wide range of prices and an eclectic selection. Dinner for two, with wine, will cost about $100.
Open Tues.-Sun. 6 p.m.-10 p.m. All major cards.

Mister Chu's

2465 E. Sunrise Blvd.,
Fort Lauderdale
• (305) 565-1664
CHINESE

11/20

In a food world where informality is a saleable commodity and restaurants carry the first names of their owners, Mister Chu's offers a welcome respite. There really is a Mister Chu, and a few times a year he takes time off from his other restaurants in Paris, New York and Geneva to stop by this modestly elegant spot, which is fighting an uphill battle to make you forget you're dining in a strip center. Screens give a sense of intimacy, Chinese porcelain adds a graceful note, and the careful use of black conveys a sense of sophistication without being austere. Family members run the place on Chu's behalf, following his dictate of culinary harmony. In explaining his philosophy, he talks about yin and yang, building a meal out of both cold elements that have a quieting effect (yin) and hot elements that stimulate (yang). The staff will help you construct a harmonious meal with such yin dishes as cold duck with ginger and lettuce and such yang dishes as potstickers (pan-fried dumplings with hot pepper). These influences are sometimes combined in a single dish, as with the shredded chicken and cucumber with a chili-garlic sauce and cool peanut paste. Instead of zeroing in on a single style, the menu jumps around China, from the western provinces of Szechuan and Hunan to the intricate northern style of Beijing to the elegant, seafood-based dishes from Shanghai. This culinary country-hopping gives the menu considerable variety, but the balance teeters on occasion—the western and northern dishes are the most successful, making Mister Chu's more of a yang (hot and spicy) kind of place. Don't miss the sliced duck with onions and zucchini in ginger sauce. The desserts are tasty but not authentic: chocolate cake, cheesecake and the like. There's a reasonable wine list and a good selection of beers. Mister Chu's may falter from time to time, but all in all the cooking is respectable—particularly given Florida's dearth of decent Chinese restaurants. Dinner for two, with wine, averages $60 to $70.
Open Mon.-Thurs. 11:30 a.m.-10:30 p.m., Fri.-Sat. 11:30 a.m.-11 p.m., Sun. 5 p.m.-10:30 p.m. Cards: AE, MC, V.

Runyon's

9810 W. Sample Rd.,
Coral Springs
• (305) 752-2333
STEAKHOUSE/AMERICAN

12/20

Damon Runyon, the witty, streetwise New York writer from the 1920s and 1930s, seems an unlikely patron saint for a simple, albeit convivial, shopping-center restaurant in Florida. No downtown lowlifes hang out here, and there's certainly no *Guys and Dolls* atmosphere around the popular bar. One look at the interior will confirm that this is Florida, not Broadway and 51st: plastic banquettes, lots of blond wood, and walls festooned with photos of Runyon and the sort of old-time movie stars he might have been pals with. But never mind the antiseptic decor—the food is terrific and free of pretense. Several kinds of steak are served just one way: exactly to your order. A chart on the menu outlines the various gradations in internal temperatures. These distinctions—red cool center (rare), red warm center (medium)—are pretty much ignored at many restaurants, but here they're given the kind of respect that a church accords the Ten Commandments. The chefs' jobs are made easier by the meat, which is of exceptionally high quality. All the usual steak cuts are available (porterhouse, filet mignon, New York strip), along with succulent, thick lamb chops and a two-inch-thick slab of roast beef free of that canned-beef-broth flavor found elsewhere. The seafood dishes receive the same deft treatment on the grill as the meat; we're particularly fond of the swordfish. Unfortunately, most of the accompaniments don't do the meat justice. Yorkshire pudding turned out to be a dry, lifeless popover, onion rings were doughy, and escargots were greasy. Neither are the desserts up to par, which is particularly disappointing at a steakhouse. Purchased from commercial bakeries, most of them are bland in both flavor and texture. The wine list also needs work, with its run-of-the-mill selections and too-young reds. Despite these shortcomings, Runyon's is still the best place in Broward County for a steak. Dinner for two, with wine, will cost $75 to $90.

Open Mon.-Thurs. 11 a.m.-3 p.m. & 4 p.m.-10:30 p.m., Fri. 11 a.m.-3 p.m. & 4 p.m.-11:30 p.m., Sat. 4 p.m.-11:30 p.m. All major cards.

Santa Lucia
602 E. Las Olas Blvd., Fort Lauderdale
• (305) 525-9530
ITALIAN

Santa Lucia occupies one of the simpler storefronts along Fort Lauderdale's historic and trendy Las Olas Boulevard. It's simple inside as well, but homey rather than homely: a single square dining room, painted in pale pastels and filled with a dozen well-spaced tables. The look is as clean and fresh as the cooking of owner/chef Angelo Ciampa. He follows tradition, he says, staying true to "*la cucina genuina.*" To a Neapolitan like Ciampa, genuine cooking means interfering as little as possible with natural flavors. Grilled calamari gets just a dab of olive oil, as do deftly roasted peppers with Provolone—no oil-drenched appetizers here. Among pastas, one of the best is macaroni "zi Mimi," dressed with olive oil, fresh tomatoes, basil and blackened (but not burned) garlic. For those who associate southern Italy with spaghetti drowning in tomato sauce, Santa Lucia is a refreshing reminder that Naples is, above all else, a seaport. Fish dishes play a big part in the menu, but the best are on listed on the blackboard—Ciampa goes to the Fort Lauderdale docks every morning and proudly displays his finds in a glass case near the kitchen. The marvelous whole grilled yellowtail snapper with lemon and olive oil unites the best of Florida and Italy. Other dependable selections include grouper with capers, veal scaloppine with Gorgonzola and the herb-marinated veal chop.

Desserts, such as heady sponge cake with chocolate and orange liqueur, delicate cannoli and zabaglione cake, are all tasty. The informal, dependable service is punctuated on occasion by one of Ciampa's short, fiery flashes of anger with recalcitrant ingredients or staff members. That's not what keeps the atmosphere so inviting, however—it's the affable genuineness of the cooking, setting and service. Dinner with wine runs $90 for two.
Open nightly 6 p.m.-10:30 p.m. All major cards.

Studio One Café
2447 E. Sunrise Blvd., Fort Lauderdale
• (305) 565-2052
FRENCH

11/20

Authentic French-style bistros are about as common these days as tomatoes that taste like tomatoes, but every now and then the genuine article turns up. So don't let the silly nightclubby name or the banal decor fool you—Studio One has the soul of a Parisian neighborhood bistro. From a simple piece of apple tart with an espresso to a multicourse meal with wine, this place will feed you well, amiably and affordably. The importers are French-born Laurent Tasci and his American wife, Carole, who met in Paris, where he studied cooking. In proper bistro style, Carole manages the front of the house, supervising an efficient serving staff, and Laurent oversees the bustle in the rear, turning out an eclectic collection of dishes, which are displayed on an easel-menu that is carried from table to table. The Tascis came to Florida via the French West Indies (where Laurent apprenticed as a chef), but you'd never know it from the setting—there isn't a hint of island charm in the sterile, disco-contemporary decor, notable mainly for the mirrors covering the walls. His island stint, however, is evident in the menu, which has considerable personality. He honors the bistro with such beloved starters as pâté and escargots, but the most exciting dishes keep his background in clear focus. Particularly successful first courses are the gumbolike stew of vegetables, shrimp, fish and conch and the richly flavorful red-pepper bisque, with a light briskness that does wonders to stimulate the appetite. The entrée list includes a sprinkling of conservative standards, from well-prepared lamb chops to rabbit in a savory mustard-cream sauce, but we prefer the more innovative dishes, like the blackened duck with a caramelized vanilla sauce. Though tasty, the desserts aren't memorable. Best of all are the prices: fixed-price menus, which include an appetizer, salad, entrée and dessert, range from $13.95 to $15.95, and the wine list is similarly affordable (though uncomfortably small). Two can have a most enjoyable dinner, including wine, for $50 to $60.
Open Mon.-Fri. 11:30 a.m.-2:30 p.m. & 6 p.m.-10:30 p.m., Sat. 6 p.m.-10:30 p.m. All major cards.

Victoria Park

900 N.E. 20th Ave.,
Fort Lauderdale
• (305) 764-6868
FRENCH/CARIBBEAN

Victoria Park's name might have you expecting an English garden cottage, but in fact it's a tropical-French place named for a small street nearby. Just off one of Fort Lauderdale's busiest intersections, which is populated primarily by pizza-and-pasta purveyors, this is an island of French Caribbean calm in the big city. The exterior is adorned with island colors: pink, white, coral and azure, with shutters on the windows and a welcoming sign above the door. Inside, Haitian paintings cover the walls, and foliage fills the bright pink-and-white room. The sense of soothing island refinement comes easily: owner/chef Patrick Farnault owned a restaurant in Martinique for several years, and that influence remains strong in his cooking. His dishes are as fresh to the eye as they are to the taste buds. Linguine comes topped with mussels, scallops, shiitake mushrooms and a dash of cream. Duck is cooked with raspberry vinegar and fresh ginger and poured over mixed greens. Seafood dishes are the strongest—like the Creole-style dolphin filet, made with a curious but heavenly sauce of tomatoes, white wine, dill, cilantro and ginger—but there are some good meat offerings as well, including calf's liver with red wine and herbs and grilled duck with a light sesame sauce. Although tasty, the fruit tarts and profiteroles that make up the dessert roster have less of a Caribbean touch than the rest of the cuisine. The short wine list is eclectic and well priced. Victoria Park is the quintessential neighborhood restaurant, alive with with good food and friendly, relaxed service. Dinner for two, with wine, will cost about $75.

Open Mon.-Sat. 5:30 p.m.-10:30 p.m. Cards: AE, MC, V.

QUICK BITES

Brasserie Max

Fashion Mall,
321 N. University Blvd.,
Plantation
• (305) 424-8000

A couple of years ago, Florida restaurant maven Dennis Max decided that the action had left trendy upscale places for trendy downscale places that catered to the whole family. Was he right? Well, Brasserie Max, his prototype, is crowded all the time, and he has four spinoffs in other locations. The key to this restaurant's success is its location (in Fashion Mall, one of Broward County's most fashionable shopping centers), its enticing, well-prepared menu and its reasonable prices. Full-size entrées are available, but most diners just pile on the appetizers and smaller dishes: oak-grilled pizza, fried Gulf snapper fingers (actually fish sticks, but much tastier than that bready cafeteria fare of our childhood), fried-chicken Cobb salad, grilled three-cheese sandwich with tomato and bacon. Food is served quickly, but if you want to linger, you'll be happy to delve into the good wine list, which includes eight to ten selections poured by the

glass. With wine by the glass, two can dine here for $35 to $50.
Open Sun.-Thurs. 10:30 a.m.-10 p.m., Fri.-Sat. 10:30 a.m.-11 p.m. Cards: AE, MC, V.

Café Grazia!
3850 N. Federal Hwy.,
Lighthouse Point
• (305) 942-7206

In some ways, Café Grazia! is the country cousin of the urban-chic Café Arugula five blocks south (*see* page 131). Dick Cingolani is the owner and executive chef of both places, but Grazia was designed for the modern family on the run—it's fast, it's hearty and it's modestly priced. An oak grill kicks out perfectly cooked fish dishes for less than $10, pastas are served in half portions ($4.25), service is quick and kids are welcome. Extras include a short but well-chosen wine list and excellent desserts. Factor in friendly, efficient service and it's no wonder this is one of the most popular restaurants in north Broward County. Dinner for two, including wine, runs about $45.
Open Mon.-Thurs. 11:30 a.m.-2:30 p.m. & 5 p.m.-10 p.m., Fri. 11:30 a.m.-2:30 p.m. & 5 p.m.-11 p.m., Sat. 5 p.m.-11 p.m., Sun. 5 p.m.-10 p.m. Cards: AE, MC, V.

Duffy's Diner
925 E. Cypress Creek Rd.,
Fort Lauderdale
• (305) 491-3584

Duffy's is passé, and proud of it. Booths ring the single dining room, and tables fill the middle, though they aren't big enough to hold all the plates—this place follows the old American rule of thumb that if the food is good, more of it is even better. And the food is indeed good: waffles as light as feathers, fluffy omelets, filling sandwiches. There's nothing fancy about this retro diner fare, just honest, satisfying tastes and low prices. Duffy's is the best spot around for a home-cooked breakfast or lunch, when away from home. Lunch for two runs about $10.
Open Mon.-Fri. 6:30 a.m.-4 p.m., Sat. 6:30 a.m.-2 p.m., Sun. 7 a.m.-1 p.m. No cards.

Saigon Oriental Restaurant
2031 Hollywood Blvd.,
Hollywood
• (305) 923-9256

With a decor primarily composed of darkly varnished wood, this comfortable eatery in the historic section of Hollywood resembles a corner tavern much more than an Asian restaurant. The food quickly corrects that impression—chef Hung Quoc Tao and his staff turn out some of the best Vietnamese food in Florida. The best entrées are the chicken with fish sauce and shredded ginger and any of the several Vietnamese curries. Given advance notice, the owners will make any of several marvelous special dishes, including grilled shrimp wrapped in sugar cane and Florida blue crab cooked in garlic butter. This is definitely one of Hollywood's hidden stars. And the price can't be beat: a four-course dinner for two, excluding drinks, is only $20.
Open Mon.-Fri. 11 a.m.-2 p.m. & 5 p.m.-11 p.m., Sat.-Sun. 5 p.m.-11 p.m. All major cards.

HOTELS

Luxury (From $150)

Diplomat Resort and Country Club
3515 S. Ocean Dr.,
Hollywood 33019
• (305) 457-8111
Fax (305) 458-2077

The Diplomat is your classic meeting resort, offering the throngs plenty of seaside allure set in a world all its own. (It's a good thing too, because the outlying city of Hollywood doesn't have a whole lot to offer). But with 1,000 guest rooms, two ballrooms, seven restaurants, six bars and a supper club, who needs the outside world? The star of the hotel's public area is its creatively designed swimming pool, where cascading waterfalls, caves and tunnels are interrupted only by poolside cocktail service. Situated along a 1,400-square-foot patch of sandy beach, the Diplomat offers guests plenty of water sports as well. There's an eighteen-hole golf course, twelve tennis courts and a private marina. Ask for one of the 69 recently refurbished suites or lanai rooms for a little something extra.
Singles, doubles & triples: $150-$200. Packages available.

Marriott Harbor Beach Resort
3030 Holiday Dr.,
Fort Lauderdale 33316
• (305) 525-4000
Fax (305) 766-6152

If you want to step from your room to wiggle your toes in the sand, this is the spot to stay. Situated on sixteen acres of oceanfront property, the Harbor Beach is also a full-service beach resort. Although it doesn't offer its own golf facilities, reciprocal privileges at the nearby Bonaventure Country Club allow guests to play at two eighteen-hole championship golf courses at will. There's a beautiful 8,000-square-foot swimming pool; 50 beachfront cabanas (featuring chaise lounges, showers and wet bars) provide welcome respite from a day under the insistent Fort Lauderdale sun. You won't be disappointed with the rooms, either, because they are spacious, decorated in cool colors to ward off the tropical clime, and offer an overflowing amenities basket. Don't forget the ocean view.
Singles & doubles: $150-$195.

Pier 66 Resort & Marina
2301 S.W. 17th St. Cswy.,
Fort Lauderdale 33316
• (305) 525-6666
Fax (305) 728-3551

From the overpopulated 17th Street Causeway, Pier 66 doesn't look like much. Looks can be deceiving. Actually taking up its own little 22-acre island jutting into the Intracoastal Waterway, the recently renovated Pier 66 is more like an island retreat than a downtown area Gold Coast resort. On top of its standard guest rooms, the hotel offers 42 executive guest rooms and eight two-bedroom designer suites, each with its own Jacuzzi, bar and stereo system. Why not splurge a little? The lushly landscaped island resort always compels us to do so. There's a poolside bar and grill and a 40-person hydro-therapy pool for evening relaxation, and a newly completed spa featuring all of the expected beauty and fitness treatments. A shuttle takes

guests to the beach (located just across the causeway), as well as to golf facilities and shopping complexes.
Singles & doubles: $160-$220.

Moderate (From $100)

Hollywood Beach Hilton
4000 S. Ocean Dr.,
Hollywood 33019
• (305) 458-1900
Fax (305) 458-7222

Don't let the name deceive you: the Hollywood Beach Hilton is actually across the street from the beaches. It is, admittedly, located overlooking the Intracoastal Waterway, and for water-sports enthusiasts, there are plenty of yachts to be chartered and windsurfers to be rented within a very reasonable proximity. The Hilton tends to attract the local meeting-and-lunching crowd as much as it does guests in its 306 rooms and suites. The Tower Floor accommodations are worth the extra couple of dollars, offering great views, turndown service and a private lounge.
Singles & doubles: $105-$180; concierge level: $115-$195.

Marriott Hotel & Marina
1881 S.E. 17th St.,
Fort Lauderdale 33316
• (305) 463-4000
Fax (305) 527-6705

The single biggest difference between the Marriott Hotel & Marina and Marriott Harbor Beach—just a stone's throw away from one another—is that the former overlooks the Intracoastal Waterway; the latter, the beach. The Hotel & Marina happily shuttles guests to the beach, so its Intracoastal location isn't necessarily a negative, especially for boaters who like the idea of having a rental fleet at their fingertips. The hotel appeals to business groups as readily as it does to individuals. Its cool, spacious rooms and airy public areas beckon to visitors who have spent an active day in the sun.
Singles & doubles: $120-$175.

Palm Aire Spa Resort & Country Club
2501 Palm Aire Dr. North,
Fort Lauderdale 33069
• (305) 972-3300
Fax (305) 968-2744

Well, Robin Leach likes it. (Palm Aire has made his top-ten list of the world's best spa resorts for the past couple of years). The resort is also popular with Liz Taylor, Farrah Fawcett, Paul Newman, Joanne Woodward and Liza Minnelli, all of whom have visited recently. The twenty-year-old, 700-acre spa and resort recently celebrated its twentieth anniversary to the tune of an $8 million renovation. Palm Aire stresses lifestyle changes for all of its guests, offering lectures and courses on nutrition, stress management and fitness as part of its program. Take-home souvenirs include a spa wardrobe, cookbooks and a maintenance video. Treatments focus on the therapeutic uses of baths, aromatherapy (facial massage with natural oils) and Shiatsu, Swedish and reflexology-style massage. On top of the European-style spa itself, the resort sports no less than five eighteen-hole golf courses, a country club, a racquet club and a delightful 191-room hotel.
Singles & doubles: $115-$175.

Sheraton Design Center

1825 Griffin Rd.,
Dania 22004
• (305) 920-3500
Fax (305) 920-3571

Occasionally, the Design Center of the Americas opens its four floors of magnificent, permanent showrooms to the public. (Generally, admittance is granted to designers only). That's the time to stay at the twelve-story Sheraton Design Center, whose covered walkway links the hotel with the Design Center's front door. Not surprisingly, the hotel itself is a design triumph, with an atrium lobby decorated in earth tones, wood, brass and marble, with a demure reflecting pool at the center of it all. Accommodations include 250 guest rooms and seven deluxe suites; the rooms are dressed up in art deco, with lots of smoky pinks and mauves dappling the scenery. Besides the Design Center and the Dania Jai Alai fronton (an arena where the game is played), there's not too much going on in this section of town. You can browse leisurely through the many antique shops down the street, or make a trip to the beaches, only two-and-a-half miles to the east.

Singles & doubles: $95-$145; suites: $225-$375.

Practical (Under $100)

Bahia Cabana Beach Resort

3001 Harbor Dr.,
Fort Lauderdale 33316
• (305) 524-1555
Fax (305) 764-5951

Bahia Cabana is nothing if not festive. Not at all what those in search of a quiet waterfront retreat might have in mind, the hotel loves to show off its "largest Jacuzzi on the beach" and a raucous beach bar that boating magazines consistently rank among the world's rowdiest. Characterized by its active marina, the hotel is family-owned—one of the last vestiges of family ownership in this stretch of mirror-and-glass hotels and sprawling chain resorts. Increasingly, this hotel has attracted a European crowd, lending a cosmopolitan twist to poolside chit chat. The staff is enthusiastic and the rooms adequate. Those rooms that overlook the marina are not for early-to-bed, early-to-rise types; if you want protection from the continuous hustle and bustle below, be sure to request a room on the other side of the hotel.

Singles & doubles: $85-$225. Winter packages available.

Bahia Mar Resort & Yachting Center

801 Seabreeze Blvd.,
Fort Lauderdale 33316
• (305) 764-2233
Fax (305) 764-2233

Almost three decades old, the Bahia Mar is part of Fort Lauderdale's old guard of hotels tucked within the hotel stretch between Port Everglades and downtown Fort Lauderdale. Sandwiched between the New River and the Atlantic Ocean, the resort's marina is extensive, offering an abundance of sailing, diving and ocean-fishing charters daily. The hotel building is rather nondescript, as are the 291 rooms and seven suites. The prices, though, are very competitive with the other hotels populating Seabreeze Boulevard.

Singles & doubles: $85-$145.

GOLD COAST Fort Lauderdale – Hotels

Embassy Suites–17th St. Causeway
1100 S.E. 17th St.,
Fort Lauderdale 33316
• (305) 527-2700
Fax (305) 772-5490

Although the Embassy Suites hotel is conveniently located near Ocean World, the marinas and many of the other waterfront attractions of south Fort Lauderdale, it can't escape the fact that it's also situated on just one more overpopulated commercial South Florida boulevard. There are plenty of gas stations, shopping complexes and frozen-yogurt shops in the immediate vicinity. The relatively new property consists entirely of suites, each one designed to look exactly like the others, in pastel hues, with perfectly coordinated appointments. This might be a comfort to some, but it's a disappointment to those of us in search of a bit of character.
Single & double suites: $95-$145.

Guest Quarters Suite Hotel
2670 Sunrise Blvd.,
Fort Lauderdale 33304
• (305) 565-3800
Fax (305) 561-0387

Despite the uniform decor of its suites, Guest Quarters is really a nice, centrally located, friendly hotel option. Located right in the heart of the downtown Fort Lauderdale action (you can watch the kids cruising the famous "Strip" from your room if you get one high enough), Guest Quarters is also adjacent to the sprawling Galleria Mall and just about two blocks away from the beach. The hotel boasts an exceptionally amiable management and staff; each suite features a living room, dining area, mini-bar, kitchen, balcony and two color TVs.
Single & double suites: $88-$148.

Hollywood Beach Resort Hotel
2501 N. Ocean Dr.,
Hollywood 33019
• (305) 921-0990
Fax (305) 920-9480

The sprawling Hollywood Beach Resort Hotel looks like something you might find at Walt Disney World: it's all whim, whimsy and nostalgia back to some former era that may well never have existed. Actually, the structure overtook that of a dilapidated art-deco-style hotel that once loomed over the beachfront here. Not much went on in this neck of the woods until the hotel, shopping and entertainment complex overlooking the festive Hollywood Beach Boardwalk sprang up a few years back. The hotel envelops the busy shopping center, which is packed with restaurants, movie theaters and boutiques. It's a fifteen-minute drive to Fort Lauderdale's downtown attractions, so if you stay here, you'll need some transportation.
Singles & doubles: $62-$152.

Inverrary Hotel & Conference Resort
3501 Inverrary Blvd.,
Fort Lauderdale 33319
• (305) 485-0500
Fax (305) 733-6534

The story goes that Jackie Gleason moved his television series to South Florida—lock, stock and barrel—for one reason: golf. The Great One could play here all year long, and Inverrary gained national prominence when it became the site of his annual Inverrary Golf Classic Tournament for many years to come. What was once a Hilton franchise with no real resort amenities has become, with the completion of nearly $4 million in renovations, a first-class golf resort. For duffers, the place

can't be beat. Every one of its 198 deluxe balcony guest rooms overlook the three rolling courses of Inverrary. Throw in a couple of extra bucks for "Club Level" accommodations and you'll get a Continental breakfast, wine and cheese in the evening and a host of in-room amenities—including private valet service. The extensive fitness facilities at the sprawling resort also include 30 Har-Tru tennis courts, swimming pools, croquet, volleyball, badminton, horseshoes and a jogging track. Inverrary tends to appeal to an upscale, older crowd—particularly during the high season—but a variety of packages allow the wallet-conscious golfer to stay here, too.
Singles & doubles: $84-$208. Packages available.

Riverside Hotel
620 Las Olas Blvd.,
Fort Lauderdale 33301
• (305) 467-0671
Fax (305) 462-2148

In greater Fort Lauderdale—where hyperbole seems to be the battle cry in both form and content—the Riverside Hotel is absolutely peerless. It is, in fact, one of the few intimate, full-service downtown hotels in all of Florida. The recently renovated, 50-something-year-old hotel, reigns like an understated princess over stylish Las Olas Boulevard, Fort Lauderdale's first road to the beach back in the 1930s boom years. In those days, suntans were for the underprivileged, and hotels weren't built on the beach itself, but slightly inland. The legacy of that idea thrives on the shady grounds of the Riverfront Hotel, which overlooks the New River with lush foliage and a subdued beach bar. There are two wings and a total of 116 rooms, but be sure to ask for one of the six larger, recently refurbished rooms featuring bronzed mirrors on the ceilings, draped bedposts and Queen Anne armchairs. If you're not put off by the original tile floors and faulty air-conditioning in some of the hallways (it seems the bulk of renovation dollars has been reserved for the sleeping rooms), the romantic Riverside is the best luxury hotel value in Greater Fort Lauderdale.
Singles & doubles $70-$75.

Sheraton Bonaventure Resort and Spa
250 Racquet Club Rd.,
Fort Lauderdale 33326
• (305) 389-3300
Fax (305) 384-1416

Because it is so enormous—featuring two championship golf courses, five freshwater pools, an artificially constructed waterfall and even a rain forest—it's hard to believe that the Sheraton Bonaventure is so well located. A short drive north from Fort Lauderdale's airport, the spa seems a world away from the bustle of the Gold Coast. The Bonaventure spa consistently ranks among the best in the world, with separate facilities for men and women and no less than 24 different fitness programs prescribed shortly after check-in. The Bonaventure prides itself on personalized attention, which begins at the front desk and carries through to the six restaurants, five boutiques and all of the lovely

GOLD COAST Fort Lauderdale – Hotels

amenities offered during your stay.
Singles & doubles: $85-$200; suites: $200-$400. Packages available.

Sheraton-Yankee Clipper Beach Resort
1140 Seabreeze Ave.,
Fort Lauderdale 33316
• (305) 524-5551
Fax (305) 523-5376

In 1982, the Sheraton brought 151 more nondescript beachfront rooms to the shores of Fort Lauderdale. The difference between this one and all the others, however, is that the Sheraton-Yankee Clipper Beach Resort is on the right side of the tracks, offering rooms that open out directly onto an overpopulated beach. The folks here offer up that island feeling night and day with plenty of tropical fare, including poolside barbecue parties, limbo lessons and lounges called the "Port Bar" and the "Wreck Bar," the latter of which attempts to re-create the atmosphere of a sunken Spanish galleon. Just relax and breathe, and order what any hearty Spanish sailor would order.
Singles & doubles: $55-$130; suites $135-$325.

Sheraton-Yankee Trader Resort
321 N. Atlantic Blvd.,
Fort Lauderdale 33304
• (305) 467-1111
Fax (305) 462-2342

The Sheraton-Yankee Trader Resort, the more northern of the two beachfront Sheratons that have been confused by visitors to Fort Lauderdale since the early 1970s, could use a little updating. Even its brochure, which features a model in gold lamé whooping it up with a disco date in the "Staying Alive" tradition, smacks of outdatedness. It is, admittedly, located in the thick of the Fort Lauderdale action; the only thing separating it from the beach is the famous "Strip." There is plenty to do on the property, too, with tennis courts, bars, restaurants, a disco and a Broadway-style dinner theater on the grounds. The hotel has long been a popular favorite among conventioneers, which individual guests might find more daunting than the passé decor.
Singles, doubles & triples: $65-$140.

Traders Ocean Resort
1600 S. Ocean Blvd.,
Pompano Beach 33062
• (305) 941-8400
Fax (305) 941-1024

Traders Pompano Beach locale offers an entirely separate Greater Fort Lauderdale experience. Just north of downtown, Traders is an unassuming little hotel which nonetheless offers 200 feet of beachfront nirvana, satisfactory rooms, some of them with ocean views, plus efficiency apartments and suites and a casual restaurant and lounge. If you want to enjoy the beach and standard amenities, plus save a few bucks by cooking in your room, Traders is more than adequate.
Singles & doubles: $54-$99.

NIGHTLIFE

Bars

Burt & Jack's
Berth 23,
Port Everglades,
Fort Lauderdale
• (305) 522-5225

Yes, the Burt of this bar is the one and only Burt Reynolds. The actor was raised in the nearby town of Jupiter, and has a ranch there today. As for Jack, we don't know who he is, other than that he's some guy named Jack Jackson. We have never run into either Burt or Jack here, (although admittedly we wouldn't know Mr. Jackson if we fell over him). With its picture-perfect address at the mouth of Port Everglades, it's a lovely spot from which to watch the mega-ships cruise in and out of port.
Open Sun.-Thurs. 4:30 p.m.-11 p.m., Fri.-Sat. 4:30 p.m.-midnight. No cover. All major cards.

Shooters Waterfront Café USA
3033 N.E. 32nd Ave.,
Fort Lauderdale
• (305) 566-2855

If you have a yen to have your boat docked by a valet, this is the place for you. (If you arrive by car, the service is also available). There's a dockside patio bar and restaurant; the requisite Fort Lauderdale "hot bod" contest is held poolside on Saturday nights. Overlooking the Intracoastal Waterway (at Oakland Park Boulevard), Shooters enjoys what is probably the best, and certainly most obvious, address in the city for waterfront action.
Open daily 11:30 a.m.-2 a.m. No cover. All major cards.

Cabarets

Molokai Bar and Lounge
3599 N. Federal Hwy.,
Fort Lauderdale
• (305) 563-3272

You'll have to spring for dinner to experience the full-scale famous Islanders Revue (whose beautiful "maidens," of partially clothed calendar fame, and agile "warriors" perform native dances from the South Pacific). The Molokai Bar is an equally Polynesian spot where you can toss down tropical drinks (we were unable to get any details on the bar's famous "Mystery Drink"), served by sarong-clad maidens, and enjoy some music.
Open Mon.-Thurs. 5 p.m.-1 a.m, Sat.-Sun. 5 p.m.-2 a.m. Cover $7.95. Cards: AE, MC, V.

Comedy

The Comic Strip
1432 N. Federal Hwy.,
Fort Lauderdale
• (305) 565-8887

It began as New York City in the 1970s, but a sister Comic Strip didn't arrive in Fort Lauderdale until 1980. The club that helped launch the careers of stand-up greats including Eddie Murphy and Joe Piscopo often hosts comedy superstars today. A tired looking little venue at a none too assuming address

nonetheless offers great comics and good service.
Shows Sun.-Fri. 9:30 p.m., Sat. 8:30 p.m. & 11 p.m. Cover $7-$10 plus a 2-drink minimum. Cards: AE, MC, V.

Dance Clubs

City Limits
2520 S. Miami Rd.,
Fort Lauderdale
• (305) 524-7827

Because Fort Lauderdale has a very strict rule forcing its nightspots to close up shop by 2 a.m., City Limits (whose name aptly describes its locale) is where those nightcrawlers go who don't want the night to end. A sort of Florida version of a 1970s disco in *Saturday Night Fever* (it looks as if it had been decorated at around the time the film was made), City Limits is a great place to watch the spill-over crowd—from distinctly different Broward County bars—congregate to while away the night.
Open Mon.-Thurs. 5 p.m.-4 a.m., Fri.-Sat. 5 p.m.-6 a.m. Cover $5. Cards: AE, MC, V.

DoDa's American Country Saloon Dancehall
700 S. State Rd. 7,
Fort Lauderdale
• (305) 792-6200

It's not possible to have this much down-home country fun between here and Mickey Gilley's. It's a little-known fact that Florida is the nation's third most prolific cattle-producing state, but it's true—there are plenty of bona fide cowboys in this neck of the woods. DoDa's spit-polished dance floor looks more like a roller rink as couples glide by doing the two-step like the pros. Also on the premises is the Tepee Western Wear Boutique—in case your forgot your spurs.
Open Mon.-Tues. 5 p.m.-2 a.m., Wed.-Sat. 5 p.m.-4 a.m.; dance lessons Mon.-Thurs. 7:30 p.m.-9 p.m. Cover $3.50 Fri.-Sat. after 8:30 p.m. All major cards.

Dragon Club
401 N. Federal Hwy.,
Deerfield Beach
• (407) 360-9929

Looks like somebody's got it in for the Dragon Club's tipsy beautiful people: recently, dozens of police cars lined the roads surrounding the club at closing to impose alcohol-level tests on those driving Porsches, BMWs and other suspicious makes and models. Nevertheless, the dragons and gargoyles that share the place with clubgoers (helping to create what is, hands down, the oddest club decor in South Florida) continue to lord over the hottest club in Deerfield Beach.
Open Sun.-Thurs. 9 p.m.-3 a.m., Fri.-Sat. 10 p.m.-4 a.m. Cover $5. All major cards.

Joseph's
3200 E. Oakland Park Blvd.,
Fort Lauderdale
• (305) 565-5866

First it was opened, then it was closed, then it was opened again. We can't make any promises, but if Joseph's is in business during your visit to Fort Lauderdale, you'll find plenty of the chrome and glass and mauve tones that local architects seem to thrive on in these parts. Inside, there are six bars and four dance floors—and plenty of attitude.
Open daily 11:30 a.m.-2 a.m. Cover $5. All major cards.

Squeeze Progressive Danceteria
2 S. New River Dr.,
Fort Lauderdale
• (305) 522-2151

We don't know which is more surreal: the interior of Squeeze (which closely resembles Mr. Toad's Wild Ride, with various fluorescent body parts dangling from the ceiling) or the million-dollar Hatteras yacht dealership just across the street. Deejays here air such progressive groups as The Lords of Acid, Joined at the Head and 1,000 Homo DJs. Need we say more?
Open Mon.-Thurs. 5 p.m.-1 a.m., Fri.-Sat. 5 p.m.-2 a.m. Cover $5. Cards: AE, MC, V.

Music Clubs

The Button South
100 Ansin Blvd.,
Hallandale
• (305) 454-0001

The ambience of this rock-and-roll music club depends entirely on the rowdiness of the band playing. Each night of the week is devoted to a musical theme, from "Thunder Thursday," to "Guitar for the Practicing Musician" shows. Things get a little out of control when WSHE, a local rock station, broadcasts from the place, and as long as you can ignore the odious Ladies Night and $100 "Hot Legs" contests, you'll have some fun. Two-for-one drinks are offered every night from 8 to 10.
Open daily 8 p.m.-6 a.m. No cover. Cards: AE, MC, V.

Café 66
Pier 66 Resort & Marina,
301 S.E. 17th St. Causeway,
Fort Lauderdale
• (305) 525-6666

Recording artist Donna Allen keeps them coming to Café 66, with live performances of original soul music and dance tunes. Allen also hosts a "Midnight Revue," with dance contests and prizes on the weekends. You can sit, drink in hand, and gaze upon the million-dollar yachts docked in the marina outside. All around, a lively ambience and a truly adult Fort Lauderdale experience, which is sometimes hard to come by here in spring break territory.
Open daily 5 p.m.- 2 a.m. Shows Wed.-Sun. 9:30 p.m.-2 a.m. Midnight Revue nightly at midnight. Cover $5. All major cards.

Docksider's Bar & Grille
Guest Quarters Suite Hotel,
2670 E. Sunrise Blvd.,
Fort Lauderdale
• (305) 565-3800

Docksider's guest duo, "Wooden Ships" (named for the Crosby, Stills, Nash and Young song of the same name), lends a mellow ambience to the waterfront bar with an even-tempered acoustic and strings sound. Docksider's is a lovely place to grab a cocktail and watch as the sun goes down.
Open daily 5 p.m.-midnight., Fri.-Sat. 8 p.m.-2 a.m. Show Fri.-Sat. 8 pm.-midnight. No cover. All major cards.

Summers
219 S. Atlantic Blvd.,
Fort Lauderdale
• (305) 462-8978

More of an indoor/outdoor concert venue than a bar, Summers hosts a variety of local and national bands, with music ranging from jazz to hard rock. We could do without the South Florida imperative of the daily "Thong Bikini" contest, but when you relax poolside with a cool drink in hand, you won't fret.
Open daily 2 p.m.-2 a.m. Shows daily 2 p.m.-6 p.m. (poolside); 9 p.m-2 a.m. (inside). Concert tickets $6-$12. Cards: AE, MC, V.

SHOPS

Clothes & Jewelry

Alper Furs
801 E. Las Olas Blvd.,
Fort Lauderdale
• (305) 525-5241

Don't worry—it probably wouldn't occur to the typical Fort Lauderdale type to throw red paint your way. Florida's exclusive distributor of Black Diamond Ranch Mink, the most exclusive fur shop in South Florida, also offers a stylish selection of sable, fox, lynx, beaver and raccoon.
Open Mon.-Sat. 10 a.m.-6 p.m.

Ciro
E. Sunrise Blvd. (at A1A),
Fort Lauderdale
• (305) 563-5444

Diamonds may well be a girl's best friend, but since you can't woo a diamond out of a store with friendship alone, you may find fault with the exclusive prices elsewhere. Consider fakes: Ciro's has a wonderful selection of *faux* diamonds and pearls; and the good news is that even the most elaborate Victorian collar featuring plenty of both shouldn't run you more than $100.
Open Mon.-Sat. 10 a.m.-10 p.m., Sun. 10 a.m.-6 p.m.

The Forgotten Woman
810 E. Las Olas Blvd.,
Fort Lauderdale
• (305) 523-8801

Large-sized women (sizes 14 to 46) will find this *très* elegant shop along *très* elegant Las Olas Boulevard a refreshingly well-stocked designer boutique. An assortment of custom outfits, from sports items to evening wear, is regularly in stock.
Open Mon.-Sat. 10 a.m-6 p.m., Sun. noon-5 p.m.

Maus & Hoffman
800 E. Las Olas Blvd.,
Fort Lauderdale
• (305) 463-1472

South Florida's most exclusive shopping boulevard (after Palm Beach's Worth Avenue) wouldn't be complete without a branch of Maus & Hoffman, the preppy men's store vending plenty of Oxxford Tailored suits and sport coats. There is also plenty of cashmere and corduroy to bring home to more appropriate climes, plus a selection of women's tailored items.
Open Mon.-Sat. 10 a.m.-6 p.m, Sun. noon-5 p.m.

Moda Mario
1301 E. Las Olas Blvd.,
Fort Lauderdale
• (305) 467-3258

For the continental man, there is plenty of Italian merchandise and other Euro-garb, as well as plenty of fawning behavior, on hand at Moda Mario. The fine shop carries its own label, as well as a nice selection of La Matta Leather. An in-house café serves shoppers wine and cheese or cappuccino and pastry.
Open Mon.-Thurs. 10 a.m-8 p.m., Tues.-Wed. & Fri.-Sat. 10 a.m.-6 p.m.

Primadonna
1263 E. Las Olas Blvd.,
Fort Lauderdale
• (305) 525-6632

A little slice of Milan panache in the heart of Fort Lauderdale, Primadonna offers a wonderfully glitzy selection of Italian clothing for women. What neighboring Moda Mario does for men, this place does for women: cappuccino, espresso, pastries,

wine and a wonderful selection of clothes, beginning with its own label. There's also a shoe salon and tailor shop.
Open Mon. & Thurs. 10 a.m.-8 p.m., Tues.-Wed. & Fri.-Sun. 10 a.m.-6 p.m.

Sawgrass Mills
Flamingo Rd. (at Sunrise Blvd.), Plantation
• (305) 846-2350

We're normally wary when we hear "world's largest" anything, but Sawgrass Mills may truly be the world's largest outlet mall, as it claims to be. The cavernous West Broward mall is divided into four separate "streets": Modern Main Street, Mediterranean Main Street, Art Deco Main Street and Caribbean Main Street. Anchors include Marshalls, BrandsMart and a Sears outlet. At designer outlets such as the Ann Taylor Clearance Center, 9 West & Co. Outlet and Luria's Jewelry Exchange, you can often find some excellent buys on irregular, damaged or discontinued items.
Open Mon.-Sat. 10 a.m-10 p.m., Sun. 11 a.m.-7 p.m.

Flea Market

Fort Lauderdale Swap Shop
3291 W. Sunrise Blvd., Fort Lauderdale
• (305) 791-7927

This fancified flea market wants you to check in and never leave. To serve that purpose, there are fifteen restaurants, a movie theater, a merry-go-round and video arcade to keep the kids entertained, a farmer's market and acres of booths filled with new and used merchandise.
Open daily 10 a.m.-9 p.m.

Gifts

The Chemist Shop
817 E. Las Olas Blvd., Fort Lauderdale
• (305) 462-6587

A drugstore and gift shop, this is a great place to shop for souvenirs. Aside from standard drugstore fare, it also features unusual collectibles and gift items from around the world. Most everything is in good taste. You won't have to reckon with shelves full of kitsch (such as mugs and T-shirts decorated with neon "Your Gift from Florida" slogans)—that's all sold along the beachfront.
Open Mon.-Sat. 10 a.m.-6 p.m., Sun. noon-5 p.m.

Home

Gattle's Fine Quality Linens
2426 E. Las Olas Blvd., Fort Lauderdale
• (305) 467-7396

Ever wonder where interior designers find all of that dreamy material that creates a fairy-tale bedroom? They must go to Gattle's. Though the prices are astronomical, the shop carries a full line of Keeco brand bed coverings that will dress up your room to look like a model in an interior-design magazine.
Open Mon.-Sat. 9 a.m.-5:30 p.m.

Sporting Goods

National Football League Alumni Store
4460 N. Federal Hwy., Fort Lauderdale
• (305) 491-4766

Looking for a New York Giants sweatshirt or a Dallas Cowboys helmet? The NFL alumni store offers an unbelievably extensive selection of sportswear, equipment, stadium gear and novelties representing all 28 NGL teams, including the most obvious one: the Miami Dolphins.
Open Mon-Sat. 10 a.m.-6 p.m., Sun. 11 a.m.-4 p.m.

SIGHTS & SPORTS

Amusements

Butterfly World
Tradewinds Park, 600 W. Sample Rd., Coconut Creek
• (305) 977-4400

Butterfly World is one of the most underrated (or just least publicized) of South Florida's attractions. As educational as it is entertaining, the hands-on attraction lets you look on as literally thousands of caterpillars turn into the free-floating butterflies. All the while, Mozart and Haydn are played in the background. This will amaze children and delight adults.
Open Mon.-Sat. 9 a.m.-5 p.m., Sun. noon-5 p.m. Adults $7.50, seniors & children 3-12 $6.

International Swimming Hall of Fame
One Hall of Fame Dr., Fort Lauderdale
• (305) 462-6536

Ever wonder how Fort Lauderdale became the hottest spring break spot in the country? A number of university swim-team coaches discovered the area back in the 1930s, bringing their teams down to train in the clear waters of Greater Fort Lauderdale during spring. Thus, spring break was born, and the International Swimming Hall of Fame aims to teach you all about it—plus a variety of other swimming trivia. There's a historic display of bathing suits, the world's largest aquatic library, personal memorabilia donated by famous swimmers, and a variety of swimming-related works of art on display. At the facility's Olympic-size swimming pool, a variety of competitions and exhibitions is scheduled throughout the year.
Jan.-Dec.: open Mon.-Sat 10 a.m.-5 p.m. Oct.-May: open 11 a.m-4 p.m. Adults $3, children $1.

Ocean World
S.E. 17th St. Cswy., Fort Lauderdale
• (305) 525-6611

Where's Shamu? Don't confuse this marine park with the far superior Sea World (you'll have to go to Orlando to catch that act), but the less assuming Ocean World can also be a lot of fun. There's a dolphin and sea-lion show, a shark moat, alligators and plenty of exotic birds. Children love the petting tanks, where you can feed dolphin and get kissed by a sea lion or two. There's also a cruise boat departing regularly for tours of the Intracoastal Waterway and Port Everglades.
Open daily 10 a.m.-5 p.m.

Seminole Indian Bingo

Sterling Rd. at S.R. 441, Hollywood
• (305) 961-3220

Because the Seminole Indian tribe is technically its own nation, and therefore has immunity from federal gambling regulations, the bingo games held within the confines of the reservation have become a popular high-stakes game open to the public. Over the years, the tribe has paid out more than $100 million in cash prizes; over $35,000 is paid out nightly. Even if you don't play, you simply must watch everybody else having this much fun under such unusual circumstances.
Open nightly 7:15 p.m.-11 p.m. No cards.

Art Museum

Museum of Art
One Las Olas Blvd., Fort Lauderdale
• (305) 525-5500

Unquestionably the most important museum in South Florida, the $7.5 million Museum of Art has a permanent collection of more than 5,000 prints—plus the state's largest collection of Oceanic, West African, pre-Columbian and American Indian art. In an area long on cruise boats and short on any kind of discernible cultural life, that's no small feat. Situated in a beautiful neighborhood along Fort Lauderdale's historic New River, the museum is a must-see.
Open Tues. 11 a.m.-9 p.m., Wed.-Sat. 10 a.m.-5 p.m., Sun. noon-5 p.m. Adults $3.25, seniors $2.75, students $1.25.

Cruises

Anticipation Entertainment Yachts
305 S. Andrews Ave., Fort Lauderdale
• (305) 463-3372

Lots of yachts offer dinner and cocktail cruises along the Intracoastal Waterway, Anticipation does a particularly noteworthy job of it. With two luxury vessels, *Anticipation I* and *Anticipation II*, you can select from a variety of four-hour cruises that include marvelous gourmet dining and an open bar included. There's even a live band on board, lending a distinctly tropical touch to the cruise with everything from Reggae to Jimmy Buffet.
Sailings Mon.-Fri. 9 a.m.-5:30 p.m. & by charter. Cruises start at $49 per person.

Discovery Cruises
Pier 4, Port Everglades, Fort Lauderdale
• (305) 525-7800

If you want to take a Caribbean-style cruise aboard a full-size sailing ship, the *Discovery* is a grand way to do it. Just as if you had signed on for a weekend in the islands, you board the ship and enjoy a full day of buffet meals, a full casino and dancing—and then an afternoon in Freeport, Grand Bahama. We prefer this experience to Miami's zoolike *Seascape,* quite frankly because the crowd on board the *Discovery* tends to be a tad more civilized.
Cruise daily 8 a.m.-midnight. Bahamas cruise from $79; cruises to "nowhere" from $29; dinner cruise from $39.

Florida Princess Cruise Lines

85 Las Olas Circle,
Fort Lauderdale
• (305) 524-2322

Picture yourself and 699 of your closest friends on a luxurious miniature ship for a dinner cruise. A shot rings out. A body is discovered in the sailfish cooler. It's your job to solve the mystery. Employing dozens of local actors, plus a wonderful catering and service staff, *Florida Princess*'s Murder Mystery Dinner Cruises are loads of fun for gourmets, watersports enthusiasts, amateur sleuths and Agatha Christie buffs alike. *Cruise daily 8 a.m.-8 p.m. & by charter.*

Jungle Queen Sightseeing Cruise

801 Seabreeze Blvd.,
Fort Lauderdale
• (305) 462-5596

There are dinner cruises and there are dinner cruises, but the *Jungle Queen*'s all-you-can-eat barbecue and shrimp dinner cruises are nothing less than a bacchanalian feast. Afterward, there's a terrific Vaudeville show, but the highlight of the evening is the sing-along, participation (practically) required! *Sightseeing tours daily 10 a.m. & 2 p.m.; dinner cruises daily 7 p.m. Sightseeing cruise: adults $6.96, children $4.95. Dinner cruise $19.95 per person.*

Paddlewheel Queen

2950 N.E. 32nd Ave.,
Fort Lauderdale
• (305) 564-7659

The neatest thing about the *Paddlewheel Queen* is being in a Mississippi-style riverboat in the middle of Port Everglades, with megaton cruise ships looming over you. The 350-passenger sternwheel replica is a Fort Lauderdale favorite, with its own dining salon, dance floor and lounge. The evening cruises are presented with artfully romantic flair; the narrated daytime cruises give you a wonderful perspective on the "Venice of the Americas" from its own network of mansion-lined waterways. *Lunch cruise daily 1 p.m.-3 p.m.; evening cruise daily 7:30 p.m.-10 p.m. & by charter. Day cruise $6.95, Dinner cruise $26.95.*

Utterly Fantastic Cruises

North Ocean Blvd. at Taft St.,
Fort Lauderdale
• (305) 920-1309

Probably the smallest of the charter boats plying the waters of the Intracoastal for sightseeing forays, *Utterly Fantastic* offers a really personal, intimate experience with just 34 passengers aboard. The daily "Happy Hour" cruise can't be beat—you'll return ready to go for a wild evening in Fort Lauderdale. *Cruises daily 10:30 a.m., 1:30 p.m. & 4 p.m. Cruises by charter daily 7 p.m. & 9 p.m. Adults $7.50, children $5.*

Sports

Bar-B Ranch

4601 S.W. 128th Ave.,
Davie
• (305) 434-6175

In the literally and figuratively western city of Davie, the Bar-B ranch offers personal attention, a well-cared-for stable of horses trained for various skill levels, and acres of woods and trails. *Open Mon.-Sat. 9 a.m.-5 p.m., Sun. 9 a.m.-4:30 p.m. Adults & children $15 per hour.*

Dania Jai-Alai

301 E. Dania Beach Blvd., Dania
• (305) 945-4345

There are some 6,000 seats from which you can watch two players take each other on in the ancient Basque game of jai alai. The action occurs at breakneck speed, and we like to sit at the Clubhouse Restaraunt, perched above it all, and enjoy cocktails and snacks while watching. An ongoing strike (still unresolved at press time) prevents the best of the best players from participating, but for amateur jai alai spectators like ourselves, it's all the same excitement.

Games Tues.-Sat. noon & 7:15 p.m. Orchestra seats $1.50.

Davie-Cooper City Rodeo

S.W. 65th Ave. at Orange Dr., Davie
• (305) 437-8800

Git along little dogies, git along! It just doesn't get much more fun than this. Bareback and bronco riding, steer wrestling, bullriding, bullfighting and calf wrestling, right in the middle of South Florida. (You've got to keep driving west of the hotel scene though, so far in fact, you might feel like you've reached the Everglades). Florida is the third most prolific cattle producing station in the country, so there are lots of bona fide cowboys in residence, and it seems like most of them turn out for the rodeo on Thursday nights. In the new 5,000-seat arena, the city regularly hosts major championship events on the rodeo circuit.

Jackpot rodeo Thurs. 8 p.m. Adults $4, children $2. Championship events scheduled monthly.

Skyrider Para-Sailing

3030 Holiday Dr., Fort Lauderdale
• (305) 462-7245

The difference between Skyrider and some of the other parasailing operations you might see at beachfront hotels is that at Skyrider, you're actually seated in sort of a flying armchair. The chair is big enough for two, which means you can bring a friend along, an ideal arrangement for those of us too afraid to go it alone. Approved by the U.S. Coast Guard, the parachuted aerial chariot is towed into flight behind a 36-foot boat. Once in flight, it gives new meaning to the word sightseeing. You can choose between a dry landing and a water touchdown before you sail away.

Open daily 10 a.m.-dusk. Cost $40 per person.

Theater

Parker Playhouse

707 N.E. 8th St., Fort Lauderdale
• (305) 764-0700

Open from December through April, the Parker Playhouse generally shuns home-grown productions to host imported national touring companies. The fare on stage runs to full-blown productions of shows currently (or formerly) running on Broadway.

Open Mon.-Sat. 10 p.m.-9 p.m., Sun. noon-9 p.m.

Tours

Voyager Sightseeing Train
600 S. Seabreeze Blvd.
Fort Lauderdale
• (305) 463-0401

Local drivers may curse you and the boat you came in on, but the Voyager is a great way to get an overview of all of greater Fort Lauderdale and its attractions. The eighteen-mile trek through residential areas, downtown and Port Everglades will give you a wonderful feel for the lay of the land; you can then choose which attractions you might like to visit.
Tours 10 a.m., 2 p.m. & 4 p.m. Adults $6.50; children 3-11 $3.

Water Taxi
Between 17th St., Commercial Blvd., New River & the 7th Ave. Bridge, Fort Lauderdale
• (305) 565-5507

Let other cities have their submerged subways and crowded metrorails: Fort Lauderdale has Water Taxi service. For the boatless few of us looking to traverse the city and do a little sightseeing along the way, things don't get much better than this between here and Venice. The familiar, green-and-yellow canopied taxis pick up at waterfront stops laid out within the above boundaries, and by special arrangement elsewhere.

PALM BEACH

RESTAURANTS	154
QUICK BITES	165
HOTELS	166
NIGHTLIFE	170
SHOPS	171
SIGHTS & SPORTS	173

RESTAURANTS

Arturo's
6750 N. Federal Hwy.,
Boca Raton
• (407) 997-7373
ITALIAN

10/20

Like so many New Yorkers, Arturo Gismondi headed for Florida as he approached retirement, shutting down his namesake restaurant in the Big Apple and opening up this place. Today, his son Joe runs the show, stalking the dining area in his spotless chef's whites and toque, chatting up the regulars who have made this one of the most popular restaurants in Boca. Unfortunately, a loyal clientele doesn't always promise good cooking, and Arturo's seems to be more about appearances than substance. The surroundings are sumptuous, with elegant chande-

liers illuminating a large, lovingly decorated dining room. Tables are properly spaced, service is cool and correct, and one course after another points to the presence of a visual artist or two in the kitchen. (The chef is Joe's son, also named Arturo.) But whatever their skills in the visual arts, the culinary arts too often elude the kitchen team. Roasted peppers had just the right touch of smokiness, but the stracciatella (chicken and egg-drop soup) was bland and watery. Capellini, a pasta so thin it's almost impossible to cook correctly, came out perfectly al dente, but was drowning in a greasy pesto. The menu has a good selection of fish, but half the time the preparations are tasteless. Veal dishes are the most consistent; we've enjoyed an intensely flavored osso buco and a fine veal chop in several guises. Desserts are tasty but unremarkable. The wine list is as pricey as the menu, though there are a few good choices at manageable prices. Dinner for two, with wine, costs about $110.
Open nightly 5 p.m.-11 p.m. Cards: AE, MC, V.

Baci
344 Plaza Real, Boca Raton
• (407) 362-8500
ITALIAN

11/20

This is as close to an authentic Italian café as you're likely to find in these parts, though the high-tech, black-and-white Italian design is given a Florida twist with a lot of glass and greenery. The food is similarly styled, starting with the appetizing selection of salads (arugula with Gorgonzola, Caesar salad with chicken) and pizzas (in addition to the standards, there are toppings of spinach, shrimp, eggplant, lamb sausage, porcini mushrooms and so on) and going up to the pastas of the day and the risotto, fish and veal entrées. Service is prompt and friendly, and if these appealing flavors inspire you to whip up some Italian goodies at home, you're in luck: the restaurant includes a well-stocked retail pantry. The bar stays open until two every morning. Dinner for two, with wine, ranges from $30 to $50.
Open daily 11:30 a.m.-2:30 p.m. & 5 p.m.-11 p.m. Cards AE, MC, V.

Bice
13 Peruvian Ave., Palm Beach
• (407) 835-1600
ITALIAN

11/20

With U.S. locations in New York, Beverly Hills and now this one in Palm Beach, Bice is going after a big-bucks clientele; it has attracted said clientele so successfully that a Coconut Grove branch (and perhaps others in Florida) will be opened in 1992. Tracing its lineage to Milan, Italy, where the revered original opened in 1926, this sleek, minimalist place (with an interior notable primarily for polished, expensive woods) often gives callers a Worth Avenue address, though in fact the front door faces less-fashionable Peruvian Avenue. The gentle ambiguity of address is a telling clue about this place, where formidable prices are charged for Italian food that is almost, but not quite, first-rate. Appetizers are traditional—prosciutto with melon, carpaccio, grilled vegetables—with a few interesting variations. The beef carpaccio, for example, is matched with warmed tomato, capers and olives. Pastas are also traditional in style, though touched with the occasional pleasant surprise, as with the exquisite duck-filled ravioli with fresh sage and peppers. Fresh gnocchi, on the other hand, swims in enough cream sauce to make a thin paste. We've had flavorful entrées (quail stuffed with veal, duck breast roasted with a honey-balsamic glaze); we've had dull entrées (filet mignon with grapes, New York steak with arugula); and we've had overcooked entrées (broiled salmon with endive and tomato). The dessert selection is larger than the Italian norm, but no better; the orange cake with bittersweet chocolate and the crème brûlée are the most reliable choices. The wine list has a good selection of Italian bottles, albeit at daunting prices. In fact, the cost of dining here—about $200 for two, with wine—would give us pause even if the food was exceptional. With cooking this inconsistent, the prices seem unconscionable.

Open daily noon-3 p.m. & 6 p.m.-10:30 p.m. All major cards.

Café L'Europe
150 Worth Ave., Palm Beach
• (407) 655-4020
CONTINENTAL

Tradition is valued more than trend in Palm Beach, which is why Norbert and Lidia Goldner's low-key, old-style European restaurant fits in so well. That's not to say there's nothing new here—in fact, few kitchens balance tradition and subtle innovation so neatly. Grilled tiger shrimp on a bed of cucumber linguine and fettuccine with lobster, wild mushrooms and asparagus share menu space with such old standbys as snails with garlic butter and lobster bisque. The entrées continue this interplay of old and new, even if the kitchen occasionally goes nuts—as with the salmon encrusted with pistachios and the scallops with pine nuts. Popular standbys that do Café L'Europe's name justice include Wiener Schnitzel, venison with Spätzle and lamb with mustard and herbs. For once in a Continental restaurant, you needn't worry about suffering through tired old recipes prepared with a heavy hand—even the most traditional of dishes receives a fresh, careful treatment. And it's a sign of the chef's virtuosity that he can prepare admirable modern cuisine as well, evidenced by the delicious smoked pheasant with orange, the duck with a cabbage confit and the grilled trout with a leek beurre blanc. Desserts represent rich, decadent central-European tradition at its best, and the wine list is comprehensive. You eat this good food in a large, bright, thoroughly European room—it feels almost like an exceptionally convivial railway station, with its high ceiling and sweeping

CHAMPAGNE

Veuve Clicquot Ponsardin
MAISON FONDÉE EN 1772
REIMS
FRANCE

*"Une seule qualité:
la toute première"*

*"One quality...
the very finest"*

Madame Veuve Clicquot Ponsardin

© 1990 Club Med Sales, Inc.

Omelettes aux tomates, pain au chocolat, omelettes aux fromages, baguettes, butter brioche, omelettes aux champignons, jambon, pommes rissolées, pommes frites, bananas, oranges, apples, papaya, mangos, peaches, pears, cantaloupe, honeydew, pineapple, sausage, bacon, ham, blueberry, strawberry, cranberry and almond muffins, blueberry pancakes, pain au raisin, Swiss, Edam and cottage cheese, Brie, Camembert, crêpes, Belgian waffles, cereal, oatmeal, oeufs Benedictines, French toast, café au lait, hot chocolate, freshly squeezed orange juice, mineral water, spring water, Earl Grey, chamomile, peppermint and herbal tea, and pots of assorted jams.

[And that's only *breakfast*.]

This morning, on dozens of sunswept terraces overlooking dozens of sparkling bays, some very relaxed people are having fresh juice, and anything else they want. After playing in turquoise waters all morning, they'll return for a lunch of French breads, cheeses, salads, grilled chicken and wine. Later, they'll sip creamy piña coladas on a sugar-sand beach. Then, toward sunset, corks will pop, and the sweet aromas of veal Marsala, swordfish, soufflés and ocean breezes will mark the opening of a continental restaurant. For reservations, simply phone your travel agent or 1-800-CLUB MED.

Club Med
The antidote for civilization.

openness. A meal here doesn't come cheap: dinner with a bottle of wine will run most couples $175.
Open Mon.-Sat. 11:30 a.m.-3 p.m. & 6 p.m.-11 p.m., Sun. 6 p.m.-11 p.m. All major cards.

Charley's Crab
456 S. Ocean Blvd.,
Palm Beach
• (407) 659-1500
SEAFOOD

11/20

See review of Charley's Crab in Fort Lauderdale, page 130.

Chuck and Harold's
207 Royal Poinciana Way,
Palm Beach
• (407) 659-1440
AMERICAN

12/20

Chuck and Harold's has the next best thing to a patio overlooking the water: a sidewalk café on one of the most watchable corners in Palm Beach. This engaging spot is everything a good bistro should be. It opens for breakfast coffee and stays open straight through to end-of-evening nightcaps. Those who tire of watching the passing scene can dine in back in the lovely, light-colored atrium with its outdoorsy, patio-style decor (like so many other Palm Beach places). Several wines are poured by the glass, and a long list of light courses is served throughout the day. The food isn't particularly elegant (nor is it cheap), but it's tasty and served with good humor. Chef Michael Forzano recently introduced what he calls "rock cuisine": slabs of granite are heated for two hours, then brought to the table with raw seafood or lamb for diners to cook themselves. It may smack of Tom Sawyer's fence-painting gambit (remember how the clever boy had a friend pay *him* for the "honor" of doing Tom Sawyer's painting chore?), but it's undeniably popular. At lunch, primarily a burger-and-seafood affair, you won't go wrong with the crabcakes, among the best in South Florida, or the top-notch Cobb salad. The crabcakes show up again at dinnertime, when diners nibble on such fashionable appetizers as crispy Southwestern pizza, seared fresh tuna and fried squid. Eminently worthy entrées include the delicious pasta with lobster and goat cheese and the cioppino, an Italian bouillabaisse. On the simpler side are the grilled steaks and several types of fresh-daily local fish, which will be prepared any way you like. Lunch for two, with a glass of wine each, runs about $35; dinner for two, with a bottle of wine, ranges from $70 to $80.
Open Mon.-Thurs. 8 a.m.-midnight, Fri.-Sat. 8 a.m.-1 a.m., Sun. 8 a.m.-11 p.m. Cards: AE, MC, V.

GOLD COAST Palm Beach – Restaurants

La Finestra
171 E. Palmetto Park Rd., Boca Raton
• (407) 392-1838
ITALIAN

12/20

The name of this restaurant (*la finestra* means "window") stands for a couple of things. Its large windows give diners a view of the passing street scene outside, but the thick glass insulates them from the hustle and bustle. Soft pastels, candlelight and large tables provide a cozy warmth, and many nights chamber musicians play with muted propriety. And the kitchen looks outward through a metaphoric window. Antone Pepaj, the proprietor and chef, hails from Yugoslavia, just across the Adriatic from Italy, so it's not surprising that most of his dishes are loving, respectful interpretations of Italian originals, albeit delivered with a distinct accent. Pastas show inventive nuances, from the shredded radicchio in the fettuccine Alfredo to the extra dash of zest the anchovies give the penne putanesca (normally made with tomatoes, black olives, oil, hot peppers, garlic and parsley). Grilled dishes are erratic: we've sampled sepia (a large squid) that had little flavor of smoke or fire, but then we enjoyed a flawless yellowtail filet, savory and juicy. The simple dishes are generally the best, since the chef has the tendency to cross the line from inspiration to waste of time—as with his gluey signature dish, veal with apples and strawberries. On the other hand, the more classic veal chop with wild mushrooms is excellent. Desserts are as erratic as the rest of the cooking, but some are consistent standouts, like the bitter-chocolate cake and lemon-ricotta cheesecake. The reasonably priced wine list boasts several interesting Italian selections not generally found in restaurants. Dinner for two, with wine, costs $120.
Open Mon.-Thurs. 6 p.m.-10 p.m., Fri.-Sat. 6 p.m.-11 p.m. Cards: AE, MC, V.

The Gazebo
4199 N. Federal Hwy., Boca Raton
• (407) 395-6033
CONTINENTAL

12/20

Kathy Sellas is the ringmaster at this bustling, Old World–style spot (dark wood, closely spaced tables) north of downtown Boca, watching over her tabled brood with benevolent good humor. No matter how busy, the waiters always have a smile and an extra moment for a recommendation—you won't hear "It's all good" here. And unlike at most local restaurants, they're equally familiar with the menu and the wine list. The menu changes frequently to accommodate fresh fish and other fresh ingredients—but unfortunately, there's nothing fresh about the style of cooking, which runs to the same old Continental standards: pâté, escargots, lobster crêpes, tournedos Henry IV, chateaubriand for two, veal chop bouquetier. Not thrilling, to be sure, but the kitchen is comprised of skilled technicians who give these time-honored (or is it time-worn?) dishes a goodly amount of flavor and finesse. Usually the best and most inventive dishes are found on the daily roster of fresh fish, which can be cooked several ways; we're fond of the Florentine-style scallops (with spinach) and the Florida fishes (snapper, pom-

pano), which are tastiest when sautéed. The kitchen has a special knack with desserts, which are lighter than the typical Continental offerings. As with the food, the wine list values the classics over the innovators. No trendy Rhônes or cutting-edge boutique Californias here, just a solid, reasonably priced collection that goes back several vintages and is handled with knowledge by the staff. Dinner and wine for two costs $130 to $150.
Open Mon.-Fri. 11:30 a.m.-3 p.m. & 5:30 p.m.-10 p.m., Sat. 5:30 p.m.-10 p.m., Sun. 5 p.m.-10 p.m. All major cards.

Joe Muer Seafood

6450 N. Federal Hwy., Boca Raton
• (407) 997-6688
SEAFOOD

12/20

One of South Florida's ironies is its paucity of seafood restaurants in a land with so much coastline. Finally, a northerner came along to solve the problem in Boca Raton: one Joe Muer, who owned several restaurants in Detroit and Philadelphia before relocating here in the mid-1970s. His seemingly obvious idea of serving a large variety of fresh seafood at reasonable prices hadn't been done before, and he was quickly rewarded with a booming business. Today it's owned by Joe's grandnephew Chuck Muer, who has remained true to his uncle's insistence on fresh seafood and quick, friendly service. This isn't much of a place for romance—the dining area is large and noisy, though the designers tried to break up and soften the space with plants, banquettes and careful lighting. (For a cozier ambience, request one of the window tables set in an alcove.) The menu is as uncomplicated as the surroundings, starting with such appetizers as pristine plates of Cedar Point oysters, broiled shrimp with garlic, shallots, sherry and chopped almonds (it's better than it sounds) and, best of all, quickly steamed mussels lightly dressed with fresh ginger and vermouth. In cooler weather, the hearty clam chowder does the soul good. But it is with the entrées that the kitchen really shines: nearly every fresh Florida fish is offered daily, and each can be broiled, poached, sautéed or blackened. The heavy-handed blackening is best avoided by those wishing to actually taste their fish, but all the other methods are executed to perfection, whether you choose flounder, tuna, snapper, swordfish, lemon sole, salmon or lobster tails. If the Florida fish don't catch your fancy, you can try one of the imported offerings, such as scrod, soft-shell crabs, freshwater perch or an outstanding finnan haddie (smoked haddock). Desserts are as routine as the wine list, but they're not why you come here. You come for fresh, flavorful Florida fish prepared with care and served with good cheer. Dinner for two, with wine, costs $90.
Open Mon.-Thurs. 11:30 a.m.-2:30 p.m. & 4:30 p.m.-9:30 p.m., Fri. 11:30 a.m.-2:30 p.m. & 4:30 p.m.-10 p.m., Sat. 4:30 p.m.-10 p.m., Sun. 4:30 p.m.-9:30 p.m. Cards: AE, MC, V.

Lá Trúc

297-299 Palmetto Park Rd.,
Boca Raton
• (407) 392-4568
VIETNAMESE

12/20

The name may sound French, but the lush bamboo plant just inside the door of this simple but elegant restaurant is a subtle clue to its linguistic origin: in Vietnamese, *lá* means "leaf," and *trúc* is both the word for "branch" and a popular name for young girls. These explanations are cheerfully given by My Phuong, the manager. She moved to Boca Raton after chef Binh, her brother-in-law, decided Florida had a more agreeable climate than Connecticut, where his first restaurant was located. A modest Vietnamese community has sprung up around Boca Raton, which means that Binh can now obtain most of his fresh ingredients locally, from the shrimp and limes to the coriander and lemon grass he uses in the imperial shrimp rolls. Basic spring rolls are on the menu, but it's much more fun to try the more specialized, Vietnamese-style dishes, such as tasty beef marinated in garlic and lemon grass, wrapped in a tender la-lot leaf and grilled. The menu's delightful mix of dishes points up the sophistication and refinement of classic Vietnamese food. That's not to say Binh doesn't tamper when the need arises. He "Floridizes" some dishes, like the sea scallops sautéed with fresh orange juice, but leaves others simple, like the steamed flounder with lightly cooked fresh vegetables, a purist's dream. The desserts are a real surprise: Binh's lemon mousse is as light as a summer cloud, and even his cheesecake seems to have no calories at all. The pleasantly leisurely service is provided by waiters who treat diners like family members, honoring that delicate balance between warmth and respect. The simple, serene decor features a few Vietnamese paintings hung on walls painted the parchment color of Asian screens, and leafy plants set on the tables. Though the short wine list has a few decent items, none particularly enhance the food. That's a small quibble, though, for a place that offers such engaging service and so rewarding a cuisine. Dinner for two, including wine, costs about $75.

Open Mon.-Sat. 11 a.m.-2:30 p.m. & 5 p.m.-10 p.m., Sun. 5 p.m.-10 p.m. Cards: AE, MC, V.

Maxaluna

Crocker Center,
5050 Town Center Circle, Boca Raton
• (407) 391-7177
ITALIAN

12/20

In the late 1980s, no one had a greater influence on the South Florida food scene than restaurateur Dennis Max. Such a statement would certainly lead one to presume that he is an accomplished chef, but in fact he's a "concept man" (to borrow a Madison Avenue phrase), a visionary with a genius for synthesizing two opposite culinary approaches: what will appeal to the foodies and the trendoids and what will work in South Florida's conservative restaurant market. Quality varies from place to place in the Max empire, but none is less than very good, and two former Max establishments—Café Max and Max's Place (now called Mark's Place)—are among the best in the state. Maxaluna, a Tuscan grill, is the underachiever of the group these days. Its location may be Florida, but its look is thoroughly California: a large, lovely open space filled with blond wood, an enormous curved bar (stocked with an astonishing array of after-dinner drinks), an open kitchen and tiny tables laden with oversize plates. The good looks are undermined by these tiny tables crammed together cheek-by-jowl, but that doesn't prevent the place from always being packed with a crowd that, in its studied informality, mirrors the dressed-up rustic cooking—which may be uneven but does boast an undeniable appeal. The guiding concept of the daily-changing menu is a marriage of an Italian aesthetic with Florida's agriculture. You might find risotto with smoked chicken, Tuscan beans and escarole among the starters, or perhaps quickly cooked rounds of goat cheese served with asparagus and a miso-mint vinaigrette. This place had one of the first Tuscan oak-fired ovens in South Florida, and the kitchen uses it to great effect on fresh fish, including a thick cut of swordfish with bitter Italian broccoli and fried capers. The kitchen often stumbles when it tries to be too inventive and ends up throwing everything but the kitchen sink onto a platter, so we'd advise sticking to the more restrained dishes—except, that is, for dessert. They're outrageously decadent, especially the crème brûlée pie with fresh fruit. Although the large wine list has some excellent Californian and Italian selections (and a dozen grappas), prices are high. Dinner for two, including a relatively moderately priced bottle of wine, costs about $125.

Open Mon.-Thurs. 11:30 a.m.-2:30 p.m. & 5:30 p.m.-10:30 p.m., Fri. 11:30 a.m.-2:30 p.m. & 5:30 p.m.-11 p.m., Sat. 5:30 p.m.-11 p.m., Sun. 5:30 p.m.-10 p.m. All major cards.

Max's Grille
404 Plaza Real,
Boca Raton
• (407) 368-0080
AMERICAN

12/20

Florida restaurant pioneer Dennis Max is still full of surprises. A decade ago, he demonstrated canny insight into what people wanted from a restaurant, ending up with a stellar trio of upscale eateries. He then sold two of them (Café Max and Max's Place, which is now top-rated Mark's Place) and headed in an entirely different direction. Today, this food guru of the tropics has gone retro and pronounced that the future of dining hinges on the American family. He opened four family-style (and family-priced) restaurants in as many years, putting his unique imprint on Italian, Southwestern and French bistro food. Max's Grille, the newest, is the most upwardly mobile of these down-home places. Located in a shopping center that resembles a Disney vision of a small-town main street, it successfully imparts the feel of a Midwestern farm kitchen (albeit an exceptionally stylish one), with its country American furnishings, soaring ceiling, soft yellow lighting, roomy tables and denim-clad staff. Charles Saunders, the chef who created Maxaluna before heading west to run the kitchens at the Sonoma Mission Inn, is called the "culinary director," to acknowledge his part-time consulting role; the executive chef is Fran Casciato, another South Florida power cook. Together, they've melded a wine-country cooking style with Floridian products and flair for some interesting dishes. Too many of these taste bland in spite of their ingredients, but none is dull in conception. From the herbed flat bread topped with wood-smoked bacon, onions, spinach and sour cream to the corn fettuccine with shrimp, beans and tomatoes, each dish challenges the imagination. Some, like fresh tuna with braised endive and fennel, roasted garlic, white-bean ragoût and rosemary oil, are unnecessarily complicated, but others, like the lamb steak with a barley pilaf and the crisply fried whole Mississippi catfish, are striking in their simplicity, full of good, honest flavors. Aside from a few Champagnes, the exemplary wine list is limited to American still wines, including some of California's most intriguing. Dinner for two, with wine, costs about $80.

Open Sun.-Fri. 11:30 a.m.-2:30 p.m. & 5:30 p.m.-10:30 p.m., Sat. 5:30 p.m.-10:30 p.m. Cards: AE, MC, V.

Morada Bar & Grill
5100 Town Center Circle,
Crocker Center,
Boca Raton
• (407) 395-0805
AMERICAN

12/20

Andrew Swerskey combines flavors with the exuberance with which Jackson Pollock flung paint. His home-smoked duck comes with tricolored lentils, foie gras salad and a sesame-chile vinaigrette. His yellowfin tuna steps out in a sesame crust, with an Asian salsa and a ginger-soy aïoli. Pastel-colored sauces are gleefully squirted from squeeze bottles; cocoa powder and confectioner's sugar are sprinkled to the very edge of dessert plates. Just reading the menu is exhausting; there are so many flavors that a single meal makes you feel as if you've been dining for a week. But don't let Swerskey's culinary craziness keep you away, for in this barrage of innovation you'll find lots of worthwhile ideas. And in staid Boca Raton, a restaurant that challenges the taste buds is as rare as a snowflake in the Florida sky. Morada's recent move to larger, more contemporary quarters in Crocker Center may dismay those who loved the cozy, pink-and-white rooms of its former setting. Others will thrill at the addition of a full bar and a dance floor upstairs. Dinner for two, with wine, will run $80 to $100.

Open nightly 6 p.m.-10:30 p.m. Cards: AE, MC, V.

Roberto's

402 Plaza Real,
Boca Raton
• (407) 362-8722
ITALIAN

Roberto's, one of Palm Beach County's most popular Italian restaurants for nearly a decade, recently moved lock, stock and staff from Delray Beach to strikingly elegant new quarters in Mizner Park. Happily, the changes made by owners Roberto and Michele Tempo were only for the better. It looks like a library in an aristocratic Italian villa, with its dark wood, stately furnishings, dim lighting and luxurious comfort. The staff, watched over by maître d' Paolo Salomone, is still almost military in its precision, but the waiters now have a more focused menu to work with. What was formerly a Continental hodgepodge is now strongly Italian, with some unusual twists from Roberto, who never misses a chance to make things grand and showy. Old fans will be relieved that they can still order Roberto's extraordinary deboned, slow-roasted crispy duck with a tart cassis sauce—and new fans will appreciate the emphasis on contemporary Italian recipes, including sweetbreads with truffles, lamb with a sweet garlic sauce and a number of lovely fish creations, such as the delicious salmon with a sauce of mascarpone and pesto. The polenta with Taleggio cheese and mushrooms makes an admirable appetizer; our pasta favorites include pappardelle with fresh porcini and agnolotti with sundried tomatoes and pesto. The extravagant desserts—tiramisu, fruit tarts—are designed more for American tastes than Italian. The wine list is well above average in quality. As things go these days in pricey Boca Raton, dinner is costly but not outrageous: two will probably spend $130 to $150, including wine.
Open nightly 6:30 p.m.-10 p.m. Cards: MC, V.

St. Honoré

2401 PGA Blvd.,
Palm Beach Gardens
• (407) 627-9099
FRENCH

Not many French restaurants in America, let alone Florida, are blessed with the level of respect for tradition and the passion for clean, up-to-date flavors that you find at St. Honoré. Chef/owner Alain Jorand is responsible for these flavors, and his partner, Pierre Boutiron, for the exceptionally gracious yet relaxed atmosphere. The dining area spills onto a terrace; tables are set with Villeroy and Boch china; wine glasses are not only made of fine crystal but are, for once, the proper sizes and shapes; fresh flowers, pale terra-cotta walls and balanced lighting infuse the place with amiable warmth. Add to the setting superb waiters and a sommelier who actually suggests more appropriate but less expensive wines when you ask his advice, and you've got a restaurant that's nipping at the heels of the country's best. Jorand's menu starts off simply, with such first courses as a salad of French green beans, asparagus, beets and duck confit or a terrine of poached fresh foie gras. His more complicated dishes retain a sense of balance, as in the superb truffle-and-mush-

room-filled raviolis with a splash of warm herb vinaigrette, and in all the seafood creations, each a bastion of finesse and delicacy: fresh Florida fish (like yellowtail snapper) steamed with lemon grass, salmon steamed with juniper berries and cinnamon, shrimp sautéed with shiitake mushrooms and leeks. Meat entrées include an intriguing veal tenderloin set off with a sauce of orange and bitters, a French version of osso buco with the veal shank braised in Riesling, and delicious lightly sautéed sweetbreads with a sauce made from Earl Grey tea and fresh ginger. We're also partial to the opulent quail stuffed with foie gras and raisins. In addition to the expected French pastries is an unexpected selection of cheeses. The extensive wine list is relatively fairly priced. Dinner for two, with wine, costs about $160—a daunting sum, to be sure, but worth every penny.
Open Mon.-Sat. noon-2:30 p.m. & 6 p.m.-10 p.m., Sun. 6 p.m.-10 p.m. Cards: AE, MC, V.

Uncle Tai's
Crocker Center,
5250 Town Center Circle,
Boca Raton
• (407) 368-8806
CHINESE

12/20

The uncle is Wen Dah Tai, who studied with master chefs originally in the People's Republic of China and later in Taiwan, Japan and the Philippines. When he emigrated to the United States, he opened a restaurant in New York, where he met with wide praise and considerable prosperity. But when his lease expired in 1979 he headed west and ended up in Houston, just in time to enjoy the Texas boom days; again he prospered, soon opening a branch in Dallas. When he opened this place in Crocker Center, he baffled as many diners as he pleased. His training with China's cooking elite means that Wen's concept of fine Chinese dining is different from that of the average American, who was brought up on egg rolls and sweet-and-sour pork. In tranquil, almost formulaic surroundings rich with plenty of polished wood, Chinese screens and plants, diners sample such delicacies as lamb with scallions and frogs' legs with eggplant. Salmon, rarely seen in Chinese restaurants but a favorite of this kitchen, regularly comes in two marvelous guises: cold with hot oil and a highly spiced hot dish called "zesty salmon." Numerous dishes are marked with double asterisks, which indicates that Wen believes his is the only restaurant in the area to serve such items as sliced prawns with hot pepper and sliced duck with ginger. The polite staff will guide you through the admirably prepared menu, and the wine list has some interesting selections, though many diners opt for beer or tea. As Chinese restaurants go, Uncle Tai's is expensive—but even with a bottle of wine, dinner for two runs $65 to $75.
Open Mon.-Sat. 11:30 a.m.-10 p.m., Sun. 5 p.m.-10 p.m. Cards: AE, MC, V.

La Vieille Maison
770 E. Palmetto Park Rd.,
Boca Raton
• (407) 391-6701
FRENCH

As the owners, Leonce Picot and Al Kocab certainly set the tone and ambience here. But it is the talent of Alsatian chef Cyrille Wendling that elevates this restaurant above the others Picot and Kocab have created (such as The Down Under in Fort Lauderdale; *see* page 131). Wendling works his wonders in, as the name implies, an old house, which feels like a private home even though it now seats 200 in its rambling, antique-filled rooms. From time to time the crowd stresses the seams, but thanks to the admirable service-and-kitchen system, the place usually hums along just beautifully. The courteous waiters are only too happy to help you negotiate the lengthy menu, which takes the middle road between old- and new-fashioned interpretations of classic French dishes. For instance, the scallops quickly sautéed with garlic and served on a bed of spinach with a light mustard vinaigrette is a French classic for the 1990s—but it's balanced by such satisfying salutes to the old as the duck-pistachio pâté baked in a pastry shell. The kitchen does its best work with seafood, offering such unusual pairings as fresh pompano sautéed with butter and pecans. Other dishes well worth your attention include the two styles of duck on one plate—rich confit and sautéed fresh duck—and the sweetbreads in a light brown sauce with three kinds of mushrooms. Desserts stay on the classic side of the road, from the good apple tart to the sumptuous chocolate terrine. The wine list, which represents California nearly as well as France, boasts some terrific bargains. Despite its years, this old house still has plenty of life and vitality. Dinner for two, with wine, runs $130 to $150.
Open nightly 6 p.m.-11 p.m. All major cards.

QUICK BITES

Banana Boat
739 E. Ocean Ave.,
Boynton Beach
• (407) 732-9400

This pub perched on the Intracoastal Waterway serves down-home food with disarming informality. For a casual lunch, dinner or drink by the water, there isn't a better place for miles around, and you'll never have to wait, given the three bars and two large dining areas. The decor hails from the Davey Jones school of decorating: all harpoons, varnished wood and hanging nets. In addition to shellfish from a good raw bar, you can order such tasty things as conch fritters, huge sandwiches and any of the broiled or sautéed fresh-fish specials. Service is prompt, and prices are reasonable. Dinner for two, with wine, costs about $60; lunch is about half that.
Open Mon.-Fri. 11 a.m.-12:30 p.m., Sat.-Sun. 9 a.m.-12:30 p.m.

Tom's Place

7251 N. Federal Hwy.,
Boca Raton
• (407) 997-0920

Tom started out cooking his ribs and chicken at a much smaller place, but the increasing hordes of fans eventually forced a move. Tom's new place, which looks more like a Midwestern barn than a restaurant, is still the best place for miles around to get good barbecue and Southern home cooking. Everything is à la carte: ribs (both pork and beef) come by the slab (twenty ounces) and half slab, chicken by the piece, and such sides as candied yams, hush puppies and okra by the dish. The food is tasty, plentiful and cheap: a lunchtime feast runs about $16 for two.
Open Tues.-Fri. 11:30 a.m.-10 p.m., Sat. noon-10 p.m. No cards.

Toojay's

313 Poinciana Plaza,
Palm Beach
• (407) 659-7232

The crowd at Toojay's bridges every gap: regardless of age, social standing or lifestyle, customers come here because they love the place. At breakfast or lunch, bankers in suits rub elbows with jocks in sweatsuits at the deli take-out counter up front, while in the back, dieters sit cheek-by-jowl with culinary hedonists. The kitchen raises the salad to an art form with several intricate combinations. At dinner, the food is humble and homey: crabcakes, meatloaf, pasta and such. Breakfast for two is less than $10; an eat-in lunch or dinner for two costs anywhere from $25 to $40.
Open daily 8 a.m.-9 p.m. Cards: MC, V.

HOTELS

Luxury (From $150)

The Breakers

One S. County Rd.,
Palm Beach 33480
• (407) 655-6611
Fax (407) 659-8403

The Breakers receives our sincere admiration and respect because it is as much a wonderful museum as it is a wonderful hotel; its grace and charm begin from the ceiling down. The third of the Breakers Hotels that were built by railroad baron Henry Flagler (the first two burned down), this final design masterpiece was completed in 1926. Inspired by the Villa Medici in Florence—including hand-painted ceilings shipped in and refitted by 75 European artisans—the hotel exudes the history and lavishness of a bygone era in Palm Beach, when John D. Rockefeller, Warren G. Harding and William Randolph Hearst were regulars on the guest list at this "Palace by the Sea." Dozens of bronze and crystal chandeliers drip from the lobby, loggias and dining rooms; twenty-foot-high windows overlook courtyard gardens, fountains and the oceanfront. Today, the hotel still hosts a flurry of winter charity balls, where the blood runs blue and the ties are always black. Currently undergoing a

five-year, $50 million renovation program, the hotel is listed on the National Register of Historic Places.
Doubles: $175-$400; suites: $325-$825.

Chesterfield Hotel Deluxe
363 Cocoanut Row,
Palm Beach 33480
• (407) 659-5800
Fax (407) 659-6707

There's only room for 65 parties at the Chesterfield—65 parties with impeccable taste, of course. No matter: you won't want to share the experience with more people than that. Like its European-style counterparts in Palm Beach, the intimate hotel exudes the feeling of a downtown apartment with a great address for the winter: in Palm Beach, a block from Worth Avenue, worlds away from mundane daily concerns. There's a comfortably plush lobby, an English library, a small, country-style restaurant and an outdoor pool and spa. The rooms themselves are done in English country motifs, with bright blue-and-white florals and stripes; bathrooms are marbled and include a small amenities package.
Doubles: $145-$220; suites: $275-$450.

Moderate (From $100)

Boca Raton Resort and Club
501 E. Camino Real Dr.,
Boca Raton 33432
• (407) 395-3000
Fax (407) 391-3183

We have not a qualm about bestowing the Boca Raton Resort and Club with our highest praise. Since the early part of this century, it has retained its status as one of North America's most elegant resort estates. The resort has also managed somehow to blend ceremonious service with a friendly, welcoming ambience. There are three separate accommodations clusters spread throughout the resort's spectacular setting, which spans from the Intracoastal Waterway on one side to the Atlantic Ocean on the other. (Water lifts and shuttle buses carry guests back and forth at frequent intervals). On the resort's western side, the Cloister is made up of the reception area and original hotel. This is where the resort's impeccable Concierge Floor is located, with enormous garden view rooms and suites, access to a private, English-style library, Continental breakfast and hors d'oeuvres served daily, and Champagne and Italian cookies on arrival. Adjacent to the Cloister is the resort's signature Tower, whose pink edifice has become a Boca landmark, affording guests magnificent views of the waterway and Atlantic seascape. There are also a number of spacious golf villas, rooms and suites (some with kitchens). If beachfront accommodations are important to you, the Boca Beach Club is a bustling epicenter for local members who seem just a tad miffed about all of these hotel guests milling about (and this is the only negative aspect of the resort that we've ever stumbled upon). Even though a stay at the Cloister is priced lower than are some of the other rooms, we prefer it. Its Addison Mizner–style Spanish-Mediterranean

architecture, its marble and wood tables upon which impressionist painting jigsaw puzzles are scattered about, its tile floors and loggias and 1920s pizzazz are delightful.
Singles & doubles: $90-$270; golf villas: $95-$270.

Colony Hotel
155 Hammon Ave.,
Palm Beach 33480
• (407) 655-5430
Fax (407) 832-7318

In Palm Beach, you can't get much closer to the thick of things than you can at The Colony. For a half century, the Bermuda-style, *très* continental, pale yellow edifice has been *the* place to see and be seen, much less ostentatious than The Breakers; plenty more obvious than the Brazilian Court. Its bar is the last stop for glittering, bejeweled, die-hard socialites following a charity function or two—including Julio Iglesias, Ted Kennedy and Lee Radziwill in recent years. The rooms themselves are small and charmingly appointed; there's also a lounge, grille and gourmet dining room, as well as poolside dining under a whitewashed canopy.
Singles & doubles: $90-$140; suites: $225-$320.

Ocean Grand
2800 S. Ocean Blvd.,
Palm Beach 33480
• (407) 582-2800
Fax (407) 547-1557

Those tough Palm Beach quality-control matrons weren't going to let hoteliers build just any old hotel on this island where bank deposits are equalled only by the attitudes of their depositors. Sure, there's plenty of development in Palm Beach County in recent years (some say the developers have gone haywire), but certainly not in the city *proper*, my dears. Before the Ocean Grand opened its doors in 1989, it had been 35 years since a developer set foot on these hallowed beaches. Although the fabulous new resort is on the southern end of the island, it is on "The Island" in every sense of the word, offering 169 rooms, suites and penthouses veritably bursting with elegance worthy of their address. The beautifully landscaped resort, made up of three four-story buildings cleverly linked by glass walkways, is simply divine. There's a multilingual concierge, limousine service and complimentary transportation to Worth Avenue. And there's enough marble in these buildings to have sunk a couple of boats en route from Italy. Inside the rooms, there are stereo televisions, mini-bars, king-size beds, hair dryers and bathrobes; Grand Club level rooms are oceanfront on a private floor, with breakfast and hors d'oeuvres served daily. Two restaurants and an outdoor bar overlook the ocean, and the elegant "Living Room" lounge makes you feel like you're sitting in the home of a well-to-do local.
Singles & doubles: $125-$215.

PGA National Resort

400 Ave. of the Champions,
Palm Beach Gardens
33418
• (407) 627-2000
Fax (407) 622-0261

Want to live, sleep, breathe, eat—and even play—golf? Well, do we have the resort for you. The national headquarters for the Professional Golfers Association of America, the PGA National offers no less than five championship courses, plenty of rooms with balconies overlooking them and even a couple of packages that make it more reasonable for you to get out on them. For the rest of the duffer's entourage, there are nineteen clay tennis courts, and the largest croquet facility in the Western Hemisphere. There's a fitness center, a 26-acre lake with a variety of watersports equipment available for rental and more than 400 rooms, suites and cottage suites, inside of which you probably won't be spending much time.
Singles & doubles: $135-$153. Packages available.

Practical (Under $100)

Boca Raton Marriott Crocker Center

5150 Town Center Circle,
Boca Raton 33486
• (407) 392-4600
Fax (407) 395-8258

Shopaholics beware: there's more shopping within a couple of hundred yards of Boca Raton's Marriott than there is in most small towns throughout the rest of North America. There are also plenty of wonderful restaurants, offices and a busy Florida Turnpike entrance. Despite its commercial location, the hotel, with 28 acres of imaginatively laid out tropical gardens, manages to offer an easy ambience and unhurried feeling. A total of twelve stories, 256 rooms and sixteen suites, including two concierge levels, are attended by signature Marriott service and amenities.
Singles & doubles: $79-$164. Packages available.

Brazilian Court

301 Australian Ave.,
Palm Beach 33480
• (407) 655-7740
Fax (407) 655-0801

This must be what it's be like for those who stay with friends in Palm Beach. Each of the 134 rooms at the Brazilian Court, nestled comfortably just off the posh shopping district of Worth Avenue, is different from the next. Clustered around two separate, flower-filled courtyards abuzz with garden fountains, the hotel is just a stone's throw from the beach (a three-block walk to the east), and yet it exudes the feeling of a small hotel in the English countryside or the south of France, perhaps. Service is fine, from the 24-hour in-room attention to that of the historic Rio Bar, where the guest list over the years has included decades worth of who's whos—from Marjorie Merriwether Post to a couple of generations of Kennedys (Robert and Ethel's son, David, died of a well-publicized drug overdose here in 1984). Since then the hotel has been entirely revamped and redecorated and today, because of its inviting personality and very reasonable rates (depending on the specific

room selected), the Brazilian Court is one of those hotels you should be darn proud of yourself for having stumbled upon.
Singles & doubles: $85-$315; suites: $185-$875.

Jupiter Beach Hilton
Five North A1A,
Indiantown Rd.,
Jupiter 33477
• (407) 746-2511
Fax (407) 747-3304

This quiet and sophisticated hotel sort of stands alone on Jupiter Beach, save for the towering red lighthouse that has become a landmark. You won't mind being away from it all in this little seaside neighborhood about a half hour from Palm Beach—the 193-room Hilton property boasts a magnificent stretch of private beach, valet service, shopping shuttles, tennis courts, a fitness center and a popular local bar and grill. For celebrity oglers, Jupiter presents the best place for "Burt and Loni–watching" in the county. (Jupiter native Burt Reynolds has a ranch and petting zoo in the small community).
Singles & doubles: $75-$160; suites: $180-$1,000.

Palm Beach Polo and Country Club
13198 Forest Hill Blvd.,
West Palm Beach 33414
• (407) 793-7000
Fax (407) 798-7052

If it's good enough for His Royal Highness Prince Charles, it's good enough for you. (Actually, the prince probably stays with friends, and just visits to play the "Sport of Kings" on the nine Bermuda grass fields). At any rate, the 1,650-acre planned resort community generally ranks among the world's top-notch resort clubs, with an emphasis on equestrian activities. The club has its own resident instructor and trainer, and has carved miles of horse trails through the subtropical Big Blue Cypress Preserve adjacent to the facility. There's also an eighteen-hole golf course, nineteen tennis courts and a 25-meter swimming pool. Accommodations are set up in "villages," and you may choose from those located near the equestrian, golf or tennis facilities. If you're not staying at the complex, it does feature a 1,600-box-seat grandstand, which is open to the public during the regularly scheduled wintertime matches.
Singles, doubles & triples: $85-$295.

NIGHTLIFE

Clubs

Club Boca
7000 W. Palmetto Rd.,
Boca Raton
• (407) 368-3333

If you can't count at least a couple of dozen BMWs in the parking lot of Club Boca on any given weekend night, we think you need to raise your status consciousness. In too-too trendy Boca, land of sprawling Mediterranean-style townhouse developments and major corporate headquarters, Club Boca even puts its waitresses in tuxedo shirts (open-backed, of course). The guest dress code here requires L.L. Bean catalog purchases mixed with unnatural suntans, so we advise you take a good hard look at yourself before

you deign to enter.
Open Sun.-Thurs. 9 p.m.-3 a.m., Fri.-Sat. 10 p.m.-4 a.m. Cover $5.

Comedy

Laff Lines Comedy Theater
2401 PGA Blvd.,
Palm Beach Gardens
• (407) 634-0336

A comedy club is only as strong as its performers, and Laff Lines, a member of the Hilarities Comedy Club network, gets some of the best of them in for a week or a one-night stand. A very nicely appointed, intimate theater, the club presents a nice venue within a West Palm Beach strip mall, but we wish the establishment would get its liquor license (only beer and wine are served).
Shows Tues.-Wed. & Thurs. 8:30 p.m., Fri.-Sat. 8 p.m. & 10:30 p.m., Sun. 8:30 p.m. Cover $10. Dinner & show packages (with the adjacent Olive Garden Restaurant) from $14.95. Cards: AE, MC, V.

SHOPS

Antiques

Jack Davidson
4 Via Parigi,
Palm Beach
• (407) 655-0906

Nestled in one of the alleyways jutting off Worth Avenue, Jack Davidson is a most unique design store. On display are plenty of English and American antiques and collectibles, as well as some very affordable glassware, Victorian bamboo, lamps, linens and baskets.
Open Mon.-Sat. 9:30 a.m.-5:30 p.m.

Clothes & Jewelry

Boris-le Beau
The Esplanade,
150 Worth Ave.,
Palm Beach
• (407) 655-3702

Madison Avenue jewelry designers Madeleine van Eerde and Norman LeBeau also have a Palm Beach shop, (where else but on world-famous Worth Avenue) offering distinctive designs in gold, platinum and gemstones (much of it still designed and manufactured in New York and shipped south). The designers also take great pleasure in custom-designing pieces using your stones combined with their own creations.
Open Mon.-Sat. 10 a.m.-5:45 p.m.

Knickers
Boca Raton Resort & Club,
501 E. Camino Real,
Boca Raton
• (407) 394-5150

If you share a credit card with someone, it's probably best not to leave them waiting in the lobby of the Boca Raton Resort & Club too long. Although its inventory leans toward the slightly stuffy and definitely overpriced, Knickers nonetheless offers

jewelry and accessories, hats, bathing suits and resort wear worth taking a look at.
Open Mon.-Sat. 9:30 a.m.-6 p.m., Sun. 9:30 a.m.-4:30 p.m.

Department Stores

The Esplanade
150 Worth Ave.,
Palm Beach
• (407) 833-0868

Jutting off of Worth Avenue, The Esplanade is a two-story cluster of 48 shops, many of which, generally speaking, tend to be somewhat more affordable than those on the avenue itself. Palm Beach's Saks Fifth Avenue is located in The Esplanade, as are F.G. Bodner, Georgette Klinger, Ralph Lauren and Banana Republic.
Open Mon.-Sat. 10 a.m.-6 p.m.

Palm Beach Mall
I-95 at Palm Beach Lakes Blvd.,
West Palm Beach
• (407) 683-9186

If the sky-high prices on Worth Avenue have dampened your spirits, head west to the Palm Beach Mall, where, although prices can be just as high at the smaller boutiques, there's also a Burdines, a Lord & Taylor and a Maas Brothers/Jordan Marsh, where you at least have the option to bargain hunt.
Open Mon.-Sat. 10 a.m.-9 p.m., Sun. noon-5:30 p.m.

Town Center at Boca Raton
6000 W. Glades Rd.,
Boca Raton
• (407) 368-6000

We generally don't feel comfortable recommending sprawling suburban shopping malls—however, Boca Raton is unusually enormous, and Boca Raton is an atypically wealthy suburb. On top of Bloomingdale's, Saks Fifth Avenue and Lord & Taylor, there are some 180 shops, boutiques and restaurants to browse through. One complaint: an uneven Italian-tiled floor throughout the public areas makes walking difficult if not downright painful if you've selected the wrong shoes for the trek.
Open Mon.-Sat. 10 a.m.-9 p.m., Sun. noon-5:30 p.m.

Gifts

The Franklin Mint Gallery
6000 W. Glades Rd.,
Boca Raton
• (407) 392-4144

You don't have to send off to Philadelphia to order all of those lovely little figurines. The Franklin Mint Gallery is a veritable treasure trove of all of those elegant collector dolls, plus porcelain vases and handsome bronze and pewter sculptures.
Open Mon.-Sat. 10 a.m.-9 p.m., Sun. noon-5:30 p.m.

Home

Asadorian, Inc.
Boca Bay Plaza,
7600 N. Federal Hwy.,
Boca Raton
• (407) 997-0030

So you just purchased a little town house at Broken Sound and you're trying to make a statement with your floor coverings. Asadorian has just what you need. A family-owned operation

since 1926, Asadorian carries an enormous selection of Middle Eastern and Oriental weaves.
Open Mon-Fri. 9:30 a.m.-5:30 p.m., Sat. 10 a.m.-5 p.m.

SIGHTS & SPORTS

Amusements

The Henry M. Flagler Museum
One Cocoanut Row,
Palm Beach
• (407) 655-2833

The lavish Palm Beach home of former railroad baron Henry Morrison Flagler is a fascinating museum. The home, named Whitehall, offers a thorough retrospective on the island itself as well as the development of Florida as a tourist destination. Flagler's private railroad car, The Rambler, is on display on the grounds; the home is open to the public. Revolving exhibitions feature a variety of subjects, from antique clocks and watches to children's quilts. The Museum Store offers a terrific selection of Victorian reproductions, ornaments and unusual gift items.
Open Tues.-Sat. 10 a.m.-5 p.m. Sun. noon-5 p.m. Adults $5, children 6-12 $2.50.

Art Galleries & Museums

Norton Gallery of Art
1451 S. Olive Ave.,
West Palm Beach
• (407) 832-5194

Chicago industrialist Ralph Norton loved two things: art and Palm Beach. This wonderful private collection based on the late northerner's holdings is housed in a small, nonprofit museum, and is well worth a look. On top of the permanent collection, the Norton Gallery hosts a variety of revolving exhibits.
Open Tues.-Sat. 10 a.m.-5 p.m., Sun. 1 p.m.-5 p.m.

Patricia Judith Art Gallery
720 E. Palmetto Park Rd.,
Boca Raton
• (407) 368-3316

In addition to a variety of paintings and sculptures, Patricia Judith has recently added a contemporary glass wing. There, an extensive variety of glassware, from vases to bowls and cups, is artfully crafted and displayed.
Open Mon.-Sat. 10 a.m.-6 p.m.

Society of the Four Arts
Four Arts Plaza,
Palm Beach
• (407) 655-7226 (galleries),
(407) 655-2766 (library)

More of an exhibition hall and entertainment venue for Palm Beach's famous ball-gown set than a museum (there's only a small permanent collection), the Society of the Four Arts is worth a look during the season for its temporary themed art displays, programs films and lectures.
Open Dec. 1 to Apr. 15, Mon.-Sat. 10 a.m.-5 p.m., Sun 2 p.m.-5 p.m.

Wally Findlay Galleries
165 Worth Ave.,
Palm Beach
• (407) 655-2090

While the rest of Worth Avenue is closed for the evening, Wally Findlay is where you're likely to see a congregation of tuxedoed types oohing and ahing the works at one of the gallery's frequent openings. Specializing in impressionist, postimpressionist and modern masters, the gallery also works with a wide variety of artists American and European artists, as well as a number of artists working in primitives and pointillism.
Open Mon.-Sat. 9:30 a.m.-5:30 p.m.

Sports

The Aqua Shop
505 Northlake Blvd.,
North Palm Beach
• (407) 848-9042

If you've got your PADI (Professional Association of Diving Instructors) certification, this is where you can stop on the morning of your dive to fill your tanks. If you aren't certified yet, a variety of snorkel and scuba courses are offered here (including one exclusively for seniors). The shop also sets up charter dives in the Florida Keys and the Bahamas.
Open Mon.-Fri. 9:30 a.m.-6:30 p.m., Sat. 7:30 a.m.-6 p.m., Sun. 7:30 a.m.-4:30 p.m.

Frank's Dive Shop
301 E. Blue Heron Blvd.,
Riviera Beach
• (407) 848-7632

Situated in a nasty little neighborhood near the Port of Palm Beach, Frank's is nonetheless your best bet for diving equipment, services and instruction in central Palm Beach County. Charters to secret local lobster beds and better known Bahamian locales are also available.
Open Mon.-Fri. 8 a.m.-7 p.m., Sat. 7 a.m.-7 p.m.

Glider Rides of America
2633 Lantana Rd.,
Lantana
• (407) 965-9101

The oddest thing about taking a sailplane ride in this glass canopy-closed craft is the lack of sound. Once you cut the cord from the towplane (an honor your pilot will bestow on you, if you dare) it's just you, the wind, the water and the birds. The pilot sits in the front, and two passengers share a rather tight little seat in the back, much like an amusement park ride. Surprisingly, you can get motion sick on a sailplane ride, for us the only thing that detracted from an otherwise wonderful experience.
Open daily 9 a.m.-6 p.m. Cost $39.95-$69.95 per passenger.

Palm Beach Kennel Club
1111 N. Congress Ave.,
West Palm Beach
• (407) 683-2222

We've always found greyhound racing to be a nasty little pari-mutuel sport, but look around at the Kennel Club and everyone seems to be having a good time, at any rate. In season, there are thirteen separate races held within one performance;

the best seats are in the Paddock Dining Room, where you can enjoy drinks and dinner while watching the action below.
Open June-Sept. daily noon & 8 p.m.

Palm Beach Polo & Country Club
13198 Forest Hills Blvd.,
West Palm Beach
• (407) 798-7000

Private tailgate picnics here generally include plenty of caviar and goose-liver pâté, chased down with a nice dry Chardonnay, served on Wedgwood, with plenty of clinking Waterford. You can't get much snootier than this, and yet it's all open to the public. One of the busiest schedules of high-goal polo tournaments and leagues in the world, Palm Beach Polo is a wonderful place to spend a Sunday afternoon. For groups of 25 or more, the Royal Box (designed for the Princess of Wales, whose husband often played here before injuring himself at the sport) is available for rental.
Open Dec.-May Sun. 3 p.m.

Westfield Arabian
15565 Rte. 441 (at Atlantic Ave.),
Delray Beach
• (407) 398-2100

From polo ponies to Arabian horse breeding: that's Palm Beach County. At Westfield, visitors are always welcome to watch show and race training of the horses. A very interesting presentation of the breeding facilities (which is done by artificial insemination and embryo transfer) and conditioning sessions is well worth attending.
By appointment or Sun. 2 p.m.

Theater

Royal Poinciana Playhouse
70 Poinciana Plaza,
Palm Beach
• (407) 659-3310

With a theatrical season spanning from mid-December through mid-April, the Royal Poinciana mixes local Equity productions with those of visiting touring companies. Despite its address within the confines of a strip mall, the quality of the productions here are generally higher than those of similar houses in Miami, and well worth a look during a visit to the area.
Open Mon.-Fri. 10 a.m.-5:30 p.m., Sun. noon-5 p.m.

TREASURE COAST

INTRODUCTION	178
QUICK BITES	178
HOTELS	179
NIGHTLIFE	180
SHOPS	181
SIGHTS	183

TREASURE COAST   Introduction/Quick Bites

INTRODUCTION

Spanning roughly 100 miles of coastline on Florida's Atlantic side, the Treasure Coast is a tranquil stretch of citrus groves, small towns, quiet communities and old fishing piers. The area begins north of the Gold Coast, ending just south of Cocoa Beach, and is flanked by a chain of barrier islands. Not many locals actually call it the Treasure Coast (it's also known as the Indian River region); in fact, the alluring nickname is part of a public relations ploy to convince tourists that just a few feet off the beach lies $15 million in gold, silver and jewels that were buried in a Spanish shipwreck in 1715. The shipwreck part is true, and maybe even the treasure still lies nearby, but we wouldn't fritter away our vacation organizing dive parties.

What treasures can you find along this sun-dappled coast? Its waters do boast a magnificent bounty of finned and scaled treasures: once called the world's "sailfish capital," the area has lured such fishing enthusiasts as former U.S. Presidents Arthur, Taft, Roosevelt, Cleveland and Harding. It also lures baseball players and their fans every spring, when the L.A. Dodgers fly out to Vero Beach for spring training. You won't find Miami's nightlife or Fort Lauderdale's raucous bikinis-and-beers scene here; rather, the Treasure Coast is where you'll want to fish, dive, stroll the beaches, explore the jungleland of the barrier islands and take in a bit of old Florida.

QUICK BITES

During spring training, you may see your favorite L.A. Dodgers players hanging out in **Bobby's** (3450 Ocean Dr., Vero Beach; 407-231-6996; open daily 11:30 a.m.-1 a.m.), filling up on deli sandwiches, steaks and seafood dinners. **Mrs. Mac's Kitchen by the Sea** (1006 Easter Lilly Ln., Vero Beach; 407-231-9311; open Mon.-Sat. 9:30 a.m.-8 p.m.) specializes in hefty pita-pocket sandwiches. **Mr. Manatee's** (30 Royal Palm Blvd., Vero Beach; 407-569-9151; open Sun.-Thurs. 11 a.m.-10 p.m., Fri.-Sat. 11 a.m.-11 p.m.) serves up conch fritters and other fresh seafood, as well as chicken and steak, in a Key West–ish atmosphere.

In Fort Pierce, try **Theo Phudpuckers** (2025 Seaway Dr., Fort Pierce; 407-465-1078; open Mon.-Thurs. 11:30 a.m.-9:30 p.m., Fri.-Sat. 11:30 a.m.-11 p.m., Sun. 1 p.m.-9:30 p.m.), a beach eatery known for its oysters and seafood platters. Seafood is also the main course at the **Galley Grille** (927 N. U.S. Hwy. 1, Fort Pierce; 407-468-2081; open Mon.-Fri. 11:30 a.m.-2:30 p.m. & 5 p.m.-9 p.m., Sat.-Sun. 5 p.m.-9 p.m.). To see how Floridians do Tex-Mex, check out **Enriquo's** (3215 S. U.S. Hwy. 1, Fort Pierce; 407-465-1608; open daily Fri.-Sat. 5 p.m.-10 p.m.).

HOTELS

Club Med–The Sandpiper

3500 Morningside Blvd.,
Port St. Lucie 34952
• (407) 335-4400
Fax (407) 335-9497

The people who brought European pleasure-seekers unlocked doors, shoelessness and general vacation liberties began classing up their act in a rather unlikely locale with The Sandpiper. Situated 45 minutes north of the Palm Beach International Airport, this resort is one of two Club Med villages in the U.S. (the other is a ski resort in Colorado). Despite its decidedly less-than-exotic address along Florida's sleepy Treasure Coast, The Sandpiper is both inviting and elegant; features anomalous to the Club Med tradition include a twenty-minute shuttle ride to the ocean, enormous rooms housed in three-story riverfront lodges, and four separate restaurants from which to choose. Signature Club Med features—two golf courses and plenty of tennis and watersports, all overseen by a vivacious staff of multilingual G.O.'s (*gentil organisateurs*, or "friendly organizers")—spice up the pastel landscape at the Florida retreat. Families who pass up the Walt Disney World mecca would do well to stay here, where an elaborate Circus Workshop and four clubs for kids help Mom and Dad make a grand escape. The staff does a stellar job with the Diaper Set.

Adult all-inclusive packages $75-$175; children 6-11 $65-$110; children 4 months–5 years free.

Indian River Plantation

555 N.E. Ocean Blvd.,
Hutchinson Island
34996
• (407) 225-0003
Fax (407) 225-0003

On the grounds of a turn-of-the-century pineapple plantation, the Indian River Plantation is the most elaborate resort facility you'll find between Palm Beach and Daytona. A wonderful place for a family retreat, Indian River is the type of place you won't have to leave at all to entertain the whole gang. Cosmopolitan visitors may be disappointed with the lack of nightlife on this stretch of the Atlantic, but Indian River valiantly tries to entertain, with lots of regularly scheduled activities. On-property amenities include an in-house movie theater; weekly "turtle" walks during egg-laying season; an "aqua" driving range; and a marvelous private yacht, the Island Princess (see page 184). Although the 200 rooms within the main hotel lack oceanfront views, they are beautifully appointed, set around a quiet swimming pool. The 54 oceanfront villas are actually condominiums, some in better shape than others, but the beach views can't be beat. The newer Sandpiper wing (not to be confused with neighboring Club Med) offers 70 additional, decidedly more luxurious oceanfront suites; fully equipped kitchens can keep the meal tab low.

Singles & doubles: $90-$125; suites: $155-$275.

TREASURE COAST   Nightlife

Sheraton Beach on Hutchinson Island
10978 S. Ocean Dr., Jensen Beach 34957
• (407) 229-1000
Fax (407) 229-0253

What we'd like to know is, where's the bellman to take us up to our $100 room? (There is none that we know of, though the front desk fellow may eventually offer to chip in and help with the bags). Other than the lack of any discernible personnel in the hotel, the Sheraton offers a pleasant beachfront retreat. It's a great place to watch the sunrise over the Atlantic, and when a Space Shuttle lift-off is scheduled from neighboring Cape Canaveral, the place is bustling with onlookers.
Singles & doubles: $55-$100.

Vistana's Beach Club
10740 S. Ocean Dr., Jensen Beach 34957
• (407) 239-3100
Fax (407) 239-3131

Although it lacks the recreational amenities of Indian River Plantation (*see* page 179), Vistana's Beach Club is a pleasant little resort that shares Hutchinson Island with its higher profile neighbor. Housing some 560 two-bedroom units with fully equipped kitchens (where maids surreptitiously wash your dishes each morning), the club is a set on quiet stretch of beachfront. In-room VCRs offer a nice evening respite, and you can luxuriate in the master bathroom's roman tubs and large balconies overlooking the Atlantic.
2-bedroom units: $110-$160.

NIGHTLIFE

Scalawag's Lounge
555 N.E. Ocean Blvd. at Indian River Plantation, Stuart
• (407) 225-3700

Here's the way a Friday night on Hutchinson Island should go: the seafood buffet at Indian River Plantation, followed by a Spanish coffee at Scalawag's. There's usually a lively duo playing mellow rock, and a wonderful view of the resort. The service is chummy and attentive, as is the local custom.
Open nightly 5 p.m.-midnight. All major cards.

Summit Landing
8525 U.S. 1, Micco
• (407) 664-3029

Summit Landing's claim to fame is its patio bar, the largest one overlooking the verdant Indian River. The nightlife crowd here consists mostly of after-dinner couples and groups convening for a few drinks while the night is still young. The adjacent restaurant and raw bar serves local seafood and steaks cut to order, and much of its crowd eventually spills over to Summit Landing. You can count on plenty of good local music, a colorful cast of characters and lots of dancing at Summit Landing.
Open nightly 8 p.m.-midnight. Live bands Fri.-Sat. 8 p.m.-midnight, Sun. 4 p.m.-8 p.m. Cards: AE, MC, V.

Walter's Place
Holiday Inn,
1209 S. Federal Hwy.,
Stuart
• (407) 287-6200

Even a place as short on nightlife as the Treasure Coast can offer up a decent happy hour. Walter's has one every weeknight, 4 p.m. to 8 p.m., with plenty of good hot and cold hors d'oeuvres and even a bit of local color, unusual for a Holiday Inn lounge.
Open nightly 5 p.m.-midnight. Live music Tues.-Sat. All major cards.

SHOPS

CLOTHES

Algozzini Hawaiian Village
11335 S.E. Federal Hwy.,
Hobe Sound
• (407) 546-5373

How many shops treat you to a nice cold mai tai just for stopping by? Algozzini wants you to "Walk in, Hula Out," and the fruit and rum drinks, plus lots of gauzy flowery pieces of apparel from which to choose, certainly help. There's also an Indian-wear boutique, and lots of rare sea shells picked up off Florida's coastline and buffed up a bit.
Open Mon.-Sat. 10 a.m.-5 p.m.

Frances Brewster/ Husband's Corner
3385 Ocean Dr.
Vero Beach
• (407) 231-2051

Housed in an exceptionally beautiful building fringed by palm trees, the expansive Frances Brewster offers lovely resort wear, from bathing suits to hand-printed cotton sundresses. There's also a separate men's shop.
Open Mon.-Sat. 9 a.m.-5:30 p.m.

Very Fitting Intimate Apparel
3475 Ocean Dr.,
Vero Beach
• (407) 231-4655

Vero Beach's answer to Victoria's Secret, Very Fitting has a fine—and equally classy—selection of sleek teddies, slips, hosiery, robes and loungewear.
Open Mon.-Sat. 9:30 a.m.-5 p.m.

FOOD

Grove Shops
Village Shops,
6230 N. A1A,
Vero Beach
• No phone

Citrus groves account for some 65,000 acres of Indian River County, accounting for much of the nation's grapefruit and oranges produced in Florida. There are some 21 wholesale

packing operations in the county. Grove Shops ships Indian River fruits, juices, jellies and cheeses on a retail basis.
Open Mon.-Sat. 9:30 a.m.-5:30 p.m.

SPORTING GOODS

Center Court Tennis Outfitters
1161 Old Dixie Hwy.,
Vero Beach
• (407) 567-8211

So you forgot your tennis duds on your visit to the land of grass, clay and Laykold? Never fear—Cheryl Casano and Marie McQuillan have just what you need. Athletic shoes, rackets, sweat suits and all sorts of tennis gadgets and accessories that you never even knew you needed are on display.
Open Mon.-Fri. 10 a.m-5:30 p.m., Sat. 10 a.m.-5 p.m.

Deep Six
416 Miracle Mile Plaza,
Vero Beach
• (407) 562-2883

Probably the largest surf shop on the Treasure Coast, Deep Six consists of some 7,000 square feet of name brand surf boards, accessories, Body Glove wetsuits, scuba equipment, waterskiing accessories and just about anything you might need for anything you might think of doing on or near the water.
Open Mon.-Sat. 9 a.m.-9 p.m., Sun. 9 a.m.-4 p.m.

Mac's Bike Shop
3472 Savanna Rd.,
Jensen Beach
• (407) 334-4343

Waterfront bike trails and triathlons are the name of the game in this neck of woods, and Mac's is your source for bike rental, equipment and repairs. Mac's also holds Schwinn and Raleigh sales licenses.
Open Tues.-Fri. 10 a.m.-5 p.m., Sat. 10 a.m.-3 p.m.

St. Lucie Skyways
St. Lucie County
International Airport,
2300 Virginia Ave.,
Fort Pierce
• (407) 287-1070

You know where to get your yacht, now here's where to get your airplane or helicopter. If it flies, St. Lucie Skyways buys, charters and sells it. You can also charter a jet to anywhere, arrange helicopter service or attend the facility's FAA approved flight school.
Hours by appointment and/or charter.

Stuart Yacht
450 S.W. Salerno Rd.,
Stuart
• (407) 283-1947

In the market for a 45-foot Express Fisherman? Stuart Yacht is an excellent place to begin your search. Builders of custom yachts, both power and sail, and ranging from 30 to 80 feet in length, Stuart Yacht also provides renovation, reconstruction, refinishing and repair services.
Open daily 10 a.m.-5 p.m.

Sun Spot Surf and Beach Shop
917 Beachland Blvd.,
Vero Beach
• (407) 231-2875

Here's your shot at one-stop shopping for Billabongs, skateboards and the daily surf report. An enormous selection of active sportswear, bikinis, surfboards and Boogie boards is on display.
Open daily 10 a.m.-5 p.m.

SIGHTS

ARTS & MUSEUMS

The Center for the Arts
333 Tressler Dr., Stuart
• (407) 287-1194

The Center for the Art's "Workoutz," led by professional dancers, offer a great way to stay in shape. Pay by the class. Also offered are ballet classes and jazz-, modern- and tap-dance classes catering to individual fitness levels.
Open Mon.-Fri. 8 a.m.-7 p.m.

The Elliott Museum
825 N.E. Ocean Blvd., Stuart
• (407) 225-1961

A museum built by a son in recognition of his father, an inventor who died in relative obscurity in the 1920s, The Elliott Museum craftily exhibits a wonderful little slice of Americana, and is well worth a visit. Divided into fourteen "shops," including an apothecary, barber, blacksmith forge, clock shop and tobacco shop, the museum is chock full of interesting memorabilia. A connecting passage houses a number of Sterling Elliott's inventions, including the original quadricycle (forerunner of the motorcycle) and a terribly clever knot-tying machine.
Open daily 1 p.m.-5 p.m. Adults $2.50, children 6-13 50 cents.

Gilbert's Bar House of Refuge Museum
301 MacArthur Blvd., Stuart
• (407) 225-1875

This wonderful little oceanfront museum is rather hard to get at: you have to enter the Indian River Plantation and cut through its golf courses to the ocean to reach it. It's worth the visit. The house is the last standing member of a group of five houses commissioned in 1875 by the U.S. Life-Saving Service to offer assistance to shipwrecked sailors off the east coast of Florida. The structure continued to serve in both World Wars, and was de-activated in 1945 and later turned into a fascinating little museum. There's a Boat House with early life-saving equipment, a main house and a surfboat built according to late nineteenth-century plans.
Open Tues.-Sun. 1 p.m.-5 p.m. Adults $1, children 50 cents.

Underwater Demolition Team SEAL Museum
300 N. A1A, North Hutchinson Island
• (407) 489-3597

Opened in 1985, the UDT SEAL Museum is dedicated to the branch of the U.S. Navy that trained in this area during World War II. Some of the SEAL's (Sea, Air and Land teams') original weapons, explosives and equipment are on display; and training videos teach underwater military tactics and scuba diving.
Open Wed.-Sun. 10 a.m.-5 p.m. Admission $1.

TREASURE COAST Sights

Urca de Lima
Underwater Archaeological Preserve
2200 Atlantic Beach Blvd.,
Fort Pierce
• (407) 489-3597

In 1715, a flota of Spanish *urcas* (flat-bottomed ships), loaded with riches from Mexico and Manila, set sail from Cuba toward the Gulf Stream. Unfortunately, only a few days out, the ships were sunk by a fierce hurricane off the coast of Florida. Through the 1960s, treasure maps mistakenly placed the site of the wreck off the Florida Keys. It wasn't until the early 1980s that the surviving hull structure of the *Urca de Lima* was mapped and recorded; the wreck site lies on the first offshore reef at Fort Pierce Inlet's Pepper Park, submerged in ten feet of water just 200 yards offshore. Snorkelers must display a "divers down" flag, and must be careful not to disturb the remains of the ship.
Daylight hours only.

CHARTERS & TOURS

Captain Kidd
Fishing Charters
1606 Indian River Dr.,
Sebastian
• (407) 589-FISH

U.S. presidents who once made fishing forays to the Treasure Coast included Presidents Arthur, Taft, Roosevelt, Cleveland and Harding. The town of Stuart, at one time regarded as the "Sailfish Capital of the World," still offers a number of fishing charters. Among the best is the *Captain Kidd*, which sets sail by charter daily. The boat's crew members have loads of personality and enthusiasm: "Fishin's our mission" is their motto.
Hours daily by charter.

Island Princess
Cruises
555 N.E. Ocean Blvd.
at Indian River Plantation,
Stuart
• (407) 225-2100

There are plenty of tour boats along the Atlantic Coast offering evening charters, but the *Island Princess* is special for two reasons: the pristine scenery it traverses, and its newness. Built in 1988, the 84-foot yacht seats up to 90 passengers for dinner. You are seated in a lavishly decorated main salon, where you're offered a multicourse menu that you wouldn't have thought possible to come from a ship's galley. Evening sightseeing and cocktail cruises are also available by charter.
Evening tours by charter. All major cards.

Stuart Historic Walking Tour
Stuart Recreation Center,
201 Flagler Ave.,
Stuart

The American Association of University Women has put together a wonderful, self-guided walking tour of downtown Stuart, established more than a century ago. A slice of land cutting between the Saint Lucie and Indian rivers, the city was founded in 1880 by two Ohio brothers who established pineapple plantations here. Today, the downtown area's architectural tradition includes fine examples in Wood Frame Vernacular, art deco, Mediterranean Revival and Colonial Revival styles. For information contact the American Association of University Women, P.O. Box 95-3293, Stuart, Florida 34995-3292.
Hours vary.

SPACE COAST

COCOA BEACH 186

DAYTONA BEACH 191

COCOA BEACH

RESTAURANTS

See ORLANDO & CENTRAL FLORIDA, page 199.

QUICK BITES

The New Smyrna Beach/Cape Canaveral/Cocoa Beach area is becoming a favorite destination for inland Central Floridians (no students). **The Breakers** (518 Flagler Ave., New Smyrna Beach; 904-428-2019; open Mon.-Thurs. 11 a.m.-midnight, Fri.-Sat. 11 a.m.-2 a.m., Sun. noon-midnight) is a rustic bar offering good sandwiches, and almost every seat faces the beach. The **Cocoa Beach Pier** (formerly Canaveral Pier, 401 Meade Ave., Cocoa Beach; 407-783-7549) recently underwent renovations and has several places to eat and imbibe: **Oh, Shucks**, an outdoor raw-seafood bar; **Spinnakers**, a sandwich spot (both open daily 11 a.m.-2 a.m.); and **The Pier House**, for more formal dining in a restaurant that reaches out over the water (open daily 5 p.m.-10:30 p.m.) **Coconuts** (Minuteman Pkwy. & the Atlantic Ocean; 407-784-1422; open Mon.-Sat. 11 a.m.-2 a.m., Sun. noon-2 a.m.) is the quintessential beach restaurant, with great fish sandwiches—served with delicious sweet potato fries—and a few full meals. There's indoor dining but the deck, which overlooks the beach and the volleyball court, is really the place to be.

HOTELS

Moderate (From $100)

Radisson Suite Hotel Oceanfront
3101 N. Hwy. A1A,
Melbourne 32903
• (407) 773-9260
Fax (407) 777-3190

There's been an extensive beachfront redevelopment program in Melbourne in recent years, and the Radisson is plopped down right in the middle of 551 feet of it. One of the most uncluttered beachfront hotel stretches we know of in Florida, this area is newly equipped with wooden boardwalks and footpaths, all decorated with palm trees for shade. The Radisson offers a great deal: a suite, complete with living room, kitchen and sitting area, for the price of a room; some even have Jacuzzis. And the sixteenth-floor VIP Plaza Club accommodations include a host of amenities. The room rate also includes a very nice Continental breakfast. There's really not much going on here in this lazy

neck of the woods, but if you're looking for some comfort in a relatively untraveled locale, the Radisson is the place to find it.
Singles & doubles: $95-$159.

Practical (Under $100)

Cocoa Beach Hilton & Towers
1550 N. Atlantic Ave., Cocoa Beach 32931
• (407) 799-0003
Fax (407) 799-0344

A surprisingly well-appointed and -equipped resort hotel, the Cocoa Beach Hilton boasts about 300 rooms, some in a separate tower building that affords lovely views of the beach and waterfront. While there's no golf or tennis at the hotel, the front desk cheerfully arranges tee-times and court use at nearby facilities. There's plenty to do on-property after dark—it's a good thing, too; not much goes on in Cocoa Beach after the lights go out. Possible activities include a visit to the restaurant, lounge and pool bar, featuring local acts—for which we can't make promises. If you want more luxury, book the Towers.
Singles & doubles: $85-$140; suites: $150-$450.

Holiday Inn Cocoa Beach
1300 N. Atlantic Ave., Cocoa Beach 32931
• (407) 783-2271
Fax (407) 784-8878

You can always count on a Holiday Inn for certain things, that's our theory—and the one in Cocoa Beach is no exception. The rooms are clean, there's a children's playground and game room, the prices are reasonable and there aren't many frills. You can count on 625 feet of beachfront on 25 acres, oceanfront suites, lofts and villas, two tennis courts and a decent (if often sparsely populated) nightclub. Simple amenities in the rooms will please you. The Holiday Inn Cocoa Beach exudes the feeling of a real resort, at a moderate price.
Singles & doubles: $55-$93.

Royal Mansions Resort
8600 Ridgewood Ave., Cape Canaveral 32920
• (407) 784-8484
Fax (407) 799-2907

Just north of Cocoa Beach, where the beach thickens and gives way to Port Canaveral, Cape Canaveral Air Force Station and the John F. Kennedy Space Center, the new Royal Mansions offers a pristine, oceanfront retreat in one- and two-bedroom patio villas and penthouses. Each has a fully equipped kitchen and private Jacuzzi; there's also a heated pool with an outdoor Jacuzzi. Villas cluster in white buildings with navy-blue awnings. There's plenty of natural vegetation between the resort and the ocean. When NASA set up shop in the area in the 1950s, it took care to limit development of the area for safety reasons; the result today is the best naturally preserved stretch of beachfront in the state.
Singles: $50-$90; doubles: $65-$105; triples: $90-$150.

NIGHTLIFE

Spinnaker's
401 Meade Ave.,
Cocoa Beach
• (407) 783-7549

Well, Cocoa Beach's Pier cannot offer the liveliness of its Daytona Beach counterpart, but Spinnaker's is a pleasant place to enjoy a drink and watch the waves crash against the shoreline. During an evening Space Shuttle launch from Cape Canaveral, Spinnaker's offers an excellent view and lots of excitement.
Open nightly 5 p.m.-midnight. All major cards.

SHOPS

Antiques

Antiques, Etc.
530 E. New Haven Ave.,
Melbourne
• (407) 728-8198

Tucked into a quiet street, Antiques Etc. offers a nice selection of porcelain and fine art, as well as period furniture culled from the area.
Open Mon.-Sat. 10 a.m.-5 p.m.

The Dusty Rose Antique Mall
1101 S. Washington Ave.,
Titusville
• (407) 269-5526

Some fifteen dealers and a charming cottage teahouse present a delightful way to break up a day of touring Space Age facilities in Titusville. Located west of the Kennedy Space Center, this delightful outpost vends a wide range of country furniture, estate jewelry, linens, Depression-era glass and porcelains.
Open Mon.-Sat. 10 a.m.-6 p.m.

Home

Linger Awhile
1107 S. Washington Ave.,
Titusville
• (407) 268-2777

The pride of Jill Pope's wonderful little shop is her fabulous selection of hand-stitched quilts, available at very reasonable prices. There are also plenty of linens, gifts and gadgets, plus a delightful collection of teddy bears.
Open Wed.-Sat. 10 a.m.-6 p.m.

Sporting Goods

Ron Jon's Surf Shop
4151 N. Hwy. A1A,
Cocoa Beach
• (407) 799-8888

With billboard rentals that begin in the Florida Keys and trail north toward Georgia, Ron Jon's is quite aggressive in its promotions program. Having been quite successful at it, the enormous shop, housed in a two-story, warehouse-size building in Cocoa Beach, has become Florida's de facto embassy for beach goods. If you can use it at, on or anywhere near the water (yes, that's both salt and fresh water), Ron Jon's has it for sale or rent.
Open daily 9 a.m.-11 p.m.

SIGHTS

Amusements

Brevard Community College Planetarium Observatory
1519 Clearlake Rd., Cocoa
• (407) 631-7889

Appropriately placed because of its proximity to the Kennedy Space Center, Brevard's Planetarium beckons to astronomy enthusiasts. Cocoa is an area of Florida that is still blissfully underdeveloped; star-gazing on a clear night can be much more rewarding than in a smoggy city, even with equipment that would no doubt be more extensive. The weekend laser show, "Laser Visions," with music by Led Zeppelin, is awfully creative—if a tad loud for grown-ups.
Laser shows Fri.-Sat. 7 p.m., 9 p.m. & 10 p.m. Admission $4. Observatory open Fri.-Sat. dusk-10 p.m. (weather permitting). Adults $3, students & seniors $2.

Brevard Museum of History and Natural Science
2201 Michigan Ave., Cocoa Beach
• (407) 632-1830

This facility offers a nifty glimpse into the history of Indian River—from the Ice Age to the Space Age—through its exhibits and adjacent 22-acre nature preserve. The lifestyle of Native Americans and pioneers is depicted in various displays with informative explications, and the Johnnie Johnson Nature Trail outside the museum furnishes a view of natural Florida.
Open Tues.-Sat. 10 a.m.-4 p.m., Sun. 1 p.m.-4 p.m. Adults $2, students & seniors $1, children free.

Space Coast Science Center
1510 Highland Ave., Melbourne
• (407) 259-5572

If you've got kids who like to touch everything, then the Space Coast Science Center offers them a wonderful opportunity. Children (and adults) can pick up everything from a fossilized dinosaur egg to freeze-dried astronaut food (which they are also invited to taste). Other displays, which are sort of elaborate video games, include letting visitors navigate a high-speed chase, launch Earth into orbit, shine laser lights, watch their own heart beat and incubate turtle hatchlings.
Open Tues.-Fri. 10 a.m.-5 p.m., Sat. 10 a.m.-4 p.m. Adults $2.25, children $1.50.

U.S. Astronaut Hall of Fame
6225 Vectorspace Blvd., Titusville
• (407) 268-4716

Situated at the foot of NASA Parkway, the Mercury Seven Foundation operates the brand-new U.S. Astronaut Hall of Fame, which features videotapes, mementos and equipment donated by the original Mercury astronauts. A small and personal facility, the Hall of Fame offers a very different perspective on space travel than does neighboring Spaceport U.S.A. Also on site is the U.S. Space Camp, where children can indulge in a five-day space education program established by the Mercury astronauts. With NASA as one of its principal supporters, the simulated space-training camp gives both kids and school teach-

ers an opportunity to build rockets, enter a space shuttle and experience simulated moon walks and orbits.
Open daily 9 a.m.-5 p.m.

Arts

Cocoa Village Playhouse
300 Brevard Ave.,
Cocoa Village
• (407) 636-5050

The beautifully restored atmospheric theater, originally built in the 1920s, currently acts as Brevard Community College's theater. It also serves as a venue for many local music, drama and dance productions, as well as an annual film festival on world travel. Although we can't vouch for the quality of the home-grown and community productions, the theater's architectural splendor is worth a look, and with plenty of charming restaurants in the restored Cocoa Village area, attending a performance here makes for a wonderful evening.
Open year-round. Call for information.

Landmarks

Cocoa Village
Corner of Brevard &
Dannoy Aves.,
Cocoa Beach
• (407) 690-2284

Take the time to enjoy a charmingly restored turn-of-the-century neighborhood of cobblestone streets and former homes that are now friendly antiques shops and boutiques. Just south of SR 520 and fanning out along the banks of the Indian River, Cocoa Village is a quiet enclave of shops selling jewelry, art, antique clothes and crafts. Stores worth browsing through include Currier's-Sallee's Allee, Forget Me Not, The Country Life and Village Antiques.
Open Mon.-Sat. 10 a.m.-5 p.m., Sun. noon-5 p.m.

NASA Kennedy Space Center's Spaceport USA
Visitors Center, TWS,
Kennedy Space Center,
Merritt Island
• (904) 452-2121

If it feels like you're driving for hours along a network of highways before you reach NASA Parkway and, finally, Spaceport U.S.A., it's because you're being diverted around a series of restricted areas. On arrival, you'll be greeted by a dozen or so rockets sunning themselves in the Rocket Garden, before you begin the tour of "animatronics" displays in the extensive Visitors Center. Allow at least three hours here—it's one of Florida's four most popular attractions. *A Boy from Mars*, the center's newest film, takes a whimsical yet educational look at the life of a 10-year-old boy, son of the first Earthlings to rear a child on Mars. At the adjacent IMAX Theater, the film *The Dream is Alive*, is shown on a 70-foot screen and features three of the astronauts killed in the 1986 Space Shuttle Challenger tragedy. To ensure a place on the crowded tour, visit the facility

in the morning to take the double-decker shuttle bus tours out to the Space Shuttle launch pads.
Open daily 9 a.m.-dusk. No admission or parking fee.

Parks

Merritt Island National Wildlife Refuge
SR 402,
Titusville
• (407) 867-0667

A 71-mile-long stretch of barrier island, Merritt is the offshore, triangle-shaped land mass you can see between Melbourne in the south and New Smyrna in the north. The island boasts both the Canaveral National Seashore (SR 406) and the 140,000-acre Merritt Island National Wildlife Refuge (SR 402). Cape Canaveral sort of dangles off Merritt Island like a right arm to the east, speared up the middle by the Banana River. These nature areas feature virtually untouched flora and fauna among some of the purest beachfronts in Florida. A wintering area for migratory birds, the refuge supports nineteen wildlife species listed as endangered or threatened. This area comprises the last truly untouched expanse of land in Florida, as nearby NASA has for decades prohibited development as a safety measure.
Open Mon.-Fri. 8 a.m.-4:30 p.m., Sat. 9 a.m.-5 p.m.

DAYTONA BEACH

QUICK BITES

Every year come spring, thousands of college students descend upon Daytona Beach to overindulge in suds and sun for spring break. We figure that the restaurants still standing when the revelers leave are solid enough to be worth trying. **Kokomo's**, one of the better Marriott Hotel Boardwalk eateries (100 N. Atlantic Ave., Daytona Beach; 904-252-6232; open Sun.-Thurs. 11 a.m.-1:30 a.m., Fri.-Sat. 11 a.m.-2:30 a.m.) serves cheeseburgers, mahimahi and marlin sandwiches, as well as full dinners of shrimp and crab legs, in an atmosphere tailor-made for the Beach Boys. At the **Saint Regis Hotel** (509 Seabreeze Blvd., Daytona Beach; 904-252-8743; open Mon. 11:30 a.m.-2 p.m., Tues.-Fri. 11:30 a.m.-2 p.m. & 5:30 p.m.-10 p.m., Sat. 5:30 p.m.-10 p.m., Sun. 11 a.m.-2 p.m.), a circa 1886 home converted into a bed-and-breakfast and eatery, you'll get reasonably priced fresh seafood, chicken and salads for lunch and dinner. A short drive south of Daytona, **The North Turn** (4511 S. Atlantic Ave., Ponce Inlet; 904-760-6467; open daily 11 a.m.-10 p.m.) serves good sandwiches, burgers and finger foods inside and out on a huge wooden deck that faces the ocean.

HOTELS

Moderate (From $100)

Marriott Daytona Beach
100 N. Atlantic Ave., Daytona Beach 32018
• (904) 254-8200
Fax (904) 253-0275

You don't have to worry much about central location in Daytona Beach: most of the hotels, strewn in unimaginative lines along the beachfront so each room can be marketed as "ocean view," are right on top of one another. The relatively new (two years old) Marriott Daytona Beach is somewhat of an exception. It is indeed imaginatively laid out, rooms stacked like a pyramid and pointed like an arrow toward a the Atlantic. In addition to 402 standard rooms, 25 suites with wet bars provide a more luxurious alternative; the concierge floor is worth the few extra dollars, as it is at all Florida Marriotts. There's an indoor/outdoor pool—an interesting creation separating the inside section from the outside with Plexiglas—plus a health club with sauna and steam room and a plethora of watersports.
Singles & doubles: $95-$195; suites: $250-$750.

Palm Coast Sheraton
300 Clubhouse Dr., Palm Coast 32127
• (904) 445-3000
Fax (904) 445-9685

Midway between Daytona Beach and St. Augustine (approximately 30 miles north of the Daytona Beach Airport), Palm Coast is a mammoth planned community that has been busily replacing vast acres of nothingness over the last half decade. For golf and tennis enthusiasts, the area's facilities can't be beat; Sheraton guests have privileges at each of the four eighteen-hole golf courses designed by Tom Fazio and Arnold Palmer, as well as the eighteen hard-clay and grass-surface tennis courts. The hotel itself is pleasant enough, with 154 rooms and two suites situated around a quiet marina. The usual amenities are included.
Singles & doubles: $99-$300; golf packages available.

Practical (Under $100)

Daytona Beach Hilton
2637 S. Atlantic Ave., Daytona Beach 32118
• (904) 767-7350
Fax (904) 760-3651

With an enormous ballroom and lots of meeting facilities, the Daytona Beach Hilton remains a longtime favorite of visiting business groups. Never fear, independent travelers: the hotel does a nice job of separating you from the Shriners. The Hilton's 215 rooms and suites descend like a staircase to the hard-packed sands of Daytona Beach; the hotel also sports a lovely beachside pool, putting green, tennis courts and a spacious sauna and exercise room.
Singles & doubles: $60-$165; suites: $195-$500.

Indigo Lakes Hilton Resort
2620 Volusia Ave.,
Daytona Beach 32120
• (904) 258-6333
Fax (904) 254-3698

If you want to get away from the beachfront sprawl, consider Indigo Lakes. The official resort of the Ladies Professional Golfers Association (LPGA), which makes its headquarters in Daytona Beach, the 212-room facility has plenty of recreational facilities. There are golf and tennis, racquetball, archery, fitness trails and more. The rooms are adequate; the ambience, friendly.
Singles & doubles: $85-$159.

Perry's Ocean Edge Resort
2209 S. Atlantic Ave.,
Daytona Beach 32118
• (904) 255-0581
Fax (904) 258-7315

A carpet of well-tended lawn, spanning 700 feet along the beachfront behind Perry's, lends the feeling of being in Hawaii or the Caribbean (we can't think of any other Florida resort featuring such a parklike setting right on the ocean). A tropical garden solarium carries the theme inside, where there are 204 guest rooms (themselves rather plain, even those with oceanfront views). There's a kidney-shaped pool, and for warm dips into the wee hours, a separate Jacuzzi. By no means a luxury resort, Perry's is nonetheless comfortable and inviting, with a friendly staff offering distinctly personal service for lodgings in this price range.
Singles & doubles: $45-$110.

The Reef
935 S. Atlantic Ave.,
Daytona Beach 32118
• (904) 252-2581
Fax (904) 257-3608

We mention The Reef because, having undergone an extensive remodeling program over the last couple of years, it remains one of the best-appointed, centrally located Daytona Beach hotels in its price range. Most of the 236 rooms have their own balconies; efficiency rooms have been newly equipped with a range of appliances. For families, there's a huge pool deck with two swimming pools, a game room and shuffleboard—and, of course, there's the resort's signature perpetual game of volleyball underway at the beach.
Singles & doubles: $45-$113; efficiencies: $50-$125; suites: $85-$150.

NIGHTLIFE

Finky's
640 Grandview St.,
Daytona Beach
• (904) 255-5059

If you're under 21 and don't have a fake ID, Finky's is the place for you. (You'll be carded when you attempt to order a beer, not when you walk in the door). At 50 cents a draft, even the under-age crowd might be tempted. A concert club hosting national acts (Three Dog Night recently played here), Finky's rocks with dancing into the wee hours, spring-break style.
Open Tues.-Thurs. 9 p.m.-2 a.m., Fri.-Sat. 9 p.m.-4 a.m. Cards: AE, MC, V.

J's Island Patio
831 Broadway (Hwy. 92),
Daytona Beach
• (904) 253-5313

Famous for its Buffalo chicken wings (which go for fifteen cents each) and $1 beers to wash them down, J's Island Patio offers lots of beachfront raging into the early morning.
Open daily 1 p.m.-4 a.m. Live music Mon.-Thurs. 5 p.m.-4 a.m., Fri.-Sun. 1 p.m.-4 a.m. Cards: AE, MC, V.

Razzle's
611 Seabreeze Blvd.,
Daytona Beach
• (904) 257-6236

You can go barhopping at Razzle's, probably the hottest nightclub in town, without ever leaving the place: there are four bars and two dance floors in the cavernous night spot. The mood here (as in the rest of Daytona) depends largely on the time of year, ranging from spring break madness to the off-season blues.
Open daily 8 p.m.-4 a.m. Cards: AE, MC, V.

Antiques

Daytona Flea Market
I-95 at U.S. 92,
Daytona Beach
• (904) 252-1999

The folks at Daytona's flea market must be doing something right: they host more than 2 million visitors a year. (Maybe it has something to do with being located within hearing distance of the Daytona International Speedway.) The bargains you may come across at the flea market and antique showcase all depend on hitting it on the right day. We also recommend going early to beat the heat and the crowds.
Open Fri.-Sun. 8 a.m.-4 p.m.

For Heaven's Sake
15 N. Ridgewood Ave.,
Ormond Beach
• (904) 677-6640

How charming in this outpost of tongas and quarter beers to find a devotional shop. Small yet plentifully stocked, the shop offers a nice selection of religious children's books, adult-level books, bibles, gifts, CDs and inspirational tapes.
Open Mon.-Fri. 10 a.m.-6 p.m., Sat. 10 a.m.-4 p.m.

Sporting Goods

Baseball Card Exchange
30 W. Granada Blvd,
Ormond Beach
• (904) 677-1318

How appropriate here in spring-training country to have a pleasant little place to exchange baseball cards. The shop also buys, sells and trades other sports cards, as well as plenty of athletic equipment and memorabilia.
Open daily 10 a.m.-5 p.m.

Buck's Gun Rack
607 Volusia Ave.,
Daytona Beach
• (904) 252-8471

If you're a survivalist, hunter, taxidermist, archery pro or basic firearms freak, Buck can offer you a revolving charge for that Smith & Wesson of your dreams. The enormous retailer of all sorts of weaponry also buys, sells and trades new and used firearms.
Open Mon.-Sat. 10 a.m.-5:30 p.m.

SIGHTS

Amusements

Atlantic Fun Center
300 S. Atlantic Ave.,
Daytona Beach
• (904) 255-6863

How's this for one-stop-shopping: buy your beer, sandwiches, beach towels and rent one of Daytona's famous beach buggies at one place. Atlantic Fun Center is Daytona's most all-inclusive beach shop. How's this for a deal—show up at 9 a.m. for your buggy rental and you'll get the first hour free.
Open daily 9 a.m.-dusk.

Birthplace of Speed Museum
160 E. Granada Blvd.,
Ormond Beach
• (904) 672-5657

The Space Coast earned its reputation as "The Birthplace of Speed" long before the first rocket blasted off nearby. It was back in 1902 that early motorcycles and automobiles began racing on Daytona's hard-packed beaches. The museum offers a colorful look at the development of the automobile with a variety of exhibits. Highlights are a Stanley Cup replica and a Rocket Kart, the latter powered by two rocket engines.
Open Tues.-Sat. 10 a.m.-5 p.m.

The Casements
25 Riverside Dr.,
Ormond Beach
• (904) 673-4701

The former winter home of John D. Rockefeller named for its casement windows, this museum and cultural center has a wide range of exhibits, from the Hungarian Historic Room to a historical Boy Scout exhibit. The adjacent Rockefeller Gardens have been restored to their original design, and you can walk along the patio to a sparkling fountain and fish pond. The mood here is peaceful; there is an ambience of history and great wealth.
Open Mon.-Fri. 9 a.m.-5 p.m., Sat. 9 a.m.-noon. Tours every half hour Mon.-Fri. 10 a.m.-3 p.m., Sat. 10 a.m.-noon.

Woody's Jet Boats
Seabreeze Bridge,
Aloha Marina,
Daytona Beach
• (904) 254-0966

Picture a go-cart that floats: it's called a jet boat, and Woody's has lots of them. Watch the high-powered speed boats buzz around Daytona, and you'll want to rent one yourself.
Open daily 9 a.m.-6 p.m.

Arts

Seaside Music Theater
Daytona Beach
Community College,
Daytona Beach
• (904) 252-6200

If you're looking for a little culture here in partying Daytona, try a little summer stock. The Seaside Theater, a musical repertory company, presents original productions of Broadway favorites in a very well-equipped, 508-seat theater at Daytona Beach Community College.
Rotating repertory from June-Aug. Matinees and evening performances.

Landmarks

Daytona International Speedway
1801 Volusia Ave.,
Daytona Beach
• (904) 254-2700

Hardly a weekend goes by without an event at the Daytona International Speedway, which opened in 1959 as "The World Center of Racing" and the premier attraction of the sleepy little resort area. Today, the inaugural Daytona 500 remains one of the most renowned events in racing; the Speedway also hosts the prestigious annual Sun Bank 24 and the Daytona 200 By Arai (a motorcycle racing event).
Call for schedule information.

Dunlawton Sugar Mill Ruins
950 Old Sugar Mill Rd.,
Port Orange
• (904) 767-1735

The ruins of the Dunlawton Sugar Mill, considered to be the most complete and best-preserved ruins of their kind in the nation, reflect the sweet revenge of Florida's Seminole Indians. At a time when sixteen sugar plantations along the Halifax River were thriving, the Seminole Indians were furious with the U.S. government, which had ordered them to move east of the Mississippi River. It was in 1836 that the Seminoles overran the area and forced the mill owners and their slaves to move north, burning the main mansion to the ground. You can imagine their fury as you walk through the well-preserved grounds.
Tour before dusk.

Ponce de León Inlet Lighthouse
South Peninsula Dr.,
Ponce de León Inlet,
Daytona Beach
• (904) 761-1821

The view is unparalleled: if you want to get a look at all of Daytona Beach, from the International Speedway to the beaches, make the climb. Built more than a hundred years ago, this brick lighthouse remained in service until 1970, guiding mariners along the Space Coast. Now, historical displays trace the history of Florida's lighthouses; an adjacent picnic area is a delightful place to spend the afternoon.
Open daily 10 a.m.-4 p.m.

Tours

Dixie Queen River Cruises
841 Ballough Rd.
Daytona Beach
• (904) 255-1997

Daytona's own paddle-wheel steamer, an authentic replica of the 1890s vessels that traversed the Mississippi, makes for a delightful way to enjoy an evening in Daytona. You can dance under the stars as the Dixie Queen plies the waters of the Intracoastal. There are two bars, a full-service galley and some welcome air-conditioning. The food is standard, but the moonlight is beyond comparison.
Dinner cruises by charter only. Call for prices and information.

ORLANDO & CENTRAL FLORIDA

INTRODUCTION	198
RESTAURANTS	199
QUICK BITES	208
HOTELS	211
NIGHTLIFE	221
SHOPS	224
SIGHTS & SPORTS	230
BASICS	243

INTRODUCTION

AMERICA'S NEW PLAYGROUND?

Remember back in times of yore, before *glasnost* and *perestroika* had found a place in the American language? The year was 1959, and Nikita Khrushchev was touring the United States, planning to visit Disneyland, in Anaheim, California. He was denied admission because of security reasons, and grumbled loudly about this "slight" throughout the remainder of his stay.

Today, Khrushchev's choice would probably be Walt Disney World, where he could revel for 24 hours, and still not see half of it. The mega-entertainment empire has supplanted Disneyland through sheer magnitude, just as surely as Florida (some say) eventually might take California's place as this country's vacation state. Has Florida become the playground of America, with Orlando and, most specifically, Walt Disney World pumping the fantasies of fun to the other parts of the leisure body? This could be, and we'll even dare to venture that Florida could soon be the vacation playground of the world. It's no accident that Disney's EPCOT Center contains minicountries: in many parts of Orlando, you'll hear as much French, Spanish, Italian and German spoken as you will English.

What draws so many foreigners as well as visitors to Orlando from other states? The obvious lure is the massive square footage of variety in entertainment. In the same day, you can hike on Pleasure Island, jet-ski through Typhoon Lagoon, or frolic with the children at Mickey Mouse's birthday party in the Magic Kingdom Park. Working its spell more subtly on the imaginations of America—and the world—is that unmatched, indescribable Disney atmosphere, in which time halts in its tread, color bursts its bounds, the impossible becomes tangible and the collective imagination of the crowd becomes limitless—if just for a day. How does the Disney magic work? The high-tech infrastructure of the theme parks, the crack cleaning crews and sunny, smiling faces only tell part of the story.

In reality, the secret is this: there's not a soul that doesn't desire fifteen minutes of fantasy, a moment in which they can watch the absurd, the fantastic, the impossible, the past and the future come alive in front of their eyes. This explains the success of not only Orlando's Universal Studios and the Disney-MGM Studios Theme Park ("Go ahead," beckon the attractions, "star in a TV show! We know you've dreamed of it...."), but of all of the Disney empire. With these sorts of memories available to the everyman, it's no wonder that Orlando is no longer lost on the world map.

RESTAURANTS

Arthur's 27
1900 Buena Vista Dr.,
Walt Disney World Village,
Lake Buena Vista
• (407) 827-2727
CONTINENTAL

11/20

Perhaps the thin air on the 27th floor of the Buena Vista Palace blurs people's judgment; other than that, we can't figure out why this place is consistently ranked as one of the finest in the state. The food isn't bad, but it's not even the best in a two-mile radius, let alone the best in Florida. However, with a dearth of top-floor restaurants in this area, Arthur's will always receive raves for its view. To our mind, even the view does little but emphasize Florida's flatness (though if you're seated facing the Disney parks, dinner is likely to include a fireworks show or two). Bucking the trend toward simple, clear flavors, Arthur's features a good deal of rich, old-fashioned sauces: creamy Cognac-peppercorn sauce gracing beef tenderloin, Madeira-cream sauce accompanying medallions of veal, basil cream with the swordfish. If you've sensed a certain theme, you're correct—those who eschew cream sauces won't be happy here. On the other hand, appetizers are uniformly delicious, particularly the gazpacho flavored with vodka. The painfully slow service can be a little too chummy for the formal, elegant decor, which features glass alcoves and a thankfully restrained medieval theme (the place was named for the Arthur of Round Table fame). With wine, dinner for two will run $120 to $130.
Open nightly 6 p.m.-10:30 p.m. All major cards.

Black Tulip
207 Brevard Ave.,
Cocoa Village
• (407) 631-1133
AMERICAN

9/20

For years Black Tulip has been hailed as one of the finest restaurants on Central Florida's coast, receiving numerous awards and citations, many of which fill the front window. We've always considered an abundance of awards and citations to be cause for concern, a concern that proved valid here. The look is dated and rather worn: the dining room features a burlwood-table centerpiece, tree trunks rising to the ceiling, which is covered with leafy wallpaper. And although acceptable, the cooking is by no means worth going out of your way for. The best of the appetizers was the tasty (but decidedly heavy) escargots with gobs of spinach and hollandaise; less flavorful were the banal conch fritters, which fought our attempts to chew them. We enjoyed the beef tenderloin and artichokes in a lovely mustard sauce as well as the fresh-tasting dolphin and scallops baked in parchment, though it was mere seconds away from being overcooked. But the insipid roast duckling, which was advertised as being served in a sweet sauce of apples and cashews, turned up with ordinary peanuts instead. To add insult to injury, our desserts proudly wore globs of dreadful nondairy whipped topping. The wine list is notable primarily for being absolutely huge. Dinner for two, with wine, runs about $75. *Open Mon.-Sat. 11 a.m.-2:30 p.m. & 5:30 p.m.-10 p.m. Cards: AE, MC, V.*

Chatham's Place
7575 Dr. Phillips Blvd., Orlando
• (407) 345-2992
AMERICAN

After you taste the cooking of brothers Louis and Randolph Chatham, you won't be surprised to discover that they're graduates of the Culinary Institute of America—their inventive take on modern American cuisine bears the school's distinctive stamp, combining classic French techniques with marvelous American ingredients and flair. You can watch them hard at work in their kitchen via the large windows in the small dining room, which is casually decorated with blue tile and country-style wood furnishings, a place in which both the dressed-up and dressed-down feel comfortable.

The menu is small but well structured, with a bit of Southern charm in such dishes as the delicious grouper with pecan butter, a fresh, firm filet topped with rich butter, pecans and Cajun spices that successfully cut the sweetness of the nuts and butter. We were equally impressed with the filet of beef in Madeira sauce and the grilled breast of duck, its skin crisply charred and its meat rich and juicy. Appetizers range from Brie topped with a fiery jalapeño jelly to petite escargots with a garlic, basil and tomato concasse. The desserts are unabashedly American: Granny's six-layer lemon cake, made by the Chathams' own grandmother; heavenly bananas Foster, made discreetly in the kitchen instead of embarrassingly at tableside; and extraordinarily fat and sweet blackberries with ice cream. The informal but attentive service is overseen by the Chathams' mother, Bettye, who makes her guests feel like they're dining in her home—and she requests that her guests don't sully her home with cigarette smoke. You'll find plenty of good wines that suit the cuisine. Dinner for two, with wine, averages $85.
Open nightly 6 p.m.-10:30 p.m. Cards: MC, V.

Chris's House of Beef
801 John Young Pkwy., Orlando
• (407) 295-1931
STEAKHOUSE

11/20

In a town where most restaurants date back only as far as the arrival of Disney, this decades-old place is somewhat of an oddity. And it's a welcome oddity, with its tradition of preparing high-quality steaks and prime rib that have kept its loyal customers coming back for wedding receptions, special parties or just weekly fixes of meat and spuds. Don't get discouraged if you pull up and see a full parking lot; instead, check the lighted sign out front to see if "seating is available." The multilevel dining room is expansive, with huge windows overlooking the parking lot (at night they throw back a sparkling reflection) and glass-rod chandeliers that run the length of the room; the look is 1960s fancy, with curved booths and lots of red. No one comes here for the decor, though—they're here for meat, and lots of it. There are the obligatory seafood and chicken dishes, but go somewhere else if that's what you plan to order. This is a place to revel in a fine piece of prime rib, buttery smooth and juicy, or filet mignon as tender as a Schubert sonata. Many locals consider Chris's to be a fine-dining establishment, but the friendly, coffee-shop-style service never puts on airs, and you don't have to dress up—besides, any place with a salad bar can only be so *haute*. The astounding wine list, however, would fit in at any *haute* spot—it's as big as a phone book but still manages to offer many very good selections; for this it has won recognition widely. Dinner for two, with wine, runs $85 to $90.

Open Sun.-Thurs. 11:30 a.m.-10 p.m., Fri.-Sat. 11:30 a.m.-11 p.m. All major cards.

> *Remember to call ahead to reserve your table, and please, if you cannot honor your reservation, be courteous and let the restaurant know.*

Christini's

7600 Dr. Phillips Blvd., Orlando
• (407) 345-8770
ITALIAN

11/20

You may think you're in the fresh-scrubbed, sun-washed overgrown amusement park called Orlando, but if you're in Christini's, you're in New York. For one thing, it looks like it was picked up from Manhattan's Little Italy, brusque waiters and all, and plopped down on Dr. Phillips Boulevard; for another, you're likely to find it populated with more New Yorkers than locals. There are lots of folks from other places, too, because this place pursues the tourist trade with a passion. They love the masculine, old-fashioned New York–Italian setting, all sumptuous woods, polished rails and dark-red carpeting—at least, that's what we thought it looked like, but it was hard to see through the thick haze of cigar and cigarette smoke. It was hard to hear, too, what with the accordionist carrying on and the diners shouting at each other at the closely packed tables. Fortunately, those negotiating this hubbub are rewarded with some very tasty northern Italian cuisine. The kitchen sticks to the classics that date from the pre-arugula era: spaghetti al filletto, a meatless tomato sauce with fresh herbs and olive oil; fresh red snapper spiced up with white wine, capers, olives and sweet red peppers; linguine with a simple, homey red clam sauce; and that great comfort pasta, rich spaghetti carbonara.

The desserts are in the 1950s Italian tradition, which means they're best avoided, though the tartufo (spumone in a chocolate shell) is acceptable. The wine selection suits the cuisine perfectly, but nothing here comes cheaply: two will spend about $110 for dinner with wine.
Open Mon.-Sat. 6 p.m.-11 p.m. All major cards.

Le Coq au Vin
4800 S. Orange Ave., Orlando
• (407) 851-6980
FRENCH

Le Coq au Vin is simply one of the best restaurants in central Florida—and we mean "simply" literally. It's a modest country-French kind of place, housed in a log cabin–style building that once served as a model-home sales office. The nondescript café decor and Maurice Chevalier posters give it a casual, amiable French atmosphere. Owner/chef Louis Perrotte and chef Bruno Ponsot keep the style traditional with such offerings as Basque-style tournedos of beef with yellow, red and green bell peppers in a garlicky pepper-cream sauce. A firm, tasty red snapper filet is set on a bed of earthy lentils with just a touch of vinegar, a most successful country-style dish. As is usually the case in the United States, the restaurant's namesake dish is made with a hen instead of a rooster; it's also made with veal stock instead of chicken, but that just adds even more to the rich, Burgundy-wine taste—and at $10.50, which includes vegetables and new potatoes topped with caviar, it's an exceptional bargain. Accompany your meal with a bottle from the decent wine cellar and end it with an admirable crème brûlée, and you'll want for nothing. Servers make up in friendliness what they lack in speed and efficiency. Dinner for two, with wine, runs about $65.
Open Tues.-Fri. 11:30 a.m.-2 p.m. & 5:30 p.m.-10 p.m., Sat. 5:30 p.m.-10 p.m., Sun. 5:30 p.m.-9 p.m. All major cards.

Dux
Peabody Orlando, 9801 International Dr., Orlando
• (407) 352-4000
AMERICAN

11/20

The name Dux sounds so elegant and so French—you might think it's the name of a stately country château or a French luxury car. In fact, the top-of-the-line restaurant in the Peabody Orlando is a fancy misspelling of "ducks," the hotel's mascots. Ducks frolic in the lobby fountain and parade around the grounds, and representations of them are everywhere: pictures of ducks adorn the menu and the walls over the elegant banquettes, and little silver ducks sit atop the silver domes the waiters whisk off the entrées with such flourish. But you won't find the cute little quackers under the domes—the kitchen couldn't dare serve duck à l'orange after the hotel has anthropomorphized them to such an extent.

Chef William Higgins instead whips up such sophisticated dishes as seared tuna over braised leeks in a Pinot Noir sauce

and grilled filet mignon encrusted in crushed herbs. It all sounds wonderful, and occasionally it is, but too frequently the cooking falls flat. Lamb wrapped in phyllo dough sounded irresistible but turned out to be mushy, and tasted off. A perfectly good salmon filet was ruined by its accompanying whole garlic cloves, which were overwhelmingly pungent and bitter (they probably just needing more roasting time). Dishes like these try hard, and they have a welcome touch of creativity not often seen in fancy hotel restaurants, but they just don't cut it—and when you reach this stratospheric price range, you have a right to expect extraordinary cooking. The decor is everything you'd expect of a posh hotel dining room, done in those ubiquitous pale, hotel-chic neutral tones, with brocaded fabrics and pillows. Service is efficient but a bit too chatty and informal for the setting, and wines are astonishingly expensive—a very small glass of California Chardonnay cost us $8.25. Dinner for two will run about $160, even with just a glass of wine each.
Open Tues.-Sun. 6 p.m.-11 p.m. All major cards.

Jordan's Grove
1300 S. Maitland Ave., Maitland
• (407) 628-0020
AMERICAN

Jordan's Grove glows with the warmth and welcome of a dining room in a private home—and the cooking glows with vivid, well-balanced flavors. Located in a restored 1915 house, the dining area has an inviting oldtime look, with hardwood floors, beamed ceilings and polished antique tables. Given this homey atmosphere, you might expect to dine on meatloaf and mashed potatoes, but instead you're presented with some of the most creative cooking in central Florida. The menu changes daily at the whim of chefs Mark Rodriguez (who's also the owner) and Clair Epting. A curried carrot-cream sauce graces a saffron-and-scallop mousse. Homemade andouille sausage counterpoints a grilled beef tenderloin. Grilled Maine sea scallops are brilliantly matched with a blackberry-tarragon vinaigrette. This is the only place in the area that serves naturally raised beef and free-range poultry; if you've never tasted buttery, steroid-free beef, you're in for quite a treat. Dessert time brings such satisfying all-American goodies as warm blackberry-apple crisp with sweet cream and a warm macadamia-coconut tart. Although the cuisine is sophisticated, the service is far from stuffy. The extensive wine list leans heavily toward American varietals. The menu recently went à la carte, with entrées averaging $24, but a soup-to-nuts prix fixe is still available for $35. Dinner with wine will cost two from $90 to $100.
Open Tues.-Fri. & Sun. 11:30 a.m.-2:30 p.m. & 6 p.m.-10 p.m., Sat. 6 p.m.-10 p.m. All major cards.

Maison et Jardin

430 Wymore Rd.,
Altamonte Springs
• (407) 862-4410
CONTINENTAL

11/20

Locals call it "Mason Jar" to poke fun at its stuffiness, but stuffy this place remains, solidly established as the local headquarters for the old-money set. It looks like a country club with baroque flair, with its plush carpeting, stately drapes, impressive flowers and well-spaced tables; windows overlook the meticulously trimmed lawn and garden dotted with statuary. The appetizer of choice for this prosperous, conservative crowd is, of course, blini with caviar and sour cream. Prepared in the dining room (though not necessarily tableside), the light but richly flavorful blini are served with a tall glass of Stolichnaya vodka and are priced according to your choice of caviar: Icelandic, Spanish or beluga. Medallions of beef topped with smoked salmon, a light sour-cream sauce and caviar may sound fussy, but the sauce is subtle and the smoky, salty flavors of the salmon and caviar make a successful counterpoint to the beef. The chef has taken to experimenting with such exotic ingredients as kangaroo, which was nothing to get all hopped up about—its meat is notable primarily for toughness and tastelessness. Desserts run to such elegant standards as strawberries in Grand Marnier and flourless chocolate cake, both of which are first-rate. At a joint this fancy, one would certainly expect polished, professional service, but such has not been the case on our visits. When we once complained about a terribly tough pheasant, the waiter had no idea how to handle the problem, and another time our waiter didn't know the difference between Dover and petrale sole. The thorough wine list has an appropriate match for everything on the menu—except perhaps kangaroo. Dinner for two, with wine (and Icelandic caviar in the blini), runs about $145.
Open Mon.-Sat. 6 p.m.-10 p.m., Sun. 6 p.m.-9:30 p.m. All major cards.

Ming Court

9188 International Dr.,
Orlando
• (407) 351-9988
CHINESE

11/20

This little jewel has proved to Orlando that the phrase "gourmet Chinese food" is not oxymoronic. It's a notion some locals and tourists resist—we've seen several people take one look at the prices and leave without ordering. It's true that prices are higher than at the typical Chinese restaurant, but then you won't find food this good at the typical Chinese restaurant, at least not in these parts. We usually start our meal with the tasty grilled yakitori chicken marinated in fish sauce and the sweet, delicate steamed shrimp dumplings, one of several dim-sum offerings. Jumbo shrimp with lobster sauce is a good example of the chef's creativity, the mild, delicious sauce flavored with crushed black beans. Kung pao chicken bursts with a tangy, spicy, fresh flavor (no heavy cornstarch here) and boasts cashews as well as the traditional peanuts. The dining room is remarkable, a serene,

high-ceilinged space given drama with large trees; glass walls overlook a floating garden, which is separated from the very busy street outside by a wavy wall that looks like the back of a dragon. Unfortunately, the service reminds us more of a chop-suey house than a serious restaurant—waiters do little more than deliver the food. But the wine list offers plenty of worthy companions to a very good meal. Dinner for two, with wine, costs about $70.
Open nightly 5:30 p.m.-midnight. All major cards.

Park Plaza Gardens
Park Plaza Hotel,
319 Park Ave. South,
Winter Park
• (407) 645-2475
CONTINENTAL

Park Avenue, Winter Park's own little Rodeo Drive, is the perfect setting for this lovely, upscale restaurant. Located in the Park Plaza Hotel, the dining room feels like an outdoor patio, with its brick floors, trees and hanging plants; a glass-paneled roof allows for an indoor climate, so critical during a Florida summer. The talented young chef, Patrick Reilly, keeps the fare Continental, in good hotel-restaurant style, but he skillfully updates some classics and throws in a few modern creations for good measure. We've liked everything we've tried, from the woodland feuilleté with tender escargots to the exceptionally tasty salmon quesadillas, tender salmon tucked into flour tortillas with a mild, cheesy cream sauce. Entrées run the gamut from that Continental mainstay, rack of lamb, here updated with a light, herby white-wine sauce that perfectly complements the mellow flavor of the meat, to a bit of a Caribbean exotica, grouper escovitche, a thick grouper filet topped with a concasse of red, yellow and green bell peppers. Waiters are pretty well trained in the classic European style, except that they clear the plates before everyone at the table is finished eating, a minor but annoying touch of unprofessionalism. The wine selection is primarily American, and there's a good choice in every price range. Two will spend $110 for dinner with wine.
Open Mon.-Thurs. 11:30 a.m.-3 p.m. & 6 p.m.-10 p.m., Fri.-Sat. 11:30 a.m.-3 p.m. & 6 p.m.-11 p.m., Sun. 11 a.m.-3 p.m. & 6 p.m.-9 p.m. All major cards.

Portobello Yacht Club
Pleasure Island,
Walt Disney World,
Lake Buena Vista
• (407) 934-8888
ITALIAN

11/20

You can choose to believe or not to believe Disney's legend about its adult amusement area, Pleasure Island, the supposed haven of a wealthy man named Merriweather Pleasure, who supposedly built the place long ago. Whether a cynic or believer, you'll find this trattoria, with its solidly handsome setting of dark wood, highly polished brass rails and sheets of sail cloth, delightful. Operated by The Levy Restaurants, the savvy group that created a slew of Chicago hot spots, this cheerful, lively spot serves the kind of contemporary Italian food that is all the rage across the country—not completely authentic, perhaps, but full of fun and good flavors. The menu is thick with such popular standards as fried calamari (crisp and tasty) and small pizzas given a crackerlike crust in the wood-burning oven. Pastas run to such things as spaghettini alla Portobello, a tangle of pasta with Alaskan crab legs, scallops, clams, shrimp, mussels and a light, vibrant sauce of garlic, tomatoes and herbs, and perfectly al dente farfalle (butterfly pasta) primavera with peas and crunchy asparagus in a creamy sauce. Garlic-infused shrimp are grilled on a skewer of rosemary.

> *To better understand the ranking system Gault Millau uses, keep in mind that we have awarded the top restaurant in this book a 16/20. Any Florida restaurants that we rank as 13/20, 14/20, or 15/20 are therefore very good restaurants for the area; even an 11/20 or 12/20 for a moderately priced, unpretentious eatery doesn't mean that the food isn't good.*

As is always the case in the world of Walt Disney, there's a never-ending crush of humanity, so be prepared for long waits between courses. Fortunately, there are some decent Italian and American wines to keep you amused in the interims, and the friendly, dedicated waiters will make sure you don't feel neglected. We find the prices a bit high for this simple (although good) food, but that's to be expected in the Land of the Tourist, where nothing comes cheap: dinner for two, with wine, runs $80 to $85.
Open daily 11:30 a.m.-midnight. Cards: AE, MC, V.

Toscanelli
3526 N. U.S. Hwy. 17-92,
Lake Mary
• (407) 330-1299
ITALIAN

(13)

The green-and-yellow wallpaper—or what you can see of it, through all the postcards, newspaper clippings, Italian posters and . . . a picture of a geisha?—isn't especially appetizing, and neither are the cheap vinyl booths or the bare-bones decor. But one taste of the cooking and you'll be transported to the hills of Tuscany. Owners Mario and Evita Morosi serve many of the dishes found in their family's restaurant of the same name in Padova, Italy.

Two time-honored family recipes, tagliolini Marco Polo, with smoked salmon and a Parmesan-cream sauce, and filet mignon in a creamy Cognac sauce with crunchy hot peppercorns, will have you asking to be adopted by the Morosi family. The heavenly pasta e fagioli is graced with a sprig of fresh rosemary and a drizzle of extra-virgin olive oil. Even such plain-Jane dishes as bruschetta and toasted cream-cheese bread taste extraordinary; the bruschetta, for instance, is loaded up with big chunks of sweet garlic and bursts with bold flavors. Chef Mario

prepares very little in advance, so your dinner will meander along at a leisurely pace, if you know what we mean. He makes no excuses—after all, it adds to the authenticity—but he warns diners not to expect to catch a movie after dinner. The wine list could do with more Italians (this is Toscanelli, after all) and less Yugoslavians, but it isn't too difficult to find an appropriate accompaniment. Dinner for two, with wine, costs between $50 and $60.
Open Tues.-Sat. 5:30 p.m.-9:30 p.m. Cards: AE, MC, V.

Victoria & Albert's

Grand Floridian Beach Resort,
4401 Grand Floridian Way,
Walt Disney World,
Lake Buena Vista
• (407) 824-2383
AMERICAN

If you associate Disney eating with spotless fast-food operations and cheerful family restaurants, you might think this posh dining room in Disney's grandest hotel to be quite out of character. The small, circular room under a domed ceiling reflects a turn-of-the-century European opulence, with fabric-covered walls, grand furnishings and huge flower arrangements. But when you settle in for your seating, the Disney touch is immediately evident: you are served not by a waiter but by a maid and butler—and by an amazing coincidence, all the maids are named Victoria and all the butlers Albert. Before you blanch at the $75 prix-fixe menu, your only option here, remember that tables are set with Sambonet silver, Schott-Zweisel crystal and Royal Doulton china, and the daily-changing menu is personalized for your table, engraved in gold for you to take home and press into your scrapbook. Clearly, you come here more for the experience than the food, though the cooking can't be faulted. The six-course meal might include peach soup with amaretto, filet of salmon with chunky barbecue sauce (it sounds down-home but is actually quite elegant, and tasty to boot) or broiled lamb chops with goat cheese. After your main course comes a salad (served after the entrée, as in France), followed by an assortment of ripe assorted cheeses (served by Albert) and a glass of port. It's all stylish and executed with care, though none of the dishes will blow you away. Those planning to divulge state secrets over their meal should be warned about the acoustics of the domed ceiling: diners across the room may overhear every word you whisper. The sensitive of lung will appreciate the no-smoking policy. The $225 price tag for dinner for two, with wine, is worth it only for big spenders who want to feel pampered in the Disney style.
Seatings nightly 6 p.m.-6:45 p.m. & 9 p.m.-9:45 p.m. Cards: AE, MC, V.

QUICK BITES

BARBECUE	208
CAFES	208
COFFEE SHOPS & DINERS	209
CUBAN	209
HAMBURGERS & SANDWICHES	210
MIDDLE EASTERN FAST FOOD	210

BARBECUE

Bubbalou's Bodacious Bar-b-que
1471 Lee Rd.,
Winter Park
• (407) 628-1212

Here's what a barbecue shack is supposed to be like. Step up to the counter, place your order, then have a seat at one of the bulky picnic tables and someone will bring the food when it's ready. The barbecue here, whether in the form of ribs or shredded meat in the style of North Carolina, is always juicy, alive with a smoky flavor that lingers. The tomato-based "killer sauce" scalds unknowing tastebuds, so watch your step. The decor tries to be a little too cute—baseball hats hang everywhere and "good ol' boy" slogans abound, but those indulgences can be forgiven when the food is this tasty. If you spend more than $20 here, you're eating too much.
Open Mon.-Thurs. 10 a.m.-9:30 p.m., Fri.-Sat. 10 a.m.-10:30 p.m. No cards.

CAFES

Pebbles
2110 W. State Rd. 434,
Longwood
• (407) 774-7111

Could Pebbles's menu be a grazer's paradise? Let's see: tapas look traditional and good, as do the succulent bite-sized steak and chicken pieces called "thumb bits." Those with fuller appetites can try the angel-hair pasta with grilled duck or smoked salmon. The decor is quiet, with plenty of plants, light woods and earth tones. Think of this as Californian cuisine in Florida. With its late hours, Pebbles is a great place for an after-theater dinner. Dinner for two will run about $65, but you can nibble to your heart's content for $20.
Open daily 11 a.m.-11 p.m. Cards: AE, MC, V.

COFFEE SHOPS & DINERS

B-Line Diner
Peabody Hotel,
9801 International Dr.,
Orlando
• (407) 352-4000
ext. 4460

Although it's open 24 hours a day, night owls think of this as the place to go for a wee-hours snack or a soda, a listen to the jukebox, and a return to *Happy Days*. It's straight out of the 1950s, too sassy and clattery for a romantic tête-à-tête, but just right for an upbeat end to an evening you want to prolong. Order anything, from the bulging deli sandwiches to the scrambled eggs, because it's all good.
Open daily 24 hours. All major cards.

Hey! Faith's Cookin'
11654 E. Colonial Dr.,
Orlando
• (407) 658-0962

Faith Broadnax inconveniently located her country-cooking diner on the far east side of town. Still, folks who have tasted her biscuits and gravy, or sampled one of her fine Southern-style dinners, every bit of it made from scratch, will gladly make the trip to taste them again. A homey atmosphere that is reminiscent of an old-style Southern coffee shop comes with the food. Service is like what you remember Mom doing before the feminist revolution. Lunch for two won't cost more than $15.
Open Mon.-Thurs. 6:30 a.m.-4 p.m., Fri.-Sat. 6:30 a.m.-8 p.m. No cards.

Little Darlins Rock 'n' Roll Palace
5770 Irlo Bronson
Memorial Hwy.,
Kissimmee
• (407) 396-6499

The moment you stroll past the classic cars and through the two-story-high jukebox that forms the entryway, you're transported back to the world of Elvis, the Fonz, saddle shoes and poodle skirts. Food fits the mood: burgers, fries, shakes, brews and even a full bar. After sunset, the place turns into a true palace of rock 'n' roll, when such favorite 1950s and 1960s groups as The Shirelles, Fabian, and The Diamonds take the spotlight and everyone heads for the dance floor, poodle skirts atwirlin'.
Open daily noon-2 a.m. Cover $8.50 daily after 6 p.m. Cards: MC, V.

CUBAN

El Bohio Café
5756 Dahlia Dr.,
Orlando
• (407) 282-1723

One of the official adopted cuisines of Florida, Cuban food never fails to fill us up until were reeking with garlic and competely *satisfecho*. Always filled with locals—who love their plantains and a good bargain—this cheery spot serves up all the standards: Cuban sandwiches, boliche, ropa vieja (a shredded-beef dish that literally means "old clothes"), roast pork and a roast chicken special on Wednesdays that includes yellow rice, gooey fried plantains and a small salad, all for $5.50. For a quick lunch bite, midday specials are unbeatable, and dinner for two costs about $18.

Rolando's Cuban Restaurant
870 Semoran Blvd., Casselberry
• (407) 767-9677

Yes, you guessed it: black-bean soup with rice, yellow rice and chicken, and Cuban-style minced meat are some of the simplistic yet flavorful dishes here, typically Cuban, that keep us coming back for more. Add a little yuca and some fried plantains, and you have a feast with a Cuban accent. In Central Florida, no one does Cuban better than Rolando Vieitez. His rather plain dining room, with kitchen table-style seating, is comfortable and relaxing. Two will spend about $20 for dinner.
Open Mon.-Thurs. 11 a.m.-9:30 p.m., Fri.-Sat. 11 a.m.-10:30 p.m., Sun. 11 a.m.-8:30 p.m. Cards: AE, MC, V.

HAMBURGERS & SANDWICHES

Hard Rock Café
Universal Studios, 5401 Kirkman Rd., Orlando
• (407) 351-7625

How would you shape the largest Hard Rock Café in the world? Since the tradition of the Hard Rock is entertainment-oriented hyperbole, how about like a city-sized guitar? And how would you decorate it? With an enormous collection of rock memorabilia. The chain started in London and has girdled the world. Naturally, you'll come here in your London or Tokyo Hard Rock T-shirt to show you're a Hard Rock groupie, and buy an Orlando T-shirt here to wear when you hit the Hard Rock in New York. Come in from the studios, or park in the separate lot outside. Recorded rock rings nonstop, and the food features those American classics, including incredible burgers.
Open daily 11 a.m.-2 a.m. No cover. Cards: AE, MC, V.

MIDDLE EASTERN FAST FOOD

Phoenician
7600 Dr. Phillips Blvd., Orlando
• (407) 345-1001

This tiny Middle Eastern storefront restaurant occupies a strip mall in an up-upscale neighborhood. A bright, impeccably clean dining room with booth seating attempts a Mediterranean decor, featuring white latticework draped with *faux* grape vines. Mediterranean dishes dot the menu, but the best meal here is to order an array of appetizers called meze: hummus bi tahine (puréed chickpeas), baba ghanouj (puréed eggplant dip), dolmas (stuffed grape leaves) and tabouli (a salad of bulghur, chopped parsley and tomatoes). Tear off a hunk of pita bread, dip it in a little of this, spread on a little of that and enjoy. You can eat the whole meal without even picking up a fork. Dinner will run $35 for two.
Open Mon.-Wed. & Sun. 11 a.m.-10 p.m., Thurs.-Sat. 11 a.m.-11 p.m. Cards: AE, MC, V.

ORLANDO & CENTRAL FLORIDA Hotels

HOTELS

INTRODUCTION	211
TOP OF THE LINE (From $200)	212
LUXURY (From $150)	214
MODERATE (From $100)	217
PRACTICAL (Under $100)	219
INNS	219
BED & BREAKFASTS	220

INTRODUCTION

Visting Mickey and the Gang

More people visit the Walt Disney World Vacation Kingdom than any other tourist destination in the United States, so Disney inevitably plays a role in your visit to Central Florida—even if your goal is to stay as far away from the attractions as possible. Central Florida's hotels can be divided into three categories: those that are right on Walt Disney World property; those that are near Walt Disney World Resort and cater to theme-park vacationers; and those hotels that are well outside the Disney orbit.

If Disney will be the focus of your visit, there are advantages to staying on Disney turf, either in one of Walt Disney World's own hotels (the Yacht and Beach Club Resort, the Grand Floridian and seven others) or a non-Disney hotel located in the Walt Disney World Hotel Plaza (the Swan, Dolphin, Hilton, Grosvenor, Buena Vista Palace and so on). All these hotels offer free transportation throughout the Vacation Kingdom, plus ticketing, reservations, and such perks as free Disney movies. Disney hotel guests get priority when reserving for popular Walt Disney World restaurants and shows; second priority goes to Hotel Plaza guests; "outsiders" may have difficulty getting into shows at peak times.

Most hotels located outside the Disney universe can arrange theme-park ticketing and transportation, but it will cost more and be less convenient. While many hotels in the area offer free shuttles from hotel to theme parks, they don't usually offer the same flexibility as do the official Walt Disney World shuttles, which you can easily take from hotel to theme park, back to your hotel for a swim and a nap after lunch, to another theme park for dinner and another Disney park or hotel for a nightcap and show. You can also drive to the parks and pay a $3 parking fee.

Central Florida also offers a wide choice of non-Disney-related family resorts, golf and tennis resorts, downtown hotels, historic inns, and smart, fully furnished, self-catering villas. Following is a good sampling of all categories.

TOP OF THE LINE (From $200)

Disney's Grand Floridian Beach Resort
Walt Disney World,
4401 Grand Floridian Way,
Lake Buena Vista 32830
• (407) 824-3000
Fax (407) 824-3186

Victorian extravagance has been carried out in every detail of this 40-acre, scrupulously landscaped resort with its own lagoon and white-sand beach. Free transportation whisks you to and from all the Disney theme parks and to other hotels, giving you a choice of dozens of restaurants and lounges in addition to this hotel's own. Concierge rooms are all in the main building, a service which, of course, includes a bit of extra pampering; guests and their luggage are transported to satellite buildings in golf carts driven by bellboys in knickers. Victorian-decor rooms have a balcony or patio, and cable TV with (surprise!) the Disney Channel. Guests can amuse and exhaust themselves at lawn games, boating, water sports, golf or tennis; there are also exercise facilities with instructors.
Doubles: $220; suites: $300-$1,000.

Marriott Orlando World Center
8701 World Center Dr.,
Orlando 32821
• (407) 239-4200
Fax (407) 239-5777

This actually is a complete city, masquerading as a 1,503-room über-resort, near the Disney attractions. Always abuzz with conferences, the resort is eager to please the leisure traveler as well. Rooms are fine, chock full of all the standard amenities, and service perks up considerably on the concierge level. Of course, the price on that level also perks up by $30. Its 200 acres (the hotel alone covers 40 acres) includes an eighteen-hole Joe Lee–designed golf course, four swimming pools indoors and out, twelve lighted tennis courts, a full-service health club, six restaurants including a Japanese steakhouse, lounges with entertainment, shops, a children's program, and rental cars.
Rooms: $199; concierge-level rooms: $229; suites $275.

ORLANDO & CENTRAL FLORIDA   Hotels

Sonesta Villa Resort
10000 Turkey Lake Rd., Orlando 32819
• (407) 352-8051, (800) 766-3782
Fax (407) 345-5384

This sprawling, Mediterranean village nestles around a private, 300-acre lake. It's only minutes from the theme parks but is in a peaceful world apart, leaving you free to cook in your own villa and enjoy water sports on the lake when you don't feel like venturing out on the highways. The resort has its own swimming pools, boat rentals, restaurant and lounge, children's program, playgrounds, health club, laundry facilities, and grocery delivery service. Each of the 370 villas has a kitchenette, dining area, living room with sleeper sofa, one or two bedrooms, and private balcony or patio.
1-bedrooms: $195; 2-bedrooms: $265.

Walt Disney World Dolphin
1500 EPCOT Resort Blvd., Lake Buena Vista 32830
• (407) 934-4000
Fax (407) 934-4099

The largest hotel in Orlando, this 1,509-room megahotel epitomizes the new "entertainment architecture" by Michael Graves. In his design, the architect has employed the whimsical, the outrageous, the daring and the fun, and it's all wrapped in a cocoon of consummate Sheraton hospitality. Spacious rooms with offbeat decor overlook EPCOT Center. Enroll the children in Camp Dolphin; play any or all of the three golf courses avilable to guests; work out in the Body by Jake Health Studio. Along with the Swan hotel (*see* below), the Dolphin forms an enormous conference center, but leisure travelers also like its free, easy access to the Walt Disney World theme parks and its switched-on Disney sense of fantasy.
Rooms: $219-$350.

Walt Disney World Swan
1200 EPCOT Resort Blvd. Lake Buena Vista 32830
• (407) 934-3000, (800) 228-3000
Fax (407) 934-4499

Architects call it "playful" postmodern. Swans 47 feet high float atop what looks like a blimp warehouse painted bubble-gum pink, topped with waves that curl around porthole windows. Indoors, monkeys dangle, lamps swing from toucan beaks and carpeting symbolizes the beach. The sense of fun created by architect Michael Graves is total, but this Westin hotel is serious about hospitality. Rooms are spacious and bright, amenities lavish. Each room has two phones, a remote-control cable TV, a mini-bar, a safe and two robes. On the two concierge floors, extra pamperings include bathroom phones, complimentary Continental breakfast and afternoon cocktails. Car rental, a health club, a lively children's program, five restaurants and lounges and a business center—plus free Walt Disney World transportation to all Disney attractions—make this a complete resort for family or business travel. The Swan beckons you to sun on the white-sand beach, boat in the lagoon or swim in the supersize pool—anyway you slice it, it's pure luxury.
Singles & doubles: $210; suites: $425-$1,625.

ORLANDO & CENTRAL FLORIDA   Hotels

Walt Disney World Yacht and Beach Club Resort
Walt Disney World,
Lake Buena Vista 32830
• (407) 934-7639
Fax (407) 934-3450
(Yacht Club),
Fax (407) 934-3850
(Beach Club)

This massive twin resort re-invents New England, Disney-style. The effect is one of a sparkling, white-washed Massachusetts town that has been plucked from its roots and transplanted around a 25-acre pond and 2.5-acre water park. Once again, Disney triumphs in the altering of reality: Stormalong Bay is a filtered freshwater pool, yet its bottom is sand-covered, while a snorkeling lagoon is conveniently stocked with lots of live fish. The design can be credited to Robert A.M. Stern, known for his seaside homes in the Hamptons. Guests stay in crisply painted clapboard buildings, outfitted with luxury trims such as French doors, hardwood floors, brasses, antique millwork and porthole windows. Two hotels share the water park: the 635-room Yacht Club is modelled after a posh New England yacht club, complete with a galley, steakhouse, and staff clad in navy blue blazers; the 580-room Beach Club replicates a summer beach cottage, pretty and airy in chintz and gingham, wicker and pastels. From the resort, it's a cinch to walk or take a tram to EPCOT, or connect via Walt Disney World's free transportation system throughout the Vacation Kingdom.
Singles & doubles: $195.

LUXURY (From $150)

Buena Vista Palace
Walt Disney World
Hotel Plaza,
1900 Buena Vista Dr.,
Lake Buena Vista 22206
• (407) 827-2727,
(800) 327-2990
Fax (407) 827-6034

A refurbishment completed in March 1991 has freshened the Buena Vista's 1,028 guest rooms, playing cool, contemporary mauve- and pale-green fabrics against solid oak furniture. The decor won't excite the senses, but the rooms are perfectly comfortable, and many have a private balcony or patio. A recently built wing of 200 suites includes some suites with a kitchen and several palatially designed spaces that boast up to five bedrooms. Crown Level rooms come with their own concierge. Needless to say, one major advantage to staying here (if you consider this an advantage) is that the shops of the Disney Village Marketplace and Pleasure Island are just a hop, skip and a jump away. You can also hop on the free transportation network to reach Walt Disney World theme parks. If theme-park mania begins to frazzle your nerves, this 27-acre lakefront resort can distract you with its three swimming pools, three lighted tennis courts and a health club that has the newest fitness machines. There's also access to Walt Disney World championship golf courses. The lively, locally popular Laughing Kookaburra lounge offers another sort of distraction. For a more intimate drink, soar to the Top of the Palace (*see* page 223).
Rooms: $150; suites: $235-$380.

ORLANDO & CENTRAL FLORIDA   Hotels

Grenelefe
3200 S.R. 546,
Grenelefe 33844
• (813) 422-7511,
(800) 237-9549
Fax (813) 422-7511
(ask for fax)

One of Florida's premier golf, tennis, and conference resorts, this verdant hideaway on the shores of Lake Marion sprawls over 1,000 rolling acres. Free 24-hour shuttles buzz you from place to place, while others provide airport pick-up, so guests can survive happily without a car. Choose from attractive one- and two-bedroom villas that come with a complete kitchen. There's a "tree house" that sleeps four, for more adventurous travelers. Families can have fun at one of their favorite sports here, from red-hot bass fishing to boating, from nature walks to bicycling, from airboating to alligator hunting (with cameras). Play one of three championship golf courses, join the internationally acclaimed tennis program, sign up the children for the all-day activities at Recreation Village. Five swimming pools are spread among the villa clusters. The lounge has live entertainment.
2-bedrooms: $185.

Grosvenor Resort
Walt Disney World Hotel Plaza,
1850 Hotel Plaza Blvd.,
Lake Buena Vista 32830
• (407) 828-4444,
(800) 624-4109
Fax (407) 827-6314

Billing itself as the "official, affordable hotel," of the area, this Best Western resort is in the Walt Disney World Hotel Plaza, so guests can avail themselves of Walt Disney World transportation, Disney golf, theme-park-reservations services and such. Each room has a VCR (rental tapes are available), mini-bar with refrigerator, coffee maker and remote control television. Both swimming pools are heated and tennis courts are lighted. You might want to dine in the restaurant or café, drink in the pub or lobby bar, or lounge at the poolside patio.
Doubles: $145; suites: $370.

Hyatt Regency Grand Cypress
One Grand Cypress Blvd.,
Orlando 32819
• (407) 239-1234
Fax (407) 239-3891

Everything about this resort lives up to its grand name, from its size (1,500 manicured acres) to its free, internal transportation system (trolleys built in Belgium at the turn of the century.) Spacious rooms overlook lavish landscaping accented by life-size sculptures. In the Regency Club, which has its own concierge, complimentary breakfast, afternoon cocktails, and hors d'oeuvres are served. By special arrangement, you can take one of several helicopter "safaris"—to Disney attractions, Sea World, Universal Studios, downtown Orlando, or anywhere you choose, for that matter. After landing back at the helipad, you can warm up on the jogging or bicycle paths, the fitness trail or in the health club before playing the 45-hole Jack Nicklaus–designed golf course, the nine-hole Pitch 'n' Putt, or tennis, racquetball or shuffleboard. If that's still not enough for you, activities include horseback riding, a children's program, sailing the 21-acre lake, sunning on a white-sand beach, or hiking the 45-acre Audubon preserve. The pool is a spectacle of waterfalls, grottos, and meandering streamlets. The traveler in search of

superlatives in seclusion and luxury should also consider the villas of Grand Cypress (*see* page 217).
Singles & doubles: $160-$350; suites $290-$1,700.

Omni International Hotel

400 W. Livingston St., Orlando 32801
• (407) 843-6664, (800) 843-6664
Fax (407) 648-5414

Key to this hotel is that it adjoins the Centroplex, a bustling entertainment hub that includes a performing-arts center and the arena where Orlando's professional basketball team, the Magic, plays their season. You can play there, too; after taking a dip in the Omni's heated swimming pool, book a game of tennis or racquetball at Centroplex. We like this bright, modern, 300-room hotel for more than its proximity to fun and games. All the rooms are attractively decorated and spacious, and guests on the two "club" floors are pampered with robes, turndown service, free bar service and other perks. For those who are both rich and musical, the two-story presidential suite has its own grand piano. The Omni can also claim title of one of the city's hottest nightspots, the Ozone Lounge, and a friendly lobby bar in the airy atrium attracts a good crowd at cocktail hour. But, hold on: this is also the only hotel that we know of in the area that charges for parking: $5.30 per 24 hours. The 300-room Omni is heavily booked during special events, so if you think that this is the place for you, reserve early.
Doubles: $155-$170; Omni Club: $170-$185; suites: $285; Presidential Suite: $595.

Peabody Orlando

9801 International Dr., Orlando 32819
• (407) 352-4000, (800) 732-2639
Fax (407) 351-0073

Quack, if you're a lover of Anatidae! That's the duck family, for those who aren't experts in bird terminology. Read up if you're going to stay at the Peabody; fashioned after the historic Peabody in Memphis, where duck worship began, this is a hotel in the grand manner that hasn't lost its sense of whimsy. The duck motif is everywhere, and the real, live critters pad around the grounds and come to the fountain for a splash each morning and evening. Hospitality is impeccable, from the stately lobby with its grand piano, to spacious and tastefully appointed rooms. The swimming pool is heated and activities include tennis, golf privileges, fitness facilities with instructor, and a children's program. On the more exclusive Peabody Club level, Continental breakfast and refreshments throughout the day are complimentary. The café, done in white tile, stainless steel and neon, is open all the time. The hotel's signature restaurant Dux, pronounced (need we say it?) "ducks," serves overpriced American fare in a posh setting (*see* page 206). Staying here will put you nearby the Disney attractions and the convention center, which is one reason why, although there are almost 900 units

ORLANDO & CENTRAL FLORIDA   Hotels

in this splendid 27-story hotel, it's almost always heavily booked.
Rooms: $150; suites: $350-$1,200.

Stouffer Orlando
6677 Sea Harbor Dr., Orlando 32821
• (407) 351-5555, (800) 468-3571
Fax (407) 351-9994

An elegant, sky-high atrium lobby lends a sense of drama and excitement to your entrance here, from the moment you sweep through the doorway of this ten-story luxury hotel. The rest of the stay won't be quite so stimulating, but it will certainly leave you satisfied—even pampered, if you choose a "luxury" floor. A nice mix of families and conference visitors books rooms at the Stouffer. The hotel offers a heated swimming pool; in-room movies and cable TV; a massage and full-fitness center; and a shopping arcade with a barbershop and beauty salon. Sea World is a short walk away, and the hotel will provide free transportation to the theme parks. On the luxury floors, Continental breakfast is served gratis. All of the rooms are nicely appointed, with a bright, contemporary design that pleases.
Singles & doubles: $175; suites $375-$650.

Villas of Grand Cypress
One N. Jacaranda, Orlando 32819
• (407) 239-4700
Fax (407) 239-7219

This secluded, separate resort shares the ample amenities of the Hyatt Regency Grand Cypress (*see* page 215). Guests appreciate the very-private suites and villas, each with one to four bedrooms, a luxury kitchen and a private patio. It's easy to stay here and never lift a finger; Villas has its own pool, bar and golf club, plus a trolley link-up with the hotel's various services, programs, activities and restaurants.
Suites: $150-$250; villas: $150-$1,000.

MODERATE (From $100)

Compri Hotel Lake Buena Vista
8688 Palm Pkwy., Lake Buena Vista 32830
• (407) 239-8500, (800) 228-2846

A stay in one of the Compri's spacious rooms gives you all the plush comforts typical of a small (167 rooms) and attentive first-class hotel, plus a remote-control cable TV, two telephones, complimentary cooked-to-order breakfast, cocktails, late-night snacks and a free shuttle to Walt Disney World attractions. A restaurant, lounge, health club with Universal equipment and free-form swimming pool endeavor to keep guests happy. The hotel's 5,000-square-foot Compri Club functions much like the common room in other hotels' concierge floors. Without paying a premium rate, you can use the "club" to socialize, hold a small business confab, or eat your breakfast while reading the newspaper. The Club has its own bar, library and big-screen TV, plus work desks with telephones—though we hope for your sake you'll be enjoying yourself too much to remember to use them.

ORLANDO & CENTRAL FLORIDA Hotels

Directly adjacent is the children's play center with games, toys and television, where you can keep an eye on the tots.
Singles & doubles: $135.

Hawthorn Suites Villa Resort
8800 Meadow Creek Dr.,
Lake Buena Vista 32830
• (407) 239-7700
Fax (407) 239-7605

Each of the Hawthorn's fully furnished villas gives you 1,000 square feet plus, complete with a kitchen with a microwave oven, a dining area, living room and either one or two bedrooms with baths. It's a contemporary hotel for contemporary travelers, decorated in breezy fabrics and Floridian pastel hues, and providing two TVs, two phones and a VCR per villa. You'll enjoy the convenient luxury of the breakfast starter kit upon arrival; the staff will also pick up an entire grocery-shopping list of goodies for you, if you like. Villas are cleaned daily, including kitchen cleanup. As it is everyplace in Orlando, shuttle service to the Disney attractions is on the house. To complete the package, there are a restaurant and lounge, two pools and a whirlpool, a lighted tennis court, a playground and a golf course next door.
1-bedrooms: $110-$190; 2-bedrooms: $145-$250.

Hilton at Walt Disney World Village
1751 Hotel Plaza Blvd.,
Lake Buena Vista 32830
• (407) 827-4000,
(800) 782-4414
Fax (407) 827-6380

Greenery and brass aplenty greet you as you enter this Hilton's big, bustling lobby, which is always alive with a mix of leisure travelers and conference attendees. Every room has a mini-bar, a separate vanity outside the bathroom, and remote-control cable TV. With pushbutton phones, guests can control the temperature, call room service or a bellman, or receive help in case of an emergency. Hilton's Youth Hotel cares for children while parents dine; if you need a crib in your room it will come outfitted (surprise!) with a Mickey Mouse comforter. Rooms overlook the dazzling pools, spas and fountains on one side, theme parks on another and Lake Buena Vista on another. Business services include complete secretarial services and a staff photographer, and foreigners can usually find at least one staff member who speaks their language, including Hungarian, Japanese, Chinese and several Indian dialects. Pleasure Island and Typhoon Lagoon are a stroll away, and free Walt Disney World buses will cart you off to anywhere in the Vacation Kingdom.
Singles: $125-$145; doubles: $125-$155; suites: $430 & up.

Vistana Resort
8800 Vistana Center,
Orlando 32821
• (407) 239-3131
Fax (407) 239-3005

Combine the convenience of living in a luxuriously furnished condo with such hotel amenities as daily housekeeping and a guest-services staff, and resort amenities including tennis courts, four heated swimming pools, activities, playgrounds, bicycle rental, volleyball and 24-hour security—that's Vistana. Six to eight people will be quite comfortable in one of these

villas, which include a master bedroom with a king-size bed, two baths, a guest room with two double or two twin beds, and a living area with a queen-size sleeper sofa. Electronic gadgetry? You bet. Each unit has color television and VCR, washer, dryer, and full kitchen with microwave, dishwasher, and trash compacter. Some units include a whirlpool tub.
Rooms: $120-$275.

PRACTICAL (UNDER $100)

Harley Hotel
151 E. Washington St.,
Orlando 32801
• (407) 841-3220,
(800) 321-2323
Fax (407) 841-3220,
ext. 153

Business travelers love this old, downtown-Orlando hotel, located near the Centroplex and overlooking Lake Eola with its landmark fountain. Rooms are simple affairs, offering comfort and modest decor. Amenities include a big pool, underground parking, a locally popular restaurant (Café on the Park) and a lounge that features live entertainment. Oh, and for trivia hounds, the hotel's tiny escalator was at one time listed in the *Guinness Book of World Records* as the world's shortest. These days, a hotel in Japan claims that dubious honor.
Singles: $80-$110; doubles: $95-$125; studio suite $135-$150.

Park Plaza Hotel
307 Park Ave. South,
Winter Park 32789
• (407) 647-1072,
(800) 228-7220
Fax (407) 647-4081

A small wood lobby sets a European scene in this polished gem of a 27-room hotel overlooking Park Avenue and Central Park (be reminded, however, that this *is* Orlando, not Manhattan). Each room has a different look, but decor tends toward floral chintzes, original art, ceiling fans, brass or mahogany bedsteads, louvered wood shutters and comfortable parlors with reading lamps and wicker furniture. Premium rooms have balconies overlooking the Park. The best bonus is that guests can order room service from the Park Plaza Gardens restaurant (*see* page 209), which is adjacent. You may have your free Continental breakfast in bed; valet parking is complimentary.
Singles: $70; doubles: $75-$135; suites: $165.

INNS

Chalet Suzanne
U.S. 27 South,
P.O. Drawer C,
Lake Wales 33859
• (813) 676-6011,
(800) 288-6011
Fax (813) 676-1814

If you're one of those rare travelers who comes to Orlando and wants to escape the clutches of the Disney empire altogether, you'll delight in this most individual inn. Built during the war by the late Bertha Hinshaw, from whatever building materials could be scrounged up, this battered village is one of the state's most unusual lodgings. Come by car (it's about an hour away from Mickey mania, to the southwest) or private plane (Bertha's son, Carl, is a pilot himself, and keeps the grass runway immaculate). Each spacious room is completely different from the others, furnished with an eclectic combination of sublime antiques and ridiculous collectibles and lavished with lovely, funky touches: ironwork, tiles, mosaics, bricks and lamps from around the world. All rooms succeed at being unerringly hospitable. The resort has a pool, private lake, cozy bar, antique shop, pottery and, of course, the cannery where Chalet Suzanne soups are brewed. Before dinner, serve yourself to a complimentary wine tasting in the dank, dark, but superbly endowed wine cellar. *Singles & doubles: $85-$185.*

Lakeside Inn
100 Alexander St.,
Mount Dora 32757
• (904) 383-4101,
(800) 556-5016
Fax (904) 735-2642

The mellow mood of more romantic era is complete, from the Laura Ashley decor to the veranda overlooking Lake Dora. North of Orlando about 45 minutes, the Lakeside Inn was once a posh stopping point for Palm Beach–bound rail travelers. Since those days, the inn has been turned into the sort of resort that the Great Jay Gatsby would have loved. He surely would have played tennis, walked the state's longest boardwalk through Mount Dora's timeless marshlands, sailed the lake, or swum in the big, lakefront pool. Of course, you might prefer some time in your room, which retains the flowery, frilly decor of yesteryear. Surrounding the hotel are oak-shaded streets filled with trendy restaurants and antique shops. *Singles & doubles: $95-$135; suites $180.*

BED & BREAKFASTS

The Courtyard at Lake Lucerne
211 N. Lucerne Circle East,
Orlando 32801
• (407) 648-5188
Fax (407) 246-1368

Centered around a brick courtyard, with a tinkling fountain and the civilized strains of baroque music piped throughout, this tranquil haven lies only a few feet from the highway in the heart of the city. Mercifully it has been bypassed by the dirt and din of downtown. The main inn was built of Florida hardwoods in the 1880s, and following a careful restoration, it's now furnished with antiques—most of them collected in England by the present owners. One of the stained-glass windows is a Tiffany original, discovered in an Ormond Beach garage, where it had been stored for 60 years. There are six suites, each with a private bath and telephone. A second building has three Edwardian suites, including a honeymoon suite with its own whirlpool and steam shower. The complex also includes a restored 1930s apartment building that has been artfully restored and furnished in art deco, so skillfully that it fits perfectly

into the setting; stay here if you want Garbo-era decor and a kitchenette.
Victorian or art-deco suites: $85; Edwardian suites: $100-$150.

DeLand Country Inn
228 E. Howry Ave.,
DeLand 32720
• (904) 736-4244
No fax

In a quiet, small-college-town setting, this turn-of-the-century home has been lovingly restored and furnished with antiques and reproductions. You can choose from four comfortable rooms or the master suite, each with a private bath. There's a swimming pool, and from the inn you can walk to the library, Stetson University, and downtown restaurants. The owners prefer that no one smoke in their clean and well-cared-for inn, nor can pets or very young children be accommodated.
Singles & doubles: $50.

NIGHTLIFE

BARS	221
DANCE CLUBS	222
HOTEL LOUNGES	223
MUSIC CLUBS	223

BARS

Hurricane Bar
Hemingway's in the Hyatt Regency Grand Cypress,
One Grand Cypress Blvd.,
Orlando
• (407) 239-1234

Airy and tropical, this is a captivating slice of Key West, all oak floors and rattan and wicker, transplanted to a site overlooking the Grand Cypress's famous waterfalls and meandering swimming pool. Sit under a whirling ceiling fan amid Hemingway memorabilia, and think of Great American Novels as you order a "Papa Doble," a daiquiri said to have been invented by the author himself. Live music is almost exclusively local interpretations of Jimmy Buffett songs.
Open daily 11 a.m.- 1 a.m. All major cards.

Laughing Kookaboora
Buena Vista Palace,
Walt Disney World
Hotel Plaza,
Lake Buena Vista
• (407) 827-2727

This ground-level pub is as chummy and informal as the same hotel's Top of the Palace Lounge (*see* page 227) is sedate and swank. Waterfalls and greenery attempt to conjure up Australia, and 99 brands of domestic and imported beers keep the crowd loud and laughing. The spread of free happy hour snacks would sink a battleship. Things heat up as show bands and songsters take the stage.
Open daily 4 p.m.-3 a.m. All major cards.

DANCE CLUBS

Cuda Bay Club
8510 Palm Pkwy.,
Orlando
• (407) 239-8815

This popular lunch-and-dinner buffet spot really gets cooking after the sun sets, when deejays crank up the sound and spotlights, and people take to the dance floors to hop to Top 40 screamers. There are live acts too, including dancing on the outdoor deck to a reggae band on Friday night, and dancing indoors or out on Sundays to a Top 40 band, after feasting on barbecue. If you work in the hospitality industry (and can show proof of it) you can come for a lavish buffet on Monday evenings, with two-for-one drinks and no cover charge.
Open daily 11 a.m.-2 a.m. Schedule & cover vary; phone ahead for details. All major cards.

Murphy's Kokamo Kafe & Dance Palace
4736 W. Irlo Bronson
Memorial Hwy.,
Kissimmee
• (407) 396-6500/
239-7171

Start with one of the nightly drink specials, then try the all-you-can-eat seafood buffet followed by an evening of dancing to live music. Programs vary from mellow Big Bands and dancing cheek to cheek, to deafening videos and a Saint Vitus dance beat, so call ahead for information on whether tonight's show tunes are up your alley.
Open daily 4:30 p.m.-2 a.m. Cover varies ($2.50-$6). Central Florida residents are admitted free Tues.-Thurs. (bring a current driver's license for proof). No cards.

Ozone Lounge
Omni Hotel,
400 W. Livingston St.,
Orlando
• (407) 843-6664

We can't classify this as a hotel lounge, simply because it's too hip, too hot, for such a formal description. Local insiders slip in here for an evening of see-and-be-seen, or to clink glasses into the night after the theater or a game. Gather around the super-screen TV to watch a sports event, or come later (after 9 p.m.) when a live band launches into Top 40 hits and the dancing begins. Happy hour is an event in itself, with different tapas every night from 5 p.m. to 7 p.m.
Open daily 11 a.m.-1 a.m. No cover. All major cards.

Shooter's Waterfront Café U.S.A.
4315 N. Orange Blossom Trail, Orlando
• (407) 298-2855
Fax (407) 298-0428

Part of a sizzling chain of cafés in Fort Lauderdale and Miami Beach, as well as the Midwest, this is the place where the young crowd comes for the three oh-so-collegiate B's: Beach volleyball, Bikini contests and Beer. On Friday nights, dance to live bands playing soft rock and Top 40 tunes. The eats are always hearty, and the full menu is served until closing. The complex overlooks a lake, and has its own dock, sand beach and pool.
Open daily 11:30 a.m.-1:30 a.m. No cover. All major cards.

Sullivan's Trailway Lounge
1108 S. Orange Blossom Train, Orlando
• (407) 843-2934

If it's country-western, it's here—there's pickin', grinnin', hollerin' and stompin' aplenty on one of the largest dance floors in the state. Dance lessons are free on Tuesday; Wednesday is ladies' night. Give your Tony Lamas a polish and pull on your favorite jeans—this is one of the best places in the area for live country music and specialty acts.
Open Mon.-Sat. 2 p.m.-2 a.m., Sun. 6 p.m.-2 a.m. Cover $3. No cards.

HOTEL LOUNGES

Top of the Palace Lounge
Buena Vista Palace, Walt Disney World Village, Lake Buena Vista
• (407) 827-2727

In most cities, the 27th floor isn't exactly skyscraper level, but it's lofty for Orlando and, when it overlooks the $30,000 in fireworks that explode every night over EPCOT center, it's celestial stuff indeed. Meet here to view the sunset, too. It's a cozy, insider spot known for its superior vintages, the quiet elegance of attentive but invisible servers, tinkling crystal and music that soothes without intruding on a romantic tête-à-tête.
Open nightly 5 p.m.-1 a.m. All major cards.

MUSIC CLUBS

Blue Note
54 N. Orange Ave., Orlando
• (407) 843-3078

A downtown favorite for years (in its previous incarnation as Valentyne's, too), this is the place for a leisurely evening of cool jazz and blues. The menu features steaks, seafood and pasta with a Cajun touch (the owners are from New Orleans), from $11 to $30. Park in the Church Street Garage or on the street.
Open nightly 3 p.m.-2 a.m. Cover varies ($3-$5). Cards: AE, MC, V.

Church Street Station
129 W. Church St., Orlando
• (407) 422-2434

The good times roll here, sometimes so effervescently that they spill over into massive street parties. A glittering Victorian restoration of what was once Orlando's commercial heart, this (appropriately commercial) entertainment complex goes on and on. Visitors who love to whoop it up into the wee hours will have a drink at one place and dinner at another, then move on

for dancing at a third place and dessert at a fourth, then catch another show (there are 20 nightly), and cap off the night with coffee in one of the courtyards or lounges. Try Apple Annie's for bluegrass, the Orchid Garden for oldies, Cheyenne Saloon and Opera House for country-western, and Rose O'Grady's for rousing ragtime and Dixieland.
Open daily 11 a.m.-2 a.m. Admission Mon.-Thurs. after 4:30 p.m. & Fri.-Sun. after 5 p.m.: adults $14.95, children 4-12 $5.95, seniors $13.40. All major cards.

Mr. B.'s of Eatonville, Inc.
426 E. Kennedy, Eatonville
• (407) 644-5260

Located in Eatonville, one of the first black communities in the United States, this is the place for an after-dinner drink and easy listening to rhythm-and-blues, in a setting straight out of a George Raft movie. It's so laid back that you have to call ahead to find out who's playing, and if or when. When live entertainers aren't scheduled, the place transforms into a pulsating disco.
Open Thurs.-Sat., 4 p.m.-4 a.m. Cover $4. Cards: AE, MC, V.

Mulvaney's
27 W. Church St., Orlando
• (407) 839-0892

One of the best reasons to come downtown is to hang out in this most Irish of pubs, to quaff ale and listen to live folk ballads. The musicians are brought over from Ireland for their gigs here. Decent food runs to Irish stew or shepherd's pie, or Americanisms such as chicken fingers or burgers.
Open Mon.-Sat. 11 a.m.- 2 a.m., Sun. 11 a.m.-midnight. Cards: AE, MC, V.

SHOPS

INTRODUCTION	225
CLOTHES & JEWELRY	225
DEPARTMENT STORES & SHOPPING CENTERS	226
FOOD	228
LEATHER & LUGGAGE	229
SPORTING GOODS	229

INTRODUCTION

The Shopping Never Stops

Impulse shoppers, beware! All the Walt Disney World theme parks give you opportunity after opportunity (after opportunity . . .) to spend money in the shops, and lots of it. Keeping caution in mind, however, don't overlook the theme parks completely as shopping territory. All of them, even Universal Studios, are packed with stores, many hawking stratospherically priced tourist claptrap, and many others featuring arrays of fine-quality goods and exotic imports. Especially fruitful hunting is found at **EPCOT Center** (*see* page 240), where each national pavilion displays authentic goods from its homeland. At **Sid Cahuenga's One-of-a-Kind** in Disney-MGM Studios Theme Park (*see* page 240), movie posters and memorabilia beckon to the starstruck, including autographed photos and authenticated items that once belonged to famous stars. At **Universal Studios** (*see* page 233), there's **San Francisco Imports** for all manner of Asian imports, **E.T.'s Toy Closet** and **Park Plaza Jewelry and Gifts**. Wood carvers and glass blowers sell their wares at **Bayfront Crafts,** in the New England section of the park. **Sea World's** shops (*see* page 232) carry enormous selections of stuffed sea mammals, including large, fuzzy likenesses of the famous Shamu.

CLOTHES & JEWELRY

Costume Jewelry

Orlando's Secret Jewelers to the Stars
1855 W. State Rd. 434, Ste. 280,
Longwood
• (407) 332-9333

What's the secret? This jewelry looks expensive, but isn't the real thing. There, now that the secret's out, go indulge! The goods sold here are just the sort of jewelry desired by movie stars and royalty, who want to leave their real gems in the vault when they venture out among the hoi poloi. The shop, which is located above Jackson's, displays an exciting collection of unusual pieces. Designers will custom-make jewelry to order, too.
Open Mon.-Sat. 10 a.m.-5 p.m.

Discount

Denim World
7623 International Dr.,
Orlando
• (407) 351-5074

Dress the whole family in lovable, durable denim, in one sweep through this store. Anything in denim for all ages is on sale, at deeply discounted prices. Choose among established brand names such as Lee and Levi's, then pick shirts, tops and swimwear to complete the ensemble. Alterations are free.
Open Mon.-Sat. 9 a.m.-11 p.m., Sun. 10 a.m.-10 p.m.

ORLANDO & CENTRAL FLORIDA Shops

Flea World
U.S. 17-92,
Sanford
• (407) 645-1792

Central Florida is agog over flea markets, and this is the grandfather of them all. As well as the usual stalls selling everything from clothes to kitsch, there are two petting zoos for the children, an exotic animal display, entertainment, and parking for 4,000 cars. No fleas here—most of this merchandise is new, much of it discounted because of factory overstocks, irregulars or odd lots.
Open Fri.-Sun. 8 a.m.-5 p.m.

Recycled Clothing

Women's & Children's Resale Shop
3107 Edgewater Dr.,
Orlando
• (407) 425-3204

A bonanza in children's clothes, from newborn to size 10, plus bargains in women's clothing in all sizes. Orlando's original consignment shop and now twenty years old, this store's stock makes up in consistency and dependability what it lacks in style and excitement.
Open Mon.-Fri. 10 a.m.-5:30 p.m., Thurs. 10 a.m.-8 p.m., Sat. 10 a.m.-4 p.m.

Shoes

Great Western Boot Outlet
5597 International Dr.,
Orlando
• (407) 345-8103

You'll be perfectly shod for ropin' them dogies, dancin' the Texas Two Step or just strolling the city streets looking awfully hip, in authentic boots at factory outlet prices. Choose from thousands of boots in every style, color and size from such solidly established bootmakers as Tomy Lama, Justin, Nacona, Dingo, Capezio and Zodiac. The store takes credit cards, checks or gold dust.
Open Mon.-Sat. 9:30 a.m.-9 p.m., Sun. 11 a.m.-6 p.m.

DEPARTMENT STORES & SHOPPING CENTERS

Belz Factory Outlet World
5401 W. Oakridge Rd.,
Orlando
• (407) 352-9611

This enormous, 172-store bargain-hunter's bonanza calls itself "the second-most-visited tourist attraction in Orlando-land." (Guess who's first?) Name-brand stores sell sportswear, dinnerware, sporting goods, electronics, linens, luggage and much more at up to 75 percent off retail. Bring the children to ride the carnival-size carousel in Mall 2. The complex comprises two enclosed malls, three freestanding buildings and a strip mall, providing almost 600,000 square feet of shopping nirvana.
Open Mon.-Sat. 10 a.m.-9 p.m., Sun. 10 a.m.-6 p.m.

ORLANDO & CENTRAL FLORIDA Shops

Church Street Station Exchange
124 W. Pine St., Orlando
• (407) 422-2434

This enormous old warehouse complex, which includes the century-old train depot in the heart of downtown, has been refurbished (perhaps a little too enthusiastically) in glittering Victorian-era splendor. Among its 60 boutiques, there's ample opportunity for dining, noshing, drinking and gaming, all in a rather contrived Good Times atmosphere. Shop for fashions, lacy lingerie, upscale accessories for the wardrobe or home, or souvenirs. Church Street Station (*see* page 223) charges admission, but entrance to the Exchange is free.
Open daily 11 a.m.-11 p.m.

Disney Village Marketplace
Walt Disney Village, Lake Buena Vista
• (407) 828-3800

Disney merchandise is ubiquitous in shops throughout Central Florida, but nowhere is it sold in a more charming setting, and nowhere are the selections of a better quality or in larger quantity than they are here. If the idea of shopping for crystal in a theme-park mall doesn't frighten you away, you'll find this European-style collection of bountifully stocked shops to be among the nicest in the area. Stroll from one shop to another; you'll find good-quality clothing, collectibles, china, crystal, jewelry, Christmas items, hand-worked pottery, kitchen supplies and much more. It's set in parklike grounds, within walking distance of most Walt Disney World Hotel Plaza hotels.
Open daily 10 a.m.-10 p.m.

Florida Mall
8001 S. Orange Blossom Trail, Orlando
• (407) 851-6255

This enormous, 160-store mall is divided into Victorian-, Mediterranean- and art-deco-style "neighborhoods," so come just for the viewing if you're not in a buying mood. Stores range from an upscale Godiva Chocolatier to modestly priced Sears and JC Penney stores. In addition to the many specialty restaurants, there's also a food court. The mall can be reached from International Drive via Tri-County Transit No. 42 buses.
Open Mon.-Sat. 10 a.m.-9 p.m., Sun. 11 a.m.-6 p.m.

Mercado Festival Center
8445 International Dr., Orlando
• (407) 345-9337

One of the busiest, most buzzing of the area's several "festival" shopping complexes (meant to guarantee you have a Rollicking Good Time!), the Mercado hosts scads of special events, from street parties to the nightly free entertainment in the pleasant courtyard. Shop for clothing, toys, souvenirs and gifts from 50 stores. The complex also houses five specialty restaurants including the Mardi Gras dinner theater, and an international fast-food pavilion.
Open daily 10 a.m.-10 p.m.

ORLANDO & CENTRAL FLORIDA Shops

Old Town
5770 W. Irlo Bronson Memorial Hwy.,
Kissimmee
• (407) 396-4888

Once the heart of Florida's "cow town," before Kissimmee became part of the Disney megalopolis, this quaint collection of 70 shops and eateries hasn't forgotten its history. Gay Nineties decor highlights brick-laid streets; a lovely 1909 carousel is adorned with hand-carved wooden animals; an antique Ferris wheel squeaks and grinds. After browsing for gifts and souvenirs, take a breather with an ice-cold 5-cent Coke, straight out of the good ol' days. If you have the energy, peek into the Elvis Presley Museum, (*see* page 235), or stay on through the evening, for a burger and a show at Little Darlin's Rock 'n' Roll Palace (*see* page 209).
Open daily 10 a.m.-10 p.m.

Park Avenue Association
P.O. Box 11,
Park Ave.,
Winter Park
• (407) 628-1414

Within this three-block area in the center of the arty little college town of Winter Park is central Florida's answer to Rodeo Drive, second in swank only to Worth Avenue in Palm Beach. Shop for the smartest fashions and accessories, the fussiest of children's velvets, laces and furs, the most coveted in home fashions, the finest of antiques. Check out the name brands in silver, crystal and china. Brunching and browsing here is a must for both locals and discerning visitors.
Hours vary; phone ahead for information.

Quality Outlet Center
International Dr. at Grand National,
Orlando
• (407) 423-5885

This shopping center is the place for people who insist on top brand names, but who also like a shaved price. Find outlets selling Royal Doulton and Mikasa china, American Tourister luggage, Corningware, Revereware, Le Creuset cookware, linens and more at factory-outlet prices. Most of the merchandise is for the home, but there's also a large boot outlet and a T-shirt shop.
Open Mon.-Sat. 9:30 a.m.-9 p.m., Sun. 11 a.m.-6 p.m

FOOD

Goodings Supermarket
12521 S.R. 535,
Lake Buena Vista
• (407) 827-1200

The showplace store of a local chain, Goodings features entire aisles of items most markets only carry by ones and twos. Select from deli foods, complete microwave-ready meals, ready-to-eat meals, dewy fruits and vegetables, bakery specialties, meats and seafood. It also has a florist and complete pharmacy. The clincher: Goodings is always open.
Open daily 24 hours.

Orange Blossom Market
5151 S. Orange Blossom Trail, Orlando
• (407) 855-2837

Orlando's fruit growers will probably never recover from the two killer freezes of the 1980s, and many of the area's orange groves have already become building lots. Here, you can still sample the lush harvest of sunny fruits, brought in from the Indian River area and Florida's other remaining groves. Sip a glass of freshly squeezed juice and choose from an abundance of Indian River oranges and grapefruit to ship or take with you. The attached souvenir shop carries campy citrus claptrap, coconut candy, pecan logs and the like.
Open daily 8 a.m.-6 p.m.

LEATHER & LUGGAGE

Florida Briefcase
285 W. Center St. 1706, Altamonte Springs
• (407) 682-3814

A complete line of leather and eelskin briefcases is sold directly to the public at wholesale prices by this factory distributor. Also on display are wallets, business organizers, portfolios, handbags, attaché cases and carry-on luggage.
Open Mon.-Sat. 9 a.m.-5 p.m.

Stone Mountain Handbag Factory Store
Quality Outlet Center, International Dr. at Grand National, Orlando
• (407) 351-0488

The famous Stone Mountain Craftsmen's Guild sells its beautifully crafted, custom-designed leather handbags and accessories here at 20-percent to 50-percent off retail. Merchandise consists of first-quality factory overruns, closeouts or special promotional designs.
Open Mon.-Sat. 9:30 a.m.- 9 p.m., Sun. 11 a.m.-6 p.m.

SPORTING GOODS

Edwin Watts Golf Shop
7297 Turkey Lake Rd., Orlando
• (407) 345-8451

Billing itself as "the world's largest retailer of professional golf equipment," this is the place for those who live on the putting green. Choose from classic and specialty golf needs, in all the exalted, the everyday, and the more esoteric brand names, for both right and left handers, in every color, style and size.
Open Mon.-Sat. 9:30 a.m.-6 p.m.

Track Shack
1322 N. Mills Ave.,
Orlando
• (407) 898-1313

Not only *the* place to buy running shoes and other road-and-track paraphernalia, Track Shack is also the nerve center of Orlando's road race world. Check here for the latest information about where to run for fun or profit.
Open Mon.-Fri. 10 a.m.-7 p.m., Sat. 10 a.m.-5 p.m.

SIGHTS & SPORTS

AMUSEMENTS	230
EXCURSIONS	234
MUSEUMS	235
PARKS & GARDENS	237
SPORTS	237
WALT DISNEY WORLD	238

AMUSEMENTS

Cypress Gardens
2641 S. Lake Summit Dr.,
Cypress Gardens
• (813) 324-2111

One of Florida's oldest attractions, dating back to the Great Depression, this 223-acre Eden draws closer to the 21st century with some pizzazz. The gardens themselves are among the most varied, colorful and extensive in America. Float through timeless canals in silent, electric boats and lose yourself in a flowery wonderland; wander through this huge, tropical forest and gaze at centuries-old cypress trees. When shows are put on here, this simple attraction metamorphoses into a slick theme park, with nonstop entertainment, dining and shopping. For waterskiers all over the world, this is the Grail, and the entertainment extravanganzas include waterski spectaculars featuring some of the best there are. Add in the awesome *Island in the Sky* ride and you'd best budget an entire day for this spot. To get to the gardens, take I-4 going west and take Exit 23, go south on U.S. Highway 27 and take County Road 540 west. Plenty of signs will point the way from there.
Open daily 9 a.m.-6 p.m. Adults $18.95, children (3-9) $12.95.

Fort Liberty Wild West Dinner Show & Trading Post
5260 W. Hwy. 192, Kissimmee
• (407) 351-5151, (800) 347-8181

Spend all day reliving those thundering days of yesteryear, when men were men and women were something else. The complex comprises the Trading Post with a number of shops, a wax museum honoring explorers Lewis and Clark, and a Miccosukee Indian Village with alligator-wrestling demonstrations. The show during the four-course western dinner is thigh-slappingly cornball, with singing, dancing, lariat slinging, shoot-outs, and screaming Indian attacks. Unlimited beer and soft drinks come with the meal; bar drinks are available.

Open daily 10 a.m.-10 p.m. Fort Liberty complex: admission free. Dinner & show: adults $26.95, children ages 3-11 $18.95; children under 3 free. Showtimes vary with the season. Call for times and reservations. All major cards.

Fun 'n' Wheels
International Dr. at Sand Lake Rd., Osceola Square Mall, Kissimmee
• (407) 351-5651 (Orlando), (407) 870-2222 (Kissimmee)

In contrast to the expensive, all-inclusive theme parks, this old-fashioned amusement park charges no admission. You buy a string of tickets at the gate, then spend them on whatever rides and attractions you care to. Drive bumper cars or bumper boats, have a tank fight, play hoop ball, or ride the dry water slides. This is a good way to keep some money in your wallet, and have a good laugh with the kids.

Winter: open Mon.-Fri. 4 p.m.-11 p.m., Sat.-Sun. 10 a.m.-midnight. Summer: open daily 10 a.m.-midnight. Admission free. Ride tickets $1.25, or 20 tickets for $20.

King Henry's Feast
8984 International Dr., Orlando
• (407) 351-5151, (800) 347-8181

Hear Ye, Hear Ye! Watch the action as King Henry VIII presides over a mead reception, followed by a five-course banquet. If you revel in theatrics and love a jolly good giggle, the jugglers and jesters will amuse you, and the magicians and madrigal singers will entertain you. Abandon modern-day etiquette and try the olde English custom of eating with your fingers. The building, with its surrounding moat, replicates an English manor house, furnished with reproductions of sixteenth- and seventeenth-century furniture.

Open nightly. Showtimes vary; phone ahead for details. Reservations essential. Adults $26.95, children 3-11 $18.95, children under 3 free. All major cards.

Mardi Gras Entertainment Dinner
Mercado Shopping Village, 8445 International Dr., Orlando
• (407) 351-5151, (800) 347-8181

The evening starts with a two-hour jazz and cabaret show, then the music plays on as the audience is served a four-course dinner, featuring Caesar salad, soup, stuffed chicken breast, and Key lime pie, plus unlimited beer, wine, and soft drinks. It's all around fun, if you don't pay much attention to the food. To anyone whose every been fed en masse, stuffed chicken breast says it all.

Shows nightly; hours vary with the season. Reservations essential. Adults $27.95, children 3-11 $19.95, children under 3 free. All major cards.

Medieval Life/ Medieval Times Dinner and Tournament
4510 Hwy. 192, Kissimmee
• (407) 239-0214, (800) 327-4024

The only permanent "medieval" village in the nation, Medieval Life is a living museum that takes you back to the days of knights in armor, torture chambers, clashing jousts and bacchanalian feasts. Most of the artifacts are authentic to the period. You enter through a three-room architect's house, then stroll the grounds to see carpenters, glassblowers, weavers and other artisans at work. Falconry demonstrations are held throughout the day. The Dinner and Tournament features a four-course meal with sangría, beer or soda, brought on by serfs and serving wenches. Bar drinks are available at extra cost. The feasting is followed by a spectacular show of medieval games and jousting, with a cast that includes 30 horses that thunder around a 30,000 square foot arena.
Medieval Life: open daily 9 a.m.-9 p.m. Adults $6, children 3-12 $4. Castle at Medieval Times: open daily 9 a.m.-4 p.m. Admission free. Medieval Times Dinner and Tournament: showtimes vary. Reservations essential. Adults $26, children 3-12 $18, children under 3 free.

Rivership Grand Romance Cruises
433 N. Palmetto Ave., Sanford
• (407) 321-5091

The moonlight on the black velvet waters of the Saint Johns River spell romance and magic when you dine and dance aboard this showboat. On Fridays and Saturdays, the boat sails at 7:30, as you tuck into hors d'oeuvres. You choose among five entrées for dinner, then dance to contemporary favorites played by a five-piece band. On weekdays, cruises serve complimentary beer and wine with Cornish game hen. Dinner is followed by a rootin' tootin' show that conjures up the Old South days of fancy ladies and riverboat gamblers. The ship docks at 10 p.m.
Cruises vary seasonally. Reservations essential. Dinner/dance cruise $40; showboat cruise $35. Cards: AE, MC, V.

Sea World of Florida
7007 Sea World Dr., Orlando
• (407) 351-3600, (800) 327-2424
Fax (407) 363-0236

The marine version of the all-day theme parks that are Orlandoland's glory, Sea World is one of the few not under the Disney umbrella. This park easily justifies a daylong visit that starts early and ends with a luau dinner show. In a gargantuan tank with transparent walls, the famous killer whale, Shamu, and his offspring dive, twirl and show off. A special pool set aside for dolphins allows you to pat a velvety head, rub an inquisitive nose. As soon as you arrive, sit down with the day's schedule and decide how to apportion your time and shoe leather along the miles of pathways and the wealth of show and attractions. Watch the seals feed; ride the moving walkway through the

Penguin Encounter (where hundreds of the creatures go about their daily business in a re-creation of their natural Antarctic environment); walk through a transparent tunnel, surrounded by sharks on both sides; view a polished, fast-paced waterski show. Like any first-rate theme park that knows its business, this one has its own restaurants, shops, costumed characters and nonstop entertainment. On the grounds, there's a currency exchange and a 24-hour automatic teller.

Open daily 9 a.m.-10 p.m. (hours may vary seasonally). Adults $27, children 3-9 $23.

Universal Studios
1000 Universal Studios Plaza, Orlando
• (407) 363-8210

After infuriating hundreds of tourists because some of the much-heralded rides remained inoperable for weeks after the official opening, Universal Studios has at last taken its place among Florida's premier attractions. Give it a second chance. Crowds have been smaller than projected, and that means getting a dynamite day with less standing in line than at most of Orlando's attractions. This is a working studio where you'll probably see films being shot, and perhaps a celebrity or two, while you stroll among exactly re-created neighborhoods, including a New York street, the San Francisco waterfront and Hollywood Boulevard. Rides such as "Kongfrontation," "E.T. Adventure" and "Earthquake: the Big One" throw you into the middle of the action and snatch you from peril just in the nick of time. Live shows include "Nickelodeon" and "Murder, She Wrote," the movie *Ghostbusters* and a Hitchcock *Psycho* show played out in the shadow of the Bates Motel. While you wander the grounds, you'll rub elbows with Woody Woodpecker, Andy Panda, and Yogi Bear, and see Groucho Marx, Charlie Chaplin, Mae West and Marilyn Monroe characters signing autographs for wide-eyed kids. Something is going on all around you, all the time, even when you're not in one of the shows. Restaurants are dotted about the Studios: there's Mel's Diner (from the movie *American Graffiti*), a Hard Rock Café, Schwab's Pharmacy for ice-cream sodas, Chez Alcatraz (can you stand it?) for seafood and so on. Movie fanatics can easily have a full day of fun here.

Open daily 9 a.m.-11 p.m. Adults $30.74 (1 day), $51.94 (2 days) or $90.10 (annual pass); children 3-11 $24.38 (1 day), $41.34 (2 days) or $71.55 (annual pass). Parking $3 for cars, $6 for RVs.

Water Mania
6073 W. Irlo Bronson Memorial Hwy., Kissimmee
• (407) 396-2696, (800) 527-3092

The young and restless come here to splish, splash and slide through 24 acres of watery fun. Adults can send the *enfants* off to paddle around in the children's water playground. Roar down rapids in the giant raft, speed down the slides, or rocket down twisting flumes, then let the machine-generated waves wash your vacation wearies away. Be sure to slather on a good

sunscreen beforehand, and wear a substantial bathing suit (eeny bikinis have been known to come off on these roily rides).
Open seasonally. Phone ahead for times. Adults $16.95, children 3-12 $14.95, seniors $13.60.

Wet 'n' Wild
6200 International Dr., Orlando
• (407) 351-3200, (800) 992-9453

One of the nation's premier water parks, this one sprawls over 25 acres of wet thrills and spills, including the screaming, sizzling Black Hole free-fall into deliciously cool oblivion. Bring the whole family, for water fun ranging from serene and still lagoons to flumes and flashy slides.
Summer: open 10 a.m.-6 p.m. For the rest of the year, hours vary seasonally and the park is closed part of Jan. and Feb.; phone ahead for information. Adults $17.95, children 3-12 $14.95.

EXCURSIONS

Balloon Flights

Central Florida is passionate about hot-air ballooning, and for good reason. To float over farmlands fragrant with orange blossoms, or to hover silently on a misty morning within view of Cinderella's Castle can be high adventure. Choices range from simple sightseeing flights to elaborate Champagne breakfasts. Call **Balloons by Terry** (407-422-3529), **Rise & Float Balloon Tours** (407-352-8191), **Orange Blossom Balloons** (407-239-7677), **Fabco** (407-862-7737), **Fantasy Ballooning** (904-736-1010 or 800-255-1827 within Florida); or **Rosie O'Grady's Flying Circus** (407-841-8787).

Winery Tours

Lakeridge Winery & Vineyards
19239 U.S. 27 North, Clermont
• (904) 394-8627, (800) 476-8463

If you still think of Florida as the state that produced that sickly sweet orange wine that used to be sold in citrus stands next to the coconut patties, you're in for a surprise. The University of Florida has developed a new strain of heat- and humidity-tolerant grape, that can produce dry, crisp, light wines. These wines, sold under the label Lakeridge, are showing up in cellars at some of the state's best restaurants, and have made impressive showings at international wine competitions. Tour the winery after viewing an entertaining fifteen-minute slide show, then taste a spectrum of reds, whites, bubblies and blush wines. Buy wines to take along, or they'll ship for you.
Open Mon.-Sat. 10 a.m.-6 p.m., Sun. noon-6 p.m. Admission & wine-tasting free. All major cards.

ORLANDO & CENTRAL FLORIDA   Sights & Sports

MUSEUMS

The Cartoon Museum
4300 S. Semoran Blvd, Orlando
• (407) 273-0141

This delightfully intimate gallery/museum is operated as a labor of love by nostalgia buff, Jim Ivey. His collections include radio and television memorabilia, Big Little books, comics, old magazines and a vast collection of cartoon art.
Open Mon.-Sat. 11 a.m.-6 p.m., Sun. 11 a.m.-4 p.m. Admission free; please don't bring children under age 11.

Elvis Presley Museum
5770 W. Irlo Bronson Memorial Hwy., Old Town, Kissimmee
• (407) 345-9427

If you've ever wanted to believe the supermarket-tabloid myth that "Elvis Is Still Alive!," drop by this shrine to the King. Elvis's friend, Jimmy Velvet, founder and owner of the museum, keeps the King alive with the most extensive collection of Presley paraphernalia that can be found outside of Graceland, Tennessee. Ogle more than 100 items here that were worn or used or displayed by Mr. Presley himself, including some of his gold records and the skin-tight, razzle-dazzle costumes he loved.
Open daily 10 a.m.-11 p.m. Adults $4, children 7-12 & seniors $3, children 6 & under free.

Fort Christmas Museum
1300 Ft. Christmas Rd., Christmas
• (407) 568-4149

Although it's best known among locals as a place to have mail stamped with the Christmas postmark, this is actually a replica of a fort built over a three-day period, from Christmas Day to December 27, 1837, during the Second Seminole War. While other forts from the times (Fort Lauderdale, Fort Myers) have been long lost under great cities, this one remains as a reminder of these savage pioneer wars. Displays include maps, treaties, portraits and drawings, as well as the fort itself.
Open Tues.-Sat. 10 a.m.-5 p.m., Sun. 1 p.m.-5 p.m. Admission free.

Morse Museum of American Art
133 Wellbourne Ave. (just off Park Ave.), Winter Park
• (407) 644-3686

It's a miracle that so much of the estate of Louis Comfort Tiffany survives at all, let alone in a little college town miles from the Long Island mansion that yielded so many of these pieces. Much of the glass here was rescued from the ruins of the Tiffany home, which burned down. The accent is on art nouveau, with a wealth of originals by the great artist and maker of glassware, plus pieces by George Innes, René Lalique, Frank Lloyd Wright, John LaFarge and others.
Open Tues.-Sat. 9:30 a.m.-4 p.m., Sun. 1 p.m.-4 p.m. Adults $2.50, children $1.

Orange County Historical Museum
812 E. Rollins St., Orlando
• (407) 898-8320

Part of pleasant Loch Haven Park, this museum traces Orlando's past, starting in 1842 when Mosquito County (now Orange County) was founded, and continuing into the Seminole Wars, the golden age of citrus, the Big Freeze of 1894, the land boom-and-bust of the 1920s and the present-day Disney era.

Open Tues.-Fri. 9 a.m.-5 p.m., Sat.-Sun. noon-5 p.m. Admission $2.

Orlando Museum of Art at Loch Haven
Loch Haven Park, 2416 N. Mills Ave., Orlando
• (407) 896-4321

Distinguished for its pre-Columbian gallery, this small but comprehensive art museum has rotating exhibits of American and African art, and an excellent schedule of changing exhibits on loan from museums and private collections worldwide. On display are pre-Columbian pieces dating from 1200 B.C. to 1500 B.C., collected from throughout the Americas.

Open Tues.-Thurs. 9 a.m.-5 p.m., Fri. 9 a.m.-9 p.m., Sat. 10 a.m.-5 p.m., Sun. noon-5 p.m. Adults $3, children 6-12 $2, seniors & students $2, children under 5 free.

Orlando Science Center
Loch Haven Park, 810 E. Rollins St., Orlando
• (407) 896-7151

Also home of the John Young Planetarium, the museum offers daily programs on astronomy, a big-screen space show and weekend Cosmic Concerts. Exhibits, most of them inviting hands-on participation, are devoted to the physical sciences and to Florida's natural history.

Open Mon.-Thurs. 9 a.m.-5 p.m., Fri. 9 a.m.-9 p.m., Sat. noon-9 p.m., Sun. noon-5 p.m. Adults $4, children & seniors $3, families $10.

Spence-Lanier Pioneer Center
750 Bass Rd., Kissimmee
• (407) 396-8644

It's a small, developing pioneer center and museum showing how Floridians lived at the turn of the century, in a classic "possum trot" homestead. The library is rich in genealogy and Florida history.

Open Tues.-Fri. 10 a.m.-5 p.m., Sat.-Sun. 2 p.m.-5 p.m. Free.

Tupperware World Headquarters Museum
3175 N. Orange Blossom Trail, Kissimmee
• (407) 847-3111, (800) 858-7221

This, friends, is Tupperware Valhalla. A fast, free tour educates you as to how Tupperware is made; then you can view Tupperware's model home. On display in the museum is an unusual and comprehensive collection of food containers from prehistoric times to the present.

Open daily 9 a.m.-4 p.m. Admission free.

PARKS & GARDENS

Bok Tower Gardens
P.O. Box 3810 (3 miles north of Lake Wales, off U.S. 27), Lake Wales
• (813) 676-1408

A Florida landmark since 1928, this carillon tower and its surrounding gardens have a mystical sense of sanctuary, especially during the full moon, when carillon concerts are held by moonlight. One of the world's great carillons, the 57-bell, 205-foot Bok Singing Tower plays every half hour, with a 45-minute recital at 3 p.m. daily. Gardens burst into a riot of azaleas in early spring, magnolias in summer and camellias during cold months, all mirrored in reflecting pools and ringed by meandering pathways.
Open daily 8 a.m.-5 p.m. Adults $3, children under 12 free.

Leu Gardens
1730 N. Forest Ave., Orlando
• (407) 849-2620

Once a simple lakeside farm, believed to have been cultivated first before 1860, these 55 acres are now a superbly groomed showplace, ablaze with camellias in winter, mountains of azaleas in early spring, and seasonal flowers throughout the year. Stroll through the rose garden and rest in the shade of a gazebo. Explore the cactus garden, and marvel at the dozens of varieties of orchids in the conservatory. The Leu house, typical of Florida farmhouses at the turn of the century, has been restored to its original style (of the 1920s to 1930s) and is open to the public.
Open Mon. & Sun. 1 p.m.-4 p.m., Tues.-Sat. 10 a.m.-4 p.m. Adults $3, children 6-16 $1.

SPORTS

Fishing

In central Florida, you're never more than two hours away from deep-sea fishing in the Atlantic or the Gulf of Mexico. It's best to book such an excursion through your hotel's concierge or guest-services desk. Fleets of sportfishing charter boats (usually holding no more than six passengers) and "head" boats (that carry large groups of people offshore for drift fishing), are based on both coasts. Closer to home, bassing is the blockbuster fishery; the area is peppered with lakes large and small, where it's easy to find a guide with a boat, tackle and bait. If you want to book a private boat, be aware that most of the area's boat-rental services are one-person operations. Call well in advance, and be prepared to leave a detailed message with an answering service or machine. Most will put the boat on a trailer and meet you where the fish are biting best. Guides include **Bob Stonewater** (904-736-8442), **Bass Bustin' Guide Service** (407-281-0845), **Bass Challenge** (407-273-8045), **J & B Central Florida Bass Guide** (407-293-2791) and **Marty's Master Bass Fishing** (407-860-4816).

Spectator Sports

BASEBALL – The **Houston Astros** bat the ball during spring training in Kissimmee, and the team welcomes the public to demonstration games. When the Astros return to Houston, the **Florida State League Osceola Astros** play. For dates and rates, call (407) 933-5400 or (407) 239-0043. Ex-major-league players over age 35 play in the **Orlando Juice Senior Professional Association** games at **Tinker Field** (407-649-0085). The city's AA professional baseball team is the **Sunrays**, (407-872-7593).

BASKETBALL – Orlando's professional basketball team, the **Magic**, plays from November through April at the **Orlando Arena** (407-649-3200).

FOOTBALL – Annually on New Year's Day, the **Citrus Bowl Classic** draws 70,000 cheering fans to watch big-time football (call 407-423-2476 for information).

JAI ALAI – Orlando-Seminole Jai Alai (407-339-6221) opens season in Fern Park in September, and is played through January.

AT THE RACETRACK – Harness races (horse against horse, each harnessed to a two-wheeled sulkie, charge around the ring) are held at the **Ben White Raceway** (407-293-8721). Greyhound racing can be found at the **Sanford Orlando Kennel Club** in Longwood (407-831-1600) and the **Seminole Greyhound Park** in Casselberry (407-699-4510).

WALT DISNEY WORLD

What exactly *is* Walt Disney World? The term encompasses the entire Disney complex, which includes the **Magic Kingdom, EPCOT Center,** the **Disney-MGM Studios Theme Park, River Country, Discovery Island, Pleasure Island, Typhoon Lagoon,** the **Walt Disney World Village,** the **Walt Disney World Hotel Plaza,** several enormous hotel complexes, several golf courses, four interconnecting lakes, a campground and a natural preserve. All of this is spread over 30,000 acres (or, 46 square miles, a hunk of land about twice the size of Manhattan). Keep in mind the following while navigating the lakes and lagoons, boardwalks and bridges, canals and castles of this modern-day empire:

- High seasons at the Disney attractions run from just before Christmas through April, and from mid-June through August. Christmas week draws bigger crowds by far than any other time of the year.
- Disney suggests, and we agree, that you visit EPCOT Center first, then the Magic Kingdom. Children, and even adults, are often disappointed with the real-life

approach at EPCOT if they visit it second, expecting it to match the fantasy of the Magic Kingdom. But though the newer EPCOT Center is more educational than magical, it's no less interesting or exciting.
- Prices for these attractions change often. In the price schedule below, we have listed the prices effective as of February 17, 1991. These were still valid at press time, in June 1991; if they do go up again, they should only do so marginally.

WALT DISNEY WORLD ADMISSIONS
(effective February 17, 1991)

ATTRACTION	ADULT	CHILD (3 - 9)
Disney-MGM, 1-day pass	$33	$26
EPCOT Center, 1-day pass	$33	$26
Magic Kingdom, 1-day pass	$33	$26
4-day passport, all 3 parks	$111	$88
5-day passport**	$145	$116
Discovery Island	$8	$4.50
Pleasure Island		
1-evening pass	$11.95	--
annual pass	$34.95	--
River Country		
1-day pass	$12	$9.50
annual pass	$50	$50
Typhoon Lagoon		
1-day pass	$18.50	$14.75
annual pass	$75	$75
Annual pass, theme parks	$180	$155
Annual pass, renewal	$160	$135
Parking, car	$3	
Parking, RV	$6	

Special rates are available to Florida residents, with proof of address, during certain dates throughout the year. If you live in Florida, ask about the Four Season Salute.

** Provides limited admission to the Disney-MGM Studios, EPCOT Center and Magic Kingdom on any 5 days, and to Discovery Island, Pleasure Island, River Country and Typhoon Lagoon for 7 days after the first use of the passport.

ORLANDO & CENTRAL FLORIDA Sights & Sports

Discovery Island
Walt Disney World,
Lake Buena Vista
• (407) 824-4321/
934-7639

Theme park regulars think of this as the vacation from the vacation. It's an island of raw nature, with all of its raucous birdcalls and dewy tranquility. An island in Bay Lake, it supports the world's largest captive population of scarlet ibis, as many as 90 animal species including lemurs and tortoise, 250 species of plants and the world's largest walk-through aviary. Give it all day, or combine it with a visit to River Country.
Open daily 10 a.m.-6 p.m. Call ahead for information on ranger-led nature walks. See page 239 for price schedule.

Disney-MGM Studios Theme Park
Walt Disney World,
Lake Buena Vista
• (407) 824-4321/
934-7639

Hollywood's golden years, the 1930s through 1950s, are re-created in an entire city that serves not just as a theme park but as a working movie set. So you want to experience your fifteen minutes of fame? You've come to the right place. The SuperStar Television Theater allows you, through—dare we say it—the magic of modern technology to become a sitcom stand-in. You can also act in a professionally directed video, or star in a famous show ("Cheers", "The Today Show", "The Tonight Show"). Walk through the animation studios to see artists at work on upcoming films, stroll through a replica of Hollywood, California's Grauman's Chinese Theater. You probably won't want to star in the Indiana Jones stunt show. It's done live, by real people with heart-stopping action. To calm down, take the ride through Catastrophe Canyon and the backlot, which will wow even the most jaded theme-park regulars. It's easy to spend an entire day at this park.

Hungry? Perhaps you'll want to eat under the photographic gaze of famous gossip columnists Hedda Hopper or Louella Parsons at the Brown Derby. Or, commandeer a booth at the Prime Time Café. Your waitress, "Mom," will slide in beside you to ask what you'd like to eat, and she'll scold you if you don't finish your vegetables. It's all done in early 1950s style, complete with black-and-white televisions playing old sitcoms, such as "I Love Lucy" and "I Married Joan."
Open daily at 9 a.m., closings 7 p.m.-midnight, depending on the season & the day of the week. Many special events, so check ahead. See page 239 for price schedule.

EPCOT Center
Walt Disney World,
Lake Buena Vista
• (407) 824-4321/
934-7639

One of Disney's newest (opened in 1982) and most ambitious projects ever, the Experimental Prototype Community of Tomorrow is a city-sized theme park that divides into two worlds: Future World, with its modern and world-of-tomorrow exhibits, and the World Showcase, where the cultures of eleven nations are depicted (often a tad stereotypically) in exhibits that allow you to "experience" the country while keeping both feet firmly planted in Orlando. Don't expect EPCOT Center to be the fairytale land of the Magic Kingdom; it has less to do with fantasy and more to do with learning and discovery. It's no less exciting or energy-filled than the rest of Walt Disney World, though, and no less jammed to bursting with eager crowds.

At Future World, displays show us the history of humankind's attempts to adapt to and control the world we live in (with themes such as how we've harnessed energy and how we've achieved mobility over the past several million years); then they let us in on their optimistic, fantastic views of a high-tech future. There are also The Living Sea, a (dry) tour through a 6-million-gallon tankful of assorted sea creatures; The Wonders of Life, with thrill rides, films and exhibits on the human body; and *Captain Eo*, a 3-D film starring a gyrating Michael Jackson.

At World Showcase, each of eleven separate pavilions (France, Italy, Germany, Norway, the United Kingdom, the United States, Canada, Mexico, China, Japan and Morocco) takes us to a "country" and enchants us with its architecture, arts, crafts, wares, costumes, entertainment and food. Each exhibit is inspiring in its own way—France for its flowingly pastoral (if not quite realistic) film; China and Canada for their thundering, skyscraper-size 360° films; Morocco for its brasses and belly dancers; England for its street shows and prim shops; and Norway for its ancient Viking church and shivery ride through the foaming Maelstrom.

The culinary lineup at World Showcase is no less of an extravaganza than the rest of EPCOT Center. In keeping with the international theme, there is a lavishly presented restaurant for all the countries except the United States and Canada. Each paints a lovely picture of its original inspiration (though the scene tends toward the cliché in most—we don't remember seeing many accordion-playing trios wearing berets last time we visited the *real* France), and generally you can eat well. Which is the best? Let the type of cuisine determine your choice, though our top pick is the formal French restaurant, Les Chefs de France, with a menu designed and regularly updated by no less than three of the world's most renowned chefs—Paul Bocuse, Roger Vergé and Gaston Lenôtre. Though none of these great chefs actually cooks here, and the cuisine is nowhere near as exceptional as that at any of their restaurants in France, we hardly expected a culinary revelation at Walt Disney World. All the restaurants do do a fine job for places that serve several thousand customers a day. Other good bets are L'Originale Alfredo di Roma in "Italy," Mitsukoshi Restaurant Dining Room in "Japan" and Marrakesh in "Morrocco." Dinner for two, with a bottle of wine, in any country, will run between $70 and $105.

Open daily 9 a.m., but it's best to arrive at 8 a.m. Special events schedule varies. See page 239 for price schedule. All major cards.

ORLANDO & CENTRAL FLORIDA Sights & Sports

Magic Kingdom
Walt Disney World,
Lake Buena Vista
• (407) 824-4321/
934-7639

The most magical of Walt Disney World's theme parks in Florida, this Magic Kingdom Park is larger than its predecessor in California. The whole thing one is anchored by the glittering, eighteen-story Cinderella's Castle (which, though it sparkles with the promise of fantasy and fairytale, actually houses offices used by Disney executives and personnel). The Dumbo ride thrills the tots, while Haunted Mansion and the Big Thunder Mountain Railroad rattle kids into silliness and Space Mountain gives chills to thrill seekers; it's the scariest ride, only for older children and the bravest adults. Enter through the Town Square and Main Street, which are the American hometown of song and story, then explore all the park's sections from the new Mickey's Birthdayland to Tomorrowland to Fantasyland. Highlights of special nights are the Main Street Electrical Parade and the Fantasy in the Sky fireworks.

Opens daily 9 a.m. Get there well ahead of time. Closings 6 p.m.-midnight depending on the season and the day of the week. See page 239 for price schedule. All major cards.

Pleasure Island
Walt Disney World,
Lake Buena Vista
• (407) 824-3737

Designed as a theme park for adults, Pleasure Island is a world of nightclubs and restaurants, offering everything from high adventure to low comedy, superb dining to fast food, romantic cocktails in a secluded bar to deafening disco. There are seven nightclubs including the Comedy Warehouse and the Neon Armadillo, dance clubs including Mannequins and the XZFR Rockin' RollerDrome, and nonstop music ranging from jazz to Top 40 tunes. The *Empress Lilly* Riverboat, with its Baton Rouge Lounge, is anchored in Pleasure Island. No one under 21 is admitted to Mannequins—not because it's naughty but because it's the suavest of the island's dance clubs, and a unique, high-tech experience reserved for sophisticates.

Open daily noon-2 a.m. See page 239 for price schedule. All major cards.

River Country
Walt Disney World,
Lake Buena Vista
• (407) 824-4321/
934-7639

Less spectacular than Typhoon Lagoon, but more down-home, this is the old swimmin' hole laced with flume rides, corkscrews, waterfalls, rapids and swinging ropes, and rimmed with a white-sand beach. It's a cool-off spot, and a good park to combine with a visit to Discovery Island. Within Disney's Fort Wilderness Campground, it can be reached by car or via Walt Disney World transportation.

Open daily 10 a.m.-5 p.m. See page 239 for price schedule. All major cards.

Typhoon Lagoon
Walt Disney World, Lake Buena Vista • (407) 824-4321/ 934-7639

Once upon a time, so the story goes, the shrimp boat *Miss Tilly* shipwrecked on Mount Mayday, which most probably will erupt during your visit. The hulk remains stuck, hovering high over Typhoon Lagoon and its waterfalls, cascades, wandering streams (the figure on the float ahead of you may be Minnie Mouse or Goofy), water chutes and slides, and a salt-water reef where you can snorkel with real (harmless) sharks. Cowabunga, dude! The wave action in the lagoon is strong enough to surf on. Even in a state that is known for its water parks, this one is an eye-popper.

Open daily at 9 a.m. Closings vary by season. See page 239 for price schedule. All major cards.

BASICS

GETTING THERE	243
GETTING AROUND	244
AT YOUR SERVICE	245
GOINGS-ON	246

GETTING THERE

A number of major airlines serves the ever growing, booming **Orlando International Airport** (407-825-2001): **American Airlines, Bahama Air, British Airways, ComAir, Continental, Delta, Icelandair, KLM, Mexicana, Midway, Northwest Airlines, PanAm, Trans-Brazil, TWA, United Airlines** and **US Air**. The airport is located in South Orlando, about ten miles from downtown.

If you want to travel by train, **Amtrak** (1-800-USA-RAIL) serves Orlando with four trains daily from New York, Tampa and Miami. Amtrak also operates the **Auto Train**, which is a train service that picks up passengers and their cars in Lorton, Virginia (near Washington, D.C.), and makes the 850-mile trip overnight to either DeLand or Sanford, Florida (about 23 miles from Orlando).

GETTING AROUND

By Bus

Orlando and its satellite communities are served by **Greyhound-Trailways Bus Lines** (800-237-8211). Local bus service throughout Orange and Seminole counties is provided by **Tri-County Transit** (for route and scheduling information, call 407-841-8240).

By Car

You'll find all the major national car-rental companies in Orlando, and most of them—including **National, Budget, Avis, Hertz** and **Dollar**—have an agency at Orlando International Airport.

Highway I-4 runs southwest-to-northeast through Orlando from Tampa to Daytona Beach. I-75 comes into the state from Atlanta, and joins Florida's Turnpike, which leads into Orlando and south to Miami. Chief non-interstate north-south route through the city is U.S. 17-92; east-west, U.S. 50. The Beeline Expressway toll road connects with I-4 and the turkpike at Orlando, and provides quick access to the Space Coast. When you arrive, buy the newest map. Central Florida has been growing so explosively that entire communities, housing thousands of people and containing hundreds of new street names, spring up almost overnight.

By Shuttle

Mears Motor Shuttle is the best alternative to taxi service, operating around the clock and serving as a concessionaire to many hotels. Shuttles also go from hotels to attractions. Shuttle service to downtown or International Drive hotels is about $10 one-way or $17 round trip for adults, and $7 one-way or $11 round trip for children. To Lake Buena Vista hotels, shuttle fare is $12 and $21 for adults and $7 and $11 for children. Call 422-4561 in Orange County, or 933-1808 from Osceola County.

By Taxi

Listed in the Yellow Pages are a good selection of taxi companies. Rates average $2.25 for the first mile and $1.20 each additional mile; the flat rate from Orlando International Airport is $20 to most downtown hotels. Companies include **Yellow Cab** (407-699-9999); **City Cab** (407-422-5151); **Blue Taxi** (407-855-0800); and **Ace Metro**, (407-783-9574). In addition, many limousine services serve the airport and surrounding communities. Advance reservations are recommended. They include **Flamingo Road Transportation** (345-1400 from Orlando; 396-4800 from Kissimmee); **Orlando Connection** (407-422-6618); **Starr Transportation** (407-425-8495) and **Air Transportation Service** (407-857-9595).

USEFUL TELEPHONE NUMBERS

The area code for all Orlando phone numbers is (407).

Bar Association Orange County .... (407) 422-4551
Central Florida Reservations (for hotels &
 condos) .... (800) 423-8604, (407) 396-8300 ext. 5104
Central Reservations Service Corp. (free reservations through-
 out greater Orlando) .... (800) 950-0232
Cirrus ATM locations throughout Florida ...... (800) 4-CIRRUS
Council on Aging, Referral Service
 Orange County .... (407) 648-4357
 Osceola County .... (407) 846-8532
Dental Society, Orange County .... (407) 894-9798
Emergency (Ambulance, Fire, Police: for TDD service for the
 deaf, dial 911 and tap the space bar). 911
Florida Game and Freshwater Fish Commission
 (hunting and fishing licenses) .... (800) 342-9620
Florida Highway Patrol ....
 Non-emergency .... (407) 423-6400
 Turnpike Troop .... (407) 855-5382
Kissimmee/St. Cloud Resort Area reservations (books hotels,
 condos, villas, campsites.) .... (800) 333-KISS (5477)
Medical Society, Orange County .... (407) 841-6267
Missing Children Clearing House .... (800) 342-0821
Poison control .... (800) 282-3171
Rape Crisis Information .... (407) 648-3028
Spouse Abuse Hotline .... (407) 886-2856
Suicide prevention .... (407) 628-1227
Time .... (407) 646-3131
Tourist Information
 Orange County .... (407) 363-5800
 Kissimmee/St.Cloud .... (407) 847-5000
U.S. Marshal .... (407) 648-6326
Weather .... (407) 851-7510

SERVICES: WHERE TO FIND . . .

A Baby Sitter – Fairy Godmothers Child Care (407-277-3724) specializes in child care in hotels, motels and condos, and service is available around the clock. **Super Sitters** (21862 Winter Park Rd., Orlando; 407-740-5516) offers trained, bonded and insured professional sitters, available around the clock to baby sit in your hotel room. They wear photo ID.

A Drug Store – Stained glass windows set the scene for a discerning carriage trade at **Loomis Drugs** (7600 Dr. Phillips Blvd., Orlando; 407-352-1177). The store will fill your prescription and deliver it with your choice of toiletries, cosmetics or other needs to your hotel. It's also a mail depot, and can send faxes or packages via Federal Express or United Parcel Service for you. Open Mon.-Sat. 8:30 a.m.-10 p.m., Sun. 9 a.m.-9 p.m. For emergency prescriptions, dial (800) 2-WALGREENS (operated 24 hours a day by **Walgreen Drugstores**) to link up via satellite records with your prescription anywhere in the United States, including Puerto Rico.

A Foreign Exchange Counter – A foreign-exchange booth operates in the main terminal at **Orlando International Airport**. Major hotels also post exchange rates for the more common foreign funds. **Americash** foreign-exchange brokers are located in Orlando at 6227 International Drive (407-351-3363) and 7635 International Drive (407-352-5640); and in Kissimmee at 2938 Vineland Road (407-239-6688) and 5770 Irlo Bronson Highway (407-239-7640).

WEATHER

Central Florida's weather is relentlessly hot, still and muggy from June through September, with occasional relief from afternoon thunderstorms. Breezes are a few degrees cooler near the east coast. February through May and October through November provide the most pleasant, driest weather. Cold fronts, chiefly December through February, can be piercingly cold. If you come in winter, be prepared for temperatures as low as the teens.

GOINGS-ON

Orlando is a year-round city that is as busy during the muggy summer months, when families vacation, as in winter when cultural events are more frequent and hotels are abuzz with business conferences. For the latest information, write to the **Orlando/Orange County Convention & Visitors Bureau**, (7208 Sand Lake Rd., Ste. 300, Orlando FL 32819; 407-363-5832; Fax 407-363-5899). When in town, read the *Orlando Sentinel* for current events, and call theme parks for news of special events, which change according to season and time of the week or month.

January

- **Florida Citrus Bowl Classic**, New Year's Day, Orlando; (407) 423-2476.
- **Camellias** bloom throughout the area all month. Extensive camellia gardens are part of Leu Gardens, Orlando; (407) 849-2121.
- **Scottish Highland Games**, second weekend in January. Features bagpipes, haggis hurling and dance; (407) 422-8226.
- **Equestrian Events**, held throughout the year, Hyatt Grand Cypress Resort; (407) 239-4600.

February

- **Azaleas bloom** throughout Central Florida. Special celebrations include those at Ravine Gardens, Palatka (904-328-1503); Bok Tower Gardens, Lake Wales (813-676-1408); and Leu Gardens, Orlando (407-849-2121).
- **Minnesota Twins**, mid-February to early April. Spring training exhibition baseball; (407) 849-6346.
- **Osceola County Fair**, mid-February, Kissimmee. Food, rides, exhibits in the best, down-home traditions; (407) 847-5000.
- **Silver Spurs Rodeo**, mid-February, Kissimmee. Sterling rodeo classic held here for more than 80 years; (407) 847-5000.
- **World-Class Auto and Motorcycle Races**, usually held in February, March, July and October, Daytona Beach International Speedway; (800) 854-1234.

March

- **Azalea Festival**, second week in March, Palatka. A small-town classics with parades, regatta, arts-and-crafts show, beauty queen; (904) 328-1503.
- **Central Florida Fair**, early March, Orlando. Oldtime, country fair classic with rides, fun, judging of everything from hogs to homemade cakes; (407) 295-3247.
- **Houston Astros**, March-April, Kissimmee. Spring training begins, games continue through April; (407) 847-5000.
- **Kissimmee Bluegrass Festival**, first full weekend, Kissimmee. Country arts and crafts, clogging, family fun; (407) 847-5000.
- **St. Cloud Spring Fling**, mid-March, St. Cloud; (407) 847-5000.
- **Easter Sunrise Service**, Easter Sunday, Bok Tower Gardens. Features music played on the famous carillon; (813) 676-1408.

April

- **Antique Boat Festival**, early April, Mount Dora. Rides, clinics, displays of varnished old wooden craft; (904) 323-2165.
- **Bok Tower Gardens Annual International Carillon Festival**, Lake Wales. The serene forests and gardens echo with a magnificent carillon; (813) 676-1408.
- **Mount Dora Regatta**, late April, Lake Dora. More than 100 boats in twenty classes sail under the sponsorship of the state's oldest inland yacht club; (904) 383-2165.
- **William Bartram Walk Through**, Payne's Prairie near Micanopy. A nature walk in memory of the early naturalist; interpretive characters tell stories of Florida's history; (904) 466-3397.
- **Orlando Shakespeare Festival**, first three weeks, Orlando. Three weeks of play, arts and crafts, Renaissance events; (407) 246-2555.
- **Osceola County Wagon Trail and Trail Ride**. A weeklong trek through county ranchlands on horseback and in horse-drawn wagons; (407) 423-5000.

June

- **Florida Blueberry Festival**, early June, Ocala. Fun for the family; (407) 832-6397.
- **Silver Spurs Rodeo**, last weekend in June or first weekend in July. Ridin', ropin', and rasslin' for big prize money; one of the nation's oldest rodeos; (407) 847-5000.

September

- **Lake Wales Quilt Exhibition**, September to November, Lake Wales Museum and Cultural Center; (813) 676-5443.
- **Osceola Art Festival**, Lake Tohopelika. More than 150 Florida artists and photographers display and sell their work; (407) 847-5000.

October

- **Lake Mary-Heathrow Festival of the Arts**, last weekend prior to Halloween, Lake Mary. One of the state's best art shows; (407) 333-1111.
- **Lake Wales Pioneer Day**, last Sunday in October, Lake Wales. Old-fashioned Florida Cracker skills displayed; (813) 676-2317.
- **Florida State Air Fair**, late October, Kissimmee. Stunt flying and aircraft displays; (407) 847-5000.
- **Pioneer Day Festival**, Pine Castle Center of the Arts. Booths demonstrating folk arts and crafts common to the area, such as sugar-cane grinding; (407) 855-7461.

November

- **Festival of the Masters**, second weekend in November, Lake Buena Vista. One of Florida's premier art shows; (407) 824-4531.
- **Orlando Magic Basketball**, November through April, The Arena; (407) 649-3200.
- **Light Up Orlando**, mid-November, Orlando. Downtown street party with dozens of food booths, music and dancing; (407) 846-2555.
- **Longwood Arts and Crafts Festival**, weekend before Thanksgiving, Longwood. A fundraiser featuring finest local artists and artisans; (407) 363-5832.
- **Volusia County Fair**, begins first Thursdays and runs eleven days, DeLand. Livestock judging, agriculture displays, rides, midway; (904) 734-9514.

December

- **Christmas Boat Parades**, Kissimmee (407-847-5000) and DeLand (904-734-4331). Local boats festooned with lights compete for best decoration.
- **Christmas Recitals**, Bok Tower Gardens, Christmas Eve and Christmas Day, Lake Wales. Carillon music and readings; (813) 676-1408.
- **St. Cloud Art Festival**, first weekend in December, St. Cloud. Entertainment, handcrafts, food; (407) 432-9199.
- **Warbird Weekend**, late December, St. Cloud. Static and flying displays of vintage military aircraft and vehicles; (407) 847-5000.

FIRST COAST

| ST. AUGUSTINE | 250 |
| JACKSONVILLE | 255 |

ST. AUGUSTINE

RESTAURANTS	250
HOTELS	252
SHOPS	253
SIGHTS	253

RESTAURANTS

Gypsy Cab Company
829 Anastasia Blvd.,
St. Augustine
• (904) 824-8244
SEAFOOD

11/20

Gypsy Cab is one of the most popular restaurants in northeast Florida, in part because of its cheerful casualness: if you want to wear shorts, that's fine, or if you want to dress up a bit, that's fine, too. Once you get past the bold purple neon outside, there isn't much to the place other than a few photographs and paintings—owner Ned Pollack cares more about the food (he calls his seafood- and pasta-based cooking "urban cuisine") than the decor. Rich, stock-based soups are particularly fetching; we're partial to the lusty roasted eggplant soup with sun-dried tomatoes and the sweet-potato soup pierced with jalapeños. The house salad is simple and refreshing, a bed of crisp lettuces and alfalfa sprouts with a tangy dressing of soy sauce, nutritional yeast, olive oil and red-wine vinegar. Entrées include an impeccable grouper with a lively white wine—mustard sauce and creamy yet light shrimp primavera. Pollack also does good work with every sort of pasta, from lacy angel hair to sturdy Greek orzo. Save room for dessert, in particular the smooth chocolate mousse or the moist, springy Mandarin orange cake. Dinner for two, with wine, runs $60.
Open Sun.-Mon. 11 a.m.-3 p.m. & 5:30 p.m.-10 p.m., Wed.-Thurs. 11 a.m.-3 p.m. & 5:30 p.m.-10 p.m., Fri.-Sat. 11 a.m.-2 p.m. & 5:30 p.m.-11 p.m. Cards: MC, V.

Jimmy Ponce's Conch House
57 Comares Ave.,
St. Augustine
• (904) 824-2046
SEAFOOD

10/20

Jimmy Ponce unabashedly courts the tourists, and he gets them—they love the palm trees illuminated by colored flood lights and the chickee-hut dining room, thatched with palm fronds and full of brass, glass and weathered wood. Not all the cooking is as zippy and cheerful as the atmosphere, but it wasn't for nothing that Ponce's conch chowder took first prize in northeast Florida's 1988 Great Chowder Debate—this blend of ground conch, vegetable chunks and hot datil peppers unites in a vibrant medley of Caribbean flavors. On the other hand, we've been less than thrilled by the leaden, doughy conch fritters with a Key lime–mustard sauce. The cautious are best off playing it safe with the shrimp, oysters and scallops (steamed or fried) or perhaps the catch of the day, though a few of the more adventurous dishes are worth trying, particularly the scallops portofino, made with garlic, Dijon mustard and a brandied cream sauce, or the firm, meaty dolphin-fish filet sautéed with an exotic blend of lime juice, spiced rum and bananas. If you're lucky enough to be offered Caribbean bread, don't pass it up; likewise the fluffy cakes for dessert. Two will spend about $60 for dinner with wine.

Open Sun.-Thurs. 11:30 a.m.-9 p.m., Fri.-Sat. 11:30 a.m.-10 p.m. Cards: AE, MC, V.

Old City House
115 Cordova St.,
St. Augustine
• (904) 826-0781
NEW AMERICAN

12/20

This smart new place is getting raves from the locals, and with such dishes as the baked Brie, we can see why—a profusion of red and green apple slices, strawberries, blueberries and kiwi surrounds flaky pastry encasing heavenly melting cheese. The contemporary American cuisine is executed by the husband-and-wife team of John and Darcy Compton, who have a knack for making things interesting without lapsing into foolish trendiness. Entrées include grilled dolphin-fish topped with an aromatic mix of cilantro, lime juice and chopped pimiento and grilled lamb chops with a maple-mint-brandy sauce. The main ingredients are treated simply, so it's the sauces that get lively, from a maple-mustard glaze to a lemon-lime-orange butter. Desserts run to such delicious French-style goodies as chocolate-truffle custard cakes; American cuisine is represented in the delightful strawberry shortcake with a wealth of fresh berries. Cheerful waitresses toting bottomless baskets of muffins are one of the many welcoming touches in this updated old Spanish-style house, with its ceramic-tile tables and wooden chairs. Upstairs is a charming bed-and-breakfast run by Darcy's parents. Dinner for two, with wine, runs about $80.

Open Tues.-Fri. 11:30 a.m.-2:30 p.m. & 5 p.m.-10 p.m., Sat. 5 p.m.-10 p.m., Sun. 11:30 a.m.-3 p.m. & 5 p.m.-10 p.m. Cards: AE, MC, V.

Raintree
102 San Marco Ave.,
St. Augustine
• (904) 824-7211
CONTINENTAL

9/20

A mosey down the hallway, which is lined with framed awards and letters of praise, makes it clear that Raintree takes itself quite seriously—which is, of course, usually a sign of trouble. And, in fact, the food is about as exciting as a Perry Como record. It's a good-looking place, though, an admirably renovated Victorian home with glassed-in porches, candy-striped awnings and baskets of greenery and flowers, and it does a good business with both well-dressed tourists and locals living it up with

out-of-town friends. Occasionally the generic dressed-up Continental cooking comes out of the 1950s and into the early 1980s, as with the seafood crêpe in a light cream sauce pepped up with Cajun spices. Avoid the fussier dishes, such as veal Oscar topped with hollandaise or Maine lobster claw, which tastes as if it has been deflavorized. Stick to the simpler fare, perhaps the reliably tender and juicy pepper steak, a pan-broiled eight-ounce filet topped with peppercorns and flambéed with brandy. Salads bear the limp look of overrefrigeration, but desserts—such as Hungarian chocolate crêpes bulging with chocolate and walnuts—are worth a try. Dinner for two, with wine, runs $70.
Open Sun.-Thurs. 5 p.m.-9:30 p.m., Fri.-Sat. 5 p.m.-10 p.m. All major cards.

HOTELS

Luxury (From $150)

Marriott at Sawgrass
1000 TPC Blvd.,
Ponte Vedra Beach
32082
• (904) 285-7777
Fax (904) 285-0906

Just thinking about it gets us out of breath: at the Marriott, there are 99 holes of championship golf (including the PGA Tour's Tournament Players club), ten Har-Tru tennis courts, four swimming pools, an equestrian center, an exercise center, croquet and miles of beaches to be jogged when you get done with all of that. Pass the Evian. The sprawling, 550-room hotel is for sports enthusiasts, mostly. Ten years ago, there wasn't much in this neighborhood except a couple of beach houses and a lot of marshes. Maybe that's the reason that, although the facilities are beyond criticism for their physical beauty and extensiveness, the Marriott still gives off somewhat of a "manufactured" resort feeling.
Singles & doubles: $145; suites: $250-$400; beachfront villas: $200.

Moderate (From $100)

The Lodge at Ponte Vedra Beach
607 Ponte Vedra Beach Blvd.,
Ponte Vedra Beach
32082
• (904) 273-9500
Fax (904) 273-0210

Picture *Gone With the Wind*'s Tara on the Mediterranean, and you'll come close to the feeling at the lodge at Ponte Vedra Beach. The prize jewel in a crown of new developments encircling Ponte Vedra Beach, the lodge offers services and amenities virtually unheard of at most small resorts (90 rooms): twice-daily maid service, nightly turndown with homemade chocolate-chip cookies, 24-hour room service and a ceremonious, polished concierge. Rooms sparkle with terra-cotta and floral prints, and the enormous bathtubs are an inviting luxury.

So why all of the opulence in PV? Within the last year, both the Professional Golfers Association and the Association of

Tennis Professionals relocated their national headquarters to Ponte Vedra Beach; presumably, all of this opulence is meant to service the superstars and superlative-seekers visiting the town that golf built. Situated overlooking a white sand, sea oat–studded beachfront, the property stuns, and that's good.
Singles & doubles: $130-$210.

Bed & Breakfasts

Westcott House
146 Avenida Menendez,
St. Augustine 32084
• (904) 824-4301
No fax

Saint Augustine is one of this nation's most fascinating cities, established 55 years before the pilgrims landed on Plymouth Rock and 42 years before the English settled Jamestown. It was, contrary to popular misconception, the first continuously inhabited European settlement in the United States, and by the time of the American Revolution, Saint Augustine had already celebrated its 200th anniversary ten years earlier. A lovely little gingerbread-style house with only eight rooms, Westcott House loves iron railings, hanging ferns, porches and clapboard. Today, the Dennison family owns it and offers breakfast in a brick courtyard or in an opulent parlor. Although much of the town today suffers somewhat from "Disney-fication," Westcott House has plenty of the former.
Singles, doubles & triples: $75-$135.

SHOPS

Lightner Antique Mall
75 King St.,
St. Augustine
• (904) 824-2874

The Lightner Antique Mall is a hard-to-find spot that's well worth a visit. Tucked away behind the Lightner Museum/City Hall complex, the mall is situated in a cool, cavernous, underground space that was once the swimming pool of the Alcazar Hotel (the world's largest at the time, built in 1888 by railroad baron Henry Flagler). Today, the mall has ten dealers—six of which we counted closed in the summertime off-season. Be careful haggling here, as is the custom in antiquing throughout northeast Florida. Apparently we affronted a dealer regarding one maplewood dressing table mirror in doing so.
Open Mon.-Sat. 10 a.m-5 p.m., Sun. 1 p.m.-5 p.m.

SIGHTS

***Cross and Sword* Play**
A1A South & S.R. 3,
Anastasia Island
• (904) 471-1965

Each year Anastasia's Outdoor Amphitheater hosts the *Cross and Sword*, Florida's official state play, between mid-June and mid-August. The colorful spectacle depicts in words, dance and music the life of Admiral Don Pedro Menendez de Aviles, the Spanish sailor who destroyed the French Huguenots attempting

to take possession of then Spanish-controlled "La Florida" in 1565. Menendez organized a landing party of 600 soldiers, artisans and farmers in Saint Augustine amid the sound of artillery booming, trumpets playing and arriving voyagers cheering one another on. The play not only dramatizes the hooplah with colorful costumes and scenery, but also recreates the horror of battles with the local Indians, as well as the devastating hurricane that brought the settlement to near starvation and rebellion in ensuing years. Nearly 100 actors, dancers and singers perform in the two-hour spectacle. This is a good way to learn history on a midsummer's night in Florida.
Runs annually, mid-June to mid-August. Open Mon.-Sat. 8:30 p.m. Adults $6, children $4.

The Restored Spanish Quarter
St. George St.,
St. Augustine
• (904) 825-6830

Past the old Protestant cemetery (opened during the yellow-fever epidemic in 1821), through the city gate of Saint Augustine (built in 1739 and at that time providing the only access through the defense line of the north side of the city), awaits the restored Spanish Quarter, the center of Saint Augustine. Continuing south along Saint George Street, the central route of the restored eighteenth-century section of the city, you enter into the restored Spanish Quarter. Amid the ice-cream and souvenir shops, a collection of historic houses (each compelled to develop some sort of tourist "catch") feature guides conducting demonstrations, each clad in colonial clothing typical of the period. Walking south along Saint George, a variety of Spanish period houses have been converted into artists' studios, restaurants, candy stores and bakeries; others are now interesting period museums, presenting a more enlightening reason to visit.
Open daily 9 a.m.-5 p.m.

St. Augustine Historical Tours
Old State Jail,
167 San Marco Ave.,
St. Augustine
• (904) 829-3800

Departing from the parking lot of the Visitors' Center (and from fifteen major attractions) are the trolleys of Saint Augustine Historical Tours. This is one of many guided tours of the city, ranging in length from one hour to eight hours, and it is definitely recommended (especially in the summer months when taking in the area's attractions on foot is nearly impossible).
First tour 8:30 a.m., last tour 4:30 p.m. Stops at 15 major attractions.

Victory Cruises
118 Avenida Menendez,
City Yacht Pier,
St. Augustine
• (904) 824-1806

What a way to see Saint Augustine: by moonlight from the bay. During the balmy summer season, you can board the double-decker *Victory II*, which offers sightseeing cruises out to adjacent Anastasia Island and along Matanzas Bay. Use your imagination—this might be how it looked to the sailors who battled over the majestic Castillo San Marcos in the harbor. As you pass by, cruise-boat guides explain how the fort, built

between 1672 and 1695, was constructed of the shell-rock coquina, mined on Anastasia Island and ferried over to Saint Augustine. Modernized in 1756, it became the principal fortification in the Spanish defense system that served to maintain the country's control of Florida for more than 200 years.
Open Mar.-Oct. Departure 8:15 p.m. Cruise 1 hour & 15 minutes. Adults $6, children $2.50.

JACKSONVILLE

RESTAURANTS	255
QUICK BITES	258
HOTELS	259
SHOPS	261
SIGHTS	263

RESTAURANTS

Ragtime Tavern and Grill/Salud!
207 Atlantic Blvd., Atlantic Beach
• (904) 214-7877
SEAFOOD

11/20

Since the day it opened in 1983, seemingly every yuppie in Atlantic Beach has made this scene. And they're still here, drawn by the uniformly excellent seafood and the comfortable retro-American setting, rich with oak paneling, dentil molding, old brick, brass rails and beveled glass. You'll feel transported to the Big Easy, a feeling that's furthered by the red beans and rice served with dinner. There's not a speck of red meat on the menu, just enough good fish dishes to win the admiration of even the most devout carnivores. Coconut shrimp, dressed in a light, crispy batter dusted with grated coconut, are paired with a piquant honey-mustard dipping sauce. Dolphin-fish boasts a buttery lemon-peppercorn sauce well endowed with garlic and dill. A variety of fish spend a few perfect minutes on the grill, ending up seared on the outside and juicy within, so fresh you can almost feel the roll of the fishing boat under your feet. If you visit on a weekend, splurge on the Key lime lobster, marinated in lime juice and folded into a steaming mound of linguine dripping with garlic butter. The homemade Key lime cheesecake is fresh, firm, moist and tart, as it should be. Adjoining Ragtime and sharing the same owners (brothers Tom and Bill Morton) is Salud!, a trendy tapas bar done up with *faux*

Victorian fences, skylights and bright-red English phone booths. The menu includes all the fried calamari one could ever want, along with fifteen or twenty other tapas dishes (oysters, artichokes, you name it). Although it's perennially jammed, the tapas bar is a good place to hang out while you wait for a table at Ragtime. And wait you will, for its popularity is undying—and deserved. Two will spend about $70 for dinner with wine.
Open daily 11:30 a.m.-10:30 p.m. All major cards.

Sterling's Flamingo Café
3551 St. Johns Ave., Jacksonville
• (904) 387-0700
AMERICAN/ CONTINENTAL

Sterling's Flamingo Café in the tony, rather stuffy Avondale shopping district has a white-tile floor, modern-art prints, a chic older crowd and an air of casual elegance. The menu blends the conservative with the American hip, ranging from basic (but well-prepared) Continental veal sautés to such spirited dishes as woodsy crimini mushrooms stuffed with herb-dusted veal and pork. We steer clear of the dull oldtimers and stick to the tasty modernities, like the fresh, moist pompano infused with Cuervo gold tequila, lime juice and Triple Sec, topped with a dollop of guacamole that sparkles with jalapeño fire. Regulars are partial to the wild-mushroom pasta, a savory mix of spinach fettuccine, wild mushrooms, sun-dried tomatoes, prosciutto, Marsala and cream, but our favorite is the chicken Tchoupitoulas, a lively Creole combination of chicken, scallions, tasso ham and potatoes, dressed up with a graceful béarnaise that gleams with Cajun spices. Just for fun, owner/chefs Richard and Liz Grenamyer might toss a spinach soufflé the size of a pocket watch on your plate. Liz also whips up breezy crème brûlées in chocolate or vanilla and a gut-busting dessert called Death by Brownie, a mercilessly rich brownie with vanilla-almond ice cream and Grand Marnier–spiked chocolate sauce. All the details shine with finesse, from the accomplished cooking to the crisp service to the excellent wine list. Dinner for two, with wine, costs about $80.
Open Mon.-Thurs. 11 a.m.-2:30 p.m. & 5:30 p.m.-10 p.m., Fri. 11 a.m.-2:30 p.m. & 5:30 p.m.-11 p.m., Sat. 5:30 p.m.-11 p.m. All major cards.

24 Miramar
4446 Hendricks Ave., Jacksonville
• (904) 448-2424
AMERICAN/ CALIFORNIAN

It had to happen sooner or later: Californian cuisine has landed in Jacksonville. You can find it in this young, hip Lakewood bistro run by chefs Timothy and Barbara Felver, who spent time cooking at L.A.'s Spago and Chinois, two of Cal-cuisine guru Wolfgang Puck's hot spots. The couple learned their lessons well. They've created a setting as stylish and attention-getting as their food, a long, narrow space with red-silk wall hangings, striking tableaux-style murals of foodstuffs, and art-deco globe lights and wall sconces. The Felvers's cuisine is that hybrid currently called contemporary American, which means a little

American, a little Asian, a little Latin American, a little Italian—it sometimes seems to mean a little of *everything*, except perhaps the benighted cuisine of England. The Latin touch is evident in the tasty sautéed Louisiana oysters with a brisk tomato salsa. China and Japan speak up with the crisp, delicate shrimp tempura with black-bean sauce and a plum vinaigrette. Then we're off to Italy via the linguine tangled with chewy shiitakes, earthy morels and a sauce studded with savory prosciutto. Next we visit Louisiana for the peppy Cajun chicken breast with mushrooms, green onions and smoky tasso ham, and finally we hop over to France to try the graceful, tender filet mignon accompanied by shiitake and morel mushrooms sautéed with port and basil. Barbara Felvers's desserts stay mostly in France (still the capital of opulent sweets), and all of them cause diners to drift off into blissful reveries: the chocolate tower, a delicate cylinder of chocolate filled with chocolate mousse and topped with fresh raspberries; the lightest, creamiest crème brûlée we've had in ages; and a frothy layering of white-chocolate mousse and almond cake, topped with slivers of fresh strawberries and standing in a pool of raspberry sauce, a dish for which we'd forsake our mothers. The service is as well executed as the cooking, and the wine list reflects the Felvers's California training, offering several dozen Chardonnays, Cabernets, Merlots and Pinot Noirs. Dinner for two, with wine, runs about $80. *Open Mon.-Thurs. 5:30 p.m.-10 p.m., Fri.-Sat. 5:30 p.m.-11 p.m. Cards: AE, MC, V.*

The Wine Cellar
1314 Prudential Dr., Jacksonville
• (904) 398-8989
CONTINENTAL

12/20

If the culinary adventures at Sterling's Flamingo Café and 24 Miramar make you nervous, head for The Wine Cellar, a solidly traditional spot that makes no attempt to lighten or modernize the classics. But that doesn't mean the place is depressingly dated—in fact, it's one of Jacksonville's finest restaurants, where candles softly illuminate ceramic-tile floors, pink linens and hanging baskets of greenery. Though the food is nothing new, it's prepared with care and intelligence. Someday we may start our meal with the American sturgeon or Iranian sevruga caviar, but we usually choose the escargots, which is one of the few unusual dishes here, a savory, chowderlike broth with plenty of garlic and chives. The house salad is a fresh mix of pungent romaine and a caviar dressing. Entrées range from chicken Nancy (chicken medallions topped with crabmeat, asparagus and béarnaise) to a veal chop with a smoky morel-mushroom sauce. The thick, tender tournedos echo the wild-mushroom theme, this time with tiny chanterelles. Even the accompaniments are thoughtful, like the al dente broccoli with blanched leeks. The best of the many desserts are the cheesecake and the bittersweet-chocolate mousse cake. The Wine Cellar is aptly named: some 10,000 bottles are sold each year from a list that includes the humble and the great, including Louis Roederer Cristal Champagne and Château Mouton-Rothschild 1966. *Open Tues.-Fri. 11 a.m.-2 p.m. & 6 p.m.-10 p.m., Sat. 6 p.m.-10 p.m. All major cards.*

QUICK BITES

Homestead Restaurant
1712 Beach Blvd., Jacksonville Beach
• (904) 249-5240

One look tells why Homestead has been a solid family favorite for more than 40 years: dark pine-log walls chinked with cement, small kerosene-style lamps and a huge limestone fireplace in the middle of the front room. We love the homey cooking, starting with the huge, steaming-hot buttermilk biscuits that begin each meal. Fried chicken, the house specialty, is first-rate: a half bird coated in a light batter with a touch of garlic, cooked to a crispy turn in a small iron skillet and served piping hot. Other winners include fried shrimp and chicken with dumplings. Be warned about the appetizer called lizzards, a mix of chicken livers and gizzards: the livers are tasty and tender, but despite a crackling good batter, the gizzards are tougher than truck tires. Side dishes tend to be starchy: canned-tasting creamed peas, white rice, rich, thick flour gravy. Though tasty, the fruit pies aren't as good as the beloved pies of *Twin Peaks* myth. Dinner for two costs about $30.
Open Mon.-Sat. 5 p.m.-10:30 p.m., Sun. noon-10:30 p.m. All major cards.

Sun Dog Diner
207 Atlantic Blvd., Neptune Beach
• (904) 241-8221

This neodiner is a fun time-warp trip, a heady mix of curved mahogany paneling and tin ceilings that puts one in mind of an Airstream trailer. Art deco–style chrome coat trees and counter seats add to the nostalgia, as does the reproduction 1942 Wurlitzer jukebox sporting fat pastel glass tubes, tiny bubbles and tunes by such artists as the Chordettes and Buddy Holly. The decor gets your appetite piqued for a greasy burger and a chocolate shake, but one look at the menu will fling you into the '90s: grilled mahimahi glazed with jalapeño jam, soft-shell crab topped with a chile béarnaise, marvelous hearty huevos rancheros with sausage, black beans, a flour tortilla and cheese, a fresh, zesty chicken salad with sliced grapes, almonds and a dill mayonnaise, and aromatic meat loaf with a full-bodied marinara sauce. Further proof that this diner is no truck stop is the wine collection, including some twenty selections by the glass and a multitude of Champagnes. Dinner for two, with wine, costs about $40.
Open Mon.-Fri. 11 a.m.-10:30 p.m., Sat.-Sun. 8 a.m.-11 p.m. Cards: AE, MC, V.

Whitey's Fish Camp
2032 County Rd. 220,
Orange Park
• (904) 269-4198

Whitey's Fish Camp ("Famous for Our Fresh Caught Catfish") is the place to be on weekends, particularly out on the big deck, where country musicians entertain overflow crowds. Inside, it's as big as a jai alai fronton, filled with picnic tables and benches finished in polyurethane. Whitey's food is solid Southern fried, from side orders of 'gator tail to huge swamp platters loaded with shrimp, oysters, scallops, frogs' legs, deviled crab, catfish, alligator and turtle. The oysters are best in cold weather; the fried shrimp are crispy outside and tender inside all year long. Dinners are served with hush puppies, a choice of fries or baked potato and either salad or a lip-smacking sweet-and-sour cole-slaw dressed with vinegar, sugar, salt and pepper, but no mayonnaise. Two will spend about $30 for dinner with sodas.
Open Sun.-Thurs. 11 a.m.-10 p.m., Fri.-Sat. 11 a.m.-11 p.m. Cards: MC, V.

HOTELS

Moderate (From $100)

Amelia Island Plantation
Hwy. A1A South,
Amelia Island 32034
• (904) 261-6161
Fax (904) 277-5159

Located on its own little barrier island just south of Fernandina Beach, Amelia Island Plantation is a wonderful, full-service resort set upon a four-mile stretch of magnificent beachfront. It's one of those places whose allure lies in how difficult it is to reach. (The plantation is located some 29 miles north of downtown Jacksonville; from A1A south, you must board the ferry at Mayport Naval Station, which chugs you across the Saint Johns River. The view on the west side is much more promising immediately upon arrival.) Amelia Island, named after the daughter of King George III in the late eighteenth century, was discovered by the French in 1562; it's the only land mass in the United States to have been under eight separate flags of domination.

The plantation is set back off Highway A1A in a world of its own. Rooms are divided among thirteen complexes, and each has a terrace and comes with a refrigerator. The ocean view is probably your best bet. For a splurge, try one of the villas that are owned individually. There are on-property lagoons stocked with redfish and bass, five restaurants, a fitness center, a Sunken Forest trail thorough primary and secondary dune lines, sites of an Indian burial mound and an old Spanish mission. There's also a shopping village, children's playground, 45 holes of golf, 25 tennis courts and a complimentary on-site tram service that whisks guests from one point to another.
Singles & doubles: $128-$377. Villa rates upon request.

FIRST COAST Jacksonville – Hotels

Omni Jacksonville Hotel
245 Water St.,
Jacksonville 32202
• (904) 355-6664
Fax (904) 354-2970

Omni Jacksonville offers one of the most pleasant downtown hotel experiences in Florida. (That may well be, partially at least, because Jacksonville is one of the few downtowns that can still be walked around safely at just about any hour.) Situated in the heart of the revitalized downtown area, the Omni lies just a stone's throw from anywhere you'd want to be: Jacksonville Landing, with its enclave of boutiques, restaurants and nightspots on the river; the 1.2-mile-long Riverwalk, where the mimes and jugglers do the entertaining for the price of what's thrown in their hats; the Convention Center; or the Automated Skyway Express, which offers the best overview of the city there is. The hotel has 354 guest rooms, each nicely appointed with oversize bathrooms. And for those who just can't live without some of that signature Omni Club service, there are also two concierge floors. Pool, sundeck and fitness room complete the package.
Singles & doubles: $135-$160.

Practical (Under $100)

The Bailey House
27 S. 7th St.,
Fernandina Beach 32034
• (904) 261-5390
No fax

Amelia Island's interesting Centre Street, the hub of Fernandina Beach's Victorian "silk-stocking district," is laced by a century-old seaport, an embellished sprinkling of local lore and, most obviously, with ornamented Victorian architecture. Bailey House, built in 1895 by Effingham W. Bailey with plenty of Florida pine, contains stained-glass windows and gracious moldings. Note the gracious appointments: a marble table in the lobby with a painted gas globe overhead, plenty of brass and fringed Oriental rugs. Be sure to ask for an air-conditioned room in the summertime (only four have it). Don't worry yourself about shared phones and bathtubs, or the Historical Society tours marching by regularly to ogle the architecture: The Bailey House is worth a long, romantic submersion into days of yore.
Singles & doubles: $55-$85.

Bed & Breakfasts

1735 House
584 S. Fletcher Ave.,
Fernandina Beach 32034
• (904) 261-5878
No fax

Fernandina Beach, the nation's second-oldest city, prospered because of its lively shrimping industry—which still exists here. Today, a 50-block historic district presents one of the best redevelopment accomplishments in the state, with plenty of well-stocked antique shops, ice-cream parlors, bookstores and boutiques. 1735 house, named for the year Amelia Island was discovered by General James Oglethorpe on behalf of King George II of Britain, is run by a Cornell Hotel School–educated couple who escaped from the chain hotel business to open their

own inn. David and Susan Caples bought the long-abandoned house (which was built by a local doctor in the 1920s), and opened one of the finest bed-and-breakfasts in northeast Florida. The inn has five air-conditioned suites, each with its own bath; three suites have kitchens.
Singles: $50-$65; doubles: $60-$65.

SHOPS

Antiques

Beaches Antique Gallery
1210 Beach Blvd.,
Jacksonville Beach
• (904) 246-3149

You might have noticed that the seedier the neighborhood, the better the antiques—in terms of a value/price ratio, at the very least. Jacksonville Beach's antiques and curio shops are no exception, with the Beaches Antique Gallery at the heart of a rather nasty little neighborhood (sandwiched between the glorious beachfront resorts of Ponte Vedra and the glorious beachfront homes of Neptune and Atlantic Beach). A sort of antiques warehouse, the Beaches Antique Gallery actually houses 120 separate stores, allowing you to browse from Grampa's poker table on up to Tiffany vases, all under one air-conditioned roof.
Open Mon.-Sat. 10 a.m.-6 p.m., Sun 1 p.m.-6 p.m.

Eight Flags Antique Market
604 Centre St.,
Fernandina Beach
• (904) 277-8550

With more than 50 separate dealers sharing distinctly different booth spaces in this enormous shop, Eight Flags seems more like a museum celebrating Amelia Island's heritage than it does an antique shop. There's also a collection of books on Victorian antiques, dolls and collectibles.
Open Mon.-Sat. 10 a.m.-9 p.m., Sun. 1 p.m.-5:30 p.m.

Faith Wick's World of Little People
216 Centre St.,
Fernandina Beach
• (904) 261-3127

Though this shop is a quite tidy little corner space (in proportion to the "Little People" it vends, no doubt), it is one of the most interesting on Centre Street. Offering an abundance of original, antique and collector dolls, Faith Wick's isn't the spot to bring the kiddies, who might be tempted to go grab the goods. Doll collectors take their business seriously, and Faith Wick's also sells several catalog-type books detailing various doll series.
Open Mon.-Sat. 10 a.m.-9 p.m., Sun. 1 p.m.-5:30 p.m.

J. Ringhaver
3563-A St. Johns Ave.,
Jacksonville
• (904) 387-6321

We suspect that this is where Jacksonville's interior designers clamor upon receiving a residental assignment in one of the city's posh suburbs. Featuring an abundance of antiques, acces-

Lamp Post Antique Mall
3960 Oak St.,
Jacksonville
• (904) 384-9810

sories, gifts and paintings, the store represents one of the city's most exclusive antique shops.
Open Mon.-Sat. 10 a.m.- 5 p.m. & by appointment.

Situated in the heart of Jacksonville's Riverside historic district, the Lamp Post mall and offshooting side streets let you take a walk through various architectural periods (several homes in the area are listed in the National Register of Historic Places), as well as some fifteen antique shops in the immediate area. The mall itself has 26 individual showrooms chock-a-block with country furnishings, linens, quilts, art glass, porcelains, jewelry, silver and paintings.
Open Mon.-Fri. 10 a.m.-5:30 p.m., Sat. 10 a.m.-5 p.m.

Books

Book Loft
214 Centre St.,
Fernandina
• (904) 261-8991

The two-story Book Loft is kind enough to offer cookies and coffee to browsers among its 10,000 volumes. History buffs will enjoy the large collection of books on Florida's past, with a focus on Amelia Island itself and the First Coast.
Open Mon-Sat. 10 a.m.-9 p.m., Sun. 1 p.m.-5:30 p.m.

Food

Jacksonville Farmer's Market
West Beaver St. at Hwy. 90,
Jacksonville
• (904) 353-9736

Snap beans, Georgia peaches, boiled peanuts, watermelons and bushels of field-picked produce have been rolled in on farmers' carts to the Farmer's Market since the summer of 1938, when the grounds officially opened. The market's cleanliness is a pleasant surprise; seafood and butcher outlets are also located on the grounds.
Open daily 8 a.m.-5 p.m.

Gifts

The Plantation Shop
Palmetto Walk,
4800 First Coast Hwy.,
Amelia Island
• (904) 261-2030

This fragrant little outpost (from olfactory experimentation with its line of Crabtree & Evelyn products, no doubt) also vends a variety of gift items: native vine baskets, English antique collectibles and gourmet foods. Situated in the Palmetto Walk shopping center and nestled behind giant oaks, The Plantation Shop is well worth a visit.
Open Mon.-Sat. 10 a.m.- 6 p.m.

Rentals

Jerry's Kite Shop/Rent-a-Bike
112 N. 6th Ave., Jacksonville Beach
• (904) 246-9990

Though Jacksvonville Beach is none too glamorous, the custom here is to rent a bike and cycle from bar to bar along the wooden beachfront boardwalk. Jerry's, a permanent fixture on Jax Beach, with its bike rental outfit and shop, comes replete with colorful kites, windsocks and flying toys from around the world. *Open daily 9 a.m.-9 p.m.*

SIGHTS

Amusements

Jacksonville Zoological Park
8605 Zoo Rd., Jacksonville
• (904) 757-4463

Opened in 1914, when Jacksonville began to celebrate its heyday as an important deepwater port and industrial hub in the southeast, the Jacksonville Zoo has since spread out to cover 61 wooded acres with over 700 specimens of exotic species. A brand-new "Chimpanorama" allows chimps to move freely in their natural environment and put on an ongoing comedy act. Another notable feature is plenty of "hands-on" educational facilities for kids.
Open daily 9 a.m.-5 p.m. Adults $3, children 4-12 $1.50.

Excursions

Mayport Ferry Boat Ride
A1A at Mayport, Mayport
• (904) 246-2922

Two ferries, the *The Buccaneer* and *The Blackbeard*, take turns whisking cars across the Saint Johns River from Mayport to Amelia Island. The scenery is much more attractive on the Amelia Island side, with lots of expansive beaches and campgrounds, but the Mayport Naval Station side, where locals vend soft drinks and boiled peanuts as cars line up, gets top ratings for local charm.
Open daily 6 a.m.-10:30 p.m. Admission $1.50 per car.

Landmarks

Jacksonville Landing
2 Independent Dr. at the St. Johns River, Jacksonville
• (904) 353-1188

No reclaimed U.S. waterfront would be complete without a development project, and Jacksonville's downtown redevelopment program is no exception. A colorful complex of more than 100 shops and eating places and restaurants, Jax Landing is situated in the heart of downtown. We've found parking to be a near impossibility (plenty of signs pointing to very few discernible parking-lot entrances), so taxi or public transportation (via the city's new Automated Skyway rail system) might be a better bet for getting there.
Open daily 10 a.m.-9 p.m.

FIRST COAST   Jacksonville – Sights

The Riverwalk
Southern Bank of the St. Johns River, between Acosta Bridge & Main St. Bridge, Jacksonville
• (904) 396-4900

When the sun goes down, the milelong Riverwalk wakes up. Jacksonville's answer to Key West's Mallory Square, the Riverwalk attracts a cast of thousands of jugglers, musicians, sketch artists and mimes, who come to entertain those who've flocked down to the river for an evening stroll. There are plenty of restaurants in the vicinity; boats sailing by make the scenery especially colorful. The surprising thing about the Riverwalk is that you'll even see children playing there late at night (we can't think of anywhere else in Florida where the situation is similar); Jacksonville, obviously, is still considered by its residents to be just as safe as Mayberry, R.F.D.
Wed.-Sun. beginning at about 7 p.m.

Tours

Anheuser-Busch Brewery Tour
111 Busch Dr., Jacksonville
• (904) 751-8116

Workers for the "World's Largest Brewer," whose Jax Brewery produces more than 7 million gallons of beer annually, gleefully guide visitors through each step of the process. You'll walk through cool tanks, to the automatic bottling and canning facilities. At tour's end, the most popular feature is offered: free brew samples for those of drinking age.
May.-Oct.: open Mon.-Sat. 10 a.m.-5 p.m. Nov.-Apr.: open Mon.-Sat. 9 a.m.-4 p.m. Tours are complimentary.

Europa Cruise Line
4738 Ocean St., Mayport
• (904) 249-8404

If a visit to the Mayport Naval Station, where many of the U.S. navy's fleet of aircraft carriers make home port, gives you a yen for a cruise ship sail of your own, *Europa* is the way for you to spend an evening in Jacksonville. Departing from Mayport (adjacent to the Saint Johns ferry) the multilevel cruise ship offers a full casino, live bands, dancing and cocktails at sea.
Departing nightly at 6 p.m. for 5- or 6-hour cruises. Fare $39.95.

Old Town Carriage Co.
12 N. Front St., Fernandina Beach
• (904) 635-3466

Fernandina Beach's tourism infrastructure is quite a lot more tasteful than that of neighboring St. Augustine: no manufactured neon attractions, no yogurt shops, no stale rock candy for sale. Horse and buggy proves to be the most wonderful way to see the outpost of Victorian charm. Old Town Carriage will personalize your tour, depending on your interests. Honeymooners, for example, are guided throught exceptionally romantic sidestreets and hidden beachfront stretches.
Open Wed.-Sun. 1 p.m.-6 p.m. by reservation. Adults $5, children $3. Minimum $15.

PANHANDLE

INTRODUCTION	266
PENSACOLA	266
PANAMA CITY	271
TALLAHASSEE	272
GAINESVILLE	274

INTRODUCTION

Rustic, natural beauty sprawls across Florida's northwest with an abandon that's unmatched by any other region but the wild Everglades. Great pine forests are spread thickly over the land; verdant hills are crisscrossed by streams; little towns surrounded by farms and churches have never seen the likes of a strip mall or a waterpark. A beautifully preserved slice of Old Southern history, the Panhandle only has a couple of cities where you'll find modern development and grand-scale tourism. **Pensacola**, at Florida's far west tip, boasts a few top-notch seaside resorts, where visitors can dine and dance, golf, waterski and frolic on the silken, snow-white dunes gracing the Gulf shores; while a mile in from shore, the town's sixteenth-century heritage is kept alive in its oak-lined streets, antebellum mansions and historical musems. Along the coast to the east, glittering **Panama City** is the Panhandle's Coney Island. It shares Pensacola's rolling dunes and green waters, but there's not much else to commend this spot beyond the beachfront amusement strip, which appalled southern conservatives have dubbed the "Redneck's Riviera." In the center of the Panhandle lies the old, elegant, lazy-paced capital city of **Tallahassee**. Though it steadfastly remains the state's governmental center, the town has gladly left the duties of urban growth and internationalization to the de facto capital, Miami. In the east, the pretty town of **Gainesville** is centered around the University of Florida.

PENSACOLA

RESTAURANTS

Jamie's
424 E. Zaragoza St., Pensacola
• (904) 434-2911
CONTINENTAL

12/20

When foodwise Pensacolans want to initiate a romance—or cap it off with a marriage proposal—they head for this intimate restaurant, a dress-to-impress, special-occasion place aglow with candlelight. Tucked away in a restored Victorian house in the Seville district, Jamie's has hardwood floors, white linens, nineteenth-century American antiques and flickering fireplaces in all the rooms. Fortunately, there's more than just romancing going on here—lots of folks return regularly just to enjoy the very good food. Owner/chef Gary Ferafin adds a welcome touch of creative modernity to otherwise classic dishes, most of which

are paired with French reductions. Sweetbreads are a Ferafin favorite, and they're always worth trying; we sampled a particularly tasty version with a caramelized port demi-glace. Other toothsome entrées include grilled lamb chops with a mint–Pommery mustard sauce; broiled fresh snapper topped with Brie and a subtle dill beurre blanc; and a marvelous thick veal chop on a bed of Cajun mashed potatoes, topped with a morel-brandy-cream sauce. The delicious desserts are as unabashedly romantic as the setting, from the puréed chestnuts with a white-and-dark-chocolate mousse on a coffee-custard base to the white-chocolate Grand Marnier mousse with puréed raspberries and pistachios. Ferafin's dedication to fine dining is continued in the extensive wine list, boasting some 160 Californian and French selections. Dinner for two, with wine, runs $80.
Open Mon. 6 p.m.-10 p.m., Tues.-Sat. 11:30 a.m.-2:30 p.m. & 6 p.m.-10 p.m. All major cards.

HOTELS

Pensacola Hilton
200 E. Gregory St., Pensacola 32501
• (904) 433-3336, (800) 445-8667
Fax (904) 432-7572

No mere whistle stop in its heyday, this dazzling depot was a star in the L & N Railroad diadem until it was abandoned in 1971. Once derelict, the place is now a polished 212-room hotel, buzzing with business travelers, rail buffs and tourists who prefer the city to the beach. The old main concourse was converted into a series of shops and a lobby bar called Tickets. Accommodations include suites with wet bar, whirlpool and refrigerator. Those who abstain from tobacco will be glad to know that there are two nonsmoking floors. The pool is rooftop. Limousine pick-up at the airport or bus station is free, or if you park your car in the lot between 4 p.m. and 7 p.m., you'll be driven to the lobby in a horse-drawn carriage.
Singles & doubles: $88; weekend packages available.

Sandestin Beach Resort
5500 Hwy. 98 East, Destin 32541
• (904) 267-8000, (800) 277-0800
Fax (904) 267-8197

With its large choice of accommodations at the inn, plus condos and villas, this sprawling, 2,600-acre seaside resort seems more like a complete community. Choose your lodging according to your lifestyle: tennis players to the courts, golfers to the courses and sunlovers to the beach. If you have children, you can enroll them in day camp. How about hunting for doubloons on miles of white-sugar beach? There's not a reason in the world to spend time in your room, although rooms are more than servicable, with nice amenties packages. Other pluses: a shopping mart with thirty stores; the fitness center's new Nautilus machines, rental

watersports equipment. Fishing enthusiasts will find their passion best satisfied between March and November. The complex has ten swimming pools and five restaurants from which to choose.
Doubles: $60 (winter), $90 (summer); suites: $70 (winter), $135 (summer); villas: $90-$425.

Tops'l Beach & Racquet Club
5550 Hwy. 98 East,
Destin 32541
• (904) 267-9222,
(800) 476-9222
Fax (904) 267-2955

Tennis and acres of beach will keep your family hopping within this resort community—and don't forget that Sandestin provides golf privileges at a course nearby. Sporting families can enjoy the twelve tennis courts, three racquetball courts, lighted jogging and exercise paths, Nautilus and aerobics center, whirlpool, indoor/outdoor pool, sailing and other beach activities, sauna, steam room . . . you get the picture. Villas provide covered parking, cable television, telephones, washer and dryer, and a luxury kitchen with microwave, trash compactor, icemaker and dishwasher. Free trams tie it all together.
Tennis villa: $110; Beach Manor: $425.

NIGHTLIFE

Bars

McGuire's Irish Pub
600 E. Gregory St.,
Pensacola
• (904) 433-6789

Total mayhem, from the wacky decor to specials that include Poets Night, Blarney Hour (happy hour) and Wetback Night (the name is a Mexican waiter's concoction) with its $1 margaritas. Like the voice on the recording says, if you don't like crowds, don't come to McGuire's, whose slogan is Feasting, Imbibery and Debauchery. The pub brews its own ale—lite, porter and stout—and dyes it green on St. Pattie's Day. Order a deadly Irish Wake, then join in the lively Irish folk singing with a mix of college kids, sailors and fun-loving tourists of all ages. Great food, and the frozen Irish Coffee makes a lusty nightcap.
Open Mon.-Sat. 11 a.m.-midnight, Sun. 4 p.m.- 1 a.m. All major cards.

Seville Quarter
130 E. Government St.,
Pensacola
• (904) 434-6211

A clone of Orlando's ringing Church Street Station, this good-time complex cranks out happy-hour specials from 4 p.m. to 7 p.m. and hums until the wee hours. Hang out in one of the saloons, eat dinner or pub crawl to sample spots that feature jazz, mellow listening, country, dancing, bluegrass, sing-along or whatever else is on the music menu.
Open daily 11 a.m.-1 a.m. Cover $3. Cards: AE, DC, V.

Hotel Lounge

Pensacola Hilton
200 E. Gregory St., Pensacola
• (904) 433-3336

Drift from L & N Lobby Bar to the piano bar to Tickets, or target just one of the Hilton's nightspots for a long, leisurely evening. Tyler's piano bar is the place for quiet business talks or a romantic cocktail date. Tickets is the city's upscale nightclub, with live music, dancing, a bar and cozy banquettes.
Open nightly 4 p.m.-2 a.m.; Tyler's piano bar daily 5 p.m.-2 a.m. No cover. All major cards.

Music Club

Nightown
140 Palmetto St., Destin
• (904) 837-7625

In this huge, New Orleans–decor nightclub, the rafters ring with live music from two groups that wail Top 40 tunes and rock classics, with disco between sets. Nightown, which caters to the 25- to 35-year-old crowd, has one of the largest dance floors in the state. But that doesn't keep people from going out and dancing on the patio. The place is always switched on, with wild-and-crazy drink specials and nightly events. Call (904) 837-6448 for a recorded message about nightly specials.
Open nightly 8 p.m.-4 a.m. No cover. Cards: AE, MC, V.

SHOPS

Antique Mall
380 N. 9th Ave. between Gregory & Wright Sts., Pensacola
• (904) 438-3961

Browse among two-dozen stalls where vendors sell antiques of all types and periods. It's a festival of Oriental rugs, vintage clothes, old toys, keepsake quilts, European glass, china and crystal, baseball cards and pottery.
Open Mon.-Sat. 10 a.m.-5 p.m., Sun. noon-5 p.m.

Bayou Country Store
823 E. Jackson St. at 9th Ave., Pensacola
• (904) 432-5697

All ruffles, lace and crafts with a look of down-home simplicity, this family-run shop sells hand-hooked rugs, coordinated fabrics and wallpaper, bisque dolls, artificial flowers, stained-glass creations, furniture and accessories, all with a country accent.
Open Mon.-Sat. 10 a.m.-5 p.m.

Quayside Market
712 S. Palafox St., Pensacola
• (904) 433-9930

This bazaar of shops and stalls is burgeoning with antique linens, rare books, gourmet coffees, country crafts, custom jewelry, old records and trendy collectibles. Especially good selection of Depression-era glass.
Open Wed.-Sun. 10 a.m.-5 p.m.

SIGHTS

Art Galleries

The **Quayside Art Gallery** (15-17 E. Zaragoza St., Pensacola; 904-438-2363; open Mon.-Sat. 10 a.m.-5 p.m., Sun. 1 p.m.-5 p.m.), staffed by volunteers, is the largest art gallery co-op in the Southeastern United States. It features the works of two hundred artists, most of them inspired by the lucid colors, sands, shores and emerald seas of the area. Paintings prevail, but many media are represented. An interesting slice of local Floridian art can be found at the **Village Art Gallery** (110 Melvin St., Destin; 904-837-2228; open Tues.-Sat. 11 a.m.-4 p.m.), a tiny jewel of a gallery that has been in Destin for many moons, displaying the works of the area's best artists and artisans. Collectors dote on glass dinnerware that has been fired with fern fronds between the layers of glass, leaving a perfect imprint. There's always a good choice of oil and watercolors that capture the bright, liquid beauty of the region.

Historic Attractions

Pensacola came near to claiming the title of America's oldest city. It actually was colonized six years before Saint Augustine, but was abandoned in 1561 after a hurricane sank the Spanish colony's supply ships. Resettlement was a long time in coming, some 137 years. Still, it's a living museum of French and Spanish history, Dixiana and lavish Victoriana, remnants of the days when lumber barons grew rich on lush timber harvests. Historic **Pensacola Village** covers a six-block area. Take I-110 south from I-10, then turn left on S. Tarragona Street and look for the parking lot on the corner of Church Street One admission fee of $5 for adults, $4 for senior citizens and $2 for children ages 4 to 16 pays for entry to all sites, including the imposing **Wentworth Museum** (the structure was once City Hall), the French colonial creole **Lavalle House**, and the mid-Victorian **Dorr House.** The complex is open Monday through Saturday from 10 a.m. to 4:30 p.m. Between Easter and Labor Day, it's also open Sunday from 1 p.m. to 4:30 p.m. For information, call (904) 444-8905.

Northwest Florida's museum blockbuster is the **National Museum of Naval Aviation**, one of the largest air and space museums in the world. Signs throughout the area point to the Naval Air Station. Once there, follow the signs to the museum. For information, call (904) 452-3604. Admission is free; it's open daily except Thanksgiving, Christmas and New Year's Day, 9 a.m. to 5 p.m. Among the dozens of current and historic aircraft on display are an NC-4 Flying Boat (the first airplane to cross the Atlantic), the Skylab Command Module and the first F-14 Tomcat. If you're on the base during a weekend, take a free tour of the USS *Lexington*, a World War II–period ship that is during active duty as a trainer. Some scenes for the film, *Winds of War*, were shot on board. Call (904) 432-4872 for information.

Although **Fort Pickens** is one of more than a dozen brick forts built on America's coasts after the War of 1812, it has a special appeal, both because of its roistering history and because of its stunning setting on the Gulf Islands National Seashore. Along the seashore itself are picnic and swimming areas, campsites, fishing and windswept miles of dunes and sea oats. Yes, Martha, the place reeks of seclusion, if that's what you're looking for. In the ranger-led tour of Fort Pickens, you'll hear about the time the powder magazine exploded, the Civil War battle that went on all night and filled the inlet with cannonballs, and the years when the great Native American hero Geronimo was kept prisoner there. Once you reach Pensacola Beach, drive west on Fort Pickens Road, which ends at the fort. The Seashore is open every day; admission is $3 per car. Golden Age and Golden Access passports apply. For information about Fort Pickens hours and tours, call (904) 934-2600.

CRACKERS & COWS

Florida "Crackers," delightfully depicted in Marjorie Kinnan Rawlings's Pulitzer Prize–winning *The Yearling*, penned in the 1930s at Florida's Cross Creek, still populate the state in significant numbers. Much of Cracker folklore has been lost, but fishing, hunting, planting and doctoring superstitions remain, particularly in the northern portion of the state. The Crackers were named for the sound their whips made as they tended the cattle brought to Florida by the Spaniards in the sixteenth century. Today, Florida is the third largest cattle-producing state in the nation, with more than 2,000 working ranches.

PANAMA CITY

Marriott Bay Point Resort
100 Dellwood Beach Rd.,
Panama City Beach
32407
• (904) 234-3307
Fax (904) 233-1308

Soak up the yachty ambience of this resort on the shores of Grand Lagoon, and spend your days sailing, deep-sea fishing or playing the two eighteen-hole golf courses. Then there's tennis, day or night, on twelve courts. Around the grounds, you can swim in one of the five swimming pools, an indoor pool, practice your swing at a driving range, refine your putting skills at the putting green, stoke the bike on the bike paths or just settle in for lawn games. A children's program operates spring through early fall. Airy and pastel, accommodations have vaulted ceilings, some fireplaces and a view of the water, tennis courts or golf courses. Especially nice for the price.
Double: $85; double with kitchen: $100.

TALLAHASSEE

RESTAURANTS

Andrew's 2nd Act
228 S. Adams St., Tallahassee
• (904) 222-2759
CONTINENTAL

12/20

This downtown spot is a favorite with politicians and lobbyists who stroll over from the nearby Capitol, but we like it for more than just its propinquity. Its upscale Mediterranean atmosphere—thick stucco walls, elegant Spanish tiles and a warren of rooms, from the intimate to the spacious (including some with wide, heavy tables popular for board-meeting lunches)—has a cozy subterranean feel, and the waiters move with well-trained grace. The food is as Continental as Continental gets, unsullied by such trendy modernisms as jalapeño jelly or grilled polenta. But that's not to say it's overly dull or heavy. You can start your meal with such complicated but tasty dishes as smoked salmon, asparagus and peppercorns resting on a bed of linguine, or perhaps puff pastry filled with escargots, tomato, basil, spinach and a seafood-stock sauce. Then move on to the extra-tender and juicy rack of lamb Dijon, the broiled African lobster tails, the fine filet mignon or the thick veal chop with mushrooms and tomatoes in a classically syrupy glacé de viande, each accompanied with seasonal vegetables (zucchini, squash and onions in summer, broccoli polonaise in winter). Big-spending wine lovers will find such goodies as Château Margaux 1967 on the lengthy wine list; we've never been in a convivial enough mood to start with a bottle of Cristal, but it's nice to know it's there. The fussy desserts will take you back to the 1950s: bananas Foster, strawberries Romanoff, seasonal fruit crêpes. Dinner with wine costs about $80 for two.
Open Mon.-Thurs. 11:30 a.m.-1:30 p.m. & 6 p.m.-10 p.m., Fri. 11:30 a.m.-1:30 p.m. & 6 p.m.-11 p.m., Sat. 6 p.m.-11 p.m. All major cards.

Anthony's
1950 Thomasville Rd., Tallahassee
• (904) 224-1447
ITALIAN

10/20

Anthony's tries hard to be stuffy but doesn't quite pull it off, though it does give its loyal customers the glad hand. It's become quite the place to see and be seen, with a reservations list (and a wait) that can be lengthy every night of the week. In a handsome downstairs room dressed up with striped wallpaper and the occasional antique sideboard, diners chat and people-watch over decent though unremarkable steaks, pastas, seafood and several northern Italian standards, like chicken piccata, moderately seasoned with lemon, white wine, garlic and parsley.

Other specialties include pesce venetia, fettuccine topped with crabmeat, scallops and fish in a white wine–mushroom sauce, and chicken San Marino, a breast topped with prosciutto, Provolone and a robust cream sauce. The house salad is a respectable mix of fresh greens with a simple vinaigrette, and dessert runs to such basics as cannoli and espresso pies. The wine cellar is stocked with some three dozen moderately priced choices from Italy, France and America. Locals love Anthony's, but that seems to be more for the scene than the cooking; if you have to wait more than 30 minutes, it's probably not worth it. Dinner for two, with wine, costs about $60.
Open Mon.-Thurs. 5 p.m.-10 p.m., Fri.-Sat. 5:30 p.m.-10:30 p.m., Sun. 5:30 p.m.-9 p.m. Cards: AE, MC, V.

Spring Creek
Rte. 2, Crawfordville
• (904) 926-3751
SEAFOOD

11/20

The location alone makes us misty-eyed—Spring Creek sits on the Gulf Coast south of Tallahassee, in an old fishing community with one foot firmly planted in 1940 (the Saint Marks Wildlife Refuge outside the front door holds back progress). This homey spot keeps that nostalgic feeling going, with its knotty-pine paneling, limestone fireplace and terrific home cooking. Owner Leo Lovell's fishing boats bring in flawlessly fresh seafood, notably scamp, a succulent species of grouper whose moist, white meat is served in steaks three or four fingers thick. The kitchen knows how to make the most of scampi, which means they don't muck it up too much—it's simply dusted with paprika, broiled and dressed with a squeeze of fresh lemon and a golden pool of butter. The fried shrimp are works of art: about twenty fat, tender shrimp encased in a light, crispy batter. Meals start with the salad bowl, a portable salad bar of fresh scallions, tomatoes, cucumbers and lettuce. All the entrées are served with world-class hush puppies: crisp and golden-brown outside and blooming with a tease of onion. The chocolate–peanut butter pie is as sweet and smooth as any self-respecting Southern grandmother ever made. No alcohol is served, which keeps the tab low: for two, dinner costs about $30.
Open Wed.-Fri. 5 p.m.-10 p.m., Sat. noon-10 p.m., Sun. noon-9 p.m. Cards: MC, V.

The Wharf
4141 Apalachee Pkwy.,
Tallahassee
• (904) 656-2395
SEAFOOD

10/20

At the top of almost every local's list of family seafood places is The Wharf, found eight miles south of the capitol on the Apalachee Parkway. When Early and Eva Dugger opened the place five years ago, they decided to make it about as big as a blimp hangar, a soaring, uncomplicated space with different levels and lots of unfinished cedar. It was a wise decision—just about every night the week, it fills up to its 385-person capacity. On chilly winter nights, we stoke the fires with the hearty

seafood gumbo, which bucks tradition by skipping the okra. (Eva said she just started making it that way and liked it; we like it, too.) As is always the case in such a down-home place, the best entrées are the simplest, particularly the broiled or fried seafood platters, such as the fried shrimp-oyster combination, a substantial heap of fifteen juicy oysters and ten large, sweet shrimp. Also worth trying is the grouper stuffed with devil crab and cooked on a cast-iron grill. All dinners are served with salad or cole slaw and french fries, baked potato and cheese grits or potato salad. Save a little room to try the outstanding hush puppies, dark and crispy outside and tender inside. All the desserts are made here, from the classic chocolate–peanut butter pie to the standout tart-and-sweet Key lime pie, made with real Key limes, not bottled juice. The straightforward hospitality is as irresistible as the solid Southern home cooking. Alcohol is not served. Dinner for two runs about $30.
Open Sun.-Thurs. 11 a.m.-9 p.m., Fri.-Sat. 11 a.m.-10 p.m. Cards: AE, MC, V.

GAINESVILLE

RESTAURANTS

Emiliano's
7 S.E. 1st Ave.,
Gainesville
• (904) 375-7381
AMERICAN/SPANISH

10/20

This sidewalk café/bakery in downtown Gainesville is as fetching as a cheerleader's grin, positively bursting with cheerful, wholesome, collegiate charm. The casual interior—terra-cotta tile floors, brick walls, naturally finished redwood and cedar—is an ideal place to enjoy a fun dinner or just sit and schmooze for hours over a bottle of wine or a cup of coffee. Large refrigerated glass cases hold trays of freshly baked tortes, cakes and pies; woven baskets on the counter are piled with buns and croissants. A small tapas bar is loaded with good things: crocks of spicy scallop ceviche, an earthy mix of marinated Spanish olives and mushrooms, artichoke hearts stuffed with ricotta and spinach (served hot). If your appetite demands more than just a snack, try the arroz con pollo, the roasted chicken juicy and tender, the yellow rice dotted with onions, slices of garlic, cilantro and basil, or the paella chock-full of shrimp, clams and chicken (but sadly devoid of sausage). Romantics should sample the boneless chicken breast flavored with passion fruit, a dash of rum and a splash of maple sugar, a dish as seductive as a moonlit rhumba. Co-owner Wanda DePaz tells everyone unhesitatingly that she

serves the best cheesecake in town (we're not sure about it being the best, but it's certainly good) as well as flan, guava puffs and chocolate-mousse tortes. One warning: The fresh, chewy Cuban bread is so addictive you'll probably ruin your appetite. Two will spend about $40 for dinner with wine.
Open Mon. 8:30 a.m.-4 p.m., Tues.-Wed. 8:30 a.m.-10 p.m., Thurs. 8:30 a.m.-11 p.m., Fri. 8:30 a.m.-midnight, Sat. 9:30 a.m.-midnight. Cards: MC, V.

Leonardo's
706 W. University Ave., Gainesville
• (904) 378-2001
ITALIAN

10/20

Whether your affair is one of romance or political intrigue, there isn't a better place to conduct it in reassuring privacy. Everywhere you look there are nooks and crannies and quiet booths of dark, polished wood. And there's more than just cozy comfort: the kitchen turns out some mighty good food at amazingly low prices. It won't be easy, but try not to overdo it on the chewy, aromatic garlic rolls, or you won't have room for the appetizers. These are worth saving room for—particularly the house special, a plateful of artichokes stuffed with a savory mix of shrimp, pine nuts and ricotta, doused with garlic butter and basil. The Madagascar marinara, a peppery, creamy, brandy-spiked blend of grouper and capers on angel-hair pasta, had our table fighting over the last bite, and the chicken Gorgonzola played fresh broccoli florets and chopped pecans against the salty tang of the potent cheese. The meal ends on a similarly rich note, with such caloric wonders as the thick, dreamy banana-Kahlúa torte and the daunting slab of carrot cake slathered with a pistachio-butter icing. Weekend evenings, a strolling magician charms diners with juggling acts and sleight-of-hand tricks. The wine list has a decent selection of Italian and American wines, and the collegiate staff is charming. Dinner for two, with wine, runs a bargain-basement $40.
Open Sun.-Thurs. 5 p.m.-10 p.m., Fri.-Sat. 5 p.m.-11:30 p.m. Cards: MC, V.

The Sovereign
12 S.E. 2nd Ave., Gainesville
• (904) 378-6307
CONTINENTAL

12/20

The Sovereign is Gainesville's power-dining headquarters, the sort of solid place that University of Florida students hope their parents will take them to when they visit. Located in a downtown warehouse refurbished with lots of raw wood, old brick and glass, it seats a whopping 225 at tables adorned with pristine pink linens and pewter serving plates. The kitchen is the realm of chef Elmo Moser, a Swiss native who trained in France and has gained a loyal following for his unusual, skillful mix of the stolid and the innovative. The pâté de foie gras Strasbourg makes an unquestionably delicious appetizer, but at $35 a pop, only those traveling on a Pentagon expense account could afford it. We purred over the crisp-tasting ceviche, a tall glass of fresh scallops marinated in lime juice and topped with a frisky

salsa. We couldn't bring ourselves to order the beef Wellington, which sounded as dull as a Zurich burger, but the casserole of drunken fish—a mix of scallops, shrimp, flounder, snapper and clams in a broth spiked with a solid shot of bourbon—convinced us that Moser is not all Swiss staidness. That Continental classic, boneless sirloin with a bordelaise sauce, is hit-or-miss: the sturdy sauce glows with layers of flavors, but the steak is not always tender. But any faults are forgiven when dessert arrives, particularly for those wise enough to order Moser's astoundingly light and delicious chocolate-mousse cake. Wines from a United Nations of lists include 75 choices from Chile, Australia, Italy, Germany, France and California. On weekends, a pianist plays in the main dining room. Our only caveat: On autumn weekends when there's a home football game, this place is knee-deep in Florida Gator alums. Dinner for two, with wine, costs $80.
Open Mon.-Thurs. 5:30 p.m.-10 p.m., Fri.-Sat. 5:30 p.m.-10:30 p.m. All major cards.

TAMPA BAY AREA

TAMPA	278
ST. PETERSBURG	291
SARASOTA	300

TAMPA

RESTAURANTS	278
QUICK BITES	284
HOTELS	285
SHOPS	287
SIGHTS & SPORTS	288

RESTAURANTS

Armani's
Hyatt Regency Westshore
6200 Courtney Campbell Pkwy., Tampa
• (813) 281-9165/ 874-1234
ITALIAN

This romantic rooftop facing Old Tampa Bay has probably inspired more proposals of matrimony than even Elizabeth Taylor has. In an elegant northern Italian dining room—also near Tampa's airport—sumptuous sunsets are the canapés and twinkling take-offs the desserts. But save some room for the real thing. Armani's hot appetizers, rich concoctions that generally employ cream or cheese, are proof of the kitchen's ability to improve on time-honored themes. Escargots forgo their traditional garlic-butter bath for a still-garlicky place among wild mushrooms, pastry and artichoke relish. Lobster meets dumplings, and fried cheese discovers anchovies. Clearly, these are not dishes for Pritikin people, but those fretting over excess poundage will find salvation at the antipasto bar, with its array of light but tasty cold appetizers—the nightly changing display includes such good things as marinated squid and braised Belgian endive. The service hums with competence; whole armies stand poised to answer every wish. If your wish is an entrée, try one of the pasta or veal dishes, where the chef really shines, from his veal chop with Frangelico, walnuts and cream to his linguine with pine nuts and basil. Seafood—salmon, swordfish, shrimp, lobster—is also a reliable choice. The kitchen is humble enough to make pizza, but don't look for pepperoni here: one variety is topped with lobster and scallops, another with Provolone and Gorgonzola. Dinner for two, with wine, runs about $130.
Open Mon.-Thurs. 6 p.m.-10 p.m., Fri.-Sat. 6 p.m.-11 p.m. All major cards.

Bern's Steakhouse

1208 S. Howard Ave., Tampa
• (813) 251-2421
STEAKHOUSE

Everyone misses Bern's on the first drive by—its simple exterior belies its legendary status as one of the world's best steakhouses. Located near an expressway overpass, the cinderblock building exhibits a similarly dreary architectural style, but inside, it is merely garish, with red flocked wallpaper, gold statues and cheap murals. But no one comes here for the setting—they're here for some serious red meat washed down with some serious red wine. Owner Bern Laxer's intense perfectionism becomes evident on a tour of the place: he ages his own beef, grows his own produce on his own farm, roasts his own coffee, maintains his own saltwater fish tanks and even makes his own stainless steel for the huge kitchens. His two steak chefs have been grilling meat for 39 years between them. And the wines! He prints his list in his own printing shop and supervises the 7,000-label wine collection, which is understandably heavy on the French, Spanish, American and Italian reds, ranging from the rare to the everyday, the fairly priced to the overpriced. They're flawlessly stored in cellars in the restaurant and in three other buildings nearby. Laxer claims that his is the largest restaurant wine collection in the world, and we're not about to argue with him. Nor can we argue with the tableside Caesar salad (it sets the standard), the smoked fish plate, the incomparable onion soup or the 24 kinds of caviar. Steaks are sold by cut, weight and thickness, ranging from a six-ounce filet for $17.20 to a sixty-ounce strip sirloin for $143.42. Your steak is custom cut after you place your order, then grilled to your precise specifications according to a complex chart; if the taste of perfectly aged beef isn't enough, you can pair the meat with garlic butter or a good béarnaise. In true steakhouse fashion, the onion rings are crisp and tasty. Even seafood gets attention—bass, cod and sole are plucked from the kitchen's tanks and cooked simply.

After your entrées, if you want to become more intimately acquainted with dessert wines, you'll be shown upstairs to the dessert room. There, you'll be seated in private compartments made from wine barrels and equipped with TV monitors—it strikes us as *1984*-ish, but the idea is that you can watch TV shows, tapes of wine tastings or a video closeup of the pianist while you try one of the countless homemade desserts. You can even phone the pianist to request a song, the ultimate in passive entertainment. If you turn off the box you can pay better attention to the collection of some 1,500 dessert wines, liqueurs, Cognacs, ports, Armagnacs and scotches, not to mention the massive dessert menu, where you'll find such goodies as carrot cake with homemade macadamia ice cream and hot fudge. If you don't get too carried away with the wine, two of you can leave here purring for $140.

Open nightly 5 p.m.-11 p.m. All major cards.

TAMPA BAY AREA   Tampa – Restaurants

Columbia Restaurant
2117 E. 7th Ave.,
Ybor City
• (813) 248-4961
SPANISH

10/20

Columbia's owners have opened branches up and down the Gulf of Mexico coast, but none capture the passion and grandeur of this original structure, the anchor of Tampa's Latin district since 1905. Tourist popularity rides largely on atmosphere, and this place has loads of both tourists and atmosphere. Ceramic murals enliven the exterior, which occupies an entire city block along historic Seventh Avenue; inside, flamenco dancers ignite the crowd, while tall palms, archways and ornate railings set a Spanish stage for such dishes as paella, the traditional Spanish feast of fish, shellfish, squid, chicken, pork, sausage, green peppers, onions and tomatoes, all piled onto saffron-tinged rice. In this setting, even bean soup would taste special; fortunately, this bean soup would taste pretty good anywhere. This is a great place for hearty appetites not offended by olive oil, which the kitchen uses with abandon. Still, a trip to Ybor City without dinner at Columbia would be like going to Las Vegas and skipping Caesar's Palace. The ruler of this palace is Caesar Gonzmart, Ybor City's busiest hand-kisser. In 1946, Gonzmart, then an entertainer, married the granddaughter of Columbia's founder, later bringing his violin directly into the dining room. Evenings are strictly for theatrics and out-of-towners, but lunchtime brings in a good crowd of locals, to the restaurant and the attached Corner Café—a less formal, less expensive spot, perfect for a bean-soup and Cuban-sandwich lunch. Dinner for two, including wine, runs about $65.
Open Mon.-Thurs. 11 a.m.-10 p.m., Fri.-Sat. 11 a.m.-11 p.m., Sun. noon-9 p.m. All major cards.

Donatello
232 N. Dale Mabry Hwy.,
Tampa
• (813) 875-6660
ITALIAN

13

Donatello is a swell place to go in a stretch limo. With a snap of the maître d's fingers, the show begins: servers hustle to position, napkins fly, glasses fill and menus unfold, while diners luxuriate in a glitzy contemporary dining room. At evening's end, considerable-size checks are delivered to the table, and women are presented with roses. When this place opened in 1984, Tampa was still charmed by salad bars and cheeseburgers—it had little taste for northern Italian food and even less tolerance for big checks. That's all changed, and Donatello deserves part of the credit, for showing locals how a suave blending of service, setting and food can make for a restorative and relaxing evening that's worth an investment. The cooking style is classic fancy Italian, rich and showy, and though it's devoid of the simpler Italian charms of the country's new wave of trattorias, it's full of seductive flavors. Several subtly glorious cream sauces meet up with an array of pastas, seafood and first-rate veal scaloppines. Like most Italian restaurants of this ilk, Donatello prides itself on its veal—there are versions with ham, mushrooms and truffles; brandy, mushrooms and a truf-

fled wine sauce; and mushrooms, artichokes and zucchini. All of them are delicious. Much is made of tableside manner: instead of simply delivering sliced duckling, the server will first present the whole bird for inspection before whisking it away to be carved. It may be fussy, but there's no doubting the lovely effect of a leisurely meal here. With a moderately priced wine (on an otherwise pricey list), dinner for two costs about $130.
Open nightly 6 p.m.-11 p.m. All major cards.

Farmer Jones Red Barn
6150 New Tampa Hwy. (U.S. Hwy. 92), Lakeland
• (813) 686-2754
STEAKHOUSE

10/20

This place is true to its name and then some: there are actually three farmer Joneses (plus Billy Dee, the daughter of one of the farmers) at this red barn in rural Lakeland, a 35-minute drive from Tampa. Locals make the drive regularly for very good steaks at very good prices. You won't find the fancy frills and fine wine that are standard fare at Bern's in Tampa, but neither will you spend a bundle for them here. If all you want is quality beef and change back from your $100 bill, consider this alternative. Actually, the Red Barn isn't *that* low-brow: if you buy a frozen drink in a boot, you get to keep the boot. The no-nonsense atmosphere (a country-style decor with booths and lots of wood), rushed service and so-so side orders (flavorless fried green tomatoes, basic onion rings) don't affect the quality of the meat, which is well aged, tender and cooked to order. It almost rivals that at Bern's. The various cuts—T-bones, porterhouses, filet mignons, New York strips—are sold by the pound (starting at $12); you can inspect the offerings at the display near the front door, where you'll be greeted by one of the farmer Joneses or the farmer's daughter. There are a few countrified concessions for those who aren't partial to red meat, mainly fried chicken and seafood. On weekends, you'll need to make a reservation, but you certainly don't need to dress up. No one will put a napkin in your lap, no one will play violin in your ear, and no one will prattle on in a phony French accent. But they grow farm boys big out here, so don't run off without paying the tab—which will barely approach $70 for two, even if you order one of the pleasant Californian wines offered.
Open daily 11 a.m.-11 p.m. All major cards.

The Heron
Hwy. 24 & 2nd St., Cedar Key
• (904) 543-5666
CONTINENTAL/SEAFOOD

11/20

The Gulf Coast track has been beaten down pretty thoroughly, but Cedar Key is still far enough off it—specifically, about 80 miles north of Tampa—to be a great getaway. Our favorite place to eat in these parts, The Heron occupies a renovated nineteenth-century home given a cozy Victorian warmth with oak furniture, wainscoting and floral print wallpaper. Owner/chef Janice Coupe, a former English teacher, has a thing about crab. She makes it every which way: crab salad, crab quiche, crabmeat au gratin and her signature dish, a thick, creamy bisque loaded

with lump crabmeat instead of lobster. The perfect complement to the bisque is the hearts of palm salad, a beloved Cedar Key standard; The Heron's version is delicious and perfectly fresh, from the resilient light-green palm hearts to the strange dressing made with ice cream, mayonnaise and peanut butter (it's better than it sounds). Those who don't share Coupe's passion for crab have several options, from charbroiled steaks to baked shrimp and scallop dishes (all her seafood is baked or sautéed). Our favorite main course is the delicate snapper filet with a captivating fragrance of wine, lemon and garlic; a close second is the sinfully rich seafood Newburg. Homemade chocolate-rum pie and Key lime pie are equally good dessert choices. Dinner for two, with wine, is about $60.
Open Tues.-& Sun. 11:30 a.m.-2:30 p.m. & Fri.-Sat. 6 p.m.-9:30 p.m. All major cards.

J. Fitzgerald's
Sheraton Grand Hotel,
4860 W. Kennedy Blvd.,
Tampa
• (813) 286-4444
CONTINENTAL

12/20

Don't feel guilty—a meal in this intimate, sophisticated hotel dining room is worth every dime of your company's expense-account budget. It's a soothing oasis for business travelers, with its comfy upholstered furniture, attentive service and rich but not too fussy cuisine. Appetizers include a brioche filled with Pernod-doused escargots and a blue-crab and grouper bisque laced with sherry. The Caesar salad is flavorful and well balanced, but we're partial to the salad of nutty mâche (lamb's lettuce) and baked goat cheese in a sherry vinaigrette. A cool ball of sorbet after your salad clears the palate for such well-prepared entrées as breast of duck with glazed chestnuts and lamb medallions wed to a subtle green-peppercorn sauce. Tender beef or veal medallions in an array of cloud-light sauces distinguish Fitzgerald's from the typical hotel restaurant. After your main course, you'll be sorely tempted by a dessert cart laden with lovely tarts, cakes and such. Hotel restaurants don't always feel the need to make much of an effort, so it's refreshing to find one that can be recommended as a dining spot in itself. Plan on spending $90 for dinner and wine for two.
Open Mon.-Thurs. 11:30 a.m.-2 p.m. & 6 p.m.-10 p.m., Fri. 11:30 a.m.-2 p.m. & 6 p.m.-11 p.m., Sat. 6 p.m.-11 p.m. All major cards.

Jasmine Thai
13248 N. Dale Mabry Hwy.,
Tampa
• (813) 968-1501
THAI

Tampa loves Thai—or is it that Thais love Tampa? For whatever reason, Thai eateries are scattered throughout the city, and we can't remember the last time one closed for lack of interest. They vary from one-room neighborhood joints decorated with goldfish and paper mobiles to sleek, mirrored dining rooms boasting cushioned floor seating. The competition is stiff and quality uneven, but we've had consistently good meals in this streamlined chrome-and-glass storefront in Carrollwood, a suburb northwest of downtown. The kitchen takes pains over its artful

presentations, and if you request your dishes hot, your mouth will glow with a marvelous chili fire. Many Thai places play it safe with the same old standards, but Jasmine strays a bit off the straight-and-narrow, with such dishes as tornado shrimp: a platter of grilled shrimp arranged on a bed of eggplant, blanketed with green curry sauce and adorned with a julienne of vegetables. In fact, all the seafood—lobster, grouper, shrimp—is flavorful and fresh tasting. You won't find better than Jasmine's pad Thai, a traditional, slightly sweet jumble of sautéed rice noodles, shrimp, pork, eggs, peanuts, bean sprouts and scallions. The many young professionals who live nearby love this place, where two can feast, with Thai beers, for $55.
Open Mon.-Thurs. 11 a.m.-10:30 p.m., Fri.-Sat. 11 a.m.-11 p.m., Sun. 4 p.m.-10 p.m. Cards: AE, MC, V.

Mise en Place
1815 W. Platt St., Tampa
• (813) 254-5373
AMERICAN

12/20

The neighborhood is a tad scruffy, and the atmosphere isn't remarkable, but that hasn't stoppped this place from becoming one of Tampa's most popular new dinner spots. Chef Marty Blitz and his wife, Maryann, already had standing-room-only lunch crowds when they expanded and started serving dinner in 1989. If they'd just open for breakfast, we'd be tempted to move in and pay rent. Now spread over four storefronts, the dining rooms have a homey-American look, with charming curtains and lot of blue tones. The daily-changing menu is rife with American/Californian foodie standards, like Brie-and-mango quesadillas with coriander sauce, California-style pizza with duck sausage, and seafood sausage with fennel sauce. Bread baskets are paired with whole heads of mellow roasted garlic for spreading. And who wants chicken noodle soup when there's roasted red pepper–jalapeño bisque? Fortunately, Blitz has solid training behind him and doesn't get caught up in the sillier excesses of contemporary American cooking, keeping his flavors strong and clean. His lettuces get help from apples, corn, black beans and nuts, and his basil-Gorgonzola salad dressing is weaning locals from ordinary blue cheese. Good main courses are the tender rack of lamb with a hazelnut persillade (a parsley-and-garlic blend) and the roast duck with a California blueberry sauce studded with whole berries. A stone's throw from downtown Tampa and the fashionable Old Hyde Park Village, Mise en Place draws both CPAs and society matrons for lunch, for such goodies as curried-chicken-and-chutney sandwiches. Some of the waiters aren't quite polished professionals yet. Two can dine, with a bottle of wine, for $75.
Open Mon. 11 a.m.-3 p.m., Tues.-Thurs. 11 a.m.-3 p.m. & 5:30 p.m.-10 p.m., Fri. 11 a.m.-3 p.m. & 5:30 p.m.-11 p.m., Sat. 5:30 p.m.-11 p.m. Cards: MC, V.

QUICK BITES

Jimmy Mac's
113 S. Armenia Ave., Tampa
• (813) 879-0591

The owners of this burger joint could charge for the heavenly aromas wafting out to the sidewalk, and passersby would gladly pay. The plump burgers, served two dozen ways, are every bit as good as they smell—they're even tastier than most home-grilled versions. Toppings run the gamut from blue cheese to guacamole, from taco sauce to pineapples. Solo diners appreciate the food service at the lively bar, which occupies one of many rooms in this converted old house, with its wood floors and tables, fireplaces and enclosed porches. The young-professional happy-hour crowd is considerable, particularly later in the week, and nightly music keeps diners' spirits up. Burgers and beer for two run about $18.
Open Mon.-Fri. 11:30 a.m.-3 a.m., Sat. 5 p.m.-3 a.m., Sun. 4:30 p.m.-11 p.m. Cards: AE, MC, V.

Kojak
2808 Gandy Blvd., Tampa
• (813) 837-3774

Is this a rib joint or a flea market? We'd put money on both answers. Two mannequin Indians greet patrons at this south Tampa landmark—tucked in a 1920s wooden bungalow near Hillsborough Bay—and there's enough memorabilia on the walls to start an auction. But it's the tangy barbecue sauce, not the clutter, that keeps loyal fans returning. They slather it on chunky pork sandwiches and dip platters of pork ribs in it, while enjoying the cool breezes on the porch. Sides run to the cole slaw/baked beans/applesauce basics, and they're all satisfying. Refugees from downtown's office buildings eat side-by-side with soldiers from the nearby military base. Service is quick and congenial, prices are dirt cheap, and there's no need to dress up. Lunch for two costs about $15 with beer.
Open Tues.-Thurs. 11 a.m.-2 p.m. & 5 p.m.-10 p.m., Fri. 11 a.m.-10:30 p.m., Sat. noon-10 p.m., Sun. 5 p.m.-10 p.m. No cards.

Mel's Hot Dogs
4136 E. Busch Blvd., Tampa
• (813) 985-8000

Chicken sandwiches are offered, but ordering one would be like going to Tour d'Argent and ordering a green salad and water. Okay, maybe we're getting a tad hyperbolic—but these all-beef Vienna dogs are the dogs of all dogs. Plump, juicy and nearly bursting, they nestle on steamed poppyseed buns and are topped with any number of good things: spicy mustard, bacon, cheddar, chili, onions. Mel's works like this: wait in line to order, give the order-taker your name (if you don't, they'll make one up for you, and you might not like it), stake out a table and start reading the walls, which are loaded with hot dog cartoons, fan mail and newspaper stories about owner Mel Lohn. When your

basket is served, you will immediately understand why Tampa is a one-dog town. Hot dogs and sodas for two run about $10.
Open Mon.-Sat. 10 a.m.-10 p.m., Sun. 11 a.m.-9 p.m. No cards.

Skipper's Smokehouse and Oyster Bar
910 Skipper Rd., Tampa
• (813) 971-0666

Skipper's is all Florida, all the time. Even without the alligator-tail sandwiches, alligator–black bean chili and alligator-tail dinners, this hodgepodge of shacklike rooms north of Tampa would still seem born of sandy soil. It isn't just a restaurant—it's an institution. At night, outside, barefoot locals drink cheap beer and dance under the moon to excellent live blues and reggae. Lunchtime finds a more subdued crowd, including professors from the nearby University of South Florida. The food is simple, honest and fresh, and the place is loads of fun. Sandwiches and beer for two cost about $15.
Open Tues. & Thurs. 11 a.m.-10 p.m., Wed. & Fri. 11 a.m.-11 p.m., Sat. noon-11 p.m., Sun. 1 p.m.-11 p.m. Cards: AE, MC, V.

HOTELS

Luxury (From $150)

Safety Harbor Spa & Fitness Center
105 N. Bayshore Drive, Safety Harbor 34695
• (813) 726-1161
Fax (813) 726-4268

The woman in the Safety Harbor ad struts the mark of fitness in the 1990s: muscle tone. No beach-blanket cheesecake here. When you arrive at Safety Harbor Spa & Fitness Center, get ready to sweat. Not that the facility, following a recent $11-million improvement program, isn't a fine spa, with all that the term "spa" encompasses: fabulous, imaginatively presented cuisine; pastoral grounds; birds who seem as if they must be on the payroll with their dependably delivered choruses each and every morning. It's just that the emphasis at Safety Harbor in 1991 is on fitness, and while you may be pampered with a lovely loofah bath, massage, herbal wrap, pedicure and a visit to the Lancôme Skin Care Institute on site, be prepared to get down and dirty at one of the 34 fitness classes offered each day. Yes, 34. With over 200 staff members at the spa alone, the facilities are centered around two rather historic landmarks that still manage to characterize the property—state-of-the-art physiotherapy or not. The first are the Espiritu Santo mineral baths, stumbled upon by Spanish explorer Hernando DeSoto during his sixteenth century expedition. The legend goes that DeSoto's soldiers, suffering from beriberi (a debilitating disease of the nerves and digestive system), were cured when they drank from the source, once thought to be Ponce de León's elusive Fountain of Youth. The abundant springs still rejuvenate guests at the resort, as does the second historical feature, a domed rotunda, built in 1926, which still graces the airy dining room.

Enjoying a café-au-skim-milk beside a Michaele Volbracht mural of colorful and exotic birds is one heck of a way to start off another day of feeling the burn.
Singles: $178-$251; doubles: $131-$188.

Moderate (From $100)

Hyatt Regency Westshore at Tampa International Airport
6200 Courtney Campbell Cswy., Tampa 33607
• (813) 874-1234
Fax (813) 281-9168

If this is Tampa's idea of an airport hotel, we want to fly in more often. The marvelous service here begins with a cheerful valet staff (to whom we never even had to offer a claim check—each seemed to match us with our car on site) and continues upstairs to a piano bar, lounge and restaurant overlooking the marshy shores of Tampa Bay. To our eyes, the rooms are lovely; splurge for those on the Regency Club level, where each day, a creative appetizer or dessert surreptitiously arrives, and a host of other personalized amenities is offered.
Singles: $120-$165; doubles: $140-$185; Regency Club: $175-$195.

Innisbrook Resort
36750 U.S. Hwy. 19 North,
Palm Harbor 34684
• (813) 942-2000,
(800) 456-2000
Fax (813) 942-5576

Think Saint Andrews. Think Pinehurst. Think Casa de Campo. Many a golfer has thought he was at the pearly gates when his eyes saw the miles of fairways at Innisbrook. In this golf nirvana, there are 63 holes to sink before the day is done. While it is the rare Florida resort that doesn't have a golf pro or two on staff, Innisbrook's golf program is designed and overseen by a veritable "Who's Who" in golf. Former all-American golf pro Jay Overton developed the prestigious Innisbrook Golf Institute here a decade ago; today, the year-round series of comprehensive instructional programs is delivered by PGA (Professional Golfers Association) notables Lew Smither III, Bill Buttner and John Huston, plus LPGA (Ladies PGA) legends Myra Blackwelder and Laurel Kean. Lest you tire of taking swings at little white balls while at Innisbrook, there's a sophisticated tennis facility at the resort where you can take swings at yellow or orange balls. Home of the famed Australian Tennis Institute, directed by former Australian Davis Cupper Terry Addison, Innisbrook features a $1-million center with eleven Har-Tru and seven Lakold courts. There are golf and tennis instruction for all creatures great and small, including a "Zoo Crew" program for kids. When you finally drift off to sleep, you'll enjoy the spacious, plushly appointed accommodations; if you get hungry, The Island Clubhouse has several very good dining rooms, with golf-view tables, of course.
1-bedroom suites: $116-$204; 2-bedroom suites: $172-$337. Golf & tennis packages available.

Saddlebrook Resort

100 Saddlebrook Way, Wesley Chapel 33543
• (813) 973-1111
Fax (813) 973-4504

If you're reluctant to drive a great distance on your vacation, (what's a half hour among friends, really?), don't even consider Saddlebrook, which rests somewhere between Tampa, many acres of strawberry farms and nowhere. The closest resort, of sorts anyway, is a neighboring nudist camp. Although we weren't compelled to disrobe publicly, we do find this sort of solitude invigorating, and Saddlebrook is a cleverly laid-out, creatively designed and managed, full-service resort. Although inland, it is the kind of place in which you could spend a week, in what feels like the blink of an eye—and sign on for another one in the next blink. Although there are some 696 guest rooms (many of them one- and two-bedroom suites), the resort never feels crowded. There are two Arnold Palmer golf courses, 37 tennis courts, a fitness center, jogging, bicycling and a restaurant, the Cypress Room, which offers some of Florida's best hotel fare. At the heart of it all is a half-million gallon "Superpool," which looks like an inkspot dropped onto the landscape.
Singles, doubles & suites: $115-$205. Packages available.

Sheraton Grand Westshore

4860 W. Kennedy Blvd., Tampa 33609
• (813) 286-4400
Fax (813) 286-4053

Sheraton doesn't dole out the "Grand" add-on to its properties easily (there are only four others in the United States). Despite its commercial boulevard address overlooking the Westshore Shopping Mall and surrounding fast-food outlets, this one deserves the appellation. With its extraordinary lobby—filled with twinkling white lights and centered around an atrium filled with trees, fountains and a life-size Jay Seward Johnson sculpture of a man—this is clearly the place to fete for the townsfolk. In fact, we counted two weddings and a Bar Mitzvah as the glass elevator whisked us up and down to our beautiful corner suite during a weekend stay.
Singles: $99; doubles: $114; suites: $200.

SHOPS

Antiques

Village Antiques, Inc.

4323 El Prado Blvd., Tampa
• (813) 839-1761

Tampa, and indeed all of outlying Hillsborough County, is home to so many antique stores that the city's dealers jointly publish an antiques "atlas." The El Prado Antique Center is one such dealer, owner by one Colonel Moran, retired from the U.S. Air Force, who specializes in "Americana." Moran offers an enormous selection of period American furniture (eighteenth century to twentieth century), estate jewelry, Civil War pistols and swords and American paintings.
Open Mon.-Sat. 10 a.m.-5:30 p.m., Sun. noon-5:30 p.m.

Books

Three Birds Bookstore
1518 7th Ave.,
Ybor City
• (813) 247-7041

Currently undergoing a sort of bohemian renaissance into a charming community that's as artsy as it is ethnic, Ybor City is the location of a wonderful little bookstore hosting poetry read-ins, offering muffins and cheesecakes, and even selling a book or two. (But no best-sellers, romance novels or Jay McInerney, the three female owners promise).
Open Mon.-Wed. 10 a.m.-7 p.m., Thurs.-Sat. 10 a.m.-10 p.m.

Food

La Segunda Central Bakery
2512 N. 15th St,
Ybor City
• (813) 248-1531

La Segunda is such a fascinating bakery that its owners offer tours. Specializing in baking the three-foot-long loaves of Cuban bread, the family that runs this bakery has produced some 5,000 loaves a day since 1915. (The family "secret" is lining the dough with palmetto leaves before baking, which keeps the loaves straight and uniform). Dozens of other Cuban pastries and other Sanchez family specialties are baked daily at the establishment.
Open daily 9 a.m.-5 p.m.

Gifts

The Mole Hole
1605 W. Swann Ave.,
Old Hyde Park Village,
Tampa
• (813) 254-3704

If you want a gift that's a cut above the usual souvenir fare, visit Tampa's branch of the chain gift shop, the Mole Hole. Items are international, from Sorrento music boxes to Caithness paperweights to Wolfard oil lamps.
Open Mon.-Wed. & Sat. 10 a.m.- 6 p.m., Thurs.-Fri. 10 a.m.-9 p.m., Sun. noon-5 p.m.

SIGHTS & SPORTS

Amusements

Busch Gardens, The Dark Continent
4545 Busch Blvd. &
40th St.,
Tampa
• (813) 971-8282

Though quite a bit smaller and worlds less daring than the unsurpassable Walt Disney World, Busch Gardens Tampa certainly rivals that entertainment empire in creativity and value. You'll find rides, live entertainment, animal exhibits, shops and restaurants here—all housed in eight distinctly themed sections capturing the spirit of the Dark Continent, turn-of-the-century Africa. Plan to spend at least a day at the complex; one price covers admission to all attractions, most of which you won't want to miss. Among them is a sprawling zoo that ranks among the top zoos in the country, with an animal population of more than 3,300. The new koala exhibit at the park is one of only three sites in the United States where the lovable Australian creatures are exhibited (although we couldn't coax them out from behind the glass protecting their caves). Although there are plenty of rides, the real-life drama of Busch Gardens is its 60-acre re-creation of the Serengeti Plain, where 500 head of African wildlife roam "freely." It's a thrilling tour of vegetation and wildlife via air-conditioned monorail or by steam locomotive. If you are eager to learn about what you are seeing, look for Busch Gardens's Conservation Information department's mobile centers that are rolled throughout the park to educate visitors about wildlife.

Open daily 9:30 a.m.-6 p.m. Adults $26.45, children under 2 free.

Arts

Henry B. Plant Museum
401 W. Kennedy Blvd., Tampa
• (813) 253-3333

What was once the South Wing of a lavish Tampa grande dame is now the fascinating Henry B. Plant Museum. Just as Miami and Palm Beach are the jewels that were lovingly shaped by Henry Flagler and the Florida East Coast Railroad, Tampa—and indeed all of Florida's West Coast—is the legacy of one Henry Plant. The ambitious developer built the Tampa Bay Hotel (then the world's most expensive at a cost of some $3 million) in the 1890s, rivaling Flagler's eastern Florida retreats. Its Moorish architecture and thirteen silver minarets make it a Tampa landmark today. The spotlight fell on the "world's most elegant hotel" and the city springing up around it when Colonel "Teddy" Roosevelt and his Rough Riders set up their headquarters here in 1898, and the Cuba-bound troops commenced training for the Spanish American War. Many of these soldiers returned in the ensuing years, bringing their families along with them this time, and setting up residence. The museum showcases turn-of-the-century furnishings and fashions, though much of the hotel's original accoutrements were lost over the years, as the hotel lapsed into bankruptcy, was sold to the city, and eventually became the University of Tampa. Designed by J.A. Wood, the former hotel once featured a casino, two ballrooms, a grand salon, an indoor swimming pool, dining rooms and one of the first Otis Elevators in the country. Now, students Scotch-tape dance notices on marble columns.

Open Tues.-Sat. 10 a.m.-4 p.m. Suggested donation $2.

Martinez de Ybor Art Gallery
2025 E. 7th Ave., Ybor City
• (813) 247-2771

Watching artist Arnold Martinez work in his native Tampa, in the Latin Quarter, offers a glimpse into the area's rich past. Martinez developed his own painting techniques to develop coffee, tea and extract of tobacco into fascinating watercolors.
Open daily 9 a.m.-5 p.m.

Excursions

Harbour Island
777 South Island Blvd., Tampa
• (813) 228-7807

Half the fun of Harbour Island is the trip there: you may board the People Mover (from the Franklin Street Stop, downtown) for a two-minute aerial view of the channel en route to the island, or you can even drive across. Once on the island side, there's a variety of things to do—sightseeing cruises departing the Waterwalk for Davis Island and the Hillsborough River, rides aboard electric boats, gondolas (complete with a Venice-style gondolier) and pedal boats, noshing at waterfront restaurants.
Open Mon.-Sat. 10 a.m.-9 p.m., Sun. 11 a.m.-6 p.m.

Old Hyde Park Village
1509 Swann Ave., Tampa
• (813) 251-3500

The chic boutiques (among them Laura Ashley, Polo/Ralph Lauren and Godiva Chocolatier) of Old Hyde Park village are simply updated versions of what you may have found in Tampa's most fashionable suburb circa 1900. The shopping and dining area marks the northern boundary of Hyde Park, which began even before Tampa was established in 1824, as a fishing village called Spanish Town. In 1886, O.H. Platt of Hyde Park, Illinois bought twenty acres of the village, naming it for his home town. Palmettos, pines and orange groves of Hyde Park rapidly disappeared as homes sprang up forming a cross section of architectural styles, still represented throughout the elegant neighborhood today. The shops clustered along Swann Avenue tout "The Art of Acquiring" (which, if you're shopping in this area, you've probably already mastered) with plenty of designer and household items offered in pleasant surroundings.
Open Mon.-Wed. 10 a.m.-6 p.m., Thurs.-Fri. 10 a.m.-9 p.m. Some stores open Sun. noon-5 p.m.

Ybor Square
13th St. at 8th Ave., Ybor City
• (813) 247-4497

Turn-of-the-century street lamps, Spanish-style architecture, wrought-iron balconies and ornate grillwork are remnants of the day when this Tampa suburb was widely known as the "Cigar Capital of the World"—with some 200 cigar factories employing nearly 12,000 craftspeople in its heyday. Listed on the National Register of Historic Places, the buildings of an old stemmery, factory and warehouse make up Ybor Square, a shopping mall brimming with dozens of shops vending arts, crafts, specialty items, antiques and other collectibles. The lost art of cigar-making is still on display at one of this "period" carrefour's shops.
Mon.-Sat. 9:30 a.m.-5:30 p.m., Sun. noon-5:30 p.m.

Sports

Tampa Jai Alai
5125 S. Dale Mabry Blvd.,
Tampa
• (813) 831-1411

The ancient sport of the Spanish Basques, jai alai is played in Tampa at one of the nine frontons across the state. In the game, two helmeted, red sashed *pelotaris* (players) carom a *pelota*, a ball of virgin rubber and goatskin, off four walls with a *cesta*, sort of a basket-woven hockey stick. We think jai alai is the most humane of the pari-mutuels (an international player's strike ongoing at press time notwithstanding), and at the same time it can be very dangerous: the pelota frequently moves at speeds in excess of 150 m.p.h.

Open Dec.-Sept. for matinee and evening and matinee games. Call for exact times.

ST. PETERSBURG

RESTAURANTS	291
HOTELS	295
SHOPS	297
SIGHTS	298

RESTAURANTS

Basta's Cantina d'Italia
1625 4th St. South,
St. Petersburg
• (813) 894-7880
ITALIAN

10/20

With its tuxedo-clad waiters, fresh flowers and starched linens, Basta's clearly aims at a cause more noble than spaghetti with red sauce. The Fourth Street location means a quick cab ride for tourists staying in downtown hotels or out-of-towners visiting the museums, but this place is also a favorite with locals, who rightly consider it the best Italian in Saint Petersburg (granted, the competition isn't much; the better northern Italians live across the water in Tampa). Dine on a quiet weeknight and you'll enjoy service so attentive you'll think they've confused you with George and Barbara Bush; weekends get a bit more harried. Archways and wall murals convey an Italian ambience that is matched by the food, which is rife with fresh herbs, cheeses and pasta. Chunks of Fontina cheese and

TAMPA BAY AREA St. Petersburg – Restaurants

chopped olives add gusto to warm bread, and capers climb into the Caesar salad. (The made-to-order entrées take a little time, so it's wise to order an appetizer.) The main-course list is strong on seafood, both frozen and fresh; some of it, like the shrimp venezia flambé, winds up sautéed at tableside, as does steak Diane, a favorite with the regulars. Those who shy away from such fussy show-off dishes might try the chicken with rosemary. Basta's isn't steep, nor is it cheap—dinner for two, with wine, runs about $80—but it's a good choice for the money.
Open Mon.-Thurs. 11:30 a.m.-3 p.m. & 5 p.m.-10 p.m., Fri. 11:30 a.m.-3 p.m. & 5 p.m.-11 p.m., Sat. 5 p.m.-11 p.m. Cards: AE, MC, V.

The Heritage Grille Restaurant
256 2nd St. North,
St. Petersburg
• (813) 823-6382
AMERICAN

11/20

Located a short walk from many downtown hotels, this place combines both charm and sophistication in its setting: an old house with a series of small, clean-lined dining rooms separated by French doors. Save romance for another venue—the acoustics are less than perfect, and the place is better suited for a lively group with diverse tastes. Works by local painters give life to the walls, and chef James Christmas gives life to the plates. Mr. Christmas knows that the best presents don't come down chimneys—they come on dinner plates. From a sassy, crisp-crusted wild-mushroom pizza to an elegant hickory-smoked salmon with a papaya-Champagne vinaigrette, meals start out strong. They proceed to entrées wrapped in sauces that would more aptly be called potions: brews of Champagne and papaya, or red wine and cranberries, or black beans and tequila. These potions turn even a basic breast of chicken into something special. And when coupled with a small but reliably fresh array of seafood—shrimp, scallops, salmon, tuna, grouper—they give visitors to Saint Petersburg a good reason to stick around. The desserts range from the simple (apple pie) to the chic (chocolate-walnut torte), and the wine selection is decent. Service can be distracted—you may have to pull your waiter back down to earth. Dinner for two, with wine, costs about $75.
Open Mon.-Thurs. 11:30 a.m.-2:30 p.m. & 5 p.m.-10 p.m., Fri. 11:30 a.m.-2:30 p.m. & 5 p.m.-11 p.m., Sat. 5 p.m.-11 p.m. All major cards.

The Kapok Tree Restaurant
923 McMullen Booth Rd.,
Clearwater
• (813) 726-4734
AMERICAN

8/20

The only things this place has going for it is the tree. Botanists, enjoy yourselves, but diners beware—even a mammoth old kapok tree can't make up for mundane food, ambivalent service and a tacky decor. For years, this palatial restaurant has lured tourists by the busload; like a fast-food chain, it boasts of the number of diners served daily—4,000 in peak season—and hopefuls wait in line just to get a number, and then they wait to be seated. Some of them wind up in the Grand Ballroom, where

they're dwarfed by a chandelier, statues and Roman columns. Maybe all this grand pretension is the draw—we can't imagine anybody coming here for the French onion soup, whose cheese topping might make for good insulation. Or for the heavily battered fried shrimp entrée. Or for the tasteless eggplant parmigiana. The complimentary macaroni salad? Nah—though it made us nostaglic for the cafeteria fare of our school days. Are they here for the wind chimes made of dyed pink seashells, or the necklaces sold by the inch in the sprawling gift shop, or the mass-produced artwork? We hope not. It must be that tree outside, caged like a tiger and held at bay with torches—perhaps to keep it from leaving in protest.
Open daily noon-10 p.m. All major cards.

The Lobster Pot
17814 Gulf Blvd.,
Redington Shores
• (813) 391-8592
SEAFOOD

12/20

It may look like a resort chain restaurant, with its generic tropical decor and touristy, casually dressed clientele, but don't let that fool you—The Lobster Pot's selection of seafood is far broader than the norm. Owner Eugen Fuhrmann recruits crustaceans from a world away for his kitchen. The result? A menu of a dozen-plus lobster items—stuffed, steamed, flambéed with brandy, curried or bathed in a wine-and-cheese sauce. Because of the distances traveled, many are frozen, but they've been handled with care and taste almost as good as fresh. Our favorite? The simple broiled South African tails, offered seasonally as a "Best of the Tails" pick. These South African tails are delightfully sweet and slightly salty, with a tender but fleshy consistency. For more complexity, scan the menu. Lobster Bombay will appeal to those who like sweetened curry sauces (we're not among them). Nightly specials add an array of fresh fish—grouper, swordfish, red snapper—much of it grilled and drizzled with sauces; we tried snapper topped with crab and a tasty lime-ginger sauce and a delightfully simple grilled swordfish. Don't order a thing until you've indulged in the escargots Eugen, in whose buttery bath are blended flavors of curry, mango chutney, garlic and red wine—an ideal dip for the fresh-baked bread. Worthy desserts include the tangy Key lime pie and the rich peanut butter–ice cream pie. To appreciate The Lobster Pot's commitment to quality, you have to understand that Gulf beach restaurants can usually do a fine business whether they're good or not, since tourism brings new blood every day. But to keep the locals returning, you've got to be doing something right—and when locals want to show out-of-towners a good time, they head here. Dinner for two, with wine, runs about $100.
Open Mon.-Thurs. 4:30 p.m.-10 p.m., Fri.-Sat. 4:30 p.m.-11 p.m., Sun. 4 p.m.-10 p.m. All major cards.

TAMPA BAY AREA — St. Petersburg – Restaurants

The Pepper Mill
1575 S. Fort Harrison Ave.,
Clearwater
• (813) 449-2988
AMERICAN

11/20

Once you get past the incongruity of a tin-roofed cabin in the middle of urban Clearwater, The Pepper Mill's rustic decor sets a homey, inviting mood. But don't expect collard greens and grits for dinner—the place may look countrified, but the food is uptown (until you get the bill, which puts you back in the country). Urgent hunger pangs are promptly taken care of with complimentary stuffed mushrooms, followed quickly by baskets of fresh-baked poppyseed bread with strawberry butter (almost sweet enough to be on the dessert menu, but undeniably tasty). If they're offered, by all means order the muffin-sized Maryland crabcakes, which are crisp, fluffy and light, with a minimum of filler. Congeniality is the watchword here: owner David Lowrey makes the excellent tableside Caesar salad himself, and the kitchen is unusually accommodating—if you can't make up your mind on an entrée, your waiter may offer two half portions. You probably will have a hard time making up your mind, since the menu offers an endless array of meat, poultry and seafood dishes, including steaks, ribs, quail and fresh grouper. And every night there's a blackboard special, like the tasty squid-ink pasta with shrimp, scallops and snapper that we tried. Desserts are intense: the Key lime pie will leave you puckering for weeks, and the chocolate sin will satisfy a chocolate craving with just one bite. The otherwise charming staff can get a little too harried on busy weekends. Two can dine with wine for a very reasonable $60.
Open Mon.-Thurs. 11:30 a.m.-2:30 p.m. & 5 p.m.-10 p.m., Fri. 11:30 a.m.-2:30 p.m. & 5 p.m.-11 p.m., Sat. 5 p.m.-11 p.m., Sun. 4 p.m.-9 p.m. Crads: AE, MC, V.

Sabal's
315 Main St.,
Dunedin
• (813) 734-3463
CALIFORNIAN/
CONTINENTAL

11/20

A good example of the nice-things-in-small-packages cliché, this tiny restaurant in downtown Dunedin (north of Clearwater near Clearwater Bay) boasts a small-town air and a winning eccentricity. Depression-era plates, a charmingly mismatched decor and recorded classic jazz set the mood in the intimate-in-the-extreme interior—the front door opens directly into the dining room, which is unnerving when you realize you've interrupted someone's dinner. But after a short while, the music, the food and the friendly staff dissipate any claustrophobic tension. The cooking style is officially Californian, though it occasionally strays toward Continental (pardon me, but is that goat cheese on your escargots?). Some sort of bread with character—perhaps pumpkin—starts things off while you inspect the nightly changing menu. The inventive salads run to such combinations as green apple with blue cheese or hearts of palm with pine nuts and raisins. Successful main courses have included pork tenderloin with blackberry sauce, Edam and walnuts; crab-stuffed shrimp in an herb-cheese sauce; and scallops in a sauce of Brie and spinach. Sabal's has had its ups and downs over the

years, but a fresh look and an updated menu have it heading up again. With wine, dinner for two is about $65.
Open Tues.-Thurs. & Sun. 6 p.m.-11 p.m., Sat. 6 p.m.-midnight. Cards: MC, V.

The Sea Grill
3253 State Rd. 584,
Palm Harbor
• (813) 787-6129
SEAFOOD

10/20

This kitchen is so versatile at dressing seafood that the chef must have a degree in fashion. Consider the fresh grouper, a mild-flavored, firm-fleshed fish that is a Florida staple (it's so popular, the state had to slow its harvesting). Chefs are fond of it because, like veal, it tends to reflect the treatment it is given. And this kitchen treats its grouper like pampered nineteenth-century French ladies, dressing it in ornate sauces. Grouper Oscar is a sautéed filet wearing a coat of asparagus spears, blue crab and béarnaise. Grouper Roberto rests atop fresh spinach and below an earthy sauce of mushrooms, olive oil and wine. Court-bouillon grouper, poached in a Creole sauce, displays a sweet tang of honey and orange. The chalkboard menu offers other types of fish dressed similarly, and there are also concessions to beef and pasta lovers. Classic soups, attractively presented salads and American desserts round out the dinner offerings. The wine list is composed of a collection of mounted labels, a helpful touch that often allows you to discover more about a wine than its varietal and vintage. Recessed lighting and modern art lend sophistication to the storefront dining room. Large portions, careful preparation and fresh ingredients make The Sea Grill a good dinner choice in suburban Pinellas County. Dinner for two, with wine, runs about $60.
Open Mon.-Thurs. 5 p.m.-10 p.m., Fri.-Sat. 5 p.m.-11 p.m. Cards: AE, MC, V.

HOTELS

Moderate (From $100)

The Don CeSar Registry Resort
3400 Gulf Blvd.,
St. Petersburg Beach
33706
• (813) 360-1881
Fax (813) 360-1881,
ext. 584

Things just don't get any pinker than this. If you're having trouble finding the Don CeSar as you travel north along the causeway-connected barrier islands mirroring Florida's West Coast, just keep your eye out for the color pink. With fine, whimsical, Old Florida panache, it is slathered from floor to ceiling across the hotel, which even were it not dressed in such an obvious color would present itself with storybook architecture—a cross between Mad King Ludwig's castle and The Alhambra. Recently renovated by the new owners, Registry Resorts, a very sharp group of hoteliers that also operates the Registry in neighboring Naples, the Don CeSar matches the promise of its architecture with the promise of a storybook

vacation along Saint Pete Beach. The Thomas Rowe–built hotel, originally completed at the turn of the century, now boasts 277 newly decorated rooms and suites, each promising a Gulf view, two fine restaurants and a festive poolside bar and grill. Although there is no golf course on the grounds, the concierge happily arranges tee-times at neighboring courses. There are plenty of water sports available off the pristine beach, and shuttles depart the lobby regularly for shopping and sight-seeing forays.
Singles & doubles: $115-$215.

Practical (Under $100)

Belleview MIDO Resort Hotel
125 Belleview Blvd.,
Belleair Beach 34616
• (813) 442-6171
Fax (813) 443-6361

One of only two of the fabulous, turn-of-the-century Florida grande dames still currently in operation along the west coast, the Belleview Biltmore, now the Belleview MIDO, was orginally built in 1897 by railroad baron Henry Plant. The Japanese MIDO Development Co. bought it in 1990. Perched on a picturesque bluff overlooking the Gulf of Mexico, the newly renovated spot is *the* place to spend a weekend in the Saint Petersburg area. Still peppered with majestic pines and oaks, the 365-room property, unlike many hotels of its era, never burned down, due to what was then a revolutionary fire proofing procedure. It remains the largest occupied wood structure in the world. Used as Air Force barracks during World War II, the hotel was vacant for several years before being restored to former glory. Featuring Victorian antiques and Queen Anne decor, the hotel offers guided walking tours of the grand old resort daily at 11 a.m.—you may decide to check in afterward! If the lodging itself doesn't convince you, the relatively new spa facilities will.
Singles: $65-$165; doubles: $80-$180.

Tradewinds on Saint Petersburg Beach
5500 Gulf Blvd.,
St. Petersburg Beach 33706
• (813) 367-6461
Fax (813) 367-7496

Like Saint Petersburg Beach itself, Tradewinds is trying to make everybody happy all the time. There's the beach, the thirteen acres of lush landscaping (including a life-size chess set and croquet lawns), the five pools (one enclosed), the fitness center. But in Florida's good-times-for-one-and-all resorts, these outdoor celebrations are little more than standard. So Tradewinds figured out the extra mile, and went it. For families, there's a summer camp for kids: while counselors conduct Laff-A-Lympics, Pilo-Polo and parachute play, parents are shuffled off to shopping forays and museum visits in downtown Saint Pete. For newlyweds, there's a white latticework gazebo designed exclu-

sively for weddings and romantic dinners. And for just about everybody, there's the Tradewinds trademark: the gondolas. Come dinnertime, the Tradewinds Waterway, which wraps itself around the property from Palm Lagoon to Picnic Island, bustles like downtown Venice, with boatmen whisking guests to the waterfront Palm Court restaurant. Accomodations in one-, two- and three-bedroom suites with fully equipped kitchens make you feel like you're visiting friends; even the hotel rooms though, offer wet bars with refrigerators and toasters, which help save a few bucks during a visit.
Singles & doubles: $82-$199.

SHOPS

Antiques

Antique Alley
560-596 Indian Rocks Rd.,
Belleair Bluffs
• (813) 585-7242

Although it's tucked back off the beaten path, Antique Alley is worth a stop when you're driving through the Clearwater area. This section of Indian Rocks Road offers an abundance of antique shops; Antique Alley is made up of fifteen of them fanning north from West Bay Drive. The cluster takes on a festive ambience during its bi-annual shows (held in November and March).
Open Mon.-Sat. 10 a.m.-4 p.m

Gas Plant Antique Arcade
1246 Central Ave.,
St. Petersburg
• (813) 895-0368

With more than 70 dealers under one roof, Gas Plant offers more than 32,000 square feet of collectibles and antiques under one air-conditioned (an important adjective in these parts in the summertime) roof. What looks like a warehouse from the outside becomes a veritable antiques shopping mall once you get inside. With this many dealers, prices are nice and competive (if only with one another!)
Open Mon.-Sat. 10 a.m.-5 p.m., Sun. noon-5 p.m.

Clothes

Spencer's Western World
7108 66th St. North,
St. Petersburg
• (813) 544-2606

1894 Drews St.,
Clearwater
• (813) 447-2606

If your closet is crying out for a new Stetson, bullwhip, set of spurs of $695 pair of snakeskin boots, head out to Spencer's. With two locations, Spencer's offers, hands down, the largest selection of western wear on Florida's West Coast. And, they just love tourists: show them a room key from a local hotel, and they'll throw in a $10 discount as a welcome-to-town gift, if you buy a pair of boots, pardner.
Open Mon.-Sat. 10 a.m.-9 p.m., Sun. 10 a.m.-6 p.m.

SIGHTS

Arts & Museums

Back in the Woods Gallery
242 Beach Dr.,
St. Petersburg
• (813) 821-7999

Located just across the street from the Saint Petersburg Museum of Art, Back in the Woods offers a wonderful selection of art for wildlife enthusiasts. Specializing in signed and numbered prints, many from the Lowell Davis Collection of R.F.D. America. There are also plenty of books, tapes and stationery, plus gift items featuring our local fuzzy friends.
Open Wed.-Sun. 11 a.m.-5 p.m.

Salvador Dalí Museum
1000 3rd St. South,
St. Petersburg
• (813) 823-3767

Dalí was one of the twentieth century's most compelling figures, and the museum dedicated to his works is Saint Petersburg's most compelling attraction. It presents what is undoubtedly one of Florida's most extensive art collections. The museum, an unassuming pink building featuring the clean lines of modern architecture, overlooks the waterfront. Inside the museum (1000 3rd St. South; 813-823-3767) await no less than 93 Dalí oils, 200 watercolors and drawings, 1,000 graphics, sculptures and posters—plus photographs of Dalí and a 2,500-volume library with an extensive clip file of pieces written about the artists around the world. Most of these items were donated by A. Reynolds and Eleanor R. Morse, who began collecting Dalí's works in 1942. Touted as the largest display of Dalí outside Europe, the collection is so large that displays are rotated. Dalí is perhaps best known for his surrealist works created between 1927 and 1939, when his haunting imagery and dreamlike landscapes made him the toast of Paris. The Morse collection is important not only because of its sheer size, but also because it offers a clear retrospective of Dalí.
Open Mon. noon-5 p.m., Christmas through Easter only. Tues.-Sat. 10 a.m.-5 p.m., Sun. noon-5 p.m.

Excursions

Caladesi Island Ferry Service
West End of State Rd. 586,
Dunedin
• (813) 734-5263

Though they were once linked to one another by a narrow strip of sand, neither Honeymoon Island nor Caladesi Island is connected to the mainland by the bridge systems connecting the rest of the barrier islands that make up the lovely Pinellas Sun Coast. Caladesi therefore retains its pristine beauty and appealing remoteness, with 1,000 acres of little-explored scrub on the bay side of the island and three miles of nearly private white beaches on the Gulf side. This must be what it was like for Gilligan and the gang. Even on the busiest beach days, regulations limit the maximum number of visitors to the island to 850. A concession on the island offers drinks and sandwiches, and an Indian burial site (excavated earlier this century) is evidence of the island's history. Ferry service also links Caladesi with Honeymoon Island, which derives its name from an interesting history: in 1939, a New York developer purchased the island for $3,000, building 50 palm-thatched bungalows—for which he advertised free two-week honeymoons in the pages of *Life* magazine to contest winners. Some 167 newlyweds honeymooned here, and the resort thrived until World War II, when vacations here became a national security risk. The cottages were destroyed gradually by storms and beach erosion and the government banned further development on the island in 1970.

Ferry service departs hourly Mon.-Sat. 10 a.m.-5 p.m., Sun. & holidays 10 a.m.-6 p.m. Adults $4, children 3-12 $2.50. Additional service from the downtown Clearwater Marina.

Sponge Docks at Tarpon Springs
Dodacanese Blvd. at Alt. U.S. 19,
Tarpon Springs
• No phone

Although it's a bit of a drive north along the coast from Tampa and Saint Petersburg, Tarpon Springs makes for a fun day trip. At the Mediterranean-style sponging village, we recently heard greetings exchanged in Greek along the main street, Dodecanese Boulevard. Founded by 26-year-old Peloponnesian John Corcoris in 1895, Tarpon Springs was the world's sponge capital for nearly 40 years, until the "Red Tide" killed its trade. The sponge beds were regenerated in the 1950s and today, you can pick from baskets of sponges, watch the local sponge fleet come into port after a day's diving, and sample some good food offered throughout the warm, inviting streets of Tarpon Springs.

Open daily 10 a.m.-5 p.m.

Landmarks

The Pier
2nd Ave. N.E. at Beach Dr.,
St. Petersburg
• (813) 821-6164

Jutting out nearly a half mile into Saint Petersburg's bayfront is The Pier, a colorful, five-story, structure shaped like an inverted pyramid, that is Saint Pete's most vivid landmark. Recently renovated, The Pier offers not only a variety of shops and a crafts pavilion, but also dining and watersports (equipment rental of all kinds is available). Trolley rides depart from stops along the pier and tour the city; on the second floor of The Pier, an aquarium exhibits houses tropical fish, sharks and invertebrates—some of them encased in glass columns that reach up toward the ceiling.

Open Mon.-Sat. 10 a.m.-9 p.m., Sun. 11 a.m.-6 p.m.

SARASOTA

RESTAURANTS	300
HOTELS	305
SHOPS	306
SIGHTS	307

RESTAURANTS

L'Auberge du Bon Vivant
7003 Gulf of Mexico Dr.,
Longboat Key
• (813) 383-2421
FRENCH/CONTINENTAL

12/20

L'Auberge du Bon Vivant lingers deliciously in memory, long after the bittersweet flavor of its chocolate mousse has faded. More than just intimate, it is enchanting. In the shadows of candlelit tables, indoor vines overtake the windows; the decor is dignified, from the formal table settings to the soft lighting and fresh flowers. You might feel like you've unwittingly stumbled into a private bungalow that happens to be blessed with a skilled in-house chef. You'll understand our enthusiasm for this place when you realize that good French food is as rare in west-central Florida as a blizzard in a Florida summer. The chef has a way with liqueurs, carefully flavoring many of his best dishes with them: duck pâté with Cointreau, roast duckling with Curaçao, peppered steak with Cognac. House specialties include grilled rack of lamb, New York strip steak with a green-peppercorn sauce and veal sweetbreads that are first sautéed, then braised with port, mushrooms and sour cream, and finally encased in puff pastry. All these good things are prepared under the supervision of the owners, Judy and Michael Zouhar and Madeleine and Francis Hatton, who select their own seafood and produce from the market each day for their chef. They also keep a watchful eye on the dining room, where the service sometimes seems psychic—the waiters pace meals perfectly and treat each table as if the evening was special. And, in fact, an evening at L'Auberge du Bon Vivant—the Inn of Good Living—is quite special. Plan on spending about $100 for dinner for two, with a bottle from the extensive wine list.
Open Mon.-Sat. 5 p.m.-10 p.m. All major cards.

Beach Bistro
6600 Gulf Dr.,
Holmes Beach,
Anna Maria Island
• (813) 778-6444
CONTINENTAL

11/20

Sea foam and Champagne cocktails, fish schools and salmon fettuccine, syrupy sunsets and chocolate terrines—nature's beauty and the kitchen's bounty join forces in this tiny dining room on Anna Maria Island, whose huge picture windows put you almost atop the ocean. Ask for a window table and the mesmerizing Gulf of Mexico will make it hard for you to pay any attention to your food, which is worth a bit of attention. There's some ambition in the kitchen: whole chunks of snapper fill a tasty chowder, and the edible garnishes on the dinner plates—carved wedges of ratatouille-stuffed zucchini, for instance—resemble culinary-school final exams. The waterfront setting is reflected in the daily-changing fish specials, most of which are pretty elaborate: a swordfish might arrive swimming in a pool of orange sauce and sprinkled with delicate strands of rind. In fact, everything here is elaborate, sometimes too much so—the piquant hunter's sauce and creamy béarnaise on the filet Charlemagne are nice enough, but together it's overkill. The best way for two or more to handle dessert is to order the chocolate-truffle terrine and the praline Alexandra and share, alternating bites of chocolate with the homemade praline and ice cream. On the other hand, if you're heading to the gorgeous nearby beaches the next day, you'd better skip dessert. Dinner for two, with wine, runs about $100.
Open Sun.-Thurs. 5:30 p.m.-9:30 p.m., Fri.-Sat. 5:30 p.m.-10 p.m. Cards: DC, MC, V.

Bijou Café
1287 1st St.,
Sarasota
• (813) 366-8111
AMERICAN

11/20

Where better to fill up than at a converted 1920s gas station? If the Bijou were dispensing fuel these days, it would certainly be high-octane—ingredients are fresh, presentations are attractive, and the short menu is well prepared. You can sit either inside, in a plain decor among a chattering crowd, or outside on the patio, where candlelight adds a sense of intimacy. The Bijou's proximity to the theater district makes it a popular preshow stop for a drink and a light meal of appetizers. Try the pâté—(large enough to share with Goliath), made with duck, chicken livers, Cognac and spices and served with toast and fruit—and the crunchy crabcakes rémoulade, complemented with chopped beefsteak tomatoes. If you decide to skip the opera and stay for entrées, order the roast duck with a subtle fruit stuffing or the spinach ravioli smothered in a tomato-basil-cream sauce. The relaxed setting and cheerful, professional service will make you feel like a guest in a private home. Two will spend about $70 for dinner with wine.
Open Mon.-Thurs. 11:30 a.m.-2 p.m. & 5:30 p.m.-10 p.m., Fri. 11:30 a.m.-2 p.m. & 5:30 p.m.-10:30 p.m., Sat. 5:30 p.m.-10:30 p.m. Cards: DC, MC, V.

Café L'Europe

431 St. Armands Circle,
St. Armands Key,
Sarasota
• (813) 388-4415
CONTINENTAL

[13]

This is a great place to dine if you need to spend a lot of money fast—particularly if you explore the posh boutiques in the surrounding Saint Armands Circle shopping district before dinner. (In fact, you'll probably notice shopping bags resting in the unoccupied chairs at many of the tables.) Not much is new or daring about Café L'Europe, but much is enticing, starting with the warmly appointed interior (notable for its nooks and crannies, woodwork, brick walls, flowers and views of Saint Armands), a soothing haven after a grueling day wearing out the charge cards. Just save enough credit to cover the meal: a plain salad will cost you $6, and the extensive wine list tops out at $595 for a Château Margaux 1929. But we won't quibble over cost—besides, the creamy goose-liver pâté edged with chopped nuts and the appetizer of tender duck with lingonberry preserves are worth taking out a second mortgage. In fact, starters are the kitchen's strong suit; a wonderful dinner could be composed of an array of soups, salads and appetizers. The salads are particularly notable for their intriguing blends of taste and texture, as with the salad of smoked mozzarella, crunchy endive and zesty bits of tomato. If you're hidebound to the main-course tradition, you won't go wrong with the duck in a black-cherry and Cognac sauce, chicken in a curry sauce or tender lamb in a mustard sauce. Service is professional but subject to occasional forgetfulness. Dinner for two, with wine, will set you back about $125. As for the shopping, you're on your own.

Open Mon.-Sat. 11 a.m.-11 p.m., Sun. 6 p.m.-10 p.m. All major cards.

The Colony Restaurant

The Colony Beach &
Tennis Resort,
1620 Gulf of Mexico Dr.,
Longboat Key
• (813) 383-5558
AMERICAN

[13]

Surf and serves are the big draws at the famed Colony Beach and Tennis Resort, but if it were located in the middle of a barren desert, The Colony Restaurant could still draw a crowd. True, the waiters can be a bit stiff, but they're probably just wishing they were out in the sun. Huge windows on three sides of the sprawling dining room bring in an captivating view of the Gulf of Mexico. This is no intimate café—it's a full-scale resort restaurant accustomed to feeding the multitudes all day long. That's why it's especially pleasing to see such care taken with each dish. The lump-crabmeat ravioli, for instance, is positively dainty, resting beneath a light blanket of beurre blanc; the pheasant consommé en croûte is equally delicate. Rest assured that the tomatoes are vine ripened as promised, and order one of the seven salads with confidence. Nearly every variety of meat, poultry and fish can be found on the huge menu, from flavorful roast rack of lamb with tarragon-garlic sauce, to duck with currants and cream, to dull, mushy sautéed lobster and sea

scallops in an americaine sauce. The wine list is predictably massive. None of this comes cheap, of course, but no one comes to this acclaimed resort to save money. The budget-conscious should visit for Sunday brunch or a weekday lunch, when the view and food are just as delicious but prices much lower. Otherwise, dinner for two, with wine, may reach $150.
Open Mon.-Sat. 8 a.m.-11 a.m., noon-2:30 p.m. & 6 p.m.-10 p.m., Sun. 10 a.m.-2 p.m. & 6 p.m.-10 p.m. All major cards.

Harry's Continental Kitchens
525 St. Judes Dr., Longboat Key
• (813) 383-0777
AMERICAN

10/20

Even when this place was a deli, it was a hit. College students popped in for shrimp salads and cold pasta and then spread blankets at the public beach. The deli's still there, tucked behind a convenience store along Longboat Key's main drag, but now there's also a full-fledged dining room in back. When the restaurant opened, beachgoers were joined by the affluent retirees who populate this island. Today, plaid trousers complement the casual, garden-style dining room, a collection of wrought-iron furnishings and patio greenery. And today, the food is aimed at those who would rather eat such grown-up treats as Nova Scotia smoked salmon than student cheeseburgers. Mere toast tips would be an insult to the carefully constructed timbale—a shell of salmon stuffed with salmon mousse—so bagel slices are provided for spreading. Harry's cooking goes beyond that of the typical beachside restaurant, where customers seldom complain as long as the view's good. Maybe it's the lack of a view that makes the kitchen try harder. In any event, when you sample such inventive dishes as the quesadilla filled with black beans (usually found over yellow rice in these parts) and topped with avocado, salsa and sour cream, you'll agree that the food outclasses the atmosphere. Though limited, the wine selection is interesting. Dinner for two, with wine, runs about $100.
Open daily 11 a.m.-3 p.m. & 5 p.m.-10 p.m. Cards: MC, V.

Michael's on East
1212 East Ave. South, Sarasota
• (813) 366-0007
AMERICAN

12/20

Devotees of light, health-conscious contemporary American food will be delighted to find this place, an oasis in the land of cream sauces upon cream sauces. The flavors are as fresh and invigorating as the decor, a crisp, high-tech room filled with well-heeled diners and competent waiters. Typical of the kitchen is its update on the classic blini. Instead of buckwheat flour, the pancake is made of cornmeal and sweet red pepper; it's set on a pool of crème fraîche instead of topped with the usual sour cream, and it's accompanied by a wreath of julienned vegetables as well as the customary caviar. A dozen or more menu items

carry low-fat, low-sodium and low-calorie designations, and sauces are kept light, with lots of fresh herbs to spark flavors. But don't expect boring diet food. The basic house salad is enlivened with crumbled blue cheese and seasoned nuts. The grilled pork loin may be labeled low-cal, but its maple-mustard glaze bursts with good flavors. Pasta lovers can try fettuccine with fresh seafood in a light pesto-cream sauce; carnivores will like the steak in a mustard-brandy demi-glace. And those who appreciate the healthful qualities of wine will make good use of the well-chosen list, which offers sixteen selections by the glass. Cognacs, ports and cordials round out the dessert list (as if the triple fantasy pecan tart needs any help). Late-nighters should call before stopping in, since it sometimes closes earlier than the official hours. Dinner for two, including wine, runs about $110.
Open Mon. 11:30 a.m.-2 p.m. & 5 p.m.-9 p.m., Tues.-Fri. 11:30 a.m.-2 p.m. & 5 p.m.-11:30 p.m., Sat. 5 p.m.-11:30 p.m., Sun. 5 p.m.-9:30 p.m. All major cards.

Ristorante Bellini

1551 Main St., Sarasota
• (813) 365-7380
ITALIAN

10/20

Named for nineteenth-century Italian composer Vincenzo Bellini, this downtown place seldom misses a beat. The modern storefront dining room sits amid a row of secondhand shops, so it's appropriate that the kitchen sticks to the old favorites. Linguines, fettuccines and veal scaloppines have the run of the menu, along with such basics as Caesar salad and minestrone soup. All of them are nicely done. Well, almost all—order wrong and the waiter will probably let you know. Such conscientious service permeates a meal here: the maître d' keeps an eye on everything, the water server won't let you go thirsty, and you'll never wait long for food. Good starters include the carpaccio, shavings of tender raw beef drizzled with lemon juice, olive oil and Parmesan, and the antipasti from the daily-changing display near the entry. Take a look at the array when you enter, let the waiter know what you'd like, and he'll put together an assortment for you. Soups of the day might include a potato purée or broccoli with sour cream. In fact, we're so fond of the appetizers that we prefer to order a few and skip the richly sauced entrées altogether, though we are fond of the pollo allo Champagne, a breast of chicken with sweet peas and a Champagne-cream sauce. Just don't eat so many appetizers that you don't have room for dessert—the tiramisu (lady fingers soaked in espresso and topped with cocoa) is worth saving room for. With wine, dinner for two may near $75.
Open Mon.-Fri. 11:30 a.m.-2 p.m. & 6 p.m.-10 p.m., Sat. 6 p.m.-10 p.m. Cards: MC, V.

HOTELS

Top of the Line (From $200)

The Colony Beach & Tennis Resort
1620 Gulf of Mexico Dr.,
Longboat Key 34228
• (813) 383-6464,
(800) 237-9443,
Fax (813) 383-7549

The folks at the Colony don't ever want you to leave their paradisial resort on Longboat Key, a twelve-mile-long barrier island stretching northward from Saint Armands Key. They go about ensuring your undying allegiance by providing a quarter mile of some of the whitest sand in the world, an enchanting view of the Gulf, 21 tennis courts with twelve USPTA pros and a variety of lessons and clinics (for which the resort is chiefly known), a tennis shop, a full fitness center and spa, exercise classes, pampering spa treatments, a beachside swimming pool, a gourmet deli and market, a creative children's program and the very good Colony Restaurant (*see* page 302), that serves up fresh American cuisine that's worth sticking around for. The all-suite resort sprawls over eighteen acres, with accommodations spaced widely apart. Each spacious suite boasts a bedroom, dining area, full kitchen, whirlpool, steamroom and balcony; tropical flowers are placed around the interior. If you'd like your room stocked with fresh fruits and other grocery goodies, the staff will gladly oblige. This all costs, but if it's hard to pay, it's harder to leave.
1-bedroom: $205-$285; 2-bedrooms: $280-$395; Lanai & Clubhouse suites: $415-$450; Penthouse suite: $775-$800.

Moderate (From $100)

Harrington House
5626 Gulf Dr.,
Holmes Beach 34217
• (813) 778-5444
No fax

Anna Maria island, the northernmost (and loveliest) of the barrier islands mirroring Florida's Central West Coast, was originally settled in 1912. One of the first settlers was Charles Roser, a baker from Ohio who made a mint when he sold a creation called the Fig Newton to Nabisco. (The City Pier that Roser constructed and his original Pine Avenue beach cottage look just about the same as they did before Tropical Storm Keith swept through Manatee County in 1988). Harrington House, where legend has it the most famous hatmaker of the 1940s, Lily Daché, stayed, is now a charming bed-and-breakfast in the middle of Anna Maria Island. Each room offers a different ambience; the home is shaded by green awnings and encircled by a whitewashed widow's walk. Nothing fancy here, just dolphins playing in the surf (we saw them more than once), pretty rooms, plenty of hospitality and a dependably wonderful breakfast served daily in a flower-filled, poolside breakfast room.
Doubles: $95-$125.

Longboat Key Club

301 Gulf of Mexico Dr.,
Longboat Key 34228
• (813) 338-8821
Fax (813) 282-0113

The beaches of Longboat Key, the "Park Avenue of Sarasota," flanked by the Gulf of Mexico and Saint Armand's Bay, are surely among the world's most brilliant. (In fact, they recently placed high up in a "World's Whitest Sands" contest, judged by a Harvard geologist). The extraordinary Longboat Key club offers rooms with private balconies to celebrate all this private whiteness, as well as a golf course, eighteen Har-Tru tennis courts, bike rental and plenty of watersports. Most of the 222 condominium suites have full kitchens, washer and dryers, all of which tempt you to settle in and stay a while.
Singles & doubles: $115-$450.

Practical (Under $100)

Longboat Key Hilton

4711 Gulf of Mexico Dr.,
Longboat Key 34228
• (813) 383-2451
Fax (813) 383-7979

Do beaches get any whiter than this? Does water get any bluer? We suspect not. Legend has it that this barrier island was named for the remains of a wooden longboat, abandoned by Spanish explorer Hernando DeSoto in the sixteenth century, and later uncovered here. We've decided that he must have paddled in and sent everybody else back to the motherland. The Hilton makes staying here more affordable than some of the luxury resorts and even the sprawling condominiums nearby that are available for rental. An advantage over the latter lodging is that the Hilton offers plenty to do on property, from its swimming pool, beachfront tennis court and pool bar to shopping shuttles down to Saint Armand's circle.
Singles & doubles: $85-$160; suites: $145-$280.

SHOPS

Clothes & Jewelry

Beach Stuff and More

5600 Marina Dr.,
Holmes Beach
• (813) 778-5494

With a colorful inventory of rafts and floats outside the shop itself, Beach Stuff isn't hard to find. T-shirts, jewelry, gifts and beachwear are also for sale, as well as five sizes of small boats for wave riding.
Open Mon.-Fri. 9 a.m.-4 p.m., Sat.-Sun. 9 a.m.-6 p.m.

Sterling Anvil

5341 Gulf Dr.,
Holmes Beach
• (813) 778-3636

On an off-the-beaten-track little barrier island, where we've found family-owned groceries more often than commercial boulevard fast-food joints, the Sterling Anvil is the type of surprise you may expect to stumble upon. Featuring a wide variety of original, handcrafted sterling, this shop is worth a drive along one of Florida's most beautiful, least traveled beaches to reach.
Open Mon.-Sat. 9:30 a.m.-5 p.m.

SIGHTS

Arts & Museums

Asolo State Theater
John & Mable Ringling Museum of Art,
5401 Bayshore Rd.,
Sarasota
• (813) 351-8000

The Asolo is by far the most acclaimed theater in the state of Florida. At the front of the John & Mable Ringling Museum complex, the Asolo Theater, said to be the only authentic eighteenth century Italian theater in the United States, was originally built in 1728. John Ringling had it dismantled piece by piece and restored to its original horseshoe shape in 1950, when he had it moved to its present site. In 1965, the Florida Legislature named the Asolo an official State Theater; it now houses the Asolo/Florida State University Conservatory of Professional Training, which offers a two-year program culminating in a Master of Fine Arts. Recently, some ornate interior plaster work from the Dunfermline Opera House in Scotland was added to the "new" Asolo—located at the northeast corner of the Ringling Museum complex—offering a mix of European influences, improved acoustics and additional seating.
Performances Nov.-July. Curtain 8:15 p.m. Call for schedule.

John & Mable Ringling Museum of Art
5401 Bay Shore Rd.,
Sarasota
• (813) 355-5101

By far the most fascinating arts complex in Florida—if not the entire Southeast United States—the John & Mable Ringling Museum is an ensemble of structures. To use the term "museum" is an understatement: the complex is comprised of art galleries, the winter home of John and Mable Ringling (the wacky Ca' d'Zan, "House of John," with architectural features borrowed from such divergent spots as one of the Gothic Doges' Palaces in Venice and the tower of the old Madison Square Garden in New York City), the Asolo State Theater, Circus Galleries and 66 acres of manicured lawns and gardens, all situated along Sarasota's magnificent bayfront. Ringling and his wife collected for their dream museum between 1924 and 1931, gathering important works by Rubens and Van Dyck, as well as other major artists from the Renaissance and Baroque periods. The restored Rubens Gallery anchors a massive modernization program recently completed at the smashing complex. That, plus North Galleries One through Six, show off newly rediscovered architectural detail (revealed accidentally during the recent restorations), including carved, gilt-wood panels. The Old Master collection comprises the museum's most impressive holdings—approximately 750 of them, in paintings, prints, drawings and sculptures.
Open Mon.-Wed. & Fri.-Sun. 10 a.m.-6 p.m, Thurs. 10 a.m.-10 p.m. Adults $8.50, children $1.75. Admission free Sat.

South Florida Museum and Bishop Planetarium
201 W. 10th St., Bradenton
• (813) 746-4131

A complex of displays set up around a shady courtyard, the South Florida Museum salutes the state's rich past, which began here in the sixteenth century with the arrival of the explorer's expedition. The DeSoto Museum remembers the conquistador with all sorts of artifacts, many of them donated by Bradenton's sister city, Barcarrota, Spain. A re-created Spanish Manor House is typical of DeSoto's day; on display in the museum is a replica of the world map that the explorer's compatriots hand-drew, revealing perplexed sixteenth-century European views of the mysterious New World. Also on hand is "Snooty," a 42-year-old manatee (an aquatic mammal resembling a sea lion with a broad, pudgy nose), who, raised in captivity, lives on hand-fed carrots and lettuce, offered before a delighted crowd several times daily. (To give credit where it's due, it was Ponce de León who provided us with the first written reference to the manatee in 1513.)

Open Tues.-Fri. 10 a.m.-5 p.m., Sat.-Sun. 1 p.m.-5 p.m. Adults $3, children $2.

Van Wezel Performing Arts Center
777 N. Tamiami Trail, Sarasota
• (813) 953-3366

The Van Wezel is one of those rare architectural creations that, like the Sydney Opera House, for example, literally defines a city's waterfront. An enormous pink shell opening toward the bay, the Van Wezel Performing Arts Center was designed by the Frank Lloyd Wright Foundation, hosting over the years such greats as Beverly Sill, Duke Ellington and Victor Borge. The venue also regularly welcomes the Florida West Coast Symphony and the Florida Symphonic Band; each April, the Jazz Club of Sarasota hosts a Jazz Festival at the venue.

Hosting more than 90 performances annually; schedules vary.

Gardens

Marie Selby Botanical Gardens
S. Palm Ave. at the waterfront, Sarasota
• (813) 366-5730

Settled in 1843 by homesteader Bill Whitaker, a soldier in the Second Seminole War who bought up more than a mile of Sarasota bayfront for $1.25 an acre, Sarasota still exudes plenty of antebellum charm with its splendid bayfront homes and flower filled neighborhoods. Today, nestled on a mainland sidestreet just south of the John Ringling Causeway, the presence of that earlier natural state is keenly felt at Marie Selby Botanical Gardens. The facility features one of the world's best-known orchid gardens within a magnificent bayside settling. More than 20,000 tropical plants, plus an excellent Museum of Botany and the Arts, is complemented by a narrated visitor slide show. Also a research facility, the lush grounds offer fifteen garden display areas, include the award-winning Hibiscus Garden.

Open daily 10 a.m.-5 p.m. Adults $5, children under 12 free.

Landmarks

DeSoto National Memorial
75th St.,
Palma Sola
• (813) 792-0458

Spanish explorer Hernando DeSoto's expedition arrived at Shaw Point in 1539, and he is today commemorated at the DeSoto National Memorial Park, some five miles west of downtown Bradenton. A visit here is nothing short of eery: a nature trail is shaded by some of the very same plants and trees that the Spaniards and Indians survived on. Running along the banks of the Manatee River, the trail encircles a mangrove jungle, ending at the ruins of a "tabby house," part of one of the first white settlements in Florida dating from the early 1800s. Other attractions along the trail include the DeSoto Monument, a re-creation of DeSoto's original campsite at Camp Ucita, and a visitor's center. The park offers tremendous insight into life in this region in DeSoto's era with park employees—costumed in sixteenth-century garb during the winter season—lecturing groups and demonstrating weapons and food preparations of the time.
Open daily 8 a.m.-5:30 p.m. Admission $1.

Gamble Plantation
3708 Patten Ave.,
Ellenton
• (813) 722-1017

Beneath graceful live oaks at Ellenton sits a plantation teeming with the ghosts of a colorful past. It is the former home of Virginian Major Robert Gamble, who settled in Manatee County in 1844. Civil War blockade runner Captain Archibald McNeill bought the home after the war ended. With a price on his head, family friend Judah P. Benjamin, Secretary of State of the Confederacy, hid out for three days in the mansion before his escape to England. There, Benjamin later become legal counsel to Queen Victoria. Although Union marauders burned the 3,500-acre plantation's sugar mill after the Civil War, and only a china plate is left of the original Gamble Plantation appointments, the home was left intact. On the bucolic grounds, you may stroll thrugh the ruins of a sugar mill; inside the antebellum plantation there's a fourteen-pound iron, a fat feather bed and a dining room table set for an antebellum feast.
Open daily 9 a.m.-5 p.m.; tours depart hourly. Admission $1.

St. Armands Circle
John Ringling Blvd. at
Blvd. of the Presidents,
Sarasosta
• (813) 388-1554

Saint Armands Circle, designed more than 60 years ago by circus magnate John Ringling and today featuring some 140 galleries and boutiques, is one of the more novel places in the state to shop. Situated on island almost all its own, the Circle itself is marked by exotic plants and Italian statuary from Ringling's personal collection (including an ancient Roman general and Greco-Roman gods and goddesses). Surrounding the circle is the "Ring of Fame," a total of 36 plaques honoring famous circus performers throughout history.
Open daily; hours vary.

SHELL COAST

FORT MYERS	312
NAPLES	317
SANIBEL & CAPTIVA ISLANDS	329

FORT MYERS

RESTAURANTS	312
QUICK BITES	315
HOTELS	315
SHOPS	316
SIGHTS	316

RESTAURANTS

Flutes
Royal Palm Square
1400 Colonial Blvd.,
Fort Myers
• (813) 278-1600
AMERICAN/
CALIFORNIAN

12/20

Except for some waterfront establishments, picturesque restaurants are rare in these parts. Even rarer are places in which the cuisine is as winsome as the setting. Flutes is a blessed exception. It takes full advantage of the wealth of palms, tropical foliage and exotic birds that fill the courtyards in Royal Palm Square, Fort Myers's loveliest shopping center. Tables on the porch allow for meals under the sun or stars, and the small, colorful, contemporary dining room affords an unobstructed view of the lush courtyard and open kitchen. The kitchen is centered around a grill, which is put to excellent use in such dishes as grilled vegetable gazpacho, grilled soft-shell crabs and even grilled poppyseed cake (with vanilla ice cream and mango chunks). For balance, there are a variety of salads, such as the warm goat-cheese medallions with mixed greens and a piquant mango-chutney vinaigrette, and pastas, like the fettuccine with al dente vegetables and a basil-cream sauce. The good tastes will have you cleaning your plates, but save room for the homey desserts, particularly the Oreo cheesecake or the brownies with ice cream, Belgian chocolate sauce and fresh fruit. Two of the proprietors also own a wine shop nearby, which explains the rotating collection of unusual, albeit somewhat pricey, wines by the glass and the lengthy list of bottles. Dinner for two, with wine, runs about $85.
Open Mon.-Thurs. 11:30 a.m.-9:30 p.m., Fri.-Sat. 11:30 a.m.-10:30 p.m. Cards: AE, MC, V.

Peter's La Cuisine

2224 Bay St.,
Fort Myers
• (813) 332-2228
CONTINENTAL

14

From power lunches to romantic dinners, savvy locals hold their important meals at Peter's. It may not have a waterfront view (or a view of anything but the street, for that matter), but the interior is certainly easy on the eye, with its high ceiling, white linens, modern art, tall windows and well-dressed clientele. Besides, views would just distract you from Peter Schmid's terrific cooking. We've had many a memorable dinner here, including one that began with a suave, creamy lobster bisque, progressed to an inventive salad of brussel sprouts, walnuts and venison, and reached its peak with salmon grilled to smoky perfection, with a lightly crisped crust and flaky, juicy flesh. Schmid is a master at presentations—it must take him as long to arrange the accompanying vegetables as it does to cook the entrées, and the desserts are visual stunners. Our favorite is the white- and dark-chocolate mousses accompanied by fresh fruit and a fresh-fruit sauce, served on a black plate dusted with powdered sugar. Happily, the desserts taste as good as they look. Service is snappy, and the third-floor bar features live jazz several nights a week. Dinner for two, with wine, runs about $120.
Open Mon.-Fri. 11:30 a.m.-2 p.m. & 5:30 p.m.-9:30 p.m., Sat. 5:30 p.m.-9:30 p.m. All major cards.

The Prawn Broker

13451-16 McGregor Blvd.,
Fort Myers
• (813) 489-2226
SEAFOOD

11/20

Seafood is the bait the Prawn Broker uses to lure diners—and its daily customer catch is consistently impressive. These crowds aren't interested in cutting-edge cuisine, just plenty of fresh, carefully cooked local seafood, plus a few species from afar. Worthy starters include the oysters Romanoff (plump and fresh enough to stand up to the sour cream, shallots and caviar on top), stone crab claws (in season), peel-and-eat shrimp and various kinds of smoked fish. Crustacean lovers will revel in the fresh local shrimp prepared a multitude of ways (beer-battered, almond-fried, skewered). Other good main-course bets include the platters of assorted seafood, either broiled or fried, and, for meat eaters, the flavorful grilled-to-order steaks. The large contemporary dining rooms, with their windows overlooking a charming cluster of shops, are usually crammed to capacity, making this a poor choice for couples seeking quiet and romance. But families, groups and those who don't mind a little chaos will love the tasty seafood, speedy service and reasonable prices. Those who enjoy cooking at home should take note of the retail fish market inside the restaurant. With wine, dinner for two costs about $75.
Open Mon.-Sat. 4:30 p.m.-10 p.m., Sun. 4:30 p.m.-9 p.m. All major cards.

Sangeet

Villas Plaza
U.S. 41 & Crystal Dr.,
Fort Myers
• (813) 278-0101
INDIAN

12/20

Those who fear Indian food for its notorious five-alarm spicing are missing out on one of the world's great culinary joys, rich with vivid, exciting (and not necessarily hot) flavors. Sangeet is an ideal spot for an introduction to Indian cooking; these people want nothing more than for you to enjoy your meal, and you'll be served fiery food only if you request it. In a handsome setting replete with evocative details—stained-glass windows, an ornate dark-wood bar, a window giving diners a view of the tandoor oven—you can sample a host of classic Indian dishes. The maharajah platter offers an assortment of assertively seasoned vegetable patties and chunks of savory tandoor-grilled chicken, all of which can be dipped in a creamy mint chutney or spicy-sweet tamarind sauce. Chicken à la pondicherry is the house specialty for good reason: boneless chicken is sautéed tableside with tomato chutney, garlic, nuts and a blend of spices, then set ablaze for drama. When you add fragrant basmati rice, fresh naan breads and such desserts as the fruit malabar (flambéed fresh fruits with a dash of cinnamon and rum, served over vanilla ice cream), you have a meal that's a sensory knock-out. Vegetarians, take note of the abundance of meatless dishes. Service is attentive, though the kitchen's cook-to-order policy makes for a lengthy dinner. For two, the lunch buffet, a spread of tasty dishes, costs $15; dinner with wine is about $85.
Open Tues.-Fri. 11:30 a.m.-2:30 p.m. & 5 p.m.-10 p.m., Sat.-Sun. 5 p.m.-10 p.m. All major cards.

Siam Hut

1873 Del Prado Blvd.,
Cape Coral
• (813) 772-3131
THAI

Wherever Thais have settled in the U.S., you'll find hordes of non-Thais whose passion for Thai food runs deep and strong. Fort Myers is one such place—and with Thai food this good, we understand the passion. Siam Hut serves some of the best Thai cooking we've had outside of Asia. The spice-shy can ask the accommodating waiters to have the food prepared mild, and it will be—but those who revel in the hot stuff can be reassured that the dishes that are labeled hot will blaze. Although the menu doesn't stray far from the Thai norm, the dishes are prepared with more delicacy and care than elsewhere, with attention paid to every detail, down to the ornately carved vegetables. Try the beef or chicken saté (small skewers of grilled meat served with peanut sauce and cucumber salad), the Siam rolls (crisp little egg rolls with a sweet-and-sour sauce) and the classic pad Thai (a tasty tangle of rice noodles, chicken, shrimp, bean sprouts, eggs, scallions and ground peanuts). This fresh, tasty food is enjoyed in a spotless dining room, where glass-topped tables are dotted with pink linen napkins artfully shaped into flowers. Dinner for two, with wine, is an affordable $35.
Open Mon.-Fri. 11:30 a.m.-3 p.m. & 5 p.m.-10 p.m., Sat. 5 p.m.-10 p.m. Cards: MC, V.

QUICK BITES

Miami Connection
11506 S. Cleveland Ave., Fort Myers
• (813) 936-3811

At this traditional kosher-style deli, the corned beef is tender and the bagels are baked daily. All the standards are here: smoked fish, pastrami, chewy rye bread, crisp dill pickles and rugalach (cream-cheese cookies), served by a cheerful staff in a coffee-shop/deli setting. Iconoclasts can try the bagel dog, a kosher hot dog encased in bagel dough. The sandwiches cost more than at other local delis, but the portions are large and the quality consistently high. Lunch for two, with sodas, is $14.
Open Mon.-Fri. 7 a.m.-6 p.m., Sat. 8 a.m.-5:30 p.m., Sun. 8 a.m.-3 p.m. No cards.

Plaka
1001 Estero Blvd., Fort Myers Beach
• (813) 463-4707

Plaka II
15271 McGregor Blvd., Fort Myers
• (813) 433-5404

The two Plaka restaurants are as close to authentic Greek tavernas as any that exist in Florida. Even though the newer one is located in the heart of a shopping center, it still feels Greek, thanks to its white walls, Greek pottery, tasty food—rich moussaka, garlicky gyros, large Greek salads, honey-soaked baklava—and low prices (not to mention belly dancing on weekends). The original Plaka serves the same good food on an open-air patio overlooking Fort Myers Beach, a prime people-watching spot. Dinner for two, with a carafe of wine, costs $40.
Open Mon.-Sat. 11 a.m.-10 p.m., Sun. 11 a.m.-9 p.m. Cards: MC, V.

HOTELS

Sonesta Sanibel Harbour Resort and Spa
17260 Harbour Pointe Dr., Fort Myers 33908
• (813) 466-4000
Fax (813) 466-2150

There are so many activities and events planned at Sonesta Sanibel that management leaves a pile of guidebooks and brochures in your room to be sure you won't miss anything. The 240-room property, at the entrance to the Sanibel Causeway, offers spectacular views of both San Carlos Bay and Sanibel Island, depending on where your room is located. The 100 two-bedroom condominium units are available for nightly rental, ideal for families and large parties (they sleep six). Each offers plenty of room to spread out, with a full kitchen, living room and dining room. Sonesta's advantage over the Captiva Island resorts is its proximity to neighboring Fort Myers, where an abundance of nightlife and attractions await. Still, this is one resort you won't want to leave. There's a tennis center, boating dock, fishing pier and fitness trail, as well as a fully equipped spa and fitness center, including three outdoor pools with Jacuzzis.
Doubles: $125-$175; suites: $250-$650; 2-bedroom condominiums: $225-$450.

SHOPS

Edison Mall
12 Cleveland Ave.,
Fort Myers
• (813) 939-5464

Call it just another suburban shopping mall with two main advantages: a layout that looks like a well-tended botanical garden and shops that stay open on Sunday, while the rest of Fort Myers turns into a ghost town. Though the shops of Fifth Avenue and Third Street South in neighboring Naples are certainly more elegant, in the summer months, even the most avid shopper will be yearning for a bit of good old-fashioned air-conditioning; Edison Mall has that—and 150 shops to boot.
Open Mon.-Sat. 10 a.m.-9 p.m., Sun. noon-5:30 p.m.

The Shell Factory
2787 N. Tamiami Trail,
North Fort Myers
• (813) 995-2141

When the people at The Shell Factory say "world's largest" anything, take them seriously. With some 65,000 square feet of gift items from around the world, this emporium offers far more than its name suggests. Having marked the Fort Myers landscape for more than 50 years, the shop indeed offers what very well could be the world's largest collection of shells and black, red and angelskin coral. On top of that, The Shell Factory vends pearls, resort wear, Mexican artifacts, gourmet Florida foods and other jewelry hewn from various sea creatures.
Open daily 10 a.m.-6 p.m.

SIGHTS

Barbara B. Mann Performing Arts Hall
8099 College Pkwy.,
Fort Myers
• (813) 489-3033

This fine-arts venue is where the touring company for various Broadway hits strut their stuff in Naples. True originality, in terms of local art, is in display in the lobby of the Performing Arts Hall, an elegant space curated by noted modern artist Robert Rauschenberg, whose crown achievement here is a magnificent twenty-foot-high glass chandelier.
Open Mon.-Fri. 10 a.m.-4 p.m.

Edison Winter Home
2350 McGregor Blvd.,
Fort Myers
• (813) 334-3614/
334-7419

If you're not sold on Florida's balmy weather by the time you get to the Edison Winter Home, consider this: Thomas Alva Edison arrived here a gravely ill widower at age 38. He lived to the age of 84. Edison had selected the house from a fishing village in Maine and had it ferried in, piece by piece, along the river, which at the time presented the only gateway to his retreat. The inventor—who produced 1,097 patents in his lifetime—maintained a laboratory and office on the grounds, which today look much like they did during his life—down to his "cat nap" cot. Edison, pioneer of the synthetic rubber industry, also

worked here with both Henry Ford and Harvey Firestone to perfect the Model T. The fascinating display includes much of the equipment Edison used used through 1931, a collection of over 200 photographs, three antique cars (one of which was a gift from Henry Ford) and a lush botanical garden. Out of some 600 plants and trees, the star of the grounds is a mammoth banyan tree, 400 feet in diameter, given to the inventor by Firestone. The spirit of Mr. Edison is as keenly felt on these grounds as that of Mr. Hemingway on his former Key West retreat. You can combine this trip with a visit to the neighboring Henry Ford Winter Home.
Open Mon.-Sat. 9 a.m.-4 p.m., Sun. 12:30 p.m.-4 p.m. Adults $6, children $2.

Fort Myers Historical Museum
2300 Peck St.,
Fort Myers
• (813) 332-5955

A captivating, old Spanish/Mediterranean-style railroad depot houses the Historical Museum. Inside, a well-displayed array of Caloosa Indian artifacts points to the original settlers of the area, who inhabited Southwest Florida for thousands of years before any white settler arrived. Also displayed are a variety of turn-of-the-century innovations such as medical and transportation novelties and a beautiful, unique selection of Carnival glass. Rail buffs will delight in the 1930s railroad car, "The Esperanza."
Open Mon.-Fri. 9 a.m.-4:30 p.m., Sun. 1 p.m.-5 p.m. Adults $2, children 50 cents.

NAPLES

Welcome to Millionairetown, U.S.A. This posh, spotlessly clean seaside getaway was discovered just after the Civil War, by one General John S. Williams, a Confederate veteran from Kentucky. The general named the town Naples, in memory of his service to the King of Naples, Italy, who had awarded him honorary citizenship. For a long time, it remained a very quiet haven where the conservative rich liked to while away the winters in seclusion. The town remains a vacation retreat, but today's Naples is at once a sophisticated golfing, shopping and fishing resort and a historic center. Just a dot on the West Florida map, it is home to more money than perhaps any other wealthy suburb in the country, and is growing rapidly. Nothing so gauche as beach bars, nightclubs or mini-malls, of course, just an increasing number of elegant boutiques, elegant restaurants and mansions in the seven-figure price range.

RESTAURANTS	318
QUICK BITES	321
HOTELS	321
NIGHTLIFE	324
SHOPS	325
SIGHTS & SPORTS	326

RESTAURANTS

Chef's Garden
1300 3rd St. South, Naples
• (813) 262-5500
CONTINENTAL

Chef's Garden is a perennial member of *Florida Trend* magazine's annual list of the state's top ten restaurants, and it deserves the honor for the balanced inventiveness of its menu alone. A memorable meal might start with the smoked-duck ravioli or the spinach salad enlivened with polenta croutons and a warm pancetta dressing. It could then progress to the grilled pork loin with a plum-and-maple sauce and sweet-potato polenta, or the zesty "low country" shrimp-and-sausage stew (a gumbolike dish in the style of Louisiana), before drawing to a deeply satisfying conclusion via the crème brûlée, chocolate truffles or one of several pies and cakes. All these good things will be brought to you by efficient, unassuming waiters who answer questions and provide counsel without any raising of the eyebrows or sniffs of disdain. The dining room is a sedate setting of crisp linens, gleaming table settings, richly upholstered furnishings and a dressed-up clientele, many of whom drive over from Fort Myers. Garden buffs should request a table in the screened-in patio, whose tropical vines and foliage make it feel like a private bower. With a bottle from its impressive wine list, dinner for two costs about $125. (For a lighter meal, head upstairs to Truffles, where you'll find a bistro-style menu and a glass display case full of excellent desserts.)
Open nightly 6 p.m.-10 p.m. All major cards.

Margaux's
3080 N. Tamiami Trail (Rte. 41), Naples
• (813) 434-2773
FRENCH

12/20

If you come to Margaux's anticipating the Marseillaise and culinary fireworks, you might leave feeling a little let down. Come here for good, country French food in a comfortable, modern storefront setting, and that's exactly what you'll get. The decor in the big dining room speaks in hushed tones, with gray carpeting, pale pink walls and ceiling fans whirring above. This place is a long-time favorite of locals, many of whom are retired folks that live by the motto, "Early to Bed, Early to Rise." They arrive Early to Dine, looking forward to dishes that stay

within safe range of classic French preparations. "Safe" is often a poorly veiled euphimism for "plain old dull," but at Margaux's, it means you don't have to take risks with your palate or your wallet: you'll always get competently prepared, recognizable dishes. For starters, there's pasta topped with escargots, and grilled shrimp with garlic and parsley. One special, veal shank served with mushrooms and green vegetables, was fine, though the sauce on the side lost some of its meat-juice character and had a thick, gooey texture. Still, the sauce didn't detract from the tasty and well-cooked piece of meat. Sweetbreads with lobster is a good choice from the menu. The rich chocolate desserts might tempt sweet tooths, but we have found the best finish to be the local strawberries, refreshing and full of sweet flavor. The list of French and American wines includes no surprises and, unfortunately, no vintages, but what is offered goes nicely with the fare. Service is friendly and professional. Expect to spend about $70 for two, with a modest wine.
Open Mon.-Fri. 11:30 a.m.-2 p.m. & 5 p.m.-9 p.m., Sat.-Sun. 5 p.m.-9 p.m.

Ritz-Carlton Hotel Dining Room
280 Vanderbilt Beach Rd.,
Naples
• (813) 598-3300
CONTINENTAL

The Naples Ritz-Carlton out-Ritzes even its impressive siblings. Although only a few years old, this Mediterranean-style palace is consistently rated among the country's best by critics and consumers, for its breathtaking natural beauty, incomparable service and restrained good taste. The same praise holds true for The Dining Room, one of the most civilized and grand restaurants in Florida, with its soft colors, high ceilings, two enormous chandeliers, elegant fabrics, live music, small dance floor, seductive menu and dizzying prices. It's the sort of place where the captain opens your napkin and places it on your lap. You can start with tuna carpaccio, crab-filled ravioli with morels and thyme, or a flawlessly prepared Caesar salad. Lest you think the fare too conservative, know that a mixed-fruit strudel and a honey-lavender sauce accompany the duck, and a mango–lemon grass sauce graces the nut-encrusted pompano. Less adventurous diners can take refuge in the perfectly grilled veal chop with vegetables. Whatever you order, save room for the feather-light Grand Marnier soufflé with chocolate sauce. The serving staff moves with the grace of the Bolshoi Ballet (no pirouettes to your table, however); in fact, what truly distinguishes this restaurant is the level of service—from sommelier to bus boy—which about as good as it gets in America, or anywhere else. The lengthy wine list is a grab bag of mostly excellent French and American wines. Dinner for two, with wine, will set you back $150.
Open nightly 6 p.m.-10 p.m. All major cards.

Sign of the Vine

980 Solana Rd., Naples
• (813) 261-6745
INTERNATIONAL

[14]

Take an ordinary house, install a couple of ambitious and creative chefs, and before long the food-wise will beat a path to the door. At least that's the case at Sign of the Vine, which inspires diners to pass by tonier Naples addresses in favor of this modest house situated on a quiet residential street off U.S. 41. Owner-chefs John and Nancy Christiansen gave personality to the several rooms and beautiful enclosed porch with funky and rococo art-deco details, old wrought-iron chandeliers and a working fireplace in the main room. The hand-lettered menus, which change every six weeks, are presented in a silver picture frame. What's offered is always a variety of meats and seafood, each accompanied by an unusual chutney, biscuit or garnish. Preparations are complicated. A representative dinner might begin with Brie baked to the gooey, just-melted stage and topped with a raspberry purée, or perhaps a torta, a perfect blend of goat cheese, black beans, guacamole and sour cream on a crispy flour tortilla. Homemade relishes would follow: red grapes in balsamic vinegar, peaches in brandy and cloves. Then you'd enjoy a salad of baby lettuces, orange slices, walnuts and pomegranates in a light honey-mustard dressing, followed by a refreshing intermezzo, perhaps a Granny Smith apple sorbet with Calvados, and a memorable entrée, such as Jack's lobster hash: lobster chunks, mushrooms, artichokes and scallions in a Pernod-laced cream sauce, served with vegetable baklava. If the warm bread pudding is offered, order it: it's firm and just sweet enough, with a buttery, whiskey-spiked brown-sugar sauce. You'll finally be presented with a silver tray bearing Nancy's chocolate fudge and candied walnuts. Service is leisurely but attentive, sometimes too much so; last time we visited, the waitstaff described every dish and preparation, including mentioning that a dish was "topped with al dente fresh tomato sauce." Hmmm. The wine list, while small, has something for everyone, from a $20 domestic Chardonnay to a $500 1966 Château Haut-Brion. Dinner for two, with wine, is about $120. *Open Mon.-Sat. 6 p.m.-10 p.m. Cards: AE.*

Villa Pescatore

8920 N. Tamiami Trail, Naples
• (813) 597-8119
ITALIAN/SEAFOOD

12/20

As at the other restaurants owned by Cuisine Management Inc. (Chef's Garden, Truffles and Bayside), low-key elegance combined with imaginative cuisine—in this case, an Italian take on fresh local seafood—draws a steady stream of prosperous locals. They feel pampered but not intimidated in this traditionally elegant setting of crystal chandeliers and sparkling white linens, and the professional serving staff makes sure the mood doesn't get broken. You'll find all manner of fish and shellfish on the menu, but we're partial to the fresh shrimp. A winning meal would start with the crisp shrimp-and-scallop risotto cakes on a delicate lemon-basil beurre blanc and continue on to the grilled

prosciutto-wrapped shrimp or the sun-dried tomato linguine with shrimp, lobster and mussels. Cap it off with one of a goodly assortment of Italian and French desserts, and you'll want for nothing. With wine, dinner for two costs about $120.
Open nightly 6 p.m.-10 p.m. All major cards.

QUICK BITES

Bayside, A Seafood Grill and Bar
4270 Gulfshore Blvd., Naples
• (813) 649-5552

Bayside's upstairs dining room concentrates on more elegant dining, but the downstairs bar caters to the walk-in, just-want-a-bite crowd. Though the bar doesn't have quite the view of Venetian Bay that you'll find upstairs, it is a thoroughly comfortable place, with a clubby look and inviting, overstuffed chairs. The eclectic menu (soups, appetizers, light entrées, desserts) allows you to create a fun, international meal: you can start with Cuban black beans with chorizo, continue with soft-shell crab in an Asian mustard sauce and finish with chocolate truffles. Dinner for two, with wine, costs about $60.
Open daily 2:30 p.m.-midnight. All major cards.

HOTELS

Luxury (From $150)

Marriott Marco Island Resort
400 S. Collier Blvd., Marco Island 33937
• (813) 394-2511
Fax (813) 394-4645

With a midisland location overlooking the Gulf of Mexico and 736 rooms (including 61 one- and two-bedroom suites), the Marriott hums as the center of activity on an otherwise laid-back Marco Island. On entering, you are welcomed by a cool atrium, with windows and airy ferns below its cathedral ceiling. Most rooms at the Marriott have oceanfront balconies and terraces. There are several different accommodations to choose from: the Tower and Penthouse, the main section of the resort, which has one- and two-bedroom suites as well as the standard room; the Lanai, a separate section of suites each with a sofa in the living room that folds out to a bed; and the Villas, two-bedroom, individual villas on the beach or golf course. With three restaurants, two bars, three pools, sixteen tennis courts and three-and-a-half miles of beachfront, the Marriott offers a pleasant retreat. Guests, however, may find themselves escaping to Naples (on the mainland and fifteen miles to the north) in search of a bit of culture and nightlife. Quinn's, the Marriott's nightclub (see page 324), is one of the nicer venues in town, especially when its resident jazz duo plays.
Tower rooms: $155-$230; Tower suites: $560-$820; Lanai: $360-$600; Villas: $250-$400.

Moderate (From $100)

Radisson Suite Beach Resort
600 S. Collier Blvd.,
Marco Island 33937
• (813) 394-4100
Fax (813) 394-0419

Settled in the late nineteenth century when Captain W.D. "Bill" Collier set up a clam dredge and planted an orange grove here, Marco Island was virtually "created" as a resort by the development corporation that set out to tame the offshore jungle in the 1960s. Today, the most poignant reminder of Captain Bill is his cream- and blue-shuttered house, later converted to an inn, which stands as a monument to the pioneer in the Olde Marco section of Marco Island. The island's original hotel contrasts with the flashier resorts along the beach, those separated from the lazy shores of the Gulf of Mexico by an environmentally protected expanse of vivid-green sea oats. One such resort is the 212-suite Radisson Suite Beach Resort. Because each of the suites was designed to face the ocean, the resort's architecture is rather drab, and unless it is full to the gills, the hotel gives off a cavernous feeling, and cries for company. Rooms are fine, with the expected amenities. We admit that for reclusives this is an asset, but be forewarned to bring someone with you on your visit to Marco: this is not the kind of place where you're likely to meet people.
1-bedroom suites: $109-$249; 2-bedroom suites: $139-$399.

Registry Resort Naples
475 Seagate Dr.,
Naples 33940
• (813) 597-3232
Fax (813) 597-3147

The innovative architecture of the Registry Resort precludes having to be shuttled around from point to point, and yet offers an abundance of amenities. It's shaped like a staircase descending to the sea, with a host of resort facilities clustered neatly around it. The fifteen tennis courts, extravagant pool area, golf courses and fitness center, in addition to the well-equipped beach club and fitness center, are all centrally located, beautifully landscaped and easily accessible. The resort has 424 elegantly appointed guest rooms and suites. Service here leaves you feeling exactly the way you should on a vacation: relaxed and pampered.
Singles & doubles: $105-$149; suites: $250.

Ritz-Carlton Hotel
280 Vanderbilt Beach Rd.,
Naples 33963
• (813) 598-3300
Fax (813) 598-6690

Set within a protected mangrove swamp, the Ritz-Carlton Hotel lives up to its name. What's that supposed to mean? Well, even if you don't stay here, be sure not to miss afternoon tea in the lobby lounge, with its grand piano and Waterford chandeliers twinkling in the background—and hallways lined in eighteenth- and nineteenth-century oils. The hotel has an extraordinary sense of place. If you're a guest here, get ready for pampering, especially if you select from the 72 guest rooms and eleven suites of the Ritz Carlton Club. With the sweeping ocean views, French doors, 24-hour room service and a touch

of extra coddling from the staff, you can "put on the Ritz" with signature style. To fully appreciate the spectacular views, make sure you choose a room facing outward rather than into the courtyard. The grounds aren't as frenetic as many of the area's sportier resorts; instead the Ritz-Carlton offers an understated swimming pool area crowned with just one Jacuzzi and a fitness center, and a wide expanse of beach that offers miles of pleasant walking.
Singles & doubles: $115-$280; club level: $250-$360.

Practical (Under $100)

Naples Beach Hotel & Golf Club
851 Gulf Shore Blvd. North,
Naples 33940
• (813) 261-2222
Fax (813) 261-8019

General John S. Williams, the founding father of this historic resort town, opened the small Naples Beach Hotel in the late 1800s, with his friend and Louisville publisher, Walter N. Haldeman. Later sold to Henry B. Watkins, the hotel became the Naples Beach Hotel & Golf Club, and it's still owned and operated hands-on by the Watkins family today. Amid a couple of four-hotel resorts and plenty of luxury condos, the Naples Beach Hotel retains a sort of de facto queenship over Naples, although even its nicest rooms compare neither in elegance nor youth to its neighbors. The hotel's golf course is well known among enthusiasts, and the annual summer jazz festivals held on the hotel's lawn draw locals and hotel guests alike, who picnic under the stars while the band plays. The hotel's beach bar was constructed before zoning regulations got nasty, which makes it the only one in Naples situated directly on the beach.
Doubles: $55-$135; efficiencies: $75-$155; suites: $80-$205.

Vanderbilt Inn on the Gulf
11000 Gulf Shore Dr. North,
Naples 33963
• (813) 597-3151
Fax (813) 597-3099

The northernmost of Naples's gulf-front hotels, the Vanderbilt Inn is a lovely little 150-room resort situated on the shores of Vanderbilt Beach. Though it's only an eight-minute drive into town, the inn seems worlds away from the glitz and glamour of Olde Naples and exudes the feeling of a classic, island-style resort. The Vanderbilt recently received a facelift for all of the efficiency rooms and public areas, so expect to get value for the price. Its Chickee Hut Beachside Bar (designed by a Miccosukee craftsman) says "Southwest Florida." The poolside bustles with generally friendly and lively folk. On the beach, if a volleyball game is in progress, beware: watch too long and you'll be recruited.
Doubles: $70-$185.

NIGHTLIFE

Bars

The Pub on Linwood
2408 Linwood Ave.,
Naples
• (813) 774-2408

Is all this unnaturally cheerful sunshine getting to you? Step into a bit of Britain in a rather unlikely locale: south of SR 84 and Airport Road in Naples. The owners of The Pub on Linwood, two boisterous British transplants, Viv and Brian Stuart, offer plenty of ales on tap: Bass, Watney's, Harp and Guinness; no fruiti-tutti drinks or paper umbrellas, though. Other things plentiful here are dartboards, British accents and atmosphere.
Open Sun.-Thurs. 11 a.m.-midnight, Fri.-Sat. 11 a.m.-2 p.m. Cards: AE, MC, V.

Cabarets

Naples Dinner Theatre
10251 Piper Blvd.,
Naples
• (813) 597-6031

While many of Florida's smaller communities have dinner theaters offering something different to do on an evening out, Naples's splendid little theatrical venue remains worth a drive from Miami or Palm Beach. No, it's not the food (which is of the usual dinner-theater fare of mystery chicken and green items variety), nor the originality of the plays themselves (which are standard dinner theater Broadway hits). It is the energy of a splendid cast brought to Naples each season, as well as the 1890s ambience of the venue. Seating arrangement is in a four-tiered, horseshoe-shaped theater; service is silent and cheerful, dinner-theater style at its best.
Tickets $24-$35.50. Performances Tues.-Sat. 8:15 p.m.; buffet dinner 6 p.m. All major cards.

Jazz

Quinn's
Marriott's Marco Island Resort,
400 S. Collier Blvd.,
Marco Island
• (813) 394-2511

On an island definitely known more for its smashing sunsets than for what goes on after them, all the hotels are required to offer beachfront bars to entertain at least their clientele. But Quinn's, in the Marco Island Resort, offers something special: a wonderfully breezy jazz clarinet and piano duo. Serving up one of the best piña coladas we've sampled statewide, Quinn's Monday night jazz shows, with Bob Snyder and Bobby Gideon, provide the perfect setting for an evening in Marco Island.
Open daily 5 p.m.-midnight. All major cards.

SHOPS

Antiques

Thalheimer's Auction Gallery
2095 E. Tamiami Trail,
Olde Naples
• (813) 774-4666

Thalheimer family auctions are a dependable smorgasbord of items from around the world—porcelain, crystal, tapestries, carpets and gems—ranging from junk to some very nice objets d'art.
Auction dates vary; inspection hours by appointment.

Clothes

Hubbards, Ltd.
5400 Taylor Rd.,
Olde Naples
• (813) 566-3242

Tired of paying Olde Naples (read: inflated) prices? Sacrifice the ambience for that of this Airport Road–area shop, and choose from a selection of Ultrasuede and a line of designer clothing, much of which is marked off between 30 and 60 percent below retail.
Open Thurs.-Sat. 9 a.m.-5 p.m., Mon.-Wed. by appointment.

Ruff Hewn
839 5th Ave. South,
Olde Naples
• (813) 649-6608

Not only does Ruff Hewn offer plenty of rugged outdoor clothing (of the Banana Republic variety) for both men and women, but it also stocks a full selection of accessories and gifts celebrating the great outdoors: from fly-fishing outfits to signed wildlife prints and originals.
Open Mon.-Sat. 10 a.m.-5:30 p.m.

Food

Fantozzi's
1148 3rd St. South,
Olde Naples
• (813) 262-4808

Stop by Fantozzi's and pack your own gourmet lunch for a picnic on the old Naples Pier. Create your own, or choose from those lunch and dinner entrées that the food and wine specialists regularly make to go—from Quiche Lorraine to Cobb Salad. For souvenir shopping, there is a variety of gift items, as well as Indian River fruit shipped nationwide.
Open Mon.-Sat. 9:30 a.m.-5:30 p.m.

Gifts

Glenna Moore
465 5th Ave. South,
Olde Naples
• (813) 263-4121

Baubles, bangles and beads, plus plenty of art porcelains, glass, silver, folk arts and fine quilts make this charming ten-year-old shop worth a look. Glenna Moore is always interested in buying and bartering, which makes her novel selection different each time you visit.
Open Mon.-Sat. 10 a.m.-5:30 p.m.

Sporting Goods

Nevada Bob's
4500 N. Tamiami Trail,
Olde Naples
• (813) 263-4999

Neopolitans (of the Floridian variety, at least) love their golf courses, and Nevada Bob aims to get you equipped for your day's eighteen holes at much better prices than you're likely to find at the resorts' pro shops. Offering discounts on lines from Cleveland Classics to MacGregor and Mark Scot, the shop also repairs clubs, and how's this for a twist: offers video analysis of your strokes on an indoor range and putting green. Nevada Bob's "The Golfing Lady" boutique-within-a-store offers actionwear and golf collections, also at reasonable and discounted prices.
Open daily 10 a.m.-6 p.m.

SIGHTS & SPORTS

Arts

Four Winds Gallery
340 13th Ave. South,
Olde Naples
• (813) 263-7555

If you're doing a room in the popular Southwestern motif, start at Four Winds. Specializing in Native American art and jewelry (contemporary, historic and traditional), this shop often has Seminole and Miccosukee items that are more than a cut above what you might find on the gift shops of the reservations.
Open Mon.-Sat. 10 a.m.-5:30 p.m.

Harmon-Meek Gallery
386 Broad Ave. South,
Olde Naples
• (813) 261-2637

Established in 1964, Harmon-Meek has for some 26 seasons represented twentieth-century American artists, often in revolving one-person exhibitions. Regardless of whose work is being displayed during your visit, you'll be greeted by a friendly staff and an airy, museumlike gallery where even those who aren't buying are welcome to take in the artwork.
Open Mon.-Sat. 10 a.m.-5 p.m.

Helios Gallery
363 12th Ave. South,
Olde Naples
• (813) 434-2288

With affiliate galleries in Washington D.C. (the Zygos Galleries) and in Athens, Greece, the Helios gallery has an appropriate number of neo-Classical sculptures on display. Director Matina Konstandinidis also regularly hosts revolving exhibitions of contemporary art from around the world, making Helios one of the most diverse galleries in Naples.
Open Mon.-Sat. 10 a.m.-5 p.m.

McNichols Art Gallery
368 5th Ave. South,
Olde Naples
• (813) 261-7891

Owners of one of the oldest galleries in Naples, the McNichols family, many of whose members count among the artists displaying their works here, deserves credit for its ardent sensitivity to the local landscape. Porcelain dolls, murals and paintings on display depict everything from Seminole Indian women crushing corn to sunsets over Naples Pier.
Open Mon.-Sat. 10 a.m.-5:30 p.m.

Naples Art Gallery
Windsor Plaza,
275 Broad Ave. South,
Olde Naples
• (813) 262-4551

For nearly a quarter century, this gallery has presented prominent American painters, sculptors and—perhaps most notably—glass artisans. (An alcove area is devoted entirely to the gallery's studio glass collection).
Open Mon.-Sat. 10 a.m.-5:30 p.m.

Excursions

Eden of the Everglades
Hwy. 29,
Everglades City
• (800) 543-3367

Visitors traversing Southwest Florida between Naples and Miami are often disappointed to find the Everglades much less dramatic than the "River of Grass" so eloquently paid homage by the area's champion, author Marjorie Stoneman Douglas. In order to really see and appreciate the unique ecosystem of the national park, you must head south of bustling Route 441 and take a guided tour. One of the best-known of the are tour operators is Eden of the Everglades, where hour-long jungle-pontoon-boat tours visit the Everglades Zoo (guaranteeing a glimpse at typical Everglades wildlife, even if in captivity). Still, the attraction offers some novelty: the zoo was designed and built by native Seminole Indians. Among its current inhabitants are panthers, bobcats, numerous alligators and ten acres of exotic birds.
Tours daily, hourly 11 a.m-4 p.m.; zoo open daily 10 a.m.-5 p.m.

Jungle Larry's Zoological Park & Caribbean Gardens
1590 Goodlette Rd.,
Naples
• (813) 262-5409,
(800) 330-2287

It may look like just another commercial highway, but behind the fast-food outlets of Goodlette road awaits Jungle Larry's Zoological Park and Caribbean Gardens, one of those wacky Florida attractions reserved for those with a sense of humor and abiding curiosity. Acre upon acre of colorful tropical gardens is overseen by the former Ohio TV personality and animal trainer "Jungle Larry," who also trains and displays many of his favored beasts at the park. Tram tours through one of the nation's oldest botanical gardens (more than 52 acres of them) are as educational as they are relaxing, but don't miss the tiger feeding and

lecture for an up-close brush with jungle greatness. A petting zoo allows the kids to get up close and pat some woolly heads, and picnic and playground areas on the grounds make for a nice place to while away the afternoon.
Jan.-Apr.: open Mon.-Fri. 9:30 a.m.-5:30 p.m. May-Dec.: open Tues.-Fri. 9:30 a.m.-5:30 p.m. Adults $9.95, children $5.95.

Landmarks

Third Street South
1262 3rd St.,
Olde Naples
• (813) 649-6707

The "e" in Olde (Naples) adds a considerable amount to the price of the goods sold in this historic neighborhood. On Third Street South, a shady street lined with 85 shops, galleries and eateries, all skirted with wrought iron stairways, balconies and planters filled with flowering trees, we're charmed enough not to notice. The best shops stretch from Broad Avenue South to Fourteenth Avenue South. Men's and women's apparel is plentiful on the street, as are creative crafts and housewares clearly meant for nice houses.
Open Mon.-Sat. 10 a.m.-5 p.m.

Sports

Naples–Fort Myers Kennel Club
Old 41,
Bonita Springs
• (813) 597-7181

If you want to participate in an old Florida favorite—watching out over your cocktail as muzzled greyhounds chase a "rabbit" around a track—Naples–Fort Myers might be your kind of place. Offering year-round racing, gourmet dining and a welcome mat for kids, the track features five distances to be run over a quarter-mile oval. Betting to win, place, show, quiniela, trifecta or tri-super to win up to a $1 million jackpot is hair-raising for a pari-mutuel novice, and, of course, a must for the avid gambler visiting Southwest Florida.
Races Mon.-Tues. & Thurs.-Sat. 7:45 p.m., Wed. noon.

Naples Trolley Tours, Inc.
Vanderbilt Inn on the Gulf,
11000 Gulf Shore Dr. North,
Naples
• (813) 262-7300

Ding, ding, goes the trolley . . . ! As the song promises, you can't have this much fun anywhere between Naples and San Francisco. A welcome sight for shoppers "doing" the well-stocked Fifth Avenue and Third Street South shopping areas, the bright blue trolleys pick up at each of Naples's major hotels. This also affords the curious an opportunity to make an on-site inspection of the resorts they didn't choose; we suspect a return visit or two is traditionally decided upon during a trolley stop.
Open Mon.-Sat. 8:30 a.m.-4:30 p.m., Sun. 11:30 a.m.-3:30 p.m. Adults $5, children under 12 $3.

SANIBEL & CAPTIVA ISLANDS

In this ever louder, busier, faster-moving world, the few remaining havens of tranquillity become more precious all the time. One of those places, a hushed tropical oasis, can be found if you drive west on Florida Highway 867, until you leave the Florida mainland and begin to cross the Gulf of Mexico. The pair of islets, Sanibel and Captiva, lie about three miles along the highway from the mainland, stretching another twenty miles into the Gulf of Mexico like a tarpon tail in motion. You won't want to spend your days on these tiny islands doing anything more than shell-hunting (for some of the world's most beautiful and exotic shells), fishing for tarpon and grouper, bird-watching, bicycling and filling up on fresh fish, fresh fruit and fresh air.

RESTAURANTS	329
QUICK BITES	332
HOTELS	333
SHOPS	334
SIGHTS	335

RESTAURANTS

The Bubble Room
15001 Captiva Rd., Captiva Island
• (813) 472-5558

4320 N. Tamiami Trail, Naples
• (813) 263-3434
AMERICAN

11/20

Virtually anyone who's ever set foot on Captiva has been to the Bubble Room. This explains why it's always full to bursting point and why it doesn't bother to take reservations. An hour's wait is not uncommon, and during the winter season, expect to wait even longer. With decor that is unabashed kitsch—a mishmash of 1930s, 1940s and 1950s memorabilia—there's plenty to look at while awaiting a seat, including campy life-size statues, glass baubles and bubbles and lots of twinkling, candle-shaped, Christmas bubble lamps from which the restaurant took its name. While waiting, keep your impatience at bay with thoughts of the garlicky Bubble Bread baked with Roquefort cheese and oregano, and the heavenly, sticky cinnamon buns. Served up by khaki-clad Bubble Scouts, this food is not for the dainty eater or the seeker of nouvelle creations: it's as American as American gets, and straight out of an era gone by. Sure bets are Prime Ribs Weismuller, a 32-ounce slab of aged beef that covers the plate; the Eddie Fisherman, a black grouper poached in a paper bag;

and the Agatha Grill, a mixed grilled of quail, pork, filet mignon and sausage. Dinners come with a large Greek or house salad and four vegetables. Although portions are huge, it's worth saving room for dessert: There are some sixteen choices each night, including Very Moist Chocolate and Chocolate Cappuccino Cheesecake. Your Bubble Scout will happily wrap one to go. Dinner for two, including cocktails, runs about $100.
Open daily 11:30 a.m.-2:30 p.m. & 5:30 p.m.-10 p.m. All major cards.

The Greenhouse
Captiva Village Square,
14970 Captiva Rd.,
Captiva Island
• (813) 472-6006
AMERICAN

Captiva is blessed with a number of cozy restaurants staffed with inspired chefs who are defining Southwest Florida's tropical, casual cuisine. This place is one of the best examples of the genre. A tiny place decorated with plans, charming table lanterns and art-for-sale, The Greenhouse draws as many local food-lovers as tourists. They return again and again to be wowed by salads dotted with edible flowers, wondrous crabcakes with a lime mayonnaise, and tortillas stuffed with lobster, bean sprouts, salsa and red cabbage. Local seafood and exotic fruits figure prominently in the roster of inventive appetizers and entrées, and desserts wallow in decadence, as with the meringue topped with ice cream, nuts, fresh fruit, a wisp of chocolate sauce and a mound of whipped cream. The open kitchen displays The Greenhouse's professionalism: no one ever clatters pots, mutters obscenities or leaves a dirty dish hanging about, and attentive servers make sure that all flows smoothly from pan to plate. With wine, two will spend $120 for dinner.
Open nightly 5:45 p.m.-9:30 p.m. Cards: MC, V.

Jean-Paul's French Corner
708 Tarpon Bay Rd.,
Sanibel Island
• (813) 472-1493
FRENCH

Nestled behind a helter-skelter flower garden is one of the area's most enduring and reliable restaurants, a haven of country-French cooking and charm. The sound of people enjoying themselves wafts out the door along with the captivating aromas of garlic and wine; inside is a café-style setting of terra-cotta floors, paneled walls, big pots of flowers and recorded French music. Though the atmosphere isn't formal, the service is first-rate—waiters are well informed and gracious, never unctuous or uppity—and the food is heavenly. Appetizers include classically prepared French onion soup, escargots, soft-shell crabs and a regularly changing pâté du chef, perhaps a creamy blend of chicken livers, pork and spinach in a currant sauce. Those partial to duck will find a kitchen that knows what to do with it; order it crispy and it comes just that way, not scorched or charred, the meat inside moist but not greasy. Desserts run to such delicious standards as profiteroles (choux pastry filled with vanilla cream and topped with chocolate sauce and almonds) or coupe maison (huge strawberries in a smooth rasp-

berry sauce). This traditional cooking may not sparkle with inventiveness, but it does sparkle with freshness, care and deeply satisfying flavors. Dinner for two, with wine, costs about $110.
Seatings Mon.-Sat. 6 p.m. & 8:30 p.m. Cards: MC, V.

The Mad Hatter
6460 Sanibel-Captiva Rd.,
Sanibel Island
• (813) 472-0033
NEW AMERICAN

The pristine beauty of Sanibel's gulf waters attracts hundreds of thousands of vacationers each year. Those same waters also attract millions of fierce mosquitoes and gnats, but in the front-row seats inside The Mad Hatter you'll be cool, protectd and distracted by a gorgeous sunset view—while sampling some of the area's most inventive cooking. Within this unassuming wooden bungalow is a light, tropical decor, notable mainly for its pastel prints, large windows, touches of *Alice in Wonderland* whimsy and a mere baker's dozen tables. A paean to the wonderful diversity of America's cuisine, the menu combines the best of Southern, Southwestern, Californian and even Japanese cooking, without lapsing into the silliness of the restaurant's namesake. Marinated and grilled quail rests on a mound of fresh corn and crunchy fried okra. The grilled veal chop meets polenta, grilled radicchio and a smoked tomato-pancetta sauce. Basil, grilled eggplant and pink peppercorns jazz up a splendid slab of tuna. Don't let foolish concerns about health and weight prevent you from trying one of the superb desserts, such as the warm apple Kuchen topped with Frangelica-laced whipped cream. The service and wine list are on a par with the food. Dinner for two, with wine, costs $125.
Open Tues.-Sun. 5 p.m.-9:30 p.m. Cards: AE, MC, V.

Mucky Duck
Andy Rosse Ln.,
Captiva Island
• (813) 472-3434

5500 Estero Blvd.,
Fort Myers
• (813) 463-5519
SEAFOOD

11/20

The Captiva Mucky Duck is about as gulf-front as it gets. A few years ago, during a nasty tropical storm, the water came so close to the building, it nearly became water-borne. A successful renourishment project has returned the Duck and its flamboyant owner, Victor Mayeron, to drier ground. It's safe to say that as long as it remains on land, the restaurant's loyal clientele will keep it afloat. Within the British-style pub is good food at moderate prices (by Sanibel/Captiva standards, that is). Fragrant tomato-based New England clam chowder, bacon-wrapped barbecued shrimp and fish-and-chips are among the well-prepared dishes. The definitely non-British Mayeron is apt to be found socializing with Captiva patrons. The Fort Myers Beach "Duck" is a bit more formal than the original on Captiva. One drawback: neither restaurant takes reservations except for large groups, both are small and fill up quickly. But then there are worse places to wait for a table that on a gulf beach. Dinner for two, including two beers, will cost about $60.
Captiva: open Mon.-Sat. 11:30 a.m.-2:30 p.m. & 5 p.m.-9:30 p.m. Fort Myers: open daily same hours. Cards: AE, MC, V.

Windows on the Water

Sundial Beach & Tennis Resort,
1451 Middle Gulf Dr.,
Sanibel Island
• (813) 472-4151
SEAFOOD/AMERICAN

Executive chef Peter Harman calls his handiwork "Gulf Coast cuisine," which seems an apt enough name for this effervescent blend of Florida seafood, tropical fruits and a dash of New Orleans zest (Harman trained with famed chef Paul Prudhomme). While the restaurant's name focuses on what's outside—a gorgeous view of the Gulf of Mexico—what's inside merits equal attention. The bronzed swordfish, a fresh filet piqued with a blend of seventeen herbs and spices, possesses the spirit (if not the bite) of the blackened version. The tuna with peppercorns and the Caribbean-style pork tenderloin are equally good bets, accompanied by such things as a Florida fruit salad or a watercress salad with a Burgundy-poached pear and Montrachet toast. The Key lime pie is among the best we've had, and the chocolate bayou cake will satiate even hard-core chocoholics. The comfortable space, in hues of teal, peach and blue, is filled with as many locals as tourists. Service is a bit slow. Dinner for two, with wine, costs about $100.
Open Mon.-Sat. 7:30 a.m.-10:30 a.m., 11:30 a.m.-3 p.m. & 5:30 p.m.-9:30 p.m., Sun. 7:30 a.m.-9:30 a.m., 11 a.m.-2 p.m. & 5:30 p.m.-9:30 p.m. All major cards.

QUICK BITES

The Sunshine Café

Captiva Village Square,
14970 Captiva Rd.,
Captiva Island
• (813) 472-6200

If you feel too underdressed after a day on the beach to venture into one of the island's more formal restaurants, head for the Sunshine Café. At one of the five tables inside the cramped, minimalist café, or one of the five on the porch, you can order beach grub such as simple cheeseburgers, or more complex smoked pork loin with tandoori spices and fresh-fruit chutney. There's always a grilled local fish of the day, along with at least three gooey desserts. You can order every dish to go to make a terrific picnic on the beach. A full dinner for two, with wine, costs about $85, but you'll spend much less on a light meal.
Open Wed.-Mon. 11:30 a.m.-9 p.m. No cards.

HOTELS

South Seas Plantation

Captiva Island 33924
• (813) 472-5111
Fax (813) 472-7541

How pretentious to grab the whole island as its address. Then again, South Seas *is* Captiva, always has been. A seventeenth-century pirate's retreat and a nineteenth-century lime-and-coconut plantation, the island didn't become popular among the well heeled until the Jazz Age, when boatloads of adventurous flappers and Hemingway pretenders sailed in for fishing forays. As a full-service resort, South Seas Plantation has only been in operation for the last couple of decades—but has it ever been in operation. The facilities here are so extensive that it is impossible to walk the 330 acres of grounds: a trolley shuttles guests from classes at Steve Colgate's Off-Shore Sailing School to lunch and tennis lessons with touring pro Virginia Wade. Since getting to the resort requires a healthy 35-mile drive from downtown Fort Myers, it's a lucky thing there's so much going on here. Dining ranges from candlelight dinners to a bona fide pizza parlor, and—we think this has to be some sort of record—there are eighteen swimming pools on property. With 600 units at the hotel, it's difficult to sum up the accommodations, but as a general rule, you do get what you pay for—from in-room whirlpools to magnificent golf, marina or oceanfront views. *Doubles: $190-$360.*

Sundial Beach & Tennis Resort

1451 Middle Gulf Dr.,
Sanibel Island 33957
• (813) 472-4151
Fax (813) 472-0554

The people at Sundial take their fun pretty seriously. From dawn to well past dark, you may elect to participate in a series of activities that's nothing if not well thought out—anything from Aquacize to Shellcraft, Sand Sculpture and Family Pictionary. There are thirteen tennis courts, bike and nature trails and plenty of virgin shelling, Sanibel's favorite pastime. Public areas are beautifully appointed with lots of whites, peaches and paddle fans splashed about; accommodations range from comfortable to extremely comfortable, if not the lap of luxury. Fresh "Gulf Coast" cuisine comes out of the kitchen at Windows on the Water (*see* page 332), the resort's better restaurant.
1-bedroom unit: $116-$172; 2-bedroom unit: $137-$221.

'Tween Waters Inn

Captiva Rd.,
Captiva Island 33924
• (813) 472-5161
Fax (813) 472-0249

The waters this inn is "'tween" are those of Pine Island Sound and the Gulf of Mexico. At sunset, its hard to say which is lovelier: both are purple, and command your attention much like a mighty French Impressionist. The resort features a bustling marina (Captain Mike Fuery's Shelling Charters is one of the shelling and fishing boats that makes this home port) and a friendly, Old Florida ambience. The hotel's Old Captiva House has been a favorite island eatery for years; there's also a waterfront café and pizzeria. Other than that, 'Tween Waters doesn't really try to compete with its more sophisticated, full-service resort competitors. If you want to rent canoes, or relax on a wooden sundeck around just one swimming pool, or rent bikes and canoes and shop for fishing tackle in a Mayberry R.F.D.-style marina store, 'Tween Waters is the place for you.
Doubles: $75-$235.

SHOPS

Islander Trading Post
1446 Periwinkle Way,
Sanibel Island
• (813) 395-0888

Sanibel's Periwinkle Way, where the mode of shop-hopping transportation, by rule, is the bicycle, is home to a number of delightful little crafts shops. One of these is the Islander Trading Post, where you can select from a number of locally crafted souvenirs. You can also make your own scented candles here, and choose your own candle holder from a large inventory.
Open Mon.-Fri. 10 a.m.-6 p.m., Sat. 10 a.m.-5 p.m., Sun. noon-5 p.m.

The Lion's Paw
1025 Periwinkle Way,
Sanibel Island
• (813) 472-0909

Clothing, jewelry and accessories—and plenty of local charm—are for sale at The Lion's Paw. The prices here are generally more reasonable on comparable items to those you might find in Olde Naples; if you stumble upon one of the shop's regular clearance sales, prices are even more attractive.
Open Mon.-Fri. 10 a.m.-6 p.m., Sat.-Sun. noon-5 p.m.

SIGHTS

Captain Mike Fuery's Shelling Charters
'Tween Waters Inn Marina,
Captiva Rd.,
Captiva Island
• (813) 472-3459

Sanibel's sands harbor some of the finest seashells in the world, so fine, in fact, that the bent-over posture of the typical beach walker is referred to as the "Sanibel Stoop." An exuberant Captain Fuery will explain it all to you—the shell population here is so plentiful because of the youth of the island, and due to its position perpendicular to the coast, allowing the island to act as a giant net, catching shells being swept north and south by the currents. And Fuery knows just where to find them. The charters depart regularly, guided by the local expert on shelling, for hidden off-shore islands sure to yield the finest specimens.
Hours by charter. Half-day shelling tours $160, half-day fishing tours $180.

J.N. "Ding" Darling Wildlife Refuge
Sanibel-Captiva Rd.,
Captiva Island
• (813) 472-1100

Situated on the north side of twelve-mile-long Captiva Island, this 5,000-acre wilderness sanctuary is edged with mangroves and shallow bays—an excellent natural habitat for the numerous wading birds who reside at the complex. The preserve was named for "Ding," a Pulitzer prize-winning cartoonist and winter resident of the islands who designed the first stamp of the 1934 "Migratory Bird Hunting Stamp" program. Enjoy an afternoon exploring the Wildlife Drive, the Canoe Trail, the Boardwalk, the Observation Tower and the various Foot Trails of the sanctuary.
Driving fees $3, bicycling or walking fees $1.

MAPS

FLORIDA	336-337
MIAMI & VICINITY	338
ORLANDO & VICINITY	339
THE FLORIDA KEYS	340

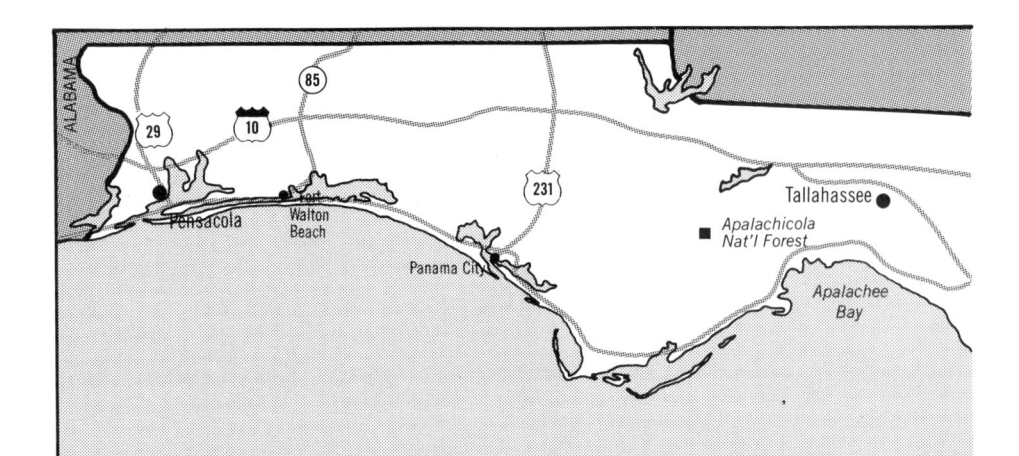

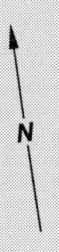

FLORIDA

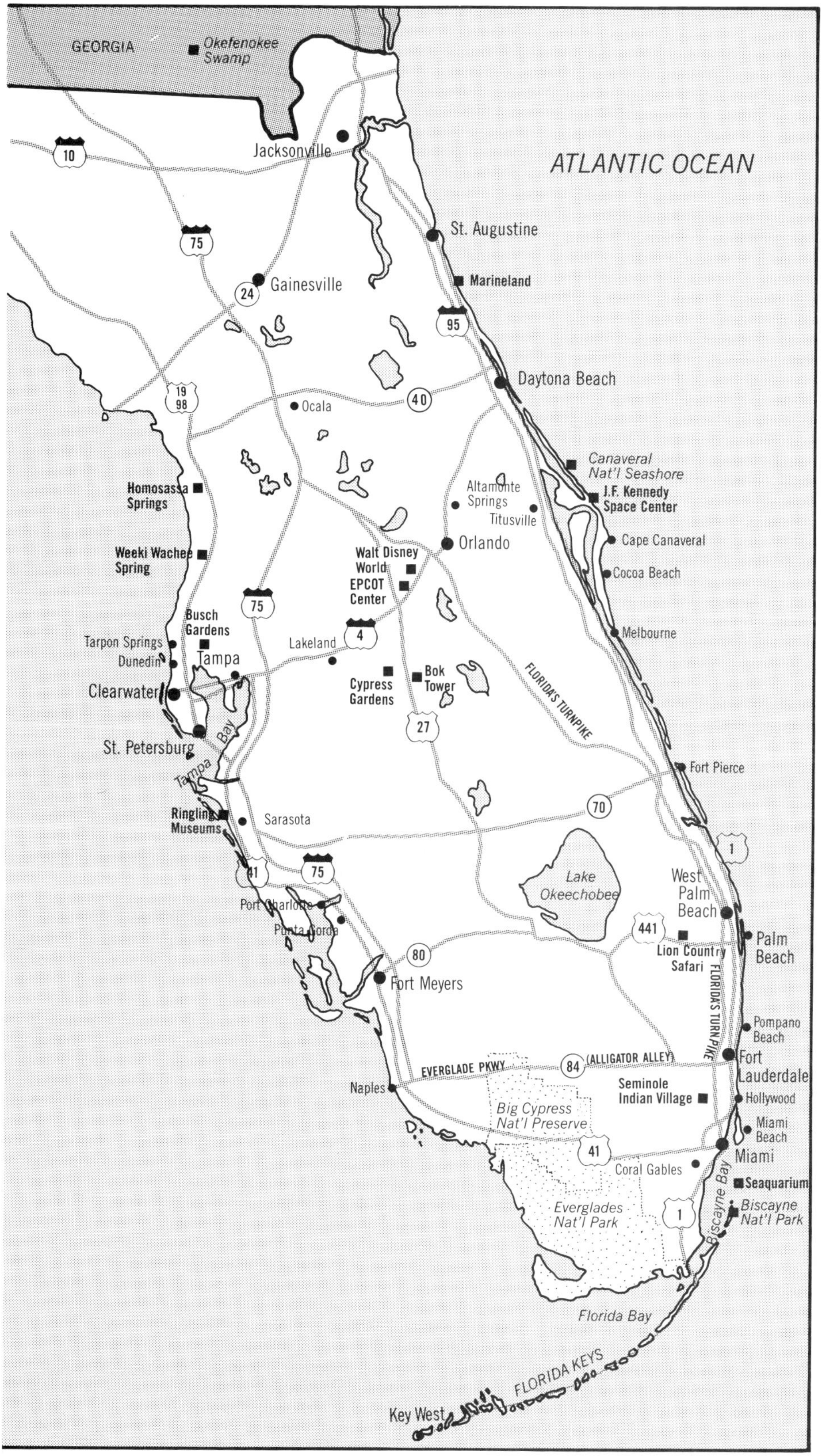

GEORGIA
Okefenokee Swamp
ATLANTIC OCEAN
10
Jacksonville
St. Augustine
75
Gainesville
24
Marineland
95
Daytona Beach
19
98
40
Ocala
Canaveral Nat'l Seashore
J.F. Kennedy Space Center
Altamonte Springs
Titusville
Homosassa Springs
Weeki Wachee Spring
Orlando
Cape Canaveral
Walt Disney World
EPCOT Center
Cocoa Beach
75
Busch Gardens
4
Melbourne
Tarpon Springs
Lakeland
Dunedin
Tampa
Cypress Gardens
Bok Tower
Clearwater
FLORIDA'S TURNPIKE
27
St. Petersburg
Tampa Bay
Fort Pierce
70
Ringling Museums
Sarasota
1
41
75
Lake Okeechobee
West Palm Beach
Port Charlotte
Punta Gorda
441
Lion Country Safari
Palm Beach
80
Fort Meyers
FLORIDA'S TURNPIKE
Pompano Beach
EVERGLADE PKWY
84
(ALLIGATOR ALLEY)
Fort Lauderdale
Naples
Seminole Indian Village
Hollywood
Big Cypress Nat'l Preserve
Miami Beach
41
Miami
Coral Gables
Biscayne Bay
Seaquarium
Everglades Nat'l Park
1
Biscayne Nat'l Park
Florida Bay
FLORIDA KEYS
Key West

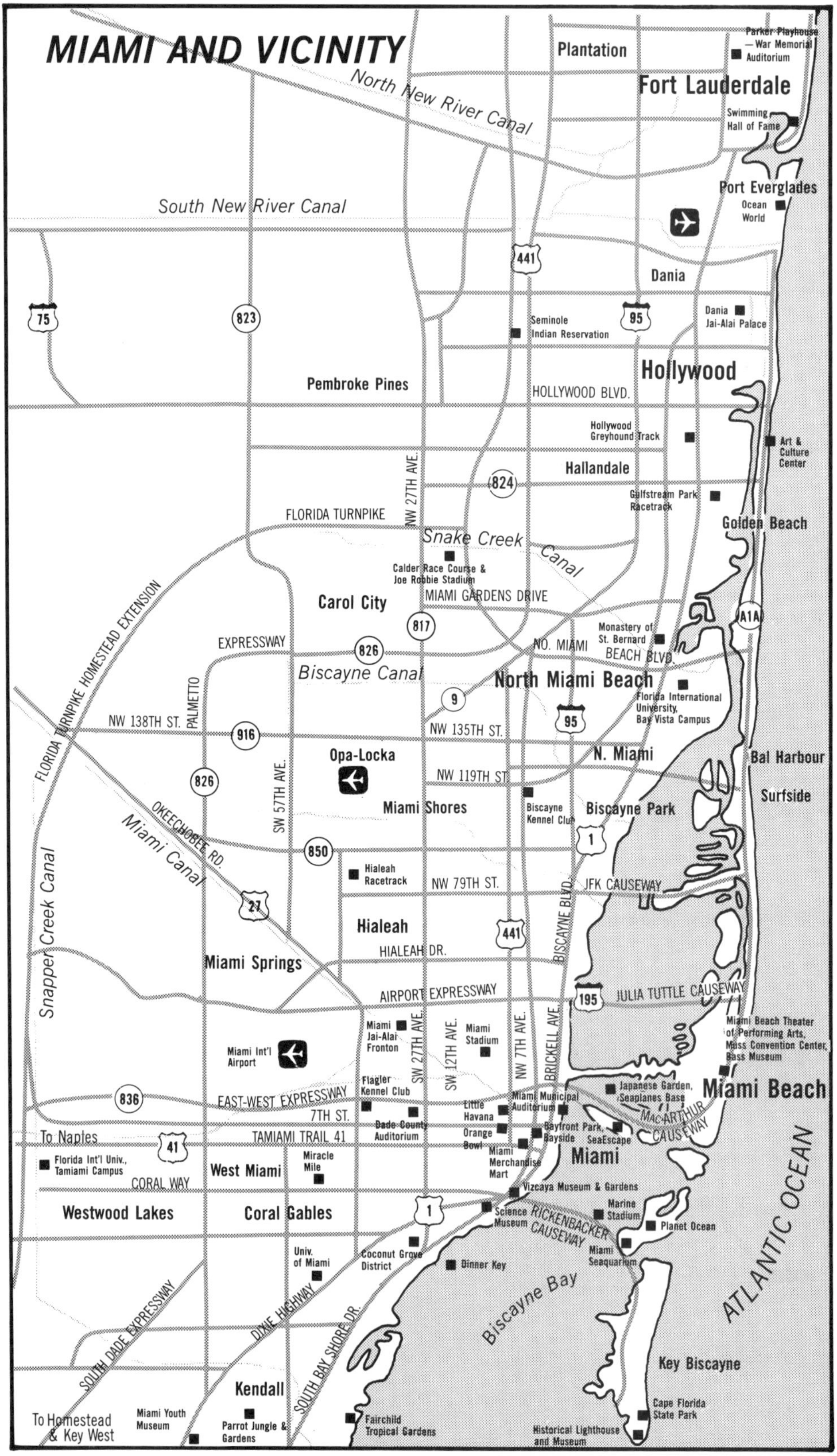

MIAMI AND VICINITY
Plantation
Parker Playhouse — War Memorial Auditorium
Fort Lauderdale
North New River Canal
Swimming Hall of Fame
Port Everglades
South New River Canal
Ocean World
441
Dania
75
823
95
Dania Jai-Alai Palace
Seminole Indian Reservation
Hollywood
Pembroke Pines
HOLLYWOOD BLVD.
Hollywood Greyhound Track
Art & Culture Center
NW 27TH AVE.
Hallandale
824
Gulfstream Park Racetrack
FLORIDA TURNPIKE
Golden Beach
Snake Creek Canal
Calder Race Course & Joe Robbie Stadium
FLORIDA TURNPIKE HOMESTEAD EXTENSION
MIAMI GARDENS DRIVE
Carol City
A1A
817
Monastery of St. Bernard
EXPRESSWAY
826
NO. MIAMI BEACH BLVD.
Biscayne Canal
9
North Miami Beach
Florida International University, Bay Vista Campus
PALMETTO
NW 138TH ST.
916
NW 135TH ST.
95
Opa-Locka
N. Miami
Bal Harbour
NW 119TH ST.
826
Surfside
SW 57TH AVE.
Miami Shores
Biscayne Kennel Club
Biscayne Park
OKEECHOBEE RD.
Miami Canal
1
850
Hialeah Racetrack
NW 79TH ST.
JFK CAUSEWAY
Snapper Creek Canal
27
BISCAYNE BLVD.
Hialeah
441
HIALEAH DR.
Miami Springs
AIRPORT EXPRESSWAY
195
JULIA TUTTLE CAUSEWAY
Miami Jai-Alai Fronton
SW 27TH AVE.
SW 12TH AVE.
Miami Stadium
NW 7TH AVE.
BRICKELL AVE.
Miami Beach Theater of Performing Arts, Miss Convention Center, Bass Museum
Miami Int'l Airport
Flagler Kennel Club
Japanese Garden, Seaplanes Base
Miami Beach
836
EAST-WEST EXPRESSWAY
Miami Municipal Auditorium
MACARTHUR CAUSEWAY
7TH ST.
Little Havana
Dade County Auditorium
To Naples
TAMIAMI TRAIL 41
Orange Bowl
Bayfront Park, Bayside
SeaEscape
41
Miami Merchandise Mart
Miami
Florida Int'l Univ., Tamiami Campus
Miracle Mile
West Miami
CORAL WAY
Vizcaya Museum & Gardens
Westwood Lakes
Coral Gables
1
Science Museum
RICKENBACKER CAUSEWAY
Marine Stadium
Planet Ocean
Miami Seaquarium
Univ. of Miami
Coconut Grove District
Dinner Key
ATLANTIC OCEAN
SOUTH DADE EXPRESSWAY
DIXIE HIGHWAY
SOUTH BAY SHORE DR.
Biscayne Bay
Key Biscayne
Kendall
Cape Florida State Park
To Homestead & Key West
Miami Youth Museum
Parrot Jungle & Gardens
Fairchild Tropical Gardens
Historical Lighthouse and Museum

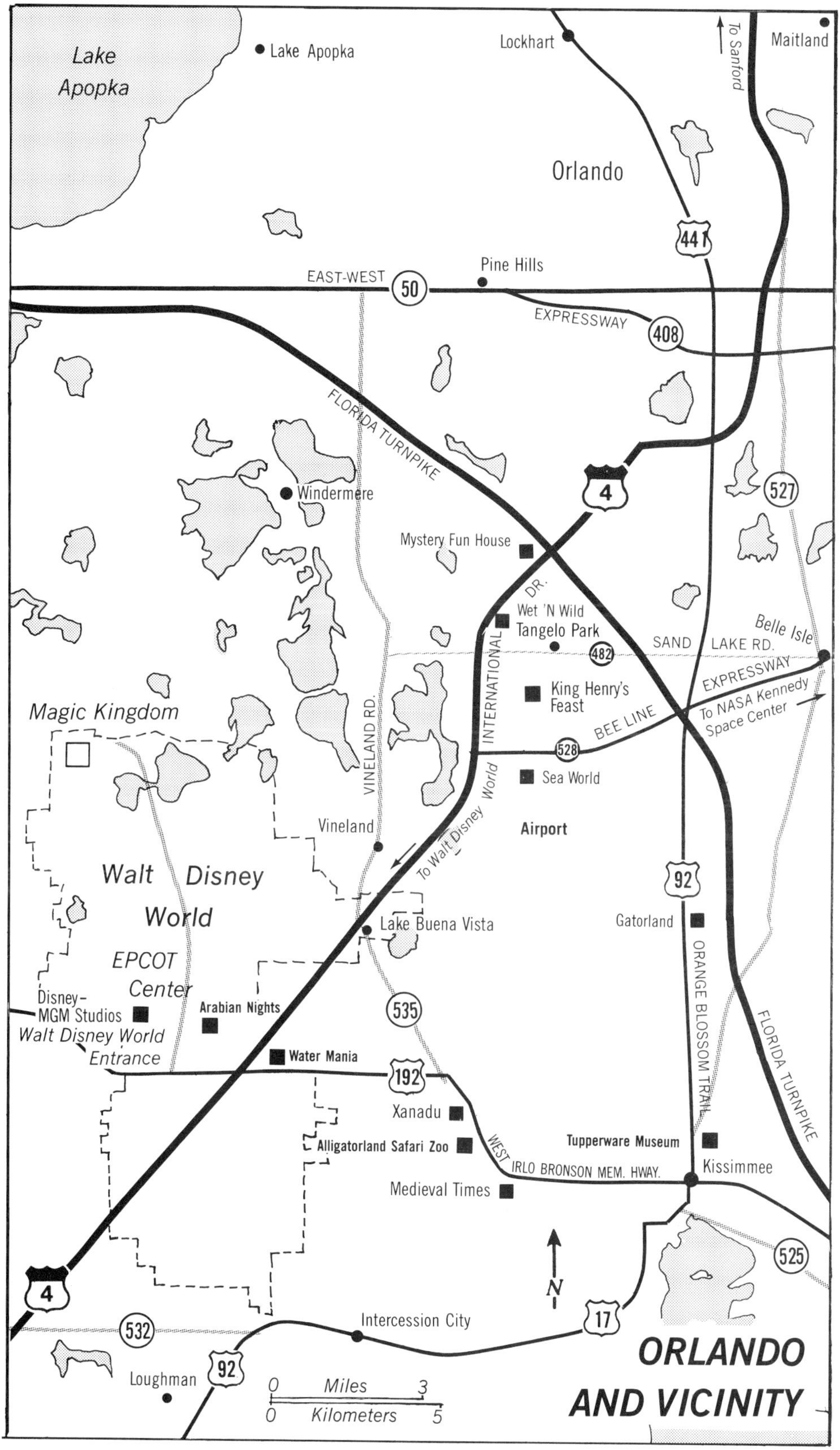

Lake Apopka
Lake Apopka
Lockhart
To Sanford
Maitland
Orlando
441
Pine Hills
EAST-WEST
50
EXPRESSWAY
408
FLORIDA TURNPIKE
4
527
Windermere
Mystery Fun House
INTERNATIONAL DR.
Wet 'N Wild
Tangelo Park
482
SAND LAKE RD.
Belle Isle
EXPRESSWAY
King Henry's Feast
BEE LINE
To NASA Kennedy Space Center
Magic Kingdom
VINELAND RD.
528
Sea World
To Walt Disney World
Airport
Vineland
Walt Disney World
92
Lake Buena Vista
Gatorland
EPCOT Center
ORANGE BLOSSOM TRAIL
Disney-MGM Studios
Arabian Nights
535
Walt Disney World Entrance
Water Mania
FLORIDA TURNPIKE
192
Xanadu
WEST IRLO BRONSON MEM. HWAY.
Alligatorland Safari Zoo
Tupperware Museum
Kissimmee
Medieval Times
N
525
4
532
Intercession City
17
92
Loughman
0 Miles 3
0 Kilometers 5
ORLANDO AND VICINITY

THE FLORIDA KEYS

INDEX

A

Abiti Boutique, 74
Admiral Dive, 107
Adventure Yacht and Sailing, 94
Afro-Caribbean Import Export, 81
Afterdeck, The, 119
Airporter, The (Miami), 95
Air Travel, 95, 243
Akash, 22
Al Amir, 22
Alabama Jack's, 103
Alexander, The, 47
Algozzini Hawaiian Village, 181
Alhambra Antiques Center, 69
Alice's Day Off, 73
Alper Furs, 148
Altamonte Springs: *see* ORLANDO
Amelia Island: *see* Jacksonville
Amelia Island Plantation, 259
Americash, 246
Americana Bookshop & Gallery, 70
Amusements: *see* "Sights" *in specific places*
Anastasia Island: *see* St. Augustine
Andrew's 2nd Act, 272
Anheuser-Busch Brewery Tour, 264
Anna Maria Island: *see* Sarasota
Antares, 83
Anthony's, 272
Antique Alley, 297
Antique Mall, 269
Antique, Jewelry & Collectibles Show—Coconut Grove, 69
Antiques: *see* "Shops" *in specific places*
Antiques, Etc., 188
Aqua Shop, The, 174
Aragon Café, 23
Arbetter Hot Dogs, 45
Armadillo Café, 128
Armani's, 278
Art Deco District, 89
Arthur's 27, 199
Arts: *see* "Sights" *in specific places*
Arturo's, 154
Asadorian, Inc., 172
Asolo State Theater, 307
Athens Tropical Fruits and Novelties, 80
Atlantic Beach: *see* Jacksonville
Atlantic Fun Center, 195
Atlantic's Edge, 102
L'Auberge du Bon Vivant, 300
Aventura: *see* MIAMI
Aventura Mall, 77

B

B-Line Diner, 209
B. Dalton, 72
B.C. Chong, 24
Baby Baby, 73
Baby Ling, 73
Baci, 155
Back in the Woods Gallery, 298
Bahia Cabana Beach Resort, 141
Bahia Mar Resort & Yachting Center, 141
Bailey House, The, 260
Bakeries: *see* "Shops" *in specific places*
Bakery Center, 77
Bal Harbour: *see* MIAMI
Bal Harbour Shops, 77
Balloon Flights, Orlando, 234
Banana Boat, 165
Banyan Resort, The, 114

Bar-B Ranch, 152
Barbara B. Mann Performing Arts Hall, 316
Barnacle, The, 87
Bars: *see* "Nightlife" *in specific places*
Baseball: *see* "Sights & Sports" *in specific places*
Baseball Card Exchange, 194
Basketball: *see* "Sights & Sports" *in specific places*
Basta's Cantina d'Italia, 291
Bay Harbor: *see* MIAMI
Bayou Country Store, 269
Bayside, A Seafood Grill and Bar, 321
Bayside Marketplace, 78
Beach Bistro, 301
Beach Stuff and More, 306
Beaches Antique Gallery, 261
Beauty Salons: *see* "Shops" *in specific places*
Bed-and-Breakfasts: *see* "Hotels" *in specific places*
Belleair: *see* St. Petersburg
Belleview MIDO Resort Hotel, 296
Belz Factory Outlet World, 226
Bern's Steakhouse, 279
Bice, 155
Bicycle Center, 84
Bicycling: *see* "Sights & Sports" *in specific places*
Big Pine Key: *see* THE KEYS, Lower Keys
Bijou Café, 301
Bill Baggs Cape Florida State Recreation Area, 91
Birthplace of Speed Museum, 195
Biscayne Kennel Club, 93
Biscayne Miracle Mile Cafeteria, 44
Biscayne National Underwater Park, 95
Black Tulip, 199
Blue Note, 223
Blue Waters, 92
Bobby's, 178
Boca Raton: *see* Palm Beach
Boca Raton Marriott Crocker Center, 169
Boca Raton Resort and Club, 167
El Bohio Café, 209
Bok Tower Gardens, 237
Bonita Springs: *see* Naples
Books: *see* "Shops" *in specific places*
Book Loft, 262
Books & Books, 72
Bookstop, 72
Boris-le Beau, 171
Botanica La Caridad, 81
Botanical Garden Center, 83
Bottling Court, The, 122
Boynton Beach: *see* Palm Beach
Bradenton: *see* Sarasota
Brasserie Max, 137
Brazilian Court, 169
Breakers, The, 166
Brevard Community College Planetarium Observatory, 189
Brevard Museum of History and Natural Science, 189
Brickell Avenue, 89
Brigade 2506 Monument, 88
Brooks Restaurant, 129
Bubbalou's Bodacious Bar-b-que, 208
Bubble Room, The, 329
Buck's Gun Rack, 194
Buena Vista Palace, 214
Bugatti, 24

Burt & Jack's, 145
Buses, 96, 244
Busch Gardens, The Dark Continent, 288
Butterfly World, 150
Button South, The, 147

C

Cabarets: *see* "Nightlife" *in specific places*
Café Abbracci, 25
Café Arugula, 129
Café Baci, 25
Café des Artistes, 110
Café des Arts, 66
Café Grazia!, 138
Café L'Europe (Palm Beach), 156
Café L'Europe (Sarasota), 302
Café Marquesa, 110
Cafés: *see* "Quick Bites" *in specific places*
Café Seville, 130
Café 66, 147
Café Tu Tu Tango, 26
Caladesi Island Ferry Service, 298
Calder Race Course, 93
Calico Corners Decorative Fabrics, 82
Camille's, 112
Cape Canaveral: *see* Cocoa Beach
Cape Coral: *see* Fort Myers
Captain Dan's Deep Sea Fishing Charters, 92
Captain Kidd Fishing Charters, 184
Captain Mike Fuery's Shelling Charters, 334
Captain Tony's Saloon, 119
Captiva Island: *see* Sanibel & Captiva Islands
Caribbean Marketplace, 78
Carlyon Collection, 76
Carolyn Lamb, 76
Caron Cherry, 76
Car Rental, 96, 244
Cartoon Museum, The, 235
Casa Juancho, 26
Casa Rolandi, 27
Casements, The, 195
Casselberry: *see* ORLANDO
Castle Harbor Sailboats, 94
Cedar Key: *see* Tampa
Center Court Tennis Outfitters, 182
Center for the Arts, The, 183
Chalet Suzanne, 219
Charley's Crab (Ft. Lauderdale), 130
Charley's Crab (Palm Beach), 157
Charters: *see* "Sights" *in specific places*
Chatham's Place, 200
Cheeca Lodge, 104
Chef Allen's, 27
Chef's Garden, 318
Chemist Shop, The, 149
Chesterfield Hotel Deluxe, 167
Children's Shops: *see* "Shops" *in specific places*
Chris's House of Beef, 200
Christie's, 28
Christini's, 201
Chuck and Harold's, 157
Church Street Station, 223
Church Street Station Exchange, 227
Ciro, 148
City Limits, 146
Clearwater: *see* St. Petersburg

INDEX

Clermont: *see* ORLANDO
Clevelander Poolside Bar, 59
Clothes: *see* "Shops" *in specific places*
Club Boca, 170
Club Med—The Sandpiper, 179
Club Nautico, 107
Club Nu, 63
Club Tropigala at La Ronde (Fontainebleau Hilton), 62
Cocoa Beach, 186–91
　hotels, 186–87
　nightlife, 188
　quick bites, 186
　restaurants: *see* ORLANDO, 299
Cocoa Beach Hilton & Towers, 187
Cocoa Beach Pier, 186
Cocoa Village, 190
Cocoa Village Playhouse, 190
Coconut Creek: *see* Fort Lauderdale
Coconut Grove, 90
　see also MIAMI
Coconuts, 186
CocoWalk, 78
Coffee Shops: *see* "Quick Bites" *in specific places*
Colonnade, The, 48
Colony Beach & Tennis Resort, The, 305
Colony Hotel, 168
Colony Restaurant, The, 302
Columbia Restaurant, 280
Comedy: *see* "Nightlife" *in specific places*
Comic Strip, The, 145
Compri Hotel Lake Buena Vista, 217
La Concha Holiday Inn, 116
Conch Tour Train, 125
Connie Banko, 73
Cookie Bar, The, 79
Le Coq au Vin, 202
Coral Gables, 88
　see also MIAMI
Coral Gables City Hall, 88
Coral, Pearls & Gems, 74
Coral Springs: *see* Fort Lauderdale
Courtyard at Lake Lucerne, The, 220
Crawfordville: *see* Tallahassee
Cruises: *see* "Sights" *in specific places*
Crook & Crook, 85
Cross & Sword Play, 253
Crown Region, The: *see* FIRST COAST
Cuda Bay Club, 222
Curry Mansion Inn, The, 117
Cutler Ridge: *see* MIAMI
Cypress Gardens, 230

D

Dade Cycle, 92
Dade Helicopter Jet Service, 94
Dadeland Marriott, 51
Dance Clubs: *see* "Nightlife" in specific places
Dania: *see* Fort Lauderdale
Dania Jai-Alai, 153
David William Hotel, 52
Davie: *see* Fort Lauderdale
Davie-Cooper City Rodeo, 153
Daytona Beach, 191–96
　hotels, 192–93
　nightlife, 193–94
　shops, 194
　sights, 195–96
Daytona Beach Hilton, 192
Daytona Flea Market, 194
Daytona International Speedway, 196
Deco Dermots, 75

Deep Six, 182
Deerfield Beach: *see* Fort Lauderdale
DeLand Country Inn, 221
Delray Beach: *see* Palm Beach
Denim World, 225
Denmark's Art Stone, 84
Department Stores: *see* "Shops" *in specific places*
DeSoto National Memorial, 309
Destin: *see* Pensacola
Dick Clark's American Bandstand Grill, 63
Dim Sum, 111
Diners: *see* "Quick Bites" *in specific places*
Dining Galleries, 28
Diplomat Resort and Country Club, 139
Discovery Cruises, 151
Discovery Island, 240
Disney Village Marketplace, 227
Disney's Grand Floridian Beach Resort, 212
Disney-MGM Studios Theme Park, 240
Diving: *see* "Sights & Sports" *in specific places*
Dixie Queen River Cruises, 196
Doc Dammer's Saloon, 60
Docksider's Bar & Grille, 147
DoDa's American Country Saloon Dancehall, 146
Dominque's, 29
Don CeSar Registry Resort, The, 295
Donatello, 280
Doral Ocean Beach Resort, 52
Doral Resort & Country Club, 52
Doral Saturnia International Spa Resort, 47
Doubletree Hotel, 55
Down Under, The, 131
Dragon Club, 146
Duffy's Diner, 138
Dunedin: *see* St. Petersburg
Dunlawton Sugar Mill Ruins, 196
Dupont Plaza Hotel, 55
Dust & Glitter, 75
Dusty Rose Antique Mall, The, 188
Duval House, 117
Dux, 202

E

East Martello Museum, 123
Eaton Lodge, 117
Eatonville: *see* ORLANDO
Eden of the Everglades, 327
Edison Hotel, The, 56
Edison Mall, 316
Edison Winter Home, 316
Edwin Watts Golf Shop, 229
Eight Flags Antique Market, 261
Ellenton: *see* Sarasota
Elliott Museum, The, 183
Elvis Presley Museum, 235
Embassy Suites-17th St. Causeway, 142
Emiliano's, 274
Enriquo's, 178
Ensign Bitters, 63
Anticipation Entertainment Yachts, 151
EPCOT Center, 240
Epicure Market, 80
Ernest Hemingway Home & Museum, 123
Esplanade, The, 172
La Esquina de Tejas, 45

Europa Cruise Line, 264
Events: *see* Goings-On
Everglades City: *see* Naples
Everglades Hotel, The, 56
Excursions: *see* "Sights" *in specific places*

F

Fabrics: *see* "Shops" *in specific places*
F.G. Bodner, 74
Fairchild Tropical Gardens, 91
Fairy Godmothers Child Care, 245
Faith Wick's World of Little People, 261
Falls, The, 78
Fantozzi's, 325
Farmer Jones Red Barn, 281
Faro Blanco Marine Resort, 108
Fast Buck Freddie's, 122
La Ferme, 132
Fernandina Beach: *see* Jacksonville
Ferris Groves, 80
La Finestra, 158
Finky's, 193
FIRST COAST, 249–264
　see also Jacksonville, St. Augustine
Fishing: *see* "Sights & Sports" *in specific places*
Fish Market, The, 30
Flagler Greyhound Track, 93
Flea World, 226
Floral Group, The Designers, 79
FLORIDA
　Florida Reborn, 3–5
　maps, 2, 336–37
Florida Briefcase, 229
Florida Mall, 227
Florida Princess Cruise Lines, 152
Florida Yacht Charters & Sales, 94
Flowers: *see* "Shops" *in specific places*
Flutes, 312
Fontainebleau Hilton Resort and Spa, 49
Food Shops: *see* "Shops" *in specific places*
Football: *see* "Sights & Sports" *in specific places*
Foreign Exchange
　Miami, 98
　Orlando, 246
For Heaven's Sake, 194
Forge, The, 30
Forgotten Woman, The, 148
Fort Christmas Museum, 235
Fort Lauderdale, 128–154
　hotels, 139–44
　nightlife, 145–47
　quick bites, 137–38
　restaurants, 128–37
　shops, 148–50
　sights & sports, 150–53
Fort Lauderdale Swap Shop, 149
Fort Liberty Wild West Dinner Show & Trading Post, 231
Fort Myers, 312–17
　hotels, 315
　quick bites, 314
　restaurants, 312–14
　shops, 316
　sights 316–17
Fort Myers Historical Museum, 317
Fort Pickens, 271
Fort Pierce: *see* TREASURE COAST
Fort Zachary Taylor State Historic Site, 124
Four Way Street, 77
Four Winds Gallery, 326

INDEX

Frances Brewster/Husband's Corner, 181
Frances Cary Antiques, 69
Franco B., 74
Frank's Dive Shop, 174
Franklin Mint Gallery, The, 172
Full Moon Saloon, 119
Fun 'n' Wheels, 231
Furniture: see "Shops" in specific places

G

Gainesville, 274–76
　restaurants, 274–76
Galley Grille, 178
Gamble Plantation, 309
Gardens: see "Sights" in specific places
Gas Plant Antique Arcade, 297
Gattle's Fine Quality Linens, 149
Gazebo, The, 158
Georgette Klinger, 70
Gessner & Camp Salon, 70
Gilbert's Bar House of Refuge Musem, 183
Gift Shops: see "Shops" in specific places
Glenna Moore, 325
Glider Rides of America, 174
Goings-On,
　Miami, 98–100
　Orlando, 246–48
GOLD COAST, 127–176
　see also Fort Lauderdale, Palm Beach
Golf: see "Sights & Sports" in specific places
Golf Shoppe of Miami, The, 85
Goodings Supermarket, 228
Grand Bay Hotel, 50
Grand Café, The, 31
Greater Miami: see MIAMI
Great Southern Gallery, 123
Great Western Boot Outlet, 226
Grenelefe, 215
Greyhound Racing: see "Sights & Sports" in specific places
Gringo's Cantina, 119
Grosvenor Resort, 215
Grove Fitness Tanning Salon, 71
Grove Isle Yacht & Tennis Club Hotel, 50
Grove Shops, 181
Gucci, 77
Guest Quarters Suite Hotel, 142
Gypsy Cab Company, 250

H

H&H Gift Collection, 81
H.T. Chittum & Co., 106
Half Shell Raw Bar, 113
Hallandale: see Fort Lauderdale
Harbor Island Spa, 56
Harbour Island, 290
Hard Rock Café, 210
Harley Hotel, 219
Harmon-Meek Gallery, 326
Harrington House, 305
Harry's Continental Kitchens, 303
Hawk's Cay Resort and Marina, 109
Hawthorn Suites Villa Resort, 218
Helios Gallery, 326
Hemmingway, Ernest, 119, 123
Henry B. Plant Museum, 289
Henry M. Flager Museum, The, 173
Heritage Grille Restaurant, The, 292
Heron, The, 281
Hey! Faith's Cookin', 209

Hialeah: see MIAMI
Hilton at Walt Disney World Village, 218
Historic Attractions: see "Sights & Sports" in specific places
Historic Cauley Square, 78
Holiday Inn Cocoa Beach, 187
Holiday Isle, 104
Hollywood: see Fort Lauderdale
Hollywood Beach Hilton, 140
Hollywood Beach Resort Hotel, 142
Holmes Beach: see Sarasota
Home Shops: see "Shops" in specific places
Homestead Restaurant, 258
Horse Racing: see "Sights & Sports" in specific places
Hotel Lounges: see "Nightlife" in specific places
Hotel Place St. Michel, 56
Hotel Riverparc, 57
Hotel Sofitel Miami, 57
HOTELS
　about the Hotels, 16–20; by area & price, 18–20, rankings & reviews, 17
　see also specific places
Hubbards, Ltd., 325
Hungry Sailor, 60
Hurricane Bar, 221
Hyatt Key West, 113
Hyatt Regency City Center at Riverwalk, 53
Hyatt Regency Coral Gables, 51
Hyatt Regency Grand Cypress, 215
Hyatt Regency Westshore at Tampa International Airport, 286

I

Il Porcino, 132
Il Tartuffo, 133
Indian River Country: see TREASURE COAST
Indian River Plantation, 179
Indigo Lakes Hilton Resort, 193
Industry, 64
Innisbrook Resort, 286
Inns: see "Hotels" in specific places
Inter-Continental Hotel Lobby Lounge, 45
Inter-Continental Hotel Miami, 53
El Internacional Discoteca, 64
International Swimming Hall of Fame, 150
Inverrary Hotel and Conference Resort, 142
Irish Pub, The, 67
Isla Canarias, 46
Islamorada: see THE KEYS, Upper Keys
Island Arts, 123
Island City House, 118
Island Club, 64
Island Needlework, 122
Island Princess, 180
Island Silver & Spice, 106
Islander Trading Post, 334

J

J&J Rattan, 83
Jazz: see "Nightlife" in specific places
J's Island Patio, 194
J. Fitzgerald's, 282
J. Ringhaver, 261
J.N. "Ding" Darling Wildlife Refuge, 334
Jack Davidson, 171
Jack Owen's Bike Tours, 175

Jacksonville, 255–264
　hotels, 259–61
　quick bites, 258–59
　restaurants, 255–58
　shops, 261–63
　sights, 263–64
Jacksonville Beach: see Jacksonville
Jacksonville Farmer's Market, 262
Jacksonville Landing, 263
Jacksonville Zoological Park, 263
Jamie's, 266
Jasmine Thai, 282
Jean-Paul's French Corner, 330
Jerry's Kite Shop/Rent-A-Bike, 263
Jewelry: see "Shops" in specific places
Jimmy Buffett's Margaritaville, 120
Jimmy Mac's, 284
Jimmy Ponce's Conch House, 250
Joe Muer Seafood, 159
Joe's News, 72
Joe's Stone Crab, 31
John & Mable Ringling Museum of Art, 307
John James Audubon House and Gardens, 123
John Pennekamp Coral Reef State Park, 107
Jordan's Grove, 203
Joseph's, 146
Jungle Larry's Zoological Park & Caribbean Gardens, 327
Jungle Queen Sightseeing Cruise, 152
Jupiter: see Palm Beach
Jupiter Beach Hilton, 170

K

Kapok Tree Restaurant, The, 292
Keitz's American Diving Headquarters, 108
Kendall: see MIAMI
Kendall Cycle Fair, 84
Key Biscayne, 89
　see also MIAMI
Key Largo: see THE KEYS, Upper Keys
THE KEYS, 101–126
　introduction, 102
　Key West, 110–126; hotels, 113–18; nightlife, 119–20; quick bites, 112–13; restaurants, 110–12; shops, 121–22; sights, 123–26
　Lower Keys, 108–9; hotels, 108–9; shops, 109; sights, 109
　Upper Keys, 102–8; hotels, 104–5; nightlife, 105–6; quick bites, 103–4; restaurants, 102–3; shops, 106–7; sights & sports, 107–8
Key West: see THE KEYS
Key West Hand Print Fabrics, 122
Key West Island Bookstore, 121
Key West Lighthouse Museum/Southernmost attractions, 124
Key West Seaplane Service, 126
King Henry's Feast, 231
Kissimmee: see ORLANDO
Kitchen Club, The, 64
Knickers, 171
Kojak, 284
Kokomo's, 191

L

L. Valladares & Son, 121
Laff Lines Comedy Theater, 171
Landmarks: see "Sights & Sports" in specific places
Lantana: see Palm Beach

343

INDEX

Lake Buena Vista: *see* ORLANDO
Lakeland: *see* Tampa
Lake Mary: *see* ORLANDO
Lakeridge Winery & Vineyards, 234
Lakeside Inn, 220
Lake Wales: *see* ORLANDO
Lamp Post Antique Mall, 262
Last Tango in Paris, 69
Laughing Kookaboora, 222
Leather: *see* "Shops" *in specific places*
Leonardo's, 275
Les Violins Supper Club, 62
Leu Gardens, 237
Lighthouse Point: *see* Fort Lauderdale
Lightner Antique Mall, 253
Lime in the Coconut, 65
Linger Awhile, 188
Lion's Paw, The, 334
Lisa Loren Jewelers, 74
Little Darlins Rock 'n' Roll Palace, 209
Little Havana, 90
  see also MIAMI
Little Havana, Kiwanis Club of, 90
Little Palm Island, 109
Little Torch Key: *see* THE KEYS, Lower Keys
Lobster Pot, The, 293
Lodge at Ponte Vedra Beach, The, 252
Longboat Key: *see* Sarasota
Longboat Key Club, 306
Longboat Key Hilton, 306
Longwood: *see* ORLANDO
Loomis Drugs, 246
Louie's Backyard, 111
Lucky's, 66
Luggage: *see* "Shops" *in specific places*
Lulu's, 43
Luminaire, 83
Luomo, 75

M

Mac's Bike Shop, 182
Mad Hatter, The, 331
Madrid, 32
Maggie's Sand Dollar, 106
Magic: *see* "Nightlife" *in specific places*
Magic Kingdom, 242
Maison et Jardin, 204
Maitland: *see* ORLANDO
Mallory Market, 125
A Mano, 23
MAPS
  Florida, 336
  Florida's Regions, 2
  Florida Keys, The, 340
  Miami & Vicinity, 338
  Orlando & Vicinity, 339
Marathon: *see* THE KEYS, Lower Keys
Mardi Gras Entertainment Dinner, 231
Margapita, 76
Marie Selby Botanical Gardens, 308
Marina del Mar, 105
Marco Island: *see* Naples
Margaux's, 318
Marine Jewelry, 109
Mark's Place, 33
Marriott at Sawgrass, 252
Marriott Hotel & Marina, 140
Marriott Bay Point Resort, 271
Marriott Casa Marina Resort, 114
Marriott Daytona Beach, 192
Marriott Harbor Beach Resort, 139
Marriott Marco Island Resort, 321
Marriott Orlando World Center, 212

Martinez de Ybor Art Gallery, 289
Matheson Hammock Park & Marina, 91
Mato, 82
Maus & Hoffman (Miami), 75
Maus & Hoffman (Ft. Lauderdale), 148
Max's Grille, 161
Maxaluna, 160
Mayfair House, 53
Mayfair Shops in the Grove, 78
Mayport: *see* Jacksonville
Mayport Ferry Boat Ride, 263
McGuire's Irish Pub, 268
McNichols Art Gallery, 327
Medieval Life/Medieval Times Dinner and Tournament, 232
Melbourne: *see* Cocoa Beach
Mel Fisher Maritime Heritage Society Museum, 124
Mel's Hot Dogs, 284
Mental Floss, 62
La Mer Hotel, 114
Mercado Festival Center, 227
Merlinn Guest House, 118
Merritt Island: *see* Cocoa Beach
Merritt Island National Wildlife Refuge, 191
Mezzanotte, 34
MIAMI, 21–100
  basics, 95–100; foreign exchange, 98; getting there, 95–96; getting around, 96–97; goings-on, 98–100; useful telephone numbers, 97; weather & what to wear, 98
  hotels, 47–59
  map, 338
  nightlife, 59–67
  quick bites, 42–46
  restaurants, 22–42
  shops, 68–85
  sights & sports, 86–95
Miami Airport Hilton & Marina, 54
Miami Antique Auction Co., 68
Miami Beach: *see* MIAMI
Miami Beach Bicycle Center, 94
Miami City Ballet, 87
Miami Connection, 315
Miami Convention & Visitors Bureau, Greater, 90
Miami Design Preservation League, The, 89
Miami Dolphins, 93
Miami Heat, 92
Miami Jewelry Center, 74
Miami Lakes: *see* MIAMI
Miami Lakes Inn, 59
Miami Metrozoo, 86
Miami Oxygene, 73
Miami Seaquarium, 86
Miami Twice Vintage Department Store, 75
Miccosukee Indian Chickee Huts, 84
Michael's on East, 303
Ming Court, 204
Miracle Center, 79
Mise en Place, 283
Mister Chu's, 134
Moda Mario, 148
Mole Hole, The, 288
Molokai Bar and Lounge, 145
Momotombo, 46
Monty's Stone Crab, 34
Morada Bar & Grill, 162
Morgenstern's Antiques, 69

Morse Museum of American Art, 235
Mount Dora: *see* ORLANDO
Mr. B.'s of Eatonville, Inc., 224
Mr. Manatee's, 178
Mrs. Mac's Kitchen by the Sea, 178
Mucky Duck, 331
Mulvaney's, 224
Murphy's Kokamo Kafe & Dance Palace, 222
Museums: *see* "Sights" *in specific places*
Museum of Art, 151
Museum of Science and Space Planetarium, 87
Music Clubs: *see* "Nightlife" *in specific places*

N

Nails at the Beach, 71
Naples, 317–28
  hotels, 321–24
  introduction, 317
  nightlife, 324
  quick bites, 321
  restaurants, 318–21
  sights & sports, 326–28
Naples Art Gallery, 327
Naples Beach Hotel & Golf Club, 323
Naples Dinner Theatre, 324
Naples Trolley Tours, Inc., 328
Naples–Fort Myers Kennel Club, 328
NASA Kennedy Space Center's Spaceport USA, 190
National Football League Alumni Store, 150
National Museum of Naval Aviation, 270
Neighborhoods: *see* "Sights" *in specific places*
Nevada Bob's, 326
New Moon III, 93
News Café, 43
Newsstands: *see* "Shops" *in specific places*
Nightlife: *see specific places*
Nightown, 269
Norman Brothers Produce, 80
North Bay Village: *see* MIAMI
North Turn, The, 191
Norton Gallery of Art, 173

O

Ocean Grand, 168
Ocean Key House, 115
Ocean World, 150
Oh Shucks, 186
Old City House, 251
Old Hyde Park Village, 290
Old Town, 228
Old Town Carriage Co., 264
Old Town Trolley Tours, 126
Omni International Hotel (Miami), 54
Omni International Hotel (Orlando), 216
Omni Jacksonville Hotel, 260
Orange Blossom Market, 229
Orange County Historical Museum, 236
ORLANDO & CENTRAL FLORIDA, 197–248
  basics, 243–248; getting there, 243; getting around, 244; goings-on, 246–48; services, 245–46; useful telephone numbers, 145
  hotels, 211–21
  nightlife, 221–24

344

INDEX

quick bites, 208–10
restaurants, 198–207
shops, 224–30
sights & sports, 230–43
Orlando/Orange County Convention Center & Visitors Bureau, 246
Orlando Museum of Art at Loch Haven, 236
Orlando Science Center, 236
Orlando's Secret Jewelers to the Stars, 225
Ormond Beach: *see* Daytona Beach
Osteria del Teatro, 35
Ozone Lounge, 222

P

Paddlewheel Queen, 152
Palm Aire Spa Resort & Country Club, 140
Palma Sola: *see* Sarasota
Palm Beach, 154–176
  hotels, 166–70
  nightlife, 170–71
  quick bites, 165–66
  restaurants, 154–65
  shops, 171–73
  sights & sports, 173–76
Palm Beach Kennel Club, 174
Palm Beach Mall, 172
Palm Beach Polo & Country Club, 175
Palm Beach Polo and Country Club, 170
Palm Coast: *see* Daytona Beach
Palm Coast Sheraton, 192
Palm Harbor: *see* Tampa
Panama City, 271
Pan American Ocean Resort Radisson, 57
Park Avenue Association, 228
Park Central Hotel, 58
PANHANDLE, 265–276
  introduction, 266
  see also Gainesville, Panama City, Pensacola, Tallahassee
Park Plaza Gardens, 205
Park Plaza Hotel, 219
Parker Playhouse, 153
Parks: *see* "Sights & Sports" *in specific places*
Parrot Jungle & Gardens, 86
Patricia Judith Art Gallery, 173
Peabody Orlando, 216
Peacock in the Grove Café, 63
Pebbles, 208
Pelican Cove, 105
Penrod's Beach Club, 60
Pensacola, 266–72
  hotels, 267–68
  nightlife, 268–69
  restaurants, 266–67
  shops, 269
  sights, 270–71
Pensacola Hilton (bars), 269
Pensacola Hilton (hotel), 267
Pensacola Village, 270
Pepper Mill, The, 294
Perry's Ocean Edge Resort, 193
Peter's La Cuisine, 313
La Petite Pâtisserie, 79
PGA National Resort, 169
Phoenician, 210
Pier 66 Resort & Marina, 139
Pier House (Hotel), 115
Pier House Restaurant, The, 112
Pier, The, 299
Pinellas Sun Coast: *see* St. Petersburg
Plaka, 315

Plaka II, 315
Plantation: *see* Fort Lauderdale
Plantation Shop, The, 262
Pleasure Island, 242
Pompano Beach: *see* Fort Lauderdale
Ponce de León Inlet Lighthouse, 196
Ponte Vedra Beach: *see* St. Augustine
Pool Halls: *see* "Nightlife" *in specific places*
Poppi's in the Grove, 80
Portobello Yacht Club, 205
Port Orange: *see* Daytona Beach
Port St. Lucie: *see* TREASURE COAST
Prawn Broker, The, 313
Primadonna, 148
Private Clubs: *see* "Nightlife" *in specific places*
Public Transportation, 96, 244
Pub on Linwood, The, 324

Q

Quality Outlet Center, 228
Quayside Market, 269
Quick Bites: see specific places
Quinn's, 324

R

Radisson Suite Hotel Oceanfront, 186
Radisson Suite Beach Resort, 322
Ragtime Tavern and Grill/Salud!, 255
Rainbarrel, The, 106
Raintree, 251
Ramiro's, 35
Los Ranchos, 36
Rascal House, 43
Razzle's, 194
Reach, The, 115
Red Barn Theatre, The, 124
Redington Shores: *see* St. Petersburg
Reef Raiders Dive Shop, 125
Reef, The, 193
Regine's, 36, 67
Registry Resort Naples, 322
RESTAURANTS
  about the restaurants, 5–15; by area, 14–16; by cuisine, 11–14; by ranking ("Toque Tally"), 9–11; prices & credit cards, 8; rankings & toque system, 7–8
  see also specific places
Restored Spanish Quarter, The, 254
Ristorante Bellini, 304
Ritz Plaza Hotel Miami Beach, 58
Ritz-Carlton Hotel, 322
Ritz-Carlton Hotel Dining Room, 319
River Country, 242
Rivership Grand Romance, 232
Riverside Hotel, 143
Riverwalk, The, 264
Riviera Beach: *see* Palm Beach
Robert's Western Wear, 76
Roberto's, 163
Rolando's Cuban Restaurant, 210
Ron Jon's Surf Shop, 188
Roney's Health Emporium, 81
Royal Mansions Resort, 187
Royal Poinciana Playhouse, 175
Ruff Hewn, 325
Runyon's, 134
Russell House, 121

S

Sabal's, 294
Saddlebrook Resort, 287
Safety Harbor: *see* Tampa

Safety Harbor Spa & Fitness Center, 285
Saigon Oriental Restaurant, 138
Sailing: *see* "Sights & Sports" *in specific places*
Saint Armands Circle, 309
Saint Regis Hotel, 191
Sakura Gables, 37
Salmon & Salmon, 37
Salvador Dali Museum, 298
Sandestin Beach Resort, 267
Sanford: *see* ORLANDO
Sangeet, 314
Sanibel & Captiva Islands, 328–34
  hotels, 332–33
  introduction, 329
  quick bites, 332
  restaurants, 329–32
  shops, 334
  sights, 334
Santa Lucia, 135
Sarasota, 300–309
  hotels, 305–6
  restaurants, 300–304
  shops, 306
  sights, 307–9
Sawgrass Mills, 149
Scalawag's Lounge, 180
Schooner Wharf, 120
Scotty's Grocery, 81
Sea World of Florida, 232
Sea Grill, The, 295
SeaEscape, 95
Seaside Music Theater, 195
La Segunda Central Bakery, 288
Seminole Indian Bingo, 151
Semper's, 67
1735 House, 260
Seville Quarter, 268
Shades of Key West, 121
Shark Valley Tram Tours of Everglades National Park, 87
SHELL COAST, 311–34
  see also Fort Myers, Naples, Sanibel & Captiva Islands
Shell Factory, The, 316
Shell World, 107
Sheraton Bal Harbour, 48
Sheraton Beach on Hutchinson Island, 180
Sheraton Bonaventure Resort and Spa, 143
Sheraton Brickell Point on Biscayne Bay, 51
Sheraton Design Center, 142
Sheraton Grand Westshore, 287
Sheraton Key Largo Resort, 105
Sheraton River House Hotel, 54
Sheraton Royal Biscayne Beach Resort, 58
Sheraton-Yankee Clipper Beach Resort, 144
Sheraton-Yankee Trader Resort, 144
Shooter's Waterfront Café U.S.A., 145, 223
Shopping Centers: *see* "Shops" *in specific places*
Shops: *see specific places*
Shorty's Bar-B-Q, 42
Siam Hut, 314
Sights: *see specific places*
Sign of the Vine, 320
Skipper's Smokehouse and Oyster Bar, 285
Skyrider Para-Sailing, 153
Sloppy Joe's, 119

INDEX

Society Billiards, 66
Society of the Four Arts, 173
Sonesta Beach Hotel Key Biscayne, 48
Sonesta Sanibel Harbour Resort and Spa, 315
Sonesta Villa Resort, 213
South Bay Marine Store, 85
South Beach: *see* MIAMI
South Beach Furniture Company, 83
South Florida Museum and Bishop Planetarium, 308
South Seas Plantation, 332
Sovereign, The, 275
Spa Resorts: *see* "Hotels" *in specific places*
SPACE COAST, 185–96
 see also Cocoa Beach, Daytona Beach
Space Coast Science Center, 189
Spence-Lanier Pioneer Center, 236
Spencer's Western World, 297
Spinnakers, 186
Sponge Docks at Tarpon Springs, 299
Sporting Goods: *see* "Shops" *in specific places*
Sports: *see specific places*
Sports Rock Café Miami, 66
Spring Creek, 273
Spy Shops International, 82
Squeeze Progressive Danceteria, 147
St. Armands Key: *see* Sarasota
St. Augustine, 150–55
 hotels, 252–53
 restaurants, 250–52
 shops, 253
 sights, 253–55
St. Augustine Historical Tours, 254
St. Honoré, 163
St. Lucie Skyways, 182
St. Petersburg, 291–99
 hotels, 295–97
 restaurants, 291–95
 shops, 297
 sights, 298–99
Stars and Stripes Café, 38
Stefano's, 65
Sterling Anvil, 306
Sterling's Flamingo Café, 256
Stone Mountain Handbag Factory Store, 296
Stouffer Orlando, 217
Strand, The, 38
Strike Zone Charters, 109
Stringfellow's, 65
Stuart: *see* TREASURE COAST
Stuart Historic Walking Tour, 184
Stuart Yacht, 182
Stuart's Bar & Lounge, 61
Studio One Café, 136
Subtilite, 71
Sullivan's Trailway Lounge, 223
Summers, 147
Summit Landing, 180
Sun Dog Diner, 258
Sunshine Café, 332
Sun Spot Surf and Beach Shop, 182
Sundays on the Bay, 61
Sundial Beach & Tennis Resort, 333
Sunlion Jewelry, 121
SuperShuttle (Miami), 95
Super Sitters, 245
Surfcomber, 58
Surfside Watch & Silver Vault, 70

T
Tallahassee, 272–74
 restaurants 272–74

Tampa, 278–91
 hotels, 285–87
 quick bites, 284–85
 restaurants, 278–83
 shops, 287–88
 sights & sports, 288–91
TAMPA BAY AREA, 277–309
 see also Sarasota, St. Petersburg, Tampa
Tampa Jai Alai, 291
Tania Sante's Classic Collectibles, 75
Tanning Salons: *see* "Shops" *in specific places*
Tarpon Springs: *see* St. Petersburg
Taste of Sze-chuan, 39
Tavern in the Grove, 61
Taxis, 97, 244
Telephone Numbers
 Miami, 97
 Orlando, 245
La Terraza de Marti, 118
Terry's Wholesale Perfumes and Colognes, 71
Thai Toni, 39
Thalheimer's Auction Gallery, 325
Theater: *see* "Sights & Sports" *in specific places*
Theater of the Sea, 107
Thee Leathery, 76
Theo Phudpuckers, 178
Third Street South, 328
Three Birds Bookstore, 288
Tiki Bar, The, 105
Titusville: *see* Cocoa Beach
Tobacco Road, 61
Tom's Place, 166
Toojay's, 166
Top Gun, 93
Top of the Palace Lounge, 223
Top, The, 120
Tops'l Beach & Racquet Club, 268
Torrah Treasures, 82
Toscanelli, 206
Tours: *see* "Sights" *in specific places*
Town Center at Boca Raton, 172
Track Shack, 230
Traders Ocean Resort, 144
Tradewinds on St. Petersburg Beach, 296
Trattoria Pampered Chef, 81
TREASURE COAST, 178–84
 hotels, 178–80
 introduction, 178
 quick bites, 178
 shops, 181–82
 sights, 184–84
Tropics International, 66
Lá Trúc, 160
Il Tulipano, 39
Tupperware World Headquarters Museum, 236
Turnberry Isle Yacht & Country Club, 55
'Tween Waters Inn, 333
24 Miramar, 256
Typhoon Lagoon, 243

U
U.S. Astronaut Hall of Fame, 189
Uncle Tai's, 164
Underwater Demolition Team SEAL Museum, 184
Unicorn Village, 40
Universal Studios, 233
Urca de Lima Underwater Archaeological Preserve, 184
Utterly Fantastic Cruises, 152

V
Valerio Antiques, 70
Van Wezel Performing Arts Center, 308
Vanderbilt Inn on the Gulf, 323
Venetian Pool, 91
Vero Beach: *see* TREASURE COAST
Very Fitting Intimate Apparel, 181
Victor's Café, 41
Victoria & Albert's, 207
Victoria Park, 137
Victory Cruises, 254
Vidal Tan Soon, 71
La Vieille Maison, 165
Villa Pescatore, 320
Villa Vizcaya Museum and Gardens, 92
Village Antiques, Inc., 287
Village Inn, 65
Villas of Grand Cypress, 217
Vistana's Beach Club, 180
Vistana Resort, 218
Voyager Sightseeing Train

W
Wagons West, 44
Waldenbooks, 72
Walgreen Drugstores, 246
Wally Findlay Galleries, 174
Walt Disney World
 admissions information, 239
 attractions, 198, 238–243
 hotels, 211, 212, 213, 216, 217, 218
 nightlife, 222, 223
 restaurants, 198, 199, 205, 207
 shops, 225, 237
 theme parks: *see* attractions
Walt Disney World Dolphin, 213
Walt Disney World Swan, 213
Walt Disney World Yacht and Beach Club Resort, 214
Walter's Place, 181
Water Mania, 233
Water Taxi, 154
Weather
 Miami, 98
 Orlando, 246
Wesley Chapel: *see* Tampa
Westcott House, 253
Westfield Arabian, 175
West Palm Beach: *see* Palm Beach
Wet 'n' Wild, 234
Wharf, The, 273
Whitehead Street Pottery, 122
Whitney's Fish Camp, 259
Windows on the Water, 332
Windsport Catamarans & Windsurfers, 85
Wine Cellar, The, 257
Winter Park: *see* ORLANDO
Witt's End Sailing Charters, 108
Women's & Children's Resale Shop, 226
Woody's Jet Boats, 195
Wrecker's Museum, The, 124

Y
Ybor City: *see* Tampa
Ybor Square, 290
Yuca, 41

Z
Zanjabil, 82
Ziggy's Conch, 103

Gault Millau
"BEST OF" GUIDES

The guidebook series known throughout Europe for its wit and savvy now reveals the best of major U.S., European and Asian destinations. Gault Millau books include full details on the best of everything that makes these places special: the restaurants, diversions, nightlife, hotels, shops and arts. The guides also offer practical information on getting around and enjoying each area. Perfect for visitors and residents alike.

Please send me the *Best of* books checked below:

- ☐ Chicago $15.95
- ☐ France $16.95
- ☐ Germany $18.00
- ☐ Hawaii $16.95
- ☐ Hong Kong $16.95
- ☐ Italy $16.95
- ☐ London $16.95
- ☐ Los Angeles $16.95
- ☐ New England $15.95
- ☐ New Orleans $16.95
- ☐ New York $16.95
- ☐ Paris $16.95
- ☐ San Francisco $16.95
- ☐ Thailand $17.95
- ☐ Toronto $17.00
- ☐ Washington D.C. ... $16.95

Gault Millau
P.O. Box 361144
L.A. CA 90036

In the U.S., include $2 (UPS shipping charge) for the first book, and $1 for each additional book. Outside the U.S., $3 and $1.

Enclosed is my check or money order made out to Gault Millau Inc., for $_____.

CHARGE TO: _____ MASTERCARD _____ VISA _____/_____ EXP. DATE

ACCT. # _____ SIGNATURE _____

NAME _____
ADDRESS _____
CITY _____ STATE _____
ZIP _____ COUNTRY _____

André Gayot's
TASTES
with the Best of Gault Millau
THE WORLD DINING & TRAVEL CONNECTION
P.O. Box 361144, Los Angeles, CA 90036 U.S.A.

♦ All you'll ever need to know about the tables (and under the tables) of the world.
♦ The best—and other—restaurants, hotels, nightlife, shopping, fashion.
♦ What's hot, lukewarm and cold from Hollywood to Hong Kong via Paris.

Want to keep current on the best bistros in Paris? Discover that little hideaway in Singapore? Or stay away from that dreadful and dreadfully expensive restaurant in New York? **André Gayot's Tastes** tips readers off to the best and the worst in restaurants, hotel, nightlife and shopping around the world.

☐ **YES,** please enter/renew my subscription for 6 bimonthly issues at the rate of $40. (Outside U.S. and Canada, $45.)

Name_____

Address_____

City_____State_____

Zip_____Country_____

☐ **ALSO,** please send a gift subscription to: *

Name_____

Address_____

City_____State_____

Zip_____Country_____

Gift from_____
(We will notify recipient of your gift)

* With the purchase of a gift subscription or a second subscription, you will receive, FREE, the **guidebook of your choice**—a $17 value. (See order form on reverse.)

☐ CHECK ENCLOSED FOR $ _____.

☐ CHARGE TO: ____ MASTERCARD ____ VISA ___/___ Exp. date

Acct. # _____ Signature _____

☐ PLEASE SEND ME, **FREE,** THE GUIDE OF MY CHOICE: _____.

316/91